The Mammals of Texas

by

WILLIAM B. DAVIS
Professor Emeritus and Former Head
Department of Wildlife and Fisheries Sciences
Texas A&M University

and

DAVID J. SCHMIDLY
Professor and Curator of Mammals
Department of Wildlife and Fisheries Sciences
Texas A&M University

TEXAS PARKS & WILDLIFE

Nongame and Urban Program
4200 Smith School Road
Austin, Texas 78744
Revised 1994

Editor: Lisa Bradley
Project Coordinator: Noreen Damude
Art Director: Pris Martin
Design: Suzanne Davis
Cover Design: Elishea Morgan

The present revision of *The Mammals of Texas*
was funded in part by the Federal Aid in
Wildlife Restoration Act under Project W-129-M-2.

Another "Learn about Texas" publication from
TEXAS PARKS AND WILDLIFE PRESS
ISBN: 1-885696-00-0

TABLE OF CONTENTS

Order Rodentia – Continued

PREFACE

This book is devoted to mammals, which are the class of vertebrate animals possessing hair, with the females having milk-secreting glands. One group of mammals, the cetaceans (whales and dolphins) have a layer of blubber instead of hair. This class, having among its representative genera certain species that fly, others that glide, swim, climb, burrow, leap, or run, is perhaps the most versatile and adaptable of the vertebrate animal groups.

Texas, with its variety of soils, climate, vegetation, and topography, as well as extensive coastline, is the home of more than 181 distinct species of mammals. The locomotive versatility of the various members of the class is responsible in part for the occurrence of mammals in our deserts, forests, mountains, prairies, high plains, and waters.

This book represents the fifth account published by the Texas Parks and Wildlife Department detailing the kinds of mammals that occur in Texas with information about their lives and economic importance. Dr. W. P. Taylor and Dr. W. B. Davis collaborated to prepare *The Mammals of Texas*, published by the former Texas Game and Fish Commission as Bulletin No. 27, in August 1947. Recognizing the growing interest in Texas mammals and the expanding knowledge about the many kinds of mammals in the state, Dr. Davis in 1960 wrote an entirely new bulletin, designated as Bulletin No. 41, which served as an identification key to Texas mammals and also provided information on their distribution and life histories. Dr. Davis revised Bulletin No. 41 in 1966 and again in 1974.

Dwindling supplies and increasing popularity of Bulletin No. 41 prompted the Texas Parks and Wildlife Department to seek an updating of this informative publication. For this purpose, wildlife expert and mammalogist Dr. David J. Schmidly very graciously agreed to update Dr. Davis' publication and make needed revisions in the species distribution maps and other portions of the bulletin. Most of the changes were made to update the identification keys and geographic ranges of mammals in Texas and its adjacent waters. The natural history descriptions, for the most part, remain essentially as detailed by Dr. Davis in Bulletin No. 41.

Simplicity is the basic goal in organizing this book. Accounts for each species are arranged so that they contain in sequence (1) a brief description of the mammal, with special emphasis given to distinguishing features, accompanied in most cases by a photograph; (2) a description of the geographic distribution of the species in Texas, with reference to a map; and (3) a discussion of some of the basic life history of the mammal, including habitat preferences, reproduction, behavior, and food habits. This information has been taken from observations recorded by other researchers and reported in the scientific literature as well as the personal experiences of the authors based on more than 50 years of field work in Texas. On the distribution maps, counties where specimens of mammals have been reported, either in the literature or represented by a scientific specimen located in a museum collection, are indicated by black dots; the probable range for most species is shaded in.

Students of wildlife and citizens interested in conservation and natural history will find much help in this revision of *The Mammals of Texas*, by Dr. W. B. Davis (Professor Emeritus of Wildlife and Fisheries Sciences), and Dr. David J. Schmidly (Professor and Curator of Mammals in the Department of Wildlife and Fisheries Sciences) of Texas A&M University, both of whom are recognized internationally as authorities on mammals.

Andrew Sansom

Andrew Sansom
Executive Director

ACKNOWLEDGMENTS

Special thanks and appreciation are due Dr. William B. Davis, Professor Emeritus of the Department of Wildlife and Fisheries Sciences at Texas A&M University, who kindly gave permission and encouraged me to update his 1974 version of Bulletin No. 41. Dr. Davis remains the senior author of this revised version because the primary contents of the work are those of his writing and interpretation. Dr. Davis has been a student of Texas mammals for more than 50 years and he rightfully deserves acclaim as the "father" of mammalogy in the State.

My role has been to modernize the taxonomy, update the distribution maps, change the identification keys where appropriate, and otherwise make changes that reflect the current knowledge about mammalian conservation in Texas. In this regard, I have been aided by the following people who provided information, loaned specimens for study, or allowed me to examine collections under their care: the late J. Knox Jones, Jr., Clyde Jones, Robert J. Baker, Walter Dalquest, Frederick B. Stangl, Jr., James Scudday, Arthur Harris, Sarah Kerr, Mark Engstrom, Robert Dowler, Alan Chaney, Syd Anderson, Duane Schlitter, Bruce Patterson, Michael Mares, Michael Carlton, Donald Hoffmeister, Earl Zimmerman, Hugh Genoways, Terry Yates, John Baccus, James Patton, David Easterla, Kenneth Wilkins, Arthur Cleveland, John Darling, Dean Fisher, John Hafner, Brian Chapman, Robert F. Martin, Howard McCarley, Philip Myers, William E. Wilson, and Royal Suttkis. I also would like to thank the Texas Parks and Wildlife Department for inviting me to revise Bulletin No. 41 and for the technical assistance of their staff.

Several persons aided in the final stages of manuscript preparation. Dave Scarbrough, in particular, deserves special mention for working many long and tedious hours to assist with library work, prepare distribution maps, and draft revisions of the species accounts. Lisa Bradley edited and corrected the final version of the manuscript and prepared the final copies of the distribution maps. George Baumgardner assisted with listing all records of Texas mammals in the Texas Cooperative Wildlife Collection at Texas A&M University.

Most of the photographs of mammals were taken by John Tveten using animals captured by me or by my graduate students. The photographs of bats were kindly provided by Dr. Merlin Tuttle, Science Director of Bat Conservation International in Austin, Texas. Other photographs came from the files of the Texas Parks and Wildlife Department. The marine mammal illustrations were graciously provided by Pieter A. Folkens.

Financial support for the project was graciously provided by the Texas Parks and Wildlife Department. The Caesar Kleberg Wildlife Foundation, the Department of Wildlife and Fisheries Sciences at Texas A&M University, and the Texas Agricultural Experiment Station provided financial support for some of the field work and all the trips to museums and collections.

Last, but certainly not least, I want to express my appreciation to two special groups of people. The first is the forty or so graduate students who have studied mammals with me over the past 20 years. They spent many hours in the field assisting with my studies of Texas mammals. The second group is the many wonderful and dedicated Texas landowners who kindly opened the gates of their farms and ranches, and in many cases the doors to their homes, to me and my students so that we could collect, observe, and study mammals on their land. It is to this latter group, to whom Texas owes so much for the conservation of its vast natural resources, that I dedicate this new revision of *The Mammals of Texas*.

David J. Schmidly
Campus Dean, Texas A&M University at Galveston

TEXAS MAMMALS

The importance of Texas in relation to geography and wildlife is no accident. Within the state is such a wide variation of soils, climate, and topography that the resultant vegetation and animal life are unusually rich. This diverse environment supports a resident fauna of 141 species of native terrestrial mammals, a number exceeded in the United States only by California and New Mexico. In addition to the native species that occur in the area naturally, there are also 12 exotics or nonnative species that have been introduced accidentally (house mouse, roof rat, Norway rat) or intentionally (nutria, red fox, feral pig, axis deer, fallow deer, sika deer, nilgai, barbary sheep, and blackbuck) by man and have become established as a part of the freeliving fauna. An asterisk (*) beside the common name in the species accounts indicates a nonnative species.

Terrestrial mammals in Texas belong to the orders Didelphimorphia (opossums), Insectivora (shrews and moles), Chiroptera (bats), Xenarthra (armadillos), Lagomorpha (hares and rabbits), Rodentia (rodents), Carnivora (carnivores), and Artiodactyla (even-toed ungulates). In addition, Texas is bounded by the waters of the Gulf of Mexico and 28 marine mammals of the orders Cetacea (whales and dolphins), Pinnipedia (seals), and Sirenia (manatees) enter the coastal waters of the state. The number of genera and species of Texas mammals in each of these groups is given in Table 1. This total of 181 mammals does not include several large, exotic ungulates that recently have been brought into the state and are kept for the most part under high fence and two domesticated species (dog and cat) which have taken up life in the wild state in many places and have significant impacts on other mammals living in those areas.

TABLE 1. The number of genera and species of mammals in Texas.

Order	Genera	Species
Didelphimorphia (Opossums)	1	1
Insectivora (Shrews and Moles)	4	5
Chiroptera (Bats)	16	32
Xenarthra (Armadillos)	1	1
Lagomorpha (Hares and Rabbits)	2	4
Rodentia (Rodents)	28	68
Carnivora (Carnivores)	16	28
Pinnipedia (Seals)	1	1
Artiodactyla (Even-toed Ungulates)	10	14
Sirenia (Manatees)	1	1
Cetacea (Whales and Dolphins)	17	26
Totals	97	181

Texas is a keystone in understanding the distributional patterns of Recent mammals in the United States. Several species reach distributional limits within the state. The mammalian fauna includes many species that occur throughout the central United States, especially those associated with the central grasslands, others with the southeastern deciduous forests, many characteristic of the desert regions of the Mexican

Plateau and the southwestern United States, and a few associated with the mountain regions of the western United States and the tropical regions of northeastern Mexico.

Other important features of the terrestrial mammalian fauna of Texas are the number of endemic species and the variability within species as reflected by the number of described subspecies. Five species are virtually confined in their distribution to Texas. There are 243 described taxa (species and subspecies) of native land mammals in the state, and 55 of the 141 species (39%) are represented by more than one subspecies.

DIVERSITY OF LAND MAMMALS

There is considerable change in the diversity of Texas mammals with geography. To illustrate this, species diversity has been depicted along a series of quadrats positioned along two transects that traverse the state (one stretching in a west to east direction from El Paso to Beaumont and another beginning at Dalhart in the northern part of the state and continuing southeastward to Brownsville) (Figure 1). Species diversity exhibits a general decrease along the transect from El Paso to Beaumont (Figure 2, transect A). The lowest diversity is in the Blackland Prairies region (quadrats 12 and 13) and the highest is

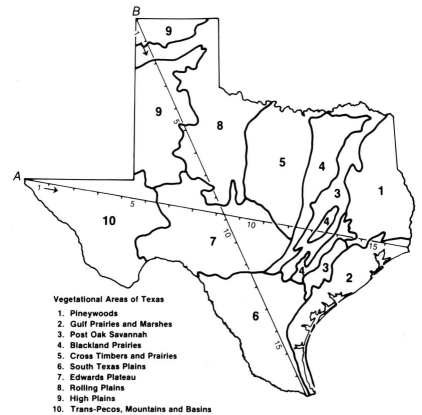

Vegetational Areas of Texas

1. Pineywoods
2. Gulf Prairies and Marshes
3. Post Oak Savannah
4. Blackland Prairies
5. Cross Timbers and Prairies
6. South Texas Plains
7. Edwards Plateau
8. Rolling Plains
9. High Plains
10. Trans-Pecos, Mountains and Basins

Figure 1.   Map of Texas showing major vegetative regions (1962) and the location of two transects along which species diversity was analyzed. Transect A stretches from El Paso to Beaumont; Transect B, from Dalhart to Brownsville. Map according to Gould, 1962, *Texas Plants: a checklist and ecological summary.* Texas Agricultural Experiment Station, MP-585.

in the Guadalupe Mountains of the Trans-Pecos (quadrat 3). Major shifts in the diversity pattern are evident on either side of the Balcones Escarpment (between quadrats 10 and 12), and between the western portion of the Edwards Plateau (quadrat 4) and the Guadalupe Mountains in the Trans-Pecos (quadrat 3).

The pattern is much more irregular, without any general trend, along the north to south transect (Figure 2, transect B). Diversity is highest in the Escarpment Breaks of the High Plains (quadrat 5), the Balcones Canyonlands of the Edwards Plateau (quadrats 10 and 11), and the subtropical brushlands of the South Texas Plains (quadrat 17). Diversity along this transect is lowest in the Rolling Plains region (quadrat 7) and the coastal sands of the South Texas Plains (quadrat 15).

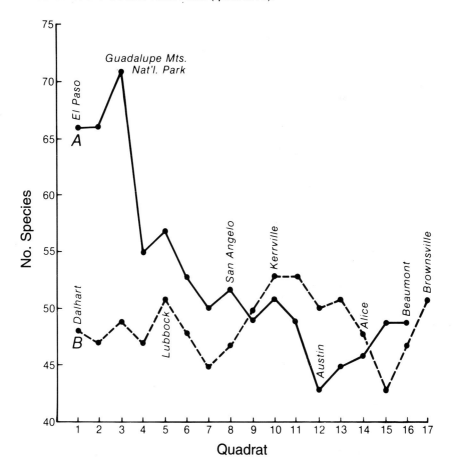

Figure 2. Species diversity plots for the quadrats along the two transects (A and B) shown in Figure 1.

Species diversity can also be viewed in terms of habitat diversity and land area. To evaluate this, the diversity of Texas mammals was examined with respect to the 10 major vegetation regions in the state. Figure 3 shows the plot of the number of species in each vegetative region versus the log of the land area for that vegetative type. The regions of lowest mammalian diversity in Texas are in the eastern half of the state (Pineywoods, Gulf Prairies and Marshes, Post Oak Savannah, Blackland Prairies, and Cross Timbers region) and on the High Plains. Areas of highest mammalian diversity are in the Trans-Pecos, Edwards Plateau, South Texas Plains, and Rolling Plains.

Two important generalizations are evident about the diversity of Texas mammals. First, there is no strong correlation between land area of the vegetation regions and species diversity. For example, the High Plains region is slightly larger in area than the Trans-Pecos region yet it supports only about half as many species of mammals. Second, those natural regions of Texas where vegetative and topographic heterogeneity are the greatest provide a broader spectrum of potential mammalian habitats and thus support a greater number of mammalian species.

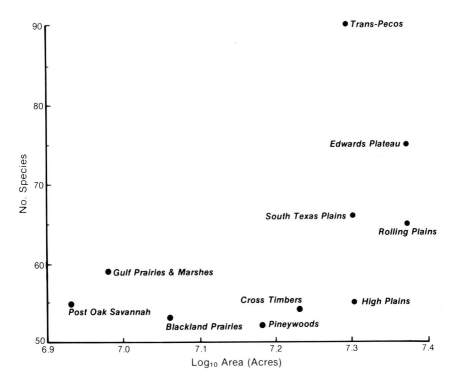

Figure 3. Plot of the number of species versus the area for each of the vegetative regions of Texas shown in Fig. 1.

GEOGRAPHIC DISTRIBUTION OF LAND MAMMALS

Texas may be conveniently arranged into four regions based on the ecological distribution of mammals. These are the Trans-Pecos, Plains Country, East Texas, and the Rio Grande Plains (Figure 4). The Trans-Pecos region includes the mountain and basin country west of the Pecos River. The Plains Country includes the High Plains, Rolling Plains, Cross Timbers area, and the Edwards Plateau. Included within the East Texas region are the Pineywoods, central Texas Woodlands, Blackland Prairies, and Coastal Prairies and Marshes. The Rio Grande Plains encompasses the South Texas brushlands. The Balcones Escarpment serves as the major physiographic barrier separating the Plains Country from East Texas and the Rio Grande Plains. The boundary between East Texas and the Rio Grande Plains is positioned between the Guadalupe and San Antonio rivers where pedocal and pedalfer soils meet.

The distributional patterns of land mammals in Texas conform to five major patterns. These are (1) ubiquitous species that range throughout most, or all, of the state (included in this group are several species that are now extinct or whose distributions have shrunk markedly in the past 150 years); (2) species that are distributed primarily in one of the four divisions of the state; (3) western species distributed in the Trans-Pecos and Plains Country; (4) western species distributed in the Trans-Pecos and Plains Country, but which also occur on the South Texas Plains; and (5) eastern species distributed principally east of the 100th meridian. Mammals assigned to each of these categories are listed. It should be noted that certain species occur slightly outside of the boundaries of the category to which they have been assigned.

The greatest number of unique elements in the mammal fauna of Texas occur in the Trans-Pecos region. Almost one-third of the 92 species of mammals that occur in the Trans-Pecos are primarily restricted in distribution to that region. Most of these mammals are species characteristic of the arid Mexican Plateau and southwestern United States or the montane woodlands of the western United States. The fewest

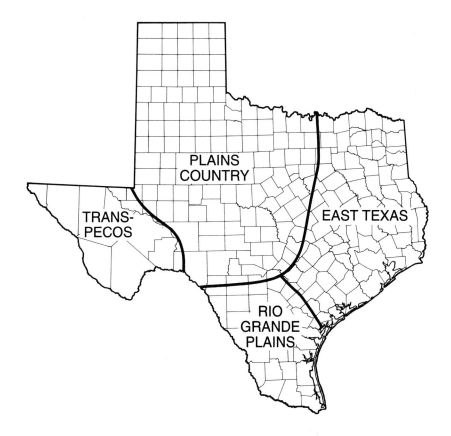

Figure 4.   Four regions of Texas based on the ecological distribution of mammals.

number of unique elements is found in the Plains Country. The 15 mammals unique to East Texas are species characteristic of the deciduous forests and coastal prairies of the southeastern United States, which reach their western distributional limits in Texas. The Rio Grande Plain supports 11 unique elements, most of which are characteristic of the tropical lowlands of northeastern Mexico and reach their northern distributional limits in south Texas.

MAMMALS GENERALLY DISTRIBUTED THROUGHOUT THE STATE

Virginia Opossum	*Didelphis virginiana* (absent from portions of the Trans-Pecos)
Silver-haired Bat	*Lasionycteris noctivagans*
Big Brown Bat	*Eptesicus fuscus* (not in Rio Grande Plains)
Eastern Red Bat	*Lasiurus borealis*
Hoary Bat	*Lasiurus cinereus*
Brazilian Free-tailed Bat	*Tadarida brasiliensis*
Eastern Cottontail	*Sylvilagus floridanus*
Black-tailed Jackrabbit	*Lepus californicus* (not in the Big Thicket of East Texas)
Hispid Pocket Mouse	*Chaetodipus hispidus* (not in the Big Thicket of East Texas)
American Beaver	*Castor canadensis*
Fulvous Harvest Mouse	*Reithrodontomys fulvescens* (not on the High Plains)
White-footed Mouse	*Peromyscus leucopus*
Deer Mouse	*Peromyscus maniculatus*
Hispid Cotton Rat	*Sigmodon hispidus*
Coyote	*Canis latrans*
Common Gray Fox	*Urocyon cinereoargenteus*
Black Bear	*Ursus americanus* (now extinct except for remnant populations in the Trans-Pecos)
Ringtail	*Bassariscus astutus*
Common Raccoon	*Procyon lotor*
Long-tailed Weasel	*Mustela frenata*
Striped Skunk	*Mephitis mephitis*
Mountain Lion	*Felis concolor* (now gone from much of the range except South Texas and the Trans-Pecos)
Bobcat	*Lynx rufus*
White-tailed Deer	*Odocoileus virginianus*
Bison	*Bos bison* (now extinct in the wild in Texas)

MAMMALS OCCURRING PRINCIPALLY IN THE TRANS-PECOS

Mexican Long-nosed Bat	*Leptonycteris nivalis*
California Myotis	*Myotis californicus* (disjunct record from Rolling Plains)
Fringed Myotis	*Myotis thysanodes* (disjunct record from Rolling Plains)
Long-legged Myotis	*Myotis volans* (disjunct record from Rolling Plains)
Yuma Myotis	*Myotis yumanensis*
Western Red Bat	*Lasiurus blossevillii*
Spotted Bat	*Euderma maculatum*
Pocketed Free-tailed Bat	*Nyctinomops femorosacca*
Western Mastiff Bat	*Eumops perotis*
Gray-footed Chipmunk	*Tamias canipes*
Texas Antelope Squirrel	*Ammospermophilus interpres* (also in western part of Edwards Plateau)
Desert Pocket Gopher	*Geomys arenarius*
Rock Pocket Mouse	*Chaetodipus intermedius*

Nelson's Pocket Mouse	*Chaetodipus nelsoni*
Desert Pocket Mouse	*Chaetodipus penicillatus*
Merriam's Kangaroo Rat	*Dipodomys merriami*
Banner-tailed Kangaroo Rat	*Dipodomys spectabilis* (also in southern part of High Plains)
Brush Mouse	*Peromyscus boylii* (also on Escarpment breaks of Rolling Plains)
Northern Rock Mouse	*Peromyscus nasutus*
Cactus Mouse	*Peromyscus eremicus* (also in extreme western part of Rio Grande Plain)
Mearns' Grasshopper Mouse	*Onychomys arenicola*
Tawny-bellied Cotton Rat	*Sigmodon fulviventer*
Yellow-nosed Cotton Rat	*Sigmodon ochrognathus*
Mexican Woodrat	*Neotoma mexicana*
Mexican Vole	*Microtus mexicanus*
Hooded Skunk	*Mephitis macroura*
Wapiti or Elk	*Cervus elaphus* (native population extinct; reintroduced into Guadalupe Mountains)
Mountain Sheep	*Ovis canadensis* (native population extinct; reintroduced into several mountain ranges)

MAMMALS OCCURRING PRINCIPALLY IN THE PLAINS COUNTRY

Thirteen-lined Ground Squirrel	*Spermophilus tridecemlineatus* (also in a narrow strip through Central Texas from the Red River and Dallas region south to Corpus Christi and east to Colorado County)
Plains Pocket Gopher	*Geomys bursarius*
Jones' Pocket Gopher	*Geomys knoxjonesi*
Llano Pocket Gopher	*Geomys texensis*
Plains Pocket Mouse	*Perognathus flavescens* (also in El Paso County)
Texas Kangaroo Rat	*Dipodomys elator*
Texas Mouse	*Peromyscus attwateri*
Prairie Vole	*Microtus ochrogaster* (subspecies *haydeni*)
Black-footed Ferret	*Mustela nigripes* (now extinct in Texas)

MAMMALS OCCURRING PRINCIPALLY IN THE RIO GRANDE PLAINS

Mexican Long-tongued Bat	*Choeronycteris mexicana*
Southern Yellow Bat	*Lasiurus ega*
Texas Pocket Gopher	*Geomys personatus*
Gulf Coast Kangaroo Rat	*Dipodomys compactus*
Mexican Spiny Pocket Mouse	*Liomys irroratus*
Coues' Rice Rat	*Oryzomys couesi*
White-nosed Coati	*Nasua narica* (also in Big Bend region of the Trans-Pecos)
Eastern Hog-nosed Skunk	*Conepatus leuconotus*
Ocelot	*Felis pardalis* (formerly more widely distributed)
Margay	*Felis wiedii* (now extinct in Texas)
Jaguarundi	*Felis yagouaroundi*

MAMMALS OCCURRING PRINCIPALLY IN EAST TEXAS

Southern Short-tailed Shrew	*Blarina carolinensis*
Southeastern Myotis	*Myotis austroriparius*
Seminole Bat	*Lasiurus seminolus*
Rafinesque's Big-eared Bat	*Plecotus rafinesquii*

Swamp Rabbit	*Sylvilagus aquaticus*
Eastern Gray Squirrel	*Sciurus carolinensis*
Eastern Flying Squirrel	*Glaucomys volans* (barely enters the Cross Timbers area of the Plains Country)
Attwater's Pocket Gopher	*Geomys attwateri*
Baird's Pocket Gopher	*Geomys breviceps*
Marsh Rice Rat	*Oryzomys palustris* (also in coastal region of Rio Grande Plain)
Eastern Harvest Mouse	*Reithrodontomys humulis*
Cotton Mouse	*Peromyscus gossypinus*
Golden Mouse	*Ochrotomys nuttalli*
Prairie Vole	*Microtus ochrogaster* (subspecies *ludovicianus*)
River Otter	*Lutra canadensis*

MAMMALS OCCURRING PRINCIPALLY IN WEST TEXAS (PLAINS REGION AND TRANS-PECOS)[1]

Western Small-footed Myotis	*Myotis ciliolabrum*
Western Pipistrelle	*Pipistrellus hesperus*
Townsend's Big-eared Bat	*Plecotus townsendii*
Rock Squirrel	*Spermophilus variegatus*
Black-tailed Prairie Dog	*Cynomys ludovicianus*
Botta's Pocket Gopher	*Thomomys bottae*
Yellow-faced Pocket Gopher	*Cratogeomys castanops*
Plains Harvest Mouse	*Reithrodontomys montanus* (also in the Blackland Prairies of East Texas)
Silky Pocket Mouse	*Perognathus flavus*
Western Harvest Mouse	*Reithrodontomys megalotis*
White-ankled Mouse	*Peromyscus pectoralis*
Piñon Mouse	*Peromyscus truei*
White-throated Woodrat	*Neotoma albigula*
Porcupine	*Erethizon dorsatum*
Swift or Kit Fox	*Vulpes velox*
Grizzly or Brown Bear	*Ursus arctos* (now extinct)
Mule Deer	*Odocoileus hemionus*

MAMMALS OCCURRING PRINCIPALLY IN WESTERN TEXAS (TRANS-PECOS AND PLAINS REGION) AND RIO GRANDE PLAINS

Desert Shrew	*Notiosorex crawfordi*
Ghost-faced Bat	*Mormoops megalophylla*
Cave Myotis	*Myotis velifer*
Pallid Bat	*Antrozous pallidus*
Big Free-tailed Bat	*Nyctinomops macrotis* (two records from East Texas)
Desert Cottontail	*Sylvilagus audubonii*
Mexican Ground Squirrel	*Spermophilus mexicanus*
Spotted Ground Squirrel	*Spermophilus spilosoma*
Merriam's Pocket Mouse	*Perognathus merriami*
Ord's Kangaroo Rat	*Dipodomys ordii*
Northern Grasshopper Mouse	*Onychomys leucogaster*
Southern Plains Woodrat	*Neotoma micropus*
Gray Wolf	*Canis lupus* (now extinct in Texas)
American Badger	*Taxidea taxus*

[1] Most of these species are distributed west of the 99th meridian.

Western Spotted Skunk	*Spilogale gracilis*
Common Hog-nosed Skunk	*Conepatus mesoleucus* (relict population in the Big Thicket probably extinct)
Collared Peccary	*Tayassu tajacu*
Pronghorn	*Antilocapra americana* (now extinct in Rio Grande Plains)

MAMMALS OCCURRING PRINCIPALLY EAST OF THE 100TH MERIDIAN

Elliot's Short-tailed Shrew	*Blarina hylophaga*
Least Shrew	*Cryptotis parva*
Eastern Mole	*Scalopus aquaticus*
Eastern Pipistrelle	*Pipistrellus subflavus*
Northern Yellow Bat	*Lasiurus intermedius*
Evening Bat	*Nycticeius humeralis*
Nine-banded Armadillo	*Dasypus novemcinctus*
Eastern Fox Squirrel	*Sciurus niger*
Northern Pygmy Mouse	*Baiomys taylori* (has spread to Plains regions)
Eastern Woodrat	*Neotoma floridana*
Woodland Vole	*Microtus pinetorum*
Common Muskrat	*Ondatra zibethicus* (also in Canadian, Pecos, and Rio Grande drainages)
Red Wolf	*Canis rufus* (now extinct in Texas)
Mink	*Mustela vison*
Eastern Spotted Skunk	*Spilogale putorius*
Jaguar	*Panthera onca* (now extinct in Texas)

Five species of mammals (all rodents) are unique to Texas in the sense that most, or all, of their known geographic range is confined to the mainland part of the state. These are:

Dipodomys elator — known from a few counties in the mesquite plains of north-central Texas and one county in Oklahoma;

Dipodomys compactus — known from the barrier islands of Texas and Tamaulipas, Mexico, and the South Texas Plains;

Geomys attwateri — known from East Texas (between the Brazos and San Antonio rivers);

Geomys personatus — known from the barrier islands of Texas and Tamaulipas, Mexico, and the South Texas Plains; and

Geomys texensis — known from eight counties in the Texas Hill Country.

There are three species of mammals (*Diphylla ecaudata, Myotis lucifugus, Myotis septentrionalis*) whose occurrence in Texas may be regarded as accidental. Resident breeding populations of these species probably never existed within the state. The Texas records for all three are far outside of their main range and only a single record exists for each in the state. Furthermore, all three are bats which are well known for their wandering movements.

CRITICAL SPECIES

Within the past 100 years, 9 species of land mammals and one marine mammal (the Caribbean monk seal) have become extirpated in Texas. A variety of factors can cause extinction, but in the case of these species, persecution and habitat alteration by man probably had more to do with their disappearance than any other single factor.

9

Overharvesting definitely seems to have caused the disappearance of the grizzly, elk, bison, and seal. Predator control activities probably had much to do with the extirpation of the gray wolf, red wolf, and the jaguar. The black-footed ferret disappeared primarily as a result of destruction of prairie dog towns, which removed most of their natural food supply. The big factors in the decline of the bighorn sheep were the introduction of domestic sheep and net wire fences into rangelands. Bighorns were unable to compete with the sheep, and the fences prevented their wandering about from one mountain range to another. The margay was probably only marginal in Texas and never represented by an established breeding population.

About 16% of the land mammals remaining in Texas today can be viewed as having some sort of biological problem that threatens or potentially threatens their existence. These are species that, in the opinion of biologists and conservation groups, currently face or likely will face serious conservation problems in the future (Table 2). State and federal agencies as well as private organizations have developed lists of rare and endangered mammals in Texas. The Texas Parks and Wildlife Department has a list of protected non-game wildlife. Similarly, the Texas Organization of Endangered Species (TOES) periodically publishes a watch-list of endangered, threatened, and peripheral vertebrates of Texas which includes mammals. The United States Fish and Wildlife Service also has produced a list of endangered and threatened species, which includes mammals listed in these categories in the Federal Register. The mammals listed in Table 2 are distributed throughout the state. There is no obvious geographic pattern or concentration of occurrence of these species within the state.

Although vigorous action must be directed to prevent direct human impacts on such species as the ocelot and jaguarundi, the continued existence and size of the populations of rare and endangered species are ultimately dependent upon availability and quality of their habitats. Therefore, for the most part, the problem of rare and endangered Texas mammals boils down to the problem of rare and endangered Texas habitats. The survival of these species is synonymous with protection and proper management of their habitats.

CONSERVATION STRATEGIES

The 20th century has proven as significant for changes made by humans in the landscape — its soils, waters, atmosphere, climate, habitats, and wildlife — as for its technological advancements. The risks as we progress toward the 21st century are not just with extinction or restriction of wildlife; there are serious economic ramifications associated with the continued loss of biological diversity. As species disappear, man's capacity to maintain and enhance agricultural, forest, and rangeland productivity decreases. And with the degradation of ecosystems, the valuable services that natural and semi-natural systems provide will be lost.

It seems inevitable that the 21st century will be as different from today's world as the current one has been from the 19th century, perhaps more so given the accelerating pace of change in lifestyle and technology. The next hundred years is likely to decide the future of wildlife in Texas and other states. Decisions will be made, directly or indirectly, as to how much and what kind of nature survives. Conservation pressures in the next century will come from a variety of sources. Habitat loss and degradation are the most important causes of wildlife decline, but overharvesting and poaching, trade in wild animal products, introduction of exotic species, pollution from pesticides and herbicides, and other causes also take a significant toll. Global warming or climate change could exacerbate the loss and degradation of biodiversity by increasing the rate of species extinction, changing

TABLE 2. List of critical mammals as defined by Texas Parks and Wildlife Department (TPW) and Department of Interior, Fish and Wildlife Service (DOI)[1].

Scientific Name, Common Name	TPW	DOI
Leptonycteris nivalis, Mexican Long-nosed Bat	E[2]	E
Choeronycteris mexicana, Mexican Long-tongued Bat		C2
Myotis austroriparius, Southeastern Myotis	T	C2
Myotis lucifugus, Little Brown Myotis		C2
Myotis septentrionalis, Northern Myotis		C2
Lasiurus ega, Southern Yellow Bat	T	C2
Euderma maculatum, Spotted Bat	T	C2
Plecotus rafinesquii, Rafinesque's Big-eared Bat	T	C2
Eumops perotis, Western Mastiff Bat		C2
Dipodomys elator, Texas Kangaroo Rat	T	C2
Oryzomys couesi, Coues' Rice Rat	T	C2
Simodon ochrognathus, Yellow-nosed Cotton Rat		C2
Canis lupus[3], Gray Wolf	E	E
Canis rufus[3], Red Wolf	E	E
Ursus americanus, Black Bear	E	PT
Nasua narica, White-nosed Coati	E	
Mustela nigripes[3], Black-footed Ferret	E	E
Conepatus leuconotus, Eastern Hog-nosed Skunk		C2
Felis pardalis, Ocelot	E	E
Felis yagouaroundi, Jaguarundi	E	E
Felis wiedii[3], Margay	E	E
Panthera onca[3], Jaguar	E	E
Trichechus manatus, West Indian Manatee	E	E
Eubalaena glacialis, Northern Right Whale	E	E
Balaenoptera musculus, Blue Whale	E	E
Balaenoptera physalus, Fin Whale	E	E
Megaptera novaeangliae, Humpback Whale		E
Physeter macrocephalus, Sperm Whale	E	E
Kogia breviceps, Pygmy Sperm Whale	T	
Kogia simus, Dwarf Sperm Whale	T	
Mesoplodon europaeus, Gervais' Beaked Whale	T	
Ziphius cavirostris, Cuvier's Beaked Whale	T	
Orcinus orca, Killer Whale	T	
Pseudorca crassidens, False Killer Whale	T	
Feresa attenuata, Pygmy Killer Whale	T	
Globicephala macrorhynchus, Short-finned Pilot Whale	T	
Steno bredanensis, Rough-toothed Dolphin	T	
Stenella frontalis, Atlantic Spotted Dolphin	T	

[1]As of January, 1992.

[2]T = Threatened; E = Endangered; C2 = Listed in Federal Register as Category 2 species (this refers to taxa for which information now in hand indicates that proposing to list the species as endangered or threatened is possibly appropriate, but for which substantial data are not currently available to biologically support a proposed rule); PT = Proposed to be listed in Federal Register as Threatened.

[3]Species considered by the authors to now be extinct in Texas.

population sizes and species distributions, modifying the composition of habitats and ecosystems, and altering their geographic extent.

Essentially the problem involves proliferating human populations and associated land conversion which is powerfully changing the form and shape of the landscape. People now constitute a pressure on the global environment that is evident everywhere. There are no longer any unoccupied frontiers; every square centimeter of the earth's surface is affected by the activities of human beings. This results in insufficient habitat for many species or situations in which habitats are isolated in separate pieces too small or too unstable to sustain viable populations of species and thus biological diversity. The theory of biogeography reveals that species richness is a function of land area. All environmental variables being equal, the greater the area, the more species it supports. Thus, as habitats are fragmented and isolated into small islands, they lose the capacity to support wildlife diversity.

Texas has a great treasure in its mammalian fauna which provides our citizens with important recreational, commercial, aesthetic, and scientific values. We are home to more than 20% of the nation's total deer population, over three-quarters of the carnivore species, and all but 10 species of bats that occur in the United States. The question is whether or not these resources can be sustained in the future. For this to happen, we must employ several conservation strategies. It has become clear in most cases that single approaches will not work successfully to conserve wildlife diversity. We must build long-range thinking and planning into conservation, and we must find ways for diverse groups, including state and federal agencies, academic institutions, private landowners and organizations, and public groups to network and explore new collaborative ventures that bring separate approaches together in a complementary way. The challenge is daunting. We face a monumental task, far beyond our existing abilities. But now is the time to look ahead, coordinate and plan, before our options are further narrowed.

There are presently about 100 areas in Texas that potentially could serve as biological reserves for the protection of species and the supporting environment. These include national parks, forests, preserves, and recreation areas; national wildlife refuges; state wildlife management areas; state parks; private wildlife foundations; and lands owned by private conservation organizations (for example, Nature Conservancy, Sierra Club, and Audubon Society). Over one million hectares of land are contained in these units which are distributed throughout the state and provide habitat for most Texas mammals.

While protected areas play a key role in the preservation of natural diversity, their ability to preserve our mammalian fauna is limited and sometimes overestimated. Their capacity for preservation is restricted by a number of internal and external factors. First, the parks and preserves of Texas are scattered throughout the state, but the geographical distribution is far from proportional. Thus, they poorly represent many of the natural areas in Texas, such as native grasslands and prairies. Second, most protected areas are too small and widely scattered to effectively preserve biological diversity. A recent publication in the scientific journal *Nature* concluded that the 14 largest national parks in western North America were too small to retain an intact mammalian fauna. No protected area in Texas is as large as the smallest of the 14 parks used in that study. Thus, a major goal of conservation must be to expand the number of protected areas to include a cross-section of all major ecosystems in the state and to link these areas via conservation corridors so they are more effective.

Protected areas alone, however, will not be sufficient to conserve mammalian diversity in Texas. To be effective in the long term, conservation strategies must consider the needs of local residents to maintain or enhance their quality of life. For this reason, conservation-based rural development is indispensable to any successful conservation strategy in Texas. With almost 98% of the state in private land, it will not be possible to conserve mammalian diversity in Texas without the support and participation of landowners. Why? — because the vast majority of wildlife habitat in Texas is privately owned. In order to retain the stability and diversity of this habitat, it must be managed and utilized by landowners in an economically and ecologically viable manner. A system of responsible wildlife management, sportsmanship, and land ethics must be developed. Aldo Leopold, the father of American conservation, recognized this more than 50 years ago when he wrote: "We need to recognize the landowner as the custodian of public game on all private lands ... and compensate him for putting his land in productive condition .... In short, make game management a partnership enterprise to which landowner, the sportsman, and the public each contribute appropriate services, and from which each derive appropriate rewards."

A basic weakness in a conservation system based wholly on economic motives is that most species of a land community have no economic value. Without a land ethic and a stewardship concern for the diversity and integrity of the land, landowners will favor those management practices which make the most money without a consideration of the whole biotic system. Landowner rights and wildlife management, including the protection of endangered species, can and must be integrated to achieve effective conservation of mammals in Texas. We must learn to manage the landscape for sustained local diversity, maintenance of ecosystem function, and renewable yields of natural resources for economic development.

We also must improve our biological knowledge about mammals. We know precious little of the life history of most mammals in Texas. In fact, for many species, our knowledge is insufficient to even accurately assess their status. Decisions as to whether a species is threatened, rare, or endangered are often based entirely on biological "guesswork" without proper knowledge of the population dynamics, reproduction, food habits, or behavior of the species considered. Future research efforts, whether they involve biologists working for state and federal agencies or scientists associated with academic institutions, should focus on correcting this problem.

Conserving wildlife, which recognizes neither ownership or boundaries, calls for good science, first-rate technology, excellent management, and a broad constituency willing to make some concessions to save it. Whether we act, and how, will depend on factors such as politics, education, socioeconomics, recreation interests, and planning capabilities. Broad-based conservation education programs, designed to diffuse conservation information to the public, must become an important priority. Without understanding of the need for action, and without commitment to that action, citizens will not contribute to the effort, nor will they cooperate with those so engaged. People must be educated to understand what the continuation — or destruction — of wildlife means to their future and that of their descendants, and they must be persuaded to act on their resulting concern in ways respectful to the diversity of wildlife and to their own cultural values.

KEY TO THE MAJOR GROUPS (ORDERS)
OF MAMMALS IN TEXAS

1. Body covered dorsally, and tail completely, by bands of bony plates; snout tapering and lacking teeth anteriorly; eight peglike teeth on each side of upper and lower jaws. Order Xenarthra, armadillos, sloths, and allies, p. 82.

   Not as above 2

2. Body torpedo-shaped; hind legs absent; front limbs developed into paddles; hairless or nearly so; live in ocean or coastal waters 3

   Not as above 4

3. Body ending in a broad, horizontally flattened, rounded fluke; no dorsal fin; muzzle squarish, covered with stout bristles; short bristlelike hairs scattered sparingly over rest of body; nostrils terminal; length 2.5 to 4.5 m. Order Sirenia, manatee and allies, p. 296.

   Body ending in horizontal, expanded (not rounded) flukes; blowhole (nostrils) on top of head; most Texas forms with dorsal fin; length 2.5 to 30 m. Order Cetacea, whales, porpoises, and dolphins, p. 298.

4. Hand and arm developed into leathery wing. Order Chiroptera, bats, p. 28.

   Hand and arm normal, not developed into a wing 5

5. Hoofed mammals; two or four toes on each foot. Order Artiodactyla, even-toed ungulates, p. 266.

   Toes usually armed with claws, not hoofs 6

6. Total of 10 upper incisors; big toe of hind foot without claw; tail prehensile. Order Didelphimorphia, opossums, p. 15.

   Total of six or less upper incisors; all toes armed with claws; tail not prehensile 7

7. Snout highly flexible and protruding conspicuously beyond mouth; eyes very small or hidden; length of head and body usually less than 150 mm. Order Insectivora, shrews and moles, p. 18.

   Snout normal, or if protruding conspicuously then length of head and body much more than 150 mm; eyes normal. 8

8. Total of two incisors in lower jaw, one on each side 9

   Total of four or more incisors in lower jaw (two or three on each side) 10

9. Total of two incisors in the upper jaw, one on each side so that incisor formula is 1/1. Order Rodentia, rodents, p. 95.

   Total of four incisors in the upper jaw, two on each side, one in front of the other in tandem; incisor formula 2/1. Order Lagomorpha, hares and rabbits, p. 86.

10. Marine dwellers, fore and hind limbs developed into flippers; tail normal or vestigial, never developed into flukes. Order Pinnipedia, seals and walruses, p. 264.

    Mainly land dwellers, limbs never developed into flippers, but hind feet may have webs between the toes. Order Carnivora, carnivores, p. 211.

ORDER DIDELPHIMORPHIA
OPOSSUM AND ALLIES

Opossums, as a group, are among the oldest, most primitive mammals of the New World. Some scientists call them "living fossils" because they have survived relatively unchanged for at least 50 million years. They are intermediate in many respects between the most primitive of all mammals, the egg-laying monotremes of Australia, and the higher placental mammals. Their chief character is the marsupium or pouch that develops on the abdomen of females. One species occurs in Texas.

Virginia Opossum (*Didelphis virginiana*). Photo by John L. Tveten.

FAMILY DIDELPHIDAE (OPOSSUMS)

VIRGINIA OPOSSUM
Didelphis virginiana Kerr

Description. A mammal about the size of a terrier dog, with long, scaly, prehensile tail; short, black, leathery ears; long, slender snout; five toes on each foot, the "big toe" on hind foot lacking a claw, thumblike and opposable; soles naked; pouch for young developed during breeding season on abdomen of female; pelage of long guard hairs and short soft underfur; two color phases — (1) grayish and (2) blackish; basal fourth or more of tail black, terminal section whitish; legs and feet blackish, toes often white or whitish. Dental formula: I 5/4, C 1/1, Pm 3/3, M 4/4 X 2 = 50. External measurements of males average: total length, 782 mm; tail, 324 mm; hind foot, 66 mm; of females, 710-320-63. Weight, 1.8-4.5 kg; males are usually larger and heavier than females.

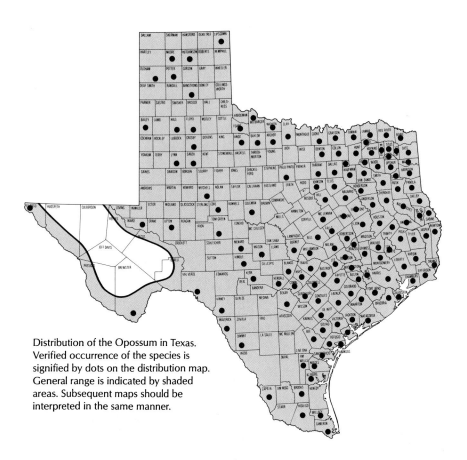

Distribution of the Opossum in Texas.
Verified occurrence of the species is
signified by dots on the distribution map.
General range is indicated by shaded
areas. Subsequent maps should be
interpreted in the same manner.

Distribution. Occurs statewide except for xeric areas of the Trans-Pecos and Llano Estacado of the Panhandle.

Habits. Opossums are primarily inhabitants of deciduous woodlands but are often found in prairies, marshes, and farmlands. In the western part of their native range they generally keep to the woody vegetation along streams and rivers, a habit which permits them to penetrate the otherwise treeless grasslands and deserts of west Texas.

Hollow trees and logs are preferred sites, but opossums will den in woodpiles, rock piles, crevices in cliffs, under buildings, in attics, and in underground burrows. Since they are not adept at digging burrows for themselves they make use of those excavated by other mammals.

Movements of opossums monitored in East Texas showed that these animals typically frequent a home range approximately 4.6 ha in size, although the minimum size of home ranges may vary from 0.12 ha to 23.4 ha. Home ranges tend to overlap considerably. In East Texas woodland habitat the density of opossums is about one opossum every 1.6 ha while in sandy, coastal parts of the state the density is about one opossum every 6 ha.

The opossum is more or less solitary and strictly nocturnal, venturing forth to feed shortly after dark. It feeds on a variety of foods, including rats, mice, young rabbits, birds, insects, crustaceans, frogs, fruits, and vegetables. Analyses of six stomachs from winter-trapped opossums in Texas revealed that the following foods (expressed in percentages) had been eaten: insects (grasshoppers, crickets, beetles, bugs, ants), 62.8; mammals (cottontails), 19.5; birds (sparrow family), 15.5; reptiles (lizards and snakes), 1.0;

16

mollusks (snails), 1.0; crustacea (crayfish), 0.2. In June the food for four opossums was about the same except that fruits and berries were added and birds were lacking.

Their mating season extends from January or February to June or July. Females, which are in heat for about 30 days, breed the first season following birth. The mating period is not longer than 36 hours and terminates with copulation, which is done in a manner similar to dogs. Young opossums have been observed as early as January 24 and as late as August 15. Usually two litters are produced — in February and June. The young, five to 21 in number, are born after a gestation of 11-12 days and each weighs about 3 grains (1/5 of a gram; 1/2,380 of a pound)! Blind, nearly helpless, hardly larger than honey bees, and embryonic in appearance they crawl unaided into the abdominal pouch of the mother, each attaching itself to a nipple. Shortly after a young one begins to nurse, the nipple swells and completely fills its mouth, thereby firmly attaching it to its mother. It remains attached until it is about 7 weeks of age, at which time it has grown large enough to detach itself. This peculiar adaptation compensates in part for the brief period of uterine development and assumes part of the function performed by the placenta in higher mammals. Since the number of teats is seldom more than 13, young born in excess of that number are doomed to die.

Mortality is high during the first year of life, and population turnover is relatively rapid. Known predators include foxes, coyotes, horned owls, and barred owls. Opossums are commonly seen killed on highways. The normal lifespan may be as low as 2 years.

The opossum is the second most commonly harvested furbearing animal in Texas, but the value of its pelt is low. During the period 1976 to 1982 the average value of an opossum pelt was only $1.83. Many trappers do not consider opossums worth "skinning out." Their fur is used primarily for trim on less expensive coats and hats.

Newborn opossums. Photo by John Wood.

ORDER INSECTIVORA
SHREWS AND MOLES

The name insectivora (insect eater) has reference to the food habits of the group as a whole. Although moles and shrews are not all strictly insectivorous, insects and other small animal life constitute the chief dietary items of most members of the group. Some kinds, the otter shrews of Africa and the star-nosed mole of America, for example, feed also upon fish. The Townsend mole of the Pacific Northwest often is a nuisance to bulb growers because of its fondness for the bulbs of many kinds of plants.

Moles, as a group, are subterranean in habit and spend most of their lives in the darkness of underground tunnels which they usually excavate for themselves. Correlated with this fossorial habit, the eyes of all moles are very small, in some species actually not opening to the outside, and of little value to them. On the other hand, their senses of touch and smell are highly developed.

Most American shrews live on the surface of the ground and occupy burrows only for sleeping or resting. Most of them have a decided preference for damp or boggy habitats where rank vegetation, surface litter, rocks, or rotting logs afford adequate protection. Some species, notably the desert shrew, are adapted to the arid regions of our western deserts. At the opposite extreme are the water shrew and the marsh shrew, neither of which occurs in Texas.

Shrews and moles are active throughout the year; the former often tunnel through snow or walk on top of it in search of food. Some species, notably the short-tailed shrew, store food for winter use, but this habit is not common. Surprisingly little is known regarding the habits of many species. The exact gestation period is not known for most species, and practically nothing is known about the growth and development of the young except that "they grow rapidly" and reach adult proportions in about 6 weeks. The length of life of shrews is thought to be less than 2 years, but specific information is lacking.

One species of mole and four species of shrews occur in Texas.

KEY TO THE INSECTIVORES OF TEXAS

1. Front feet broad and paddle-shaped; eyes non-functional. *Scalopus aquaticus* (eastern mole), p. 25.

   Front feet normal, not paddle-shaped; eyes small, but functional 2

2. Total number of teeth 30 or 32; ears nearly hidden in the fur; tail short, less than twice as long as hind foot 3

   Total number of teeth 28; ears rather conspicuous; tail more than twice as long as hind foot; total length about 80 mm. *Notiosorex crawfordi* (desert shrew), p. 23.

3. Total number of teeth 30; four upper unicuspids, with only three readily visible in lateral view; color of dorsum brownish or brownish gray. *Cryptotis parva* (least shrew), p. 21.

   Total number of teeth 32; five upper unicuspids, with four readily visible in lateral view; color of dorsum dark slate to sooty black or tinged with brown 4

4. Restricted to the pine-oak forest and pine forest regions in the eastern one-third of the state; pelage dark gray but often tinged with brown; cranial breadth usually less than 10.5 mm. *Blarina carolinensis* (southern short-tailed shrew), p. 19.

Known only from three counties in the central and coastal regions of the state; pelage not tinged with brown; cranial breadth usually greater than 10.5 mm. *Blarina hylophaga* (Elliot's short-tailed shrew), p. 21.

FAMILY SORICIDAE (SHREWS)

SOUTHERN SHORT-TAILED SHREW
Blarina carolinensis (Bachman)

Description. A rather robust, short-legged, short-tailed shrew with long, pointed, protruding snout; external ears short and nearly concealed by the soft, dense fur; tail less than half the length of head and body, usually less than twice as long as hind foot; upperparts dark slate to sooty black; underparts paler; tail black above, paler below. Dental formula: I 4/2, C 1/0, Pm 2/1, M 3/3 X 2 = 32. External measurements average: total length, 88 mm; tail, 17 mm; hind foot, 11 mm. Weight, 18-28 g.

Distribution. Eastern one-fourth of the state with a recent, disjunct record from Bastrop State Park (Bastrop County).

Habits. Short-tailed shrews occur in forested areas and their associated meadows and openings. Adequate cover and food appear to be more important in determining their presence than type of soil or vegetation.

Their burrows usually occupy two zones, one several centimeters below the surface or directly upon it and the other at a deep level, often 40-60 cm below the surface. These two levels are joined at irregular intervals. Frequently, their runs follow just beneath a log, sometimes penetrating and honeycombing the log if it is rotten and easily worked.

These creatures are short-legged and slow of gait but they always seem to be in a hurry, running along with their tails elevated at an angle. A slow-walking person can easily overtake them. They are well adapted for digging; the front feet are wide, strong, and slightly larger than the hind feet. Burrowing is accomplished by the combined use of forefeet, head, and nose. Timed individuals were capable of burrowing at the rate of about 30 cm a minute in soft soil.

Southern Short-tailed Shrew (*Blarina carolinensis*). Photo by John L. Tveten.

Like the least shrew (*Cryptotis*), *Blarina* seem to be more sociable than long-tailed shrews. Several individuals seem to use a common burrow system and seldom do they fight when two or more are placed in a cage. It appears certain that the male and female remain together during the prebreeding season.

The food habits of these shrews are strangely unshrewlike in that they consume relatively large quantities of vegetable matter (nuts, berries, and so forth). Analyses of more than 400 stomachs from East Texas revealed the following items (expressed in percentages of occurrence): insects 77.6; annelids, 41.8; vegetable matter, 17.1; centipedes, 7.4; arachnids, 6.1; mollusks (mostly snails), 5.4; vertebrates (mice and salamanders), 5.2; crustacea (mostly sowbugs), 3.7; undetermined matter, 2.4. There is considerable evidence that *Blarina* stores snails for winter use.

An interesting feature of this shrew is the poison produced by the submaxillary glands, which is present in the saliva and may be introduced into wounds made by the teeth. Injections of 6 mg of an extract prepared from the submaxillary gland are strong enough to kill mice but there is little likelihood of the venom having any serious effect on man.

The breeding season of *Blarina* extends from February through September. There appear to be two and possibly three litters of five to seven young produced in this period. The gestation period is probably between 21 and 30 days. The young are pink, blind, and helpless at birth, and they weigh slightly more than 1 g. They are relatively slow in developing; the eyes of young born in captivity were still closed on the

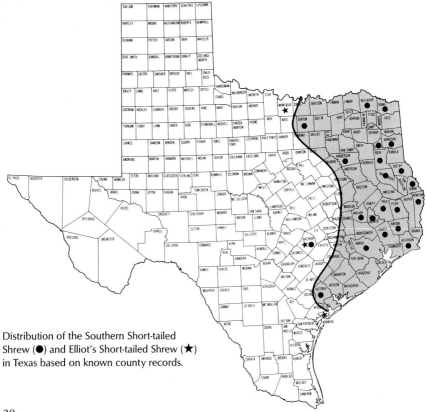

Distribution of the Southern Short-tailed Shrew (●) and Elliot's Short-tailed Shrew (★) in Texas based on known county records.

22nd day. The young are born in a special nest of grasses and other dry vegetation under a rotten log or stump or under the ground. In each instance entrance to it is gained by way of an underground tunnel. These nests are much larger than the more commonly found "resting" nests. Records indicate that very few of these shrews attain an age of 2 years.

Since the reproductive potential is high in this shrew, one can assume that its natural enemies are many. Known predators include the milk snake, black snake, red-tailed hawk, red-shouldered hawk, sparrow hawk, broadwinged hawk, barn owl, short-eared owl, barred owl, horned owl, long-eared owl, screech owl, fox, weasel, and skunk. Doubtless, others could be added to the list.

ELLIOT'S SHORT-TAILED SHREW
Blarina hylophaga Elliot

Description. Elliot's short-tailed shrew is nearly identical in appearance to the southern short-tailed shrew, *B. carolinensis*; both being tiny, slate-gray to brownish colored shrews with short tails and no external ears. *B. hylophaga* differs in having slightly larger cranial measurements and a noticeably larger fourth premolar. Also, *B. hylophaga* tends to be grayish in coloration, whereas *B. carolinensis* is often tinged with brown. Dental formula and external measurements as in *B. carolinensis*.

Distribution. Known in Texas only from Aransas, Montague, and Bastrop counties. Pleistocene fossils of this shrew are known from cave sites throughout the Hill Country.

Habits. In Aransas County, these shrews inhabit mottes of live oak trees on sandy soils, where they excavate their diminutive burrows. In Bastrop County, they have been collected in pitfall traps placed in grassy vegetation with an overstory of loblolly pine. Specimens from Montague County were obtained in a pitfall trap set in grassy vegetation several meters from some post oak trees. As with *B. carolinensis*, they may burrow extensively under leaf litter, logs, and deeply into the soil, but ground cover is not required. At Aransas Wildlife Refuge their burrows may be in areas with little or no ground cover, but are always where soft, damp soils afford easy burrowing.

As with the southern short-tailed shrew, this shrew is slightly venomous and may occasionally prey on animals larger than itself, such as mice. More frequently consumed food items are insects, arthropods, and earthworms.

Females produce two to three litters of four to six young each year. Breeding season and reproductive habits are probably similar to *B. carolinensis*. *B. hylophaga* has an average lifespan of only 2 years.

Remarks. The best way to distinguish this species from its cryptic relative, *B. carolinensis*, is to study the karyotype (number and morphology of chromosomes). That of *hylophaga* has a diploid number of 52 and a fundamental number of 60, 61, or 62; *carolinensis* has a diploid number of 37-46 and a fundamental number of 44.

LEAST SHREW
Cryptotis parva (Say)

Description. One of the smallest mammals; snout long and pointed; ears small and concealed in the short fur; eyes small; tail never more than twice as long as hind foot; fur dense; upperparts grizzled olive-brown, paler below. Dental formula: I 3/2, C 1/0, Pm 2/1, M 3/3 X 2 = 30. External measurements average: total length, 79 mm; tail 18 mm; hind foot, 10.5 mm. Weight, 4-7.5 g.

Distribution. Occurs in eastern and central portions of the state, west in the Panhandle to the New Mexico line, and to Val Verde County along the Rio Grande.

Habits. The least shrew is an inhabitant of grasslands where it utilizes the surface runways of cotton rats (*Sigmodon*) and other grassland rodents. It seldom occurs in forests but occasional individuals have been found under logs and leaf litter in moist, forested areas.

Most of its foraging seems to be done on the surface of the ground but the behavior of captive individuals suggests that occasionally they may tunnel through leaf litter and loose, damp soil, much as do moles, in search of food. The home proper is a small underground burrow or a series of shallow runways under flat stones or fallen logs. Burrows excavated in east-central Texas were about 2.5 cm in diameter, from 25 cm to 1.5 m long, and seldom more than 20 cm below the surface at the deepest point. Each burrow had an enlarged chamber at the end or in a side branch for the nest which was composed of dry, shredded blades of grass. These nests were used for rearing young or as resting places for groups of adult and half-grown shrews.

In contrast to most species of shrews, *Cryptotis* is sociable, and several individuals may be kept together in captivity without serious conflict. They sleep together and cooperate to some extent in digging tunnels and capturing food. One nest examined in December in Texas contained a dozen shrews that seemed to be established there for the winter; another examined near Nacogdoches was occupied by at least 31 individuals.

These tiny shrews are active at all hours of the day, but the peak activity comes at night. Also, they are difficult to trap except in winter when the supply of natural food is low; then they respond more readily to bait. In Texas, they tend to concentrate in favorable areas in winter and to disperse over wider areas when conditions are more favorable. That they are abundant at times in favorable areas is attested by the fact that barn owls capture and consume large numbers of them. These shrews made up 41% of the food items of a pair of barn owls as revealed by examination of owl pellets from Colorado County. In Jefferson County, 73% of the animals represented in barn owl pellets were *Cryptotis*.

The food of these tiny creatures is entirely animal matter — snails, insects, sow bugs, and other small animals. They occasionally set up housekeeping in beehives and feed upon the bees. Shrews kept in captivity preferred black crickets, then grasshoppers, sow bugs, and hard-shelled beetles in the order named. These captive shrews stored excess food in one corner of the cage, suggesting that they may behave likewise in the wild.

The breeding season extends from early March to late November. No wintertaken specimens from Texas have been in breeding condition. Females produce two or more litters each season. The young, three to six in number, are hairless, blind, and helpless and they weigh about 0.3 g each at birth. They grow rapidly and attain adult proportions in about 1 month.

Least Shrew (*Cryptotis parva*). Photo by John L. Tveten.

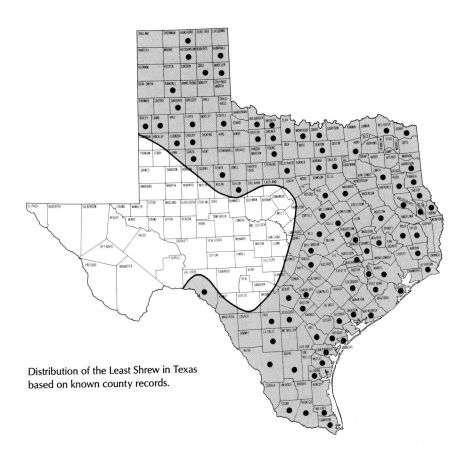

Distribution of the Least Shrew in Texas
based on known county records.

DESERT SHREW
Notiosorex crawfordi (Coues)

Description. A small shrew with conspicuous ears and long tail (more than twice as long as hind foot); upperparts lead gray; underparts paler. Dental formula: I 3/2, C 1/0, Pm 1/1, M 3/3 X 2 = 28. External measurements average: total length, 81 mm; tail, 27 mm; hind foot, 10 mm.

Distribution. Western two-thirds of state, including portions of north-central Texas and southern Texas.

Habits. Desert shrews are found in the more arid, western and southern parts of the state but do not appear to be restricted to any particular habitat. Specimens have been taken in cattail marshes, in beehives, under piles of cornstalks, among yuccas, in wood rat nests, and beneath piles of brush and refuse. In such places they construct their tiny nests of grasses and other dried vegetation. Unlike other shrews from Texas, desert shrews do not appear to construct or make use of underground burrows.

This shrew is thought to feed largely on both larval and adult insects; captive specimens have eaten a wide variety of food including mealworms, cutworms, crickets, cockroaches, houseflies, grasshoppers, moths, beetles, earwigs, centipedes, the carcasses of skinned small mammals and birds, and dead lizards. Conversely, captives refused live rodents, salamanders, scorpions, and earthworms. In captivity, desert shrews eat about 75% of their body weight each day and can subsist without drinking water.

Desert Shrew (*Notiosorex crawfordi*). Photo by John L. Tveten.

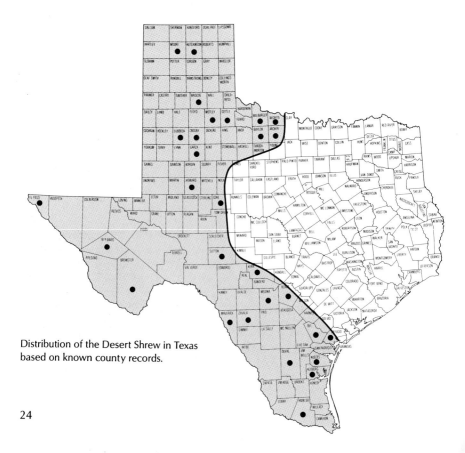

Distribution of the Desert Shrew in Texas based on known county records.

Little is known about the breeding habits of this shrew. The breeding season lasts from spring into the fall months, perhaps occasionally as late as November. Litter size averages three to five young, but it is not known if more than one litter is produced each season.

The lifespan is not known. Predators include great horned owls and barn owls.

FAMILY TALPIDAE (MOLES)

EASTERN MOLE
Scalopus aquaticus (Linnaeus)

Description. A relatively small, robust, burrowing mammal with broadened, shovel-like front feet webbed to base of claws; no visible eyes or ears; sharp-pointed nose; plushlike fur; and short, sparsely haired tail. Dental formula: I 3/2, C 1/0, Pm 3/3, M 3/3 X 2 = 36; middle upper incisors enlarged; canines small and undifferentiated; molars with W-shaped outline when viewed from biting surface. Color brown, often with silvery sheen, with suffusion of orange on nose and wrists; underparts silvery gray, faintly washed with orange. External measurements average: total length, 165 mm; tail, 29 mm; hind foot, 22 mm. Weight, 60-90 g.

Distribution. Eastern two-thirds of the state, including eastern portions of South Texas. In northern Panhandle extends to New Mexico line along Canadian River drainage. Isolated record from Presidio County.

Habits. Moles spend most of their life in underground burrows they excavate for themselves or usurp from other mammals, particularly pocket gophers (genus *Geomys*). Because of this, they are restricted in their distribution by the nature of the soil. In Texas, they occur largely in moist (not wet), sandy soils. Deep, dry sands and heavy clays are avoided.

Two types of underground burrows are used: (1) the shallow surface run, which is associated with food-getting activities, and (2) the deep burrow for protection and rearing of the young. The deep burrow is marked by conical mounds of earth the occupant has pushed to the surface, whereas the shallow burrow is marked by a meandering ridge of earth pushed up by the mole as it "swims" through the loose topsoil. Moist, well-drained fence rows, terraces, lawns, and knolls rich in organic matter are

Eastern Mole (*Scalopus aquaticus*). Photo by John L. Tveten.

25

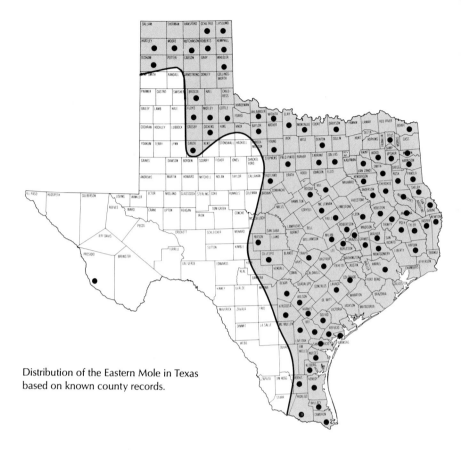

Distribution of the Eastern Mole in Texas based on known county records.

favored areas for surface burrows because in these localities food is more abundant. Certain of the surface burrows are used frequently as highways; others, especially intricate side branches, are used but once in the food-getting process and are then allowed to collapse.

Moles cannot see and spend almost all of their time underground. They may be found active at any hour of the day but generally are more active by day than by night in response to the movement of earthworms in and out of the soil. Also, they are active throughout the year.

The mole excavates its burrow by backward strokes and lateral thrusts of the front feet. Loose earth is moved and pushed to the surface by thrusts of the front feet. In excavating shallow runs the earth is merely pushed up to form a ridge, again by lateral thrusts of the front feet while the mole is turned partly on its side.

The home range of individual moles consists of several "hunting grounds" galleried with surface burrows on knolls, terraces, or along fence rows — all of them connected by a single long burrow. One burrow along a fence row in Van Zandt County was 360 m long. Such systems may be in continual use for as long as 5 years, either by one mole or by successive occupants. At times, moles travel overland in search of new locations, or, perhaps, of mates. This is evidenced by the occasional appearance of dead moles on the highways.

Throughout most of the year moles are solitary but in late winter and early spring males seek out females. In south-central Texas, the breeding season begins in February, as evidenced by the large testes of males and the swollen uteri of females. Although the breeding period may last from 3-4 months, peak activity occurs in a short period of 3-4 weeks. A single litter of two to five young is produced each year. The gestation period is about 4-6 weeks. The young are born hairless, but otherwise are miniature adults. Females reach sexual maturity in 1 year.

Moles feed largely on earthworms and grubs, although beetles, spiders, centipedes, insect larvae and pupae, and vegetable matter may also be eaten. In captivity, they have consumed mice, small birds, and ground beef.

The average daily food consumption is about 32% of the body weight of the animal, although a mole can consume more than 66% of its body weight in 18 hours. Active prey is killed by crushing it against the sides of the burrow with the front feet or by piling loose earth on the victim and biting it while thus held. Captive moles kill earthworms by biting them rapidly in several places, often nearly cutting the worm in two.

Moles do damage by their burrowing activities, especially on the greens of golf courses, in lawns, and in situations where accelerated soil erosion may result. Also, they may destroy row crops by burrowing along a row and killing the plants. It must be kept in mind, however, that the mole usually is searching out animal food and that often the larval insects taken do far more actual damage to the vegetation than does the mole. Larval June beetles, for example, feed on the roots of grasses and may, if present in large numbers, completely destroy the sod in an area. The burrowing activities of the mole also tend to aerate the soil, with beneficial results to plants.

ORDER CHIROPTERA
BATS

Chiroptera, "hand wing," alludes to the great elongation of the fingers that support the flying membrane. Among mammals, bats are unique in that they have true powers of flight; other mammals, such as flying squirrels, volplane or glide, always from a higher to a lower elevation.

Bats as a group are crepuscular or nocturnal; their eyes are small and inefficient, but their ears are usually well developed. Experiments suggest that the middle and inner ear and high-frequency vocals are highly important in guiding bats in flight and in their aerial feeding activities. Some bats hibernate in winter; others migrate seasonally.

In the temperate regions, the young are born in late spring; in the tropics there appears to be no definite breeding season — young bats may be found in every month of the year. Most bats feed on insects, but some kinds feed regularly on fruits, nectar, or fish, and some, the vampire bats, are peculiarly adapted to feed on blood.

Bats are nearly worldwide in distribution. The tropical regions are best suited for them, and there the greatest variety is found. The temperate regions are inhabited by fewer species; no bats have been recorded in the Arctic and Antarctic regions. Thirty-two species of bats occur in Texas.

In addition to the 32 species of bats living in Texas today, four others are known from fossil skeletal remains. One of these, *Myotis rectidentis*, is extinct, but the other three — *Myotis evotis*, *Macrotus californicus*, and *Desmodus rotundus* — still occur in other parts of the continent. The range of *Myotis evotis* includes almost all of the western United States from the Great Plains westward; the leaf-nosed bat *Macrotus* occupies a range from the southern parts of Arizona, Nevada, and California southward into Mexico; and *Desmodus*, the common vampire, occurs in Mexico and has been found recently about 200 km south of the Texas border near Jimenez, Tamaulipas. Intensive search may reveal the presence of both *Macrotus* and *Desmodus* in Texas.

KEY TO THE BATS OF TEXAS

1. Distinct, upwardly and freely projecting, triangular-shaped nose leaf at end of elongated snout 2

    Nose leaf absent, indistinct, or modified as lateral ridges or low mound-like structure; snout normal 3

2. Tail evident, projecting about 10 mm from dorsal side of interfemoral membrane; distance from eye to nose about twice distance from eye to ear; forearm less than 48 mm. *Choeronycteris mexicana* (Mexican long-tongued bat), p. 35.

    Tail not evident; eye about midway between nose and ear; forearm more than 48 mm. *Leptonycteris nivalis* (Mexican long-nosed bat), p. 33.

3. Thumb longer than 10 mm; hair straight, lying smoothly, glossy tipped. *Diphylla ecaudata* (hairy-legged vampire), p. 36.

    Thumb less than 10 mm; hair slightly wooly, pelage lax, not usually lying smoothly, not glossy tipped 4

4. Prominent grooves and flaps on chin; tail protruding from dorsal surface of interfemoral membrane. *Mormoops megalophylla* (ghost-faced bat), p. 31.

    No notable grooves or flaps on chin; lumps above nose or wrinkled lips possible, most faces lacking even these characteristics; tail extending to or beyond the edge of the interfemoral membrane 5

5. Tail extending conspicuously beyond free edge of interfemoral membrane 6

   Tail extending to free edge of interfemoral membrane 9

6. Forearm more than 70 mm; upper lips without deep vertical grooves. *Eumops perotis* (western mastiff bat), p. 79.

   Forearm less than 70 mm; upper lips with deep vertical grooves 7

7. Forearm less than 52 mm 8

   Forearm more than 52 mm (58-64). *Nyctinomops macrotis* (big free-tailed bat), p. 76.

8. Ears not united at base; second phalanx of fourth finger more than 5 mm. *Tadarida brasiliensis* (Brazilian free-tailed bat), p. 71.

   Ears joined at base; second phalanx of fourth finger less than 5 mm. *Nyctinomops femorosacca* (pocketed free-tailed bat), p. 75.

9. Ears proportionally large, more than 25 mm from notch to tip 10

   Ears of normal size, less than 25 mm from notch to tip 13

10. Color black with three large white spots on back, one just behind each shoulder, the other at the base of the tail. *Euderma maculatum* (spotted bat), p. 64.

    Color variable, but not black; no white spots on back 11

11. Dorsal color pale yellow; no distinctive glands evident on each side of the nose. *Antrozous pallidus* (pallid bat), p. 69.

    Dorsal color light brown to gray; distinctive glands (large bumps) evident on each side of the nose 12

12. Hairs on belly with white tips; strong contrast in color between the basal portions and tips of hairs on both back and belly; presence of long hairs projecting beyond the toes; known from eastern one-third of state. *Plecotus rafinesquii* (Rafinesque's big-eared bat), p. 66.

    Hairs on belly with pinkish buff tips; little contrast in color between basal portions and tips of hairs on both back and belly; absence of long hairs projecting beyond the toes; known from western half of state. *Plecotus townsendii* (Townsend's big-eared bat), p. 67.

13. At least the anterior half of the dorsal surface of the interfemoral membrane well furred 14

    Dorsal surface of interfemoral membrane naked, scantily haired, or at most lightly furred on the anterior third 20

14. Color of hair black, with many of the hairs distinctly silver-tipped. *Lasionycteris noctivagans* (silver-haired bat), p. 48.

    Color various, but never uniformly black 15

15. Color yellowish 16

    Color reddish, brownish, or grayish (not yellowish) 17

16. Total length more than 120 mm. *Lasiurus intermedius* (northern yellow bat), p. 60.

    Total length less than 120 mm. *Lasiurus ega* (southern yellow bat), p. 58.

17. Forearm more than 45 mm; color wood brown heavily frosted with white. *Lasiurus cinereus* (hoary bat), p. 57.

     Forearm less than 45 mm; upper parts reddish or mahogany 18

18. Upper parts brick red to rusty red, frequently washed with white 19

     Upper parts mahogany brown washed with white. *Lasiurus seminolus* (Seminole bat), p. 61.

19. Color reddish with frosted appearance resulting from white-tipped hairs; interfemoral membrane fully haired. *Lasiurus borealis* (eastern red bat), p. 55.

     Color rusty-red to brownish without frosted appearance; posterior one-third of interfemoral membrane bare or only scantily haired. *Lasiurus blossevillii* (western red bat), p. 54.

20. Tragus (projection within ear) short, blunt, and curved 21

     Tragus long, pointed, and straight 23

21. Forearm more than 40 mm. *Eptesicus fuscus* (big brown bat), p. 52.

     Forearm less than 40 mm 22

22. Forearm more than 32 mm; interfemoral membrane naked; color brown. *Nycticeius humeralis* (evening bat), p. 63.

     Forearm less than 32 mm; interfemoral membrane lightly furred on anterior third of dorsal surface; color drab to smoke gray. *Pipistrellus hesperus* (western pipistrelle), p. 49.

23. Dorsal fur tricolored when parted (black at base, wide band of light yellowish-brown in middle, tipped with slightly darker contrasting color); leading edge of wing membrane noticeably paler than rest of membrane. *Pipistrellus subflavus* (eastern pipistrelle), p. 51.

     Dorsal fur bicolored or unicolored with no light band in the middle; leading edge of wing same color as other parts of membrane 24

24. Calcar with well-marked keel 25

     Calcar without well-marked keel 27

25. Forearm more than 36 mm; foot more than 8 mm long; underside of wing furred to elbow; pelage dark brown. *Myotis volans* (long-legged myotis), p. 45.

     Forearm less than 36 mm; foot less than 8 mm long; underside of wing not furred to elbow; pelage light brown to buff brown 26

26. Hairs on back with dull reddish-brown tips; black mask not noticeable; thumb less than 4 mm long; naked part of snout about as long as the width of the nostrils when viewed from above. *Myotis californicus* (California myotis), p. 38.

     Fur on back with long, glossy, brownish tips; black mask usually noticeable; thumb less than 4 mm long; naked part of snout approximately 1.5 times the width of the nostrils. *Myotis ciliolabrum* (western small-footed myotis), p. 40.

27. Forearm more than 40 mm 28

     Forearm usually less than 40 mm 29

28. Conspicuous fringe of stiff hairs on free edge of interfemoral membrane. *Myotis thysanodes* (fringed myotis), p. 42.

No conspicuous fringe of stiff hairs on free edge of interfemoral membrane. *Myotis velifer* (cave myotis), p. 44.

29. In Texas occurring west of 100th meridian 30

    In Texas occurring east of 100th meridian 31

30. Dorsal fur usually with a slight sheen; forearm more than 36 mm; total length more than 80 mm. *Myotis lucifugus* (little brown myotis), p. 41.

    Dorsal fur usually lacking a sheen; forearm less than 36 mm; total length less than 80 mm. *Myotis yumanensis* (Yuma myotis), p. 46.

31. Ear more than 16 mm, extending more than 2 mm beyond nose when laid forward; tragus long (9-10 mm), thin, and somewhat sickle-shaped. *Myotis septentrionalis* (northern myotis), p. 42.

    Ear less than 16 mm, not extending more than 2 mm beyond nose when laid forward; tragus shorter and straight. *Myotis austroriparius* (southeastern myotis), p. 37.

FAMILY MORMOOPIDAE (MORMOOPID BATS)

GHOST-FACED BAT
Mormoops megalophylla Peters

Description. A medium-sized, reddish-brown or dark brown bat with conspicuous, leaflike appendages on chin; ears short, rounded, united across forehead; lower part of ear forming a copious pocket below eye; tail projecting dorsally from near middle of interfemoral membrane; crown of head highly arched; skull markedly shortened, cranium high and abruptly arched. Dental formula: I 2/2, C 1/1, Pm 2/3,

Ghost-faced Bat (*Mormoops megalophylla*). Photo by Merlin D. Tuttle, Bat Conservation International.

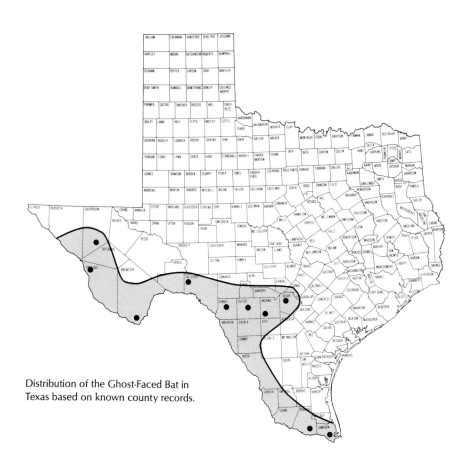

Distribution of the Ghost-Faced Bat in
Texas based on known county records.

M 3/3 X 2 = 34. External measurements average: total length, 90 mm; tail, 26 mm; foot,
10 mm; length of forearm, 54 mm.

Distribution. Known from the Apache Mountains (Culberson County),
southern Trans-Pecos, southern escarpment of the Edwards Plateau, and extreme
South Texas.

Habits. This is a colonial, cave-dwelling bat whose distribution is closely correlated with the distribution of caves, crevices, and abandoned mine tunnels which
serve as daytime roosts. A colony of about 6,000 individuals was found in Frio Cave
near Concan in February and March, 1955. This cave may serve *Mormoops* chiefly as
a winter retreat because from April through August none has been found there. In
contrast, records from Trans-Pecos Texas are from these warmer months of the year,
suggesting the possibility of seasonal migration between the two regions. Such movements have yet to be substantiated, however. At Frio Cave the population begins
building up in September, and by mid-November it approaches maximum size. Smaller
colonies of *Mormoops* inhabit Haby Cave and Valdina Farms Sinkhole in Medina
County and Webb Cave in Kinney County. They have also been taken in a railroad
tunnel near Comstock in Val Verde County. Members of a *Mormoops* colony roost
singly, spread out over the ceiling of the cave about 15 cm apart. There are no compact clusters as one finds with most cave-dwelling bats.

Mormoops also may roost in buildings. Four Texas specimens were captured in
the Junior High School at Edinburg. Students found them hanging from the rough
plaster ceiling in one of the halls. The bats apparently entered the building through
open windows at night. One specimen was captured in February, the others in January.

Their food appears to consist entirely of insects which are captured in flight. The stomachs of two *Mormoops* from Big Bend National Park were entirely filled with moths. *Mormoops* probably forages relatively high above the ground in areas unobstructed by tall vegetation. The bat is a strong, swift flier that hits a mist net with considerable force, although few of them have been caught in such nets. In Yucatan, however, *Mormoops* have been captured in mist nets set "in or near forests," and in southern Chiapas, Mexico, they have been taken in nets set across a tree-bordered, shallow stream where about a dozen species of bats came to drink.

Little data on the breeding habits of *Mormoops* in Texas are available. In Big Bend National Park two pregnant females, each containing a single embryo, were captured in mid-June. Lactating females have been captured there from mid-June to early August. In Coahuilla and Nuevo Leon, two Mexican states bordering Texas, gravid females have been captured in March, April, and May. Each gravid female contained a single embryo. Based on data collected in Central America and Mexico, it seems that in this species mating begins in late December. Sexually mature females taken between January and June are likely to be gravid or lactating; no gravid females have been reported from late June through January. Thus, it appears that the period of reproduction is confined to late winter and early spring, even in the tropics, and that each reproductively active female gives birth to only one offspring each year.

FAMILY PHYLLOSTOMIDAE (LEAF-NOSED BATS)

MEXICAN LONG-NOSED BAT
Leptonycteris nivalis (Saussure)

Description. A medium-sized bat with short ears, no tail, and a distinct nasal leaf; forearm furred above at elbow; upperparts drab brown, the hairs white basally; underparts pale drab, tips of hairs silvery. Dental formula: I 2/2, C 1/1, Pm 2/3, M 2/2 X 2 = 30. External measurements average: total length, 83 mm; foot, 17 mm; ear, 15 mm; forearm, 58 mm. Weight, 24 g.

Mexican Long-nosed Bat (*Leptonycteris nivalis*). Photo by Merlin D. Tuttle, Bat Conservation International.

33

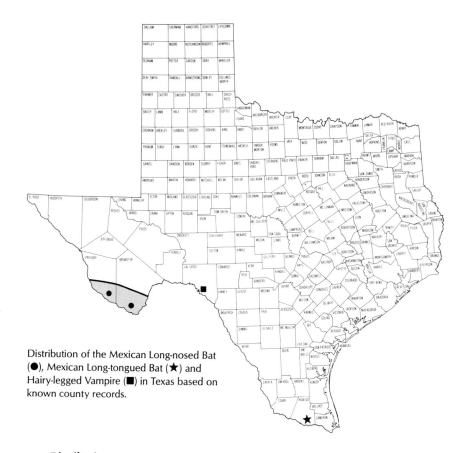

Distribution of the Mexican Long-nosed Bat
(●), Mexican Long-tongued Bat (★) and
Hairy-legged Vampire (■) in Texas based on
known county records.

Distribution. A Mexican species that enters Texas in the Big Bend region. Known in Texas from southern Brewster and Presidio Counties.

Habits. This is a colonial, cave dwelling bat that usually inhabits deep caverns. The only known colony of these bats in the United States is found in a large cave on Mt. Emory in Big Bend National Park. The number of bats using the cave fluctuates widely from year to year with yearly estimates of population numbers ranging from zero to 13,650. Reasons for this instability are unknown, but it may be that this colony forms only in years when over-population or low food supply in Mexico force the bats to move northward. This bat has recently been classified as endangered by the U.S. Fish and Wildlife Service.

At the Emory Peak cave, *L. nivalis* forms a large cluster with half-grown young and adults intermingled. Adult males and females may be present. They share the cave with a large colony of big-eared bats (*Plecotus*); each colony roosts in a different part of the cave, but not more than 6 m apart. The air in this cave in considerably cooler in summer than that outside, and a distinct breeze blows through it at all times. The cave is not used in winter; the inhabitants migrate to Mexico. This bat has a strong, musky odor similar to that of the Brazilian free-tailed bat.

L. nivalis feeds on the nectar and pollen of flowers, especially those of the century plant (*Agave* sp.). The seasonal occurrence of *L. nivalis* in Texas is probably related to food availability as their presence seems to coincide with the blooming of century plants in June. These plants open their flowers at night and attract bats with copious amounts of nectar. As the bats feed, their fur gets coated with pollen grains. When they fly to another plant in search of more food, they transfer the pollen to a new flower,

34

assisting in cross-fertilization of the plants. This mutual relationship is so strong that both the bats and the century plants cannot survive without the other. As the flower stalks of the agaves die by late summer, the bats disappear as there is nothing left for them to eat.

The breeding season is restricted to April, May, and June. Females give birth to one young annually. The young are born in Mexico, prior to the bats' arrival in Texas, and are weaned in July to August, which is the peak of the rainy season and the peak of flower abundance.

MEXICAN LONG-TONGUED BAT
Choeronycteris mexicana Tschudi

Description. A medium-sized bat with a long, slender muzzle and prominent nasal leaf. A minute tail is present and extends less than halfway to the edge of the interfemoral membrane. Color is sooty gray to brownish. Dental formula: I 2/0, C 1/1, Pm 2/3, M 3/3 X 2 = 30. External measurements average: total length, 85 mm; tail, 10 mm; foot, 14 mm; ear, 16 mm; forearm, 44 mm. Weight, 25 g.

Distribution. A Mexican species that enters the United States in extreme southern Texas, New Mexico, and Arizona. The single Texas record is from Santa Ana National Wildlife Refuge in Hidalgo County.

Habits. These bats inhabit deep canyons where they use caves and mine tunnels as day roosts. They also have been found in buildings and often are associated with big-eared bats (*Plecotus*).

C. mexicana feeds on fruit, pollen, nectar, and probably insects. Because of their longer tongue, they may be able to recover nectar from a greater variety of night-blooming plants than the other nectar feeding bat in Texas — *Leptonycteris nivalis*.

Parturition occurs from June to early July in Arizona and New Mexico with young reported as early as mid-April in Sonora, Mexico. A single young is born per female. One of us (Schmidly) collected a pregnant *C. mexicana* in May, which gave birth to a young bat shortly after capture, in the San Carlos Mountains of northern Tamaulipas, Mexico, which is no more than 241 km south of Santa Ana Wildlife Refuge. Pregnant and lactating females have been recorded in March and June in Coahuila, Mexico, to the south of the Texas border.

Mexican Long-tongued Bat (*Choeronycteris mexicana*).
Photo by Merlin D. Tuttle, Bat Conservation International.

HAIRY-LEGGED VAMPIRE

Diphylla ecaudata Spix

Description. A relatively large, sooty-brown bat with no tail; a narrow, hairy interfemoral membrane; short, rounded ears; and a short, pug-nosed snout. The dentition is highly modified with the middle upper incisors larger than the canines; the outer incisors very small and set so close to the canines that they are easily overlooked; the crowns of the outer lower incisors seven-lobed, fan-shaped, and more than twice as wide as the inner lower incisors; premolars and molars very small and probably nonfunctional. Dental formula: I 2/2, C 1/1, Pm 1/2, M 2/2 X 2 = 26. External measurements average: total length, 85 mm; foot, 13 mm; forearm, 53 mm. Weight, 30-40 g.

Distribution. From southern Texas southward to eastern Peru and Brazil. Known from Texas on the basis of one female taken May 24, 1967 from an abandoned railroad tunnel 19 km west of Comstock, Val Verde County.

Habits. This bat is primarily an inhabitant of tropical and subtropical forestlands. Its daytime retreat is normally a cave which it may share with other species of bats, but it has also been found roosting in mine tunnels and hollow trees. In the Mexican state of San Luis Potosi, Walter Dalquest found that these vampires were more solitary than the common vampire (*Desmodus*), and they did not gather in groups, even when several individuals inhabited a cave. Consequently, pools of digested blood do not form and there is only a slight odor of ammonia in the caves they inhabit. He found about 35 individuals, mostly females with young, in one cave but usually only one, two, or three were present in a given cave. These bats are shy, quick of movement, and readily take flight when molested.

The food of *Diphylla* is the blood of warm-blooded vertebrates, mainly birds, including domestic chickens. Ernest Walker reported that *Diphylla* attacks the legs and cloacal region of chickens. One bat was "observed alighting on the tail of a chicken, hanging by its hind legs and biting the exposed skin in the cloacal region, and then lapping up the blood while in an upright position."

This species seems to be reproductively active throughout the year. Pregnant females have been reported from Mexico and Central America in March, July, August, October, and November. The number of embryos per female is normally one, but one female captured July 8 in Chiapas, Mexico, contained two nearly full-term (crown-rump length 34 mm) embryos. The reproductive condition of the female captured in Texas was not recorded.

Hairy-legged Vampire (*Diphylla ecaudata*). Photo by Merlin D. Tuttle, Bat Conservation International.

Although only one specimen of the hairy-legged vampire is known from Texas, it is possible that a thorough search of the caves in the Hill Country and along the Rio Grande will reveal additional records of this species or the common vampire (*Desmodus rotundus*) which have been taken in northern Mexico no more than 200 km from the Texas border. Since *Diphylla* is a possible reservoir of bovine paralytic rabies, it is of economic importance to the cattlemen and sportsmen of Texas.

FAMILY VESPERTILIONIDAE (VESPERTILIONID BATS)

SOUTHEASTERN MYOTIS
Myotis austroriparius (Rhoads)

Description. A small bat with dense, dull, woolly fur; upperparts brownish to sooty; fur of underparts with white tips and black bases, the general white appearance contrasting sharply with the upperparts; cranium globose and normally with a low sagittal crest. Dental formula as in *M. lucifugus.* External measurements average: total length, 88 mm; tail, 36 mm; foot, 9 mm; forearm, 38 mm. Weight, 5-7 g.

Distribution. Southeastern United States; occurs westward to the Pineywoods region of East Texas.

Habits. *M. austroriparius* is predominantly a cave bat in that part of its range where suitable caves occur. But in Texas, and in most of Louisiana, it seeks out roosts in human habitations and structures. Outside of caves, it has been found in crevices between bridge timbers; in culverts and drain pipes; in boat houses, barns, and the attics of houses; and in hollow trees. The bats are usually closely associated with water and when they leave their diurnal roosts late in the evening (usually about dark), they fly to nearby ponds and streams over which they forage and from which they drink. They fly low over the water, usually within 60 cm of the surface, capturing insects. Specific foods are not known but small moths, midges, mosquitoes, and flies are probably of importance.

Southeastern Myotis (*Myotis austroriparius*). Photo by Merlin D. Tuttle, Bat Conservation International.

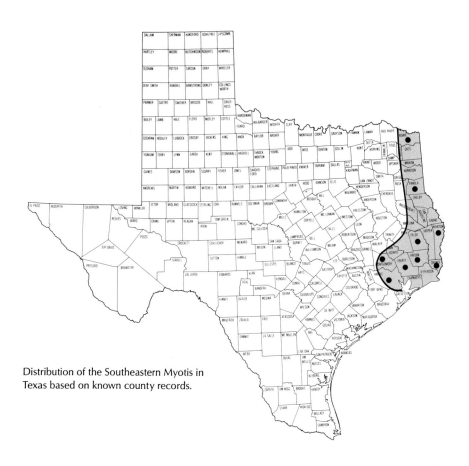

Distribution of the Southeastern Myotis in Texas based on known county records.

Where suitable caves are available, both males and females congregate in large numbers in late March and April to bear their young. In caveless areas, old buildings may serve as nursery sites. Parturition occurs in late April to late May and the young are large enough to fly 5 or 6 weeks later. The southeastern myotis is unusual among bats of the genus *Myotis* as it usually gives birth to twin offspring; other *Myotis* usually having only one young per year. At birth, the young bats weigh slightly more than 1 g each. They grow rapidly, and sexual maturity is reached in both sexes before the bats are a year old.

Their most important predators appear to be rat snakes, corn snakes, opossums, and certain species of owls. Large cockroaches may prey on newborn young that fall to the ground.

CALIFORNIA MYOTIS
Myotis californicus (Audubon and Bachman)

Description. A small *Myotis* with small foot, short forearm, and relatively long tail; ears proportionately large, extending slightly beyond snout when laid forward; ratio of foot to tibia 37 to 46, usually 43 to 46; ratio of tail to head and body 91 to 98; pelage full, long, and dull; profile of skull rises sharply to the forehead and decidedly flat-topped cranium; upperparts ochraceous tawny. Most easily confused with *M. ciliolabrum* but differs in smaller thumb (thumb and wrist together 6-7.5 mm instead of 8-8.5 mm); smaller teeth; profile of skull abruptly, rather than gradually, rising to forehead; brain case broader. Dental formula: I 2/3, C 1/1, Pm 3/3, M 3/3 X 2 = 38. External measurements average: total length, 78 mm; tail, 37 mm; foot, 5.5 mm; ear, 13 mm; forearm, 32 mm. Weight, 3-5 g.

Distribution. A western species known in Texas from the Trans-Pecos region and one disjunct record from the Panhandle (Randall County). This is one of the few species that winters in the Trans-Pecos, where it is found in desert, grassland, and wooded habitats.

Habits. These small bats are inhabitants of wooded canyons, open deciduous and coniferous forests, and brushy hillsides. Their daytime roosts are in crevices in the tops or sides of shallow caves, in cliffs and cavities, and in houses. They do not form the compact clusters typical of many other *Myotis*, but roost in small colonies of 1-25 individuals. These bats seem to use buildings more frequently than other *Myotis*. They appear on the wing much later in the evening than most species of *Myotis*.

Specific food items are unknown, but this bat appears to feed primarily on small moths and beetles that occur between, within, or below the vegetative canopy. Their flight is relatively slow, fluttery, and highly erratic.

They winter in at least part of their summer range, where they hibernate in houses or caves. They are fairly active in winter and winter records are relatively abundant from the southwestern United States. In summer, these bats seem quite transient and will use any suitable and immediately available site for shelter.

The single young is probably born in May, June or July. Pregnancy records vary from April 29 to July 6.

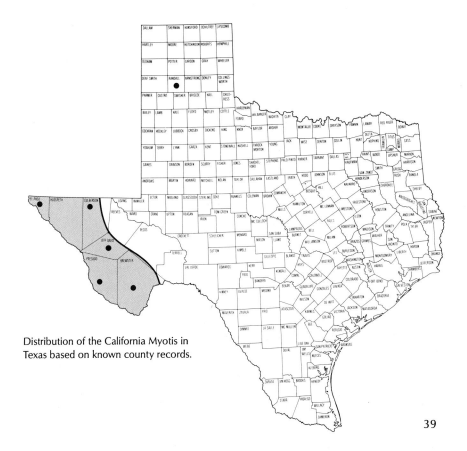

Distribution of the California Myotis in Texas based on known county records.

39

WESTERN SMALL-FOOTED MYOTIS
Myotis ciliolabrum (Merriam)

Description. A small *Myotis* with small feet, short ears, and relatively long tail; ratio of tail to head and body about 95; ratio of foot to tibia 40-45; upperparts light buff to warm buff, with slight tricolor effect; individual hairs blackish basally, succeeded by pale intermediate section and flaxen tips; underparts pale buff to nearly white; muzzle, chin, ears, and tragus blackish; sides of face from muzzle to ears blackish brown. Most easily confused with the small-footed *M. californicus* (see same for differences). Dental formula as in *M. californicus*. External measurements average: total length, 79 mm; tail, 37 mm; foot, 7 mm; ear, 13 mm; forearm, 33 mm. Weight, 4-5 g.

Distribution. Restricted in Texas primarily to the Trans-Pecos region, although two records are known from the High Plains of the Panhandle (Armstrong and Randall counties). A small, resident population may occur in this area in the vicinity of Palo Duro Canyon.

Habits. In the western United States, these bats are inhabitants of the deserts, semideserts, and desert mountains. Their daytime roosts may be in crevices and cracks in canyon walls, caves, mine tunnels, behind loose tree bark, or in abandoned houses. These bats hibernate in suitable caves or mine tunnels within the range occupied in summer. Bats observed in winter are often found wedged deeply into narrow cracks and crevices in the rock ceilings of old mines. When probed from these crevices they are able to fly, which indicates they do not go into a deep winter sleep.

Western small-footed myotises appear to have similar feeding and foraging habits as the California myotis, but their specific food habits have not been recorded. They

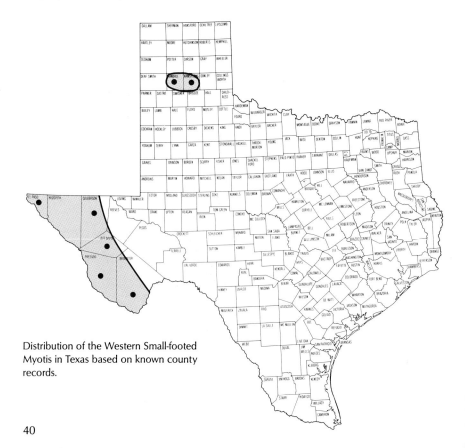

Distribution of the Western Small-footed Myotis in Texas based on known county records.

40

may feed over water and close to the ground over desert chaparral vegetation. This bat is strong enough to take off from the surface of water.

The reproductive habits of this bat are not known. Records indicate that the single young born annually appears in late May to early July.

Remarks. In previous editions of this bulletin, this bat was regarded as a subspecies of *Myotis leibii*; however, recent taxonomic work on this broadly distributed species has shown that *M. ciliolabrum* should be elevated to specific status.

LITTLE BROWN MYOTIS
Myotis lucifugus (Le Conte)

Description. A small bat; hairs of back with long, glossy tips that produce a conspicuous sheen; pelage long and full, longest hairs about 10 mm; upperparts ranging from bronzy brown to olive brown; underparts grayish with rich, buffy suffusion; interfemoral membrane sparsely haired above about to line joining knees; foot relatively large, a little more than half the length of tibia; ratio of tail to head and body less than 80; dorsal profile of skull gradually rising from relatively short rostrum. Dental formula as in *M. californicus*. External measurements average: total length, 85 mm; tail, 35 mm; foot, 9 mm; ear, 13 mm; forearm, 39.5 mm. Weight, 7-9 g.

Distribution. This species is known in Texas by only one specimen (U.S. Nat. Mus., 21083/36121) from Fort Hancock in Hudspeth County.

Habits. This bat spends the daytime in crevices in canyon walls, caves, attics, or other places of concealment and emerges shortly before dark. Its flight is erratic and relatively slow.

In the northeastern United States, these bats may migrate up to 320 km between winter and summer ranges, but in the west they are believed to hibernate near their summer range. As cold weather approaches the bats move to suitable caves, mine tunnels, or other quarters where they hibernate and sleep through the winter. During the period of preparation for winter, males and females are found together and breeding takes place, but the ova are not fertilized at that time. This habit of breeding in the fall has led some students to estimate the gestation period of this species to be 300 days; however, the period of gestation is actually 50-60 days. The sperm from the fall mating are retained in the reproductive tract of the female and fertilization of the ova does not

Little Brown Myotis (*Myotis lucifugus*). Photo by Merlin D. Tuttle, Bat Conservation International.

take place until the following spring, shortly before the bats leave their winter quarters. This ability is known as "delayed fertilization." A short breeding period may also occur in the spring. The single young is born in June or July.

Food consists of insects captured in flight. Remains of small, night-flying beetles, bugs, and flies have been identified in their stomachs. These bats forage primarily over or near water.

NORTHERN MYOTIS
Myotis septentrionalis (Trouessart)

Description. This is a small bat with dull, gray-brown pelage. Compared to other *Myotis* from Texas, *M. septentrionalis* has relatively long ears and an unkeeled calcar. As with all *Myotis*, this bat also has a narrow and sharp-pointed tragus. Dental formula as in *M. californicus*. External measurements average: total length, 78 mm; tail, 26 mm; foot, 9 mm; ear, 13 mm; forearm, 35 mm.

Distribution. Widely distributed over eastern and northern North America, this bat is known in Texas on the basis of only one specimen from Winterhaven in Dimmit County. It is doubtful that resident populations of this species occur in Texas.

Habits. This bat hibernates in caves and mine tunnels in eastern Canada and in the United States from Vermont to Nebraska. It is more solitary in its habits than other *Myotis*, generally found singly or in small groups of up to 100 individuals. In summer, this bat may occasionally be found in hollow trees, rock crevices, behind tree bark, and in buildings.

M. septentrionalis commonly forages along forest edges, over forest clearings, and occasionally over ponds but specific food habits remain unknown.

Little is known of the reproductive habits of this bat. Small nursery colonies seem the rule, and twinning may occasionally occur.

FRINGED MYOTIS
Myotis thysanodes Miller

Description. A relatively large *Myotis* with large ears and a distinct fringe of short, stiff hairs on free edge of the membrane between hind legs; tail from 75 to 81% of length of head and body; foot from 50 to 75% of length of tibia; ears projecting about 5 mm beyond snout when laid forward; pelage full and about 9 mm long on the back; upperparts uniform warm buff, tips of hairs shiny, bases fuscus black; underparts dull whitish. Dental formula as in *M. californicus*. External measurements average: total length, 86 mm; tail, 35 mm; foot, 9 mm; ear, 16.5 mm; forearm, 43 mm.

Distribution. A western bat known from Texas in the Trans-Pecos region in summer. Two specimens have been captured from northwest Texas (Crosby County), but these were probably seasonal migrants. The fringed myotis has been captured in habitats ranging from mountainous pine, oak, and pinyon-juniper to desert scrub but seems to prefer grassland areas at intermediate elevations.

Habits. These bats roost in caves, mine tunnels, rock crevices, and old buildings in colonies that may number several hundred. This is a highly migratory bat that arrives in Trans-Pecos Texas by May, at which time it forms nursery colonies. These colonies begin to disperse in October, and the winter locales and habits of this bat remain a mystery.

This species appears late in the evening to forage. They fly slowly and are highly maneuverable, allowing the bats to forage close to the vegetative canopy or about the face of small cliffs. No data are available on their specific food habits in Texas, but specimens from New Mexico contained mostly small beetles.

The single young is born in late June or early July after a gestation period of 50-60 days. Gravid females captured on June 28 each contained a single fetus nearly ready for birth. Immature individuals have been found in July and August in colonies of adult females. The young are able to fly at 16-17 days of age. As with other species of *Myotis*, adult males and females do not associate with each other in summer.

Fringed Myotis (*Myotis thysanodes*). Photo by Merlin D. Tuttle, Bat Conservation International.

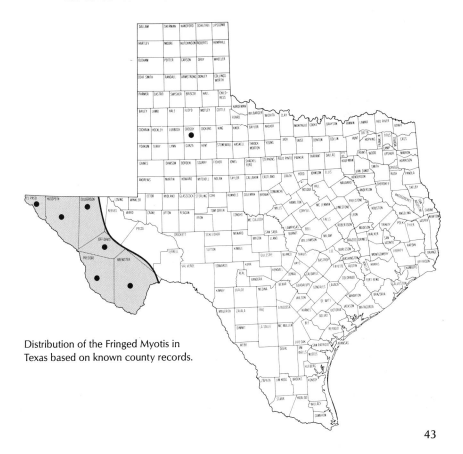

Distribution of the Fringed Myotis in
Texas based on known county records.

CAVE MYOTIS
Myotis velifer (J. A. Allen)

Description. Largest of the *Myotis* in Texas; hind foot large, more than half as long as tibia; ear short, reaching to or slightly beyond nostril when laid forward; upperparts uniform dull sepia; underparts much paler, tips of hairs pale cream buff. Dental formula as in *M. californicus.* External measurements average: total length, 90 mm; tail, 40 mm; foot, 9 mm; forearm, 42 mm.

Distribution. Occurs over most of western Texas, including South Texas, eastern portions of the Panhandle, and north-central Texas.

Habits. This species is a colonial, cave dwelling bat. They may also roost in rock crevices, old buildings, carports, under bridges, and even in abandoned cliff swallow nests. The cave myotis is the most abundant bat of the Edwards Plateau and hibernates in central Texas caves in winter. It also hibernates in the gypsum caves of the Panhandle region. The bats usually roost in clusters that may number into the thousands. Other species occasionally found with the cave myotis include big-eared bats (*Plecotus*), free-tailed bats (*Tadarida*), big brown bats (*Eptesicus*), Yuma myotis (*Myotis*), and ghost-faced bats (*Mormoops*). Although these bats may roost at the same site as the cave myotis, the different species usually segregate, with different bats inhabiting separate areas or rooms of the roosting site.

These bats appear shortly after sunset. They have been observed on several occasions coming into pools of water and open tanks in the late evening to drink. Their flight is fluttery and erratic, like that of other species of *Myotis*.

Cave myotises are opportunistic insectivores that feed on a wide variety of insects depending upon what is most available on a given night. Small moths make up the largest portion of the diet although small beetles, weevils, and antlions are also taken. Because of their larger size and stronger flight, the cave myotis may be able to forage farther abroad than other species of *Myotis*.

In Texas, females have been found with embryos as early as mid-April. On the Edwards Plateau, lactating females are frequently captured in May, suggesting that birth of the single young occurs in early May.

Remarks. There are two subspecies of this bat in Texas, and it is not clear where, or if, they intermingle. The subspecies are *M. v. incautus* in the south and *M. v. magnamolaris* in the northwestern part of the state.

Cave Myotis (*Myotis velifer*). Photo by Merlin D. Tuttle, Bat Conservation International.

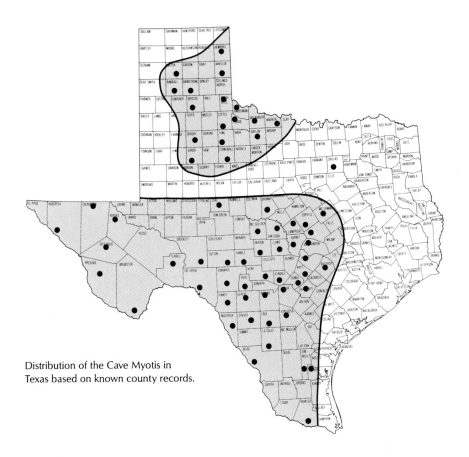

Distribution of the Cave Myotis in
Texas based on known county records.

LONG-LEGGED MYOTIS
Myotis volans (H. Allen)

Description. A rather large *Myotis*, with relatively long tail, short ears and moderately large foot; underside of wing membrane well furred out as far as line joining elbow and knee; ratio of tail to head and body averaging from 90 to 94; tibia relatively long, ratio of foot to tibia near 40; pelage full and about 7 mm long on back; profile of brain case rises abruptly from rostrum, giving a pug-nosed effect; ears short and rounded at tip. Dental formula as in *M. californicus*. External measurements average: total length, 93 mm; tail, 45 mm; foot, 7 mm; ear, 13 mm; forearm, 39 mm. Weight, 5-9 g.

Distribution. A western bat that occurs in Texas primarily in the Trans-Pecos but has also been recorded from the Rolling Plains (Knox County). This was probably a stray individual, and resident populations are not believed to inhabit the Rolling Plains.

Habits. Over much of their range, long-legged bats are forest inhabitants, and they prefer high, open woods and mountainous terrain. Nursery colonies, which may contain several hundred individuals, form in summer in places such as buildings, cliff crevices, and hollow trees. These bats apparently do not use caves as day roosts, although they may use such sites at night. The winter range and habits of this bat are not known.

These bats emerge shortly before dark to forage around cliffs, trees, and over water. Certain flyways seem to be used regularly, but the specific food preferences are not known. Evidence from New Mexico indicates they may feed mainly on small moths. The single young is born in June or early July.

45

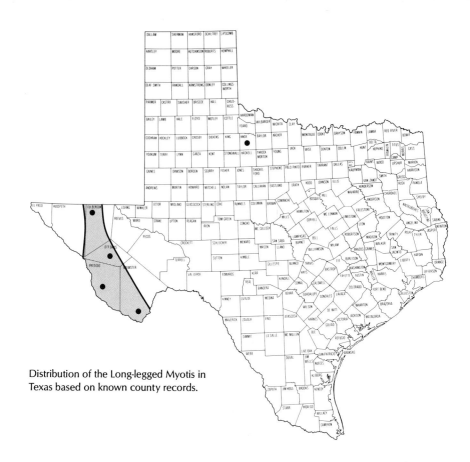

Distribution of the Long-legged Myotis in Texas based on known county records.

YUMA MYOTIS
Myotis yumanensis (H. Allen)

Description. A small bat similar to *M. lucifugus*; feet relatively large, more than half as long as tibia; ratio of tail to head and body more than 80; coloration dull, pale pinkish, or cream buff; immature individuals darker, nearly cinnamon buff; membranes pale brownish; underparts pale buff, nearly white; pelage short as compared with *M. lucifugus*; viewed from the side, the skull rises more abruptly from the rostrum than in *M. lucifugus*; dental formula as in *M. californicus*. External measurements average: total length, 78 mm; tail, 34 mm; foot, 8 mm; forearm, 34 mm.

Distribution. Restricted in Texas to the southern Trans-Pecos and Rio Grande Valley.

Habits. Surprisingly little information is available on the habits of this species in Texas. It is primarily an inhabitant of desert regions where it is most commonly encountered in lowland habitats near open water, where it prefers to forage. It roosts in caves, abandoned mine tunnels, and buildings. In the Big Bend region of Texas, it is common in summer along the Rio Grande where it comes to drink just after sundown. Its flight is fluttering and erratic, as it is in other members of the genus. No winter records are available for Texas, and it is unknown whether the Yuma myotis migrates or overwinters in the state during this season.

The stomachs of bats captured in Big Bend National Park contained moths, froghoppers and leafhoppers, June beetles, ground beetles, midges, muscid flies, caddisflies, and craneflies.

The season of partus is from May to early July, and usually only one young is born to each female.

46

Yuma Myotis (*Myotis yumanensis*). Photo by
Merlin D. Tuttle, Bat Conservation International.

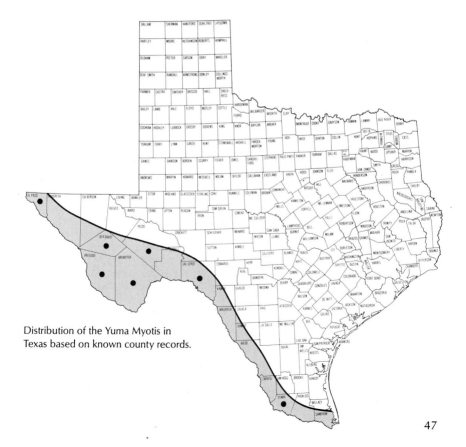

Distribution of the Yuma Myotis in
Texas based on known county records.

SILVER-HAIRED BAT

Lasionycteris noctivagans (Le Conte)

Description. A medium-sized, nearly black bat with dorsal surface of interfemoral membrane densely furred at least on the basal half and usually to near margins; upper and lowerparts sooty brown or black with white tips of hairs producing a frosted appearance; membranes and ears sooty brown or black. Dental formula: I 2/3, C 1/1, Pm 2/3, M 3/3 X 2 = 36 (upper incisors and first lower premolar very small and easily overlooked). External measurements average: total length, 100 mm; tail, 40 mm; hind foot, 8 mm; ear, 16 mm; forearm, 41 mm. Weight, 8-12 g.

Distribution. Broadly but erratically distributed across northern North America; recorded from six physiographic regions of Texas (Pineywoods, Gulf Coastal Plains, Edwards Plateau, Rolling Plains, High Plains, and Trans-Pecos, where it apparently is a fall-spring migrant).

Habits. These bats are denizens of forested areas and seldom are observed in xeric areas except in migration. Cavities in trees and spaces under loose bark are favorite daytime retreats but these bats may also use buildings.

This species is migratory, at least in part. It spends the summer in northern latitudes and winters toward the south, even crossing several hundred kilometers of ocean to reach Bermuda. Surprisingly few winter records are available; thus, the mystery of just where these bats spend the winter is still not completely solved. It is likely that many of them winter on their breeding grounds because occasional individuals have been found hibernating as far north as New York and British Columbia. Interestingly, most summer records of this bat across the southwest are of males, suggesting that geographical segregation of the sexes may occur during the warmer months. Females appear to move north in spring and summer to bear young, whereas the males remain behind at more southern locales. A small population, apparently comprised entirely of males, appears to be resident in the Guadalupe Mountains (Culberson County) during summer.

This bat typically forages in or near coniferous and/or mixed deciduous forests adjacent to ponds or other sources of water. It is a relatively late flier that often appears

Silver-haired Bat (*Lasionycteris noctivagans*). Photo by Merlin D. Tuttle, Bat Conservation International.

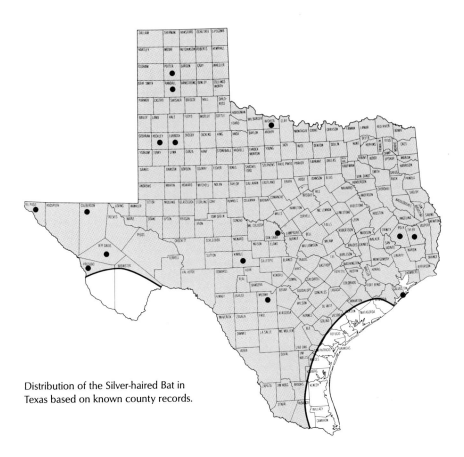

Distribution of the Silver-haired Bat in
Texas based on known county records.

after other bats have begun feeding. As with most other insectivorous bats, *Lasionycteris* is opportunistic in its feeding habits and takes a wide variety of small to medium-sized insects including moths, bugs, beetles, flies, and caddisflies.

The one or two young are born in June and July. Small maternity colonies may form in hollow trees and abandoned bird nests. The young are black and wrinkled at birth and are able to fly when about 3 weeks old.

WESTERN PIPISTRELLE

Pipistrellus hesperus (H. Allen)

Description. A small, drab-gray or smoke-gray bat with distinct, black, leathery facial mask and black membranes; tragus short, blunt, and slightly curved; underparts pale smoke-gray. Dental formula: I 2/3, C 1/1, Pm 2/2, M 3/3 X 2 = 34. External measurements average: (males), total length, 66 mm; tail, 27 mm; foot, 5 mm; forearm, 28 mm; (females), 73-30-5-28. Weight, 3-6 g.

Distribution. Western Texas east to Uvalde, Knox, and Haskell counties.

Habits. This bat is associated chiefly with rocky situations along watercourses. Its daytime retreat is in the cracks and crevices of canyon walls or cliffs, under loose rocks, or in caves.

These are among the most diurnal of bats, beginning their foraging flights very early in the evening and often remaining active throughout the early morning hours. Pipistrelles are slow bats and may be distinguished on the wing by their slow, fluttery flight which is restricted to small foraging circuits. Occasionally, individual bats have been observed on the wing during mid-day, during which time they water to alleviate stress caused by the arid environment they inhabit.

49

Western Pipistrelle (*Pipistrellus hesperus*). Photo by John L. Tveten.

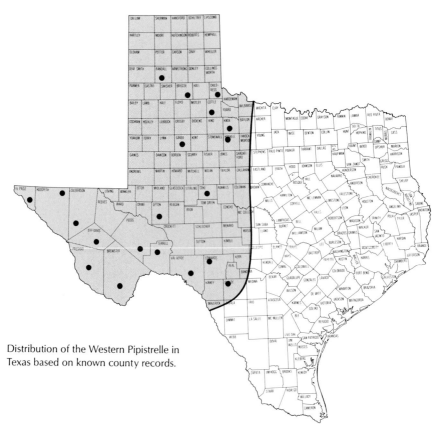

Distribution of the Western Pipistrelle in
Texas based on known county records.

Western pipistrelles forage from 2 to 15 m above ground on small, swarming insects and consume about 20% of their body weight in insects per feeding. Specific prey items include caddisflies, stoneflies, moths, small beetles, leaf and stilt bugs, leaf-hoppers, flies, mosquitoes, ants, and wasps. Stomach contents of individual bats often contain only a single species of insect, or if more than one species is present the remains are clumped together within the stomach, suggesting that they take advantage of swarming insects and feed intensively within such swarms.

The young, numbering one or two (usually two), are born in June and July after a gestation period of approximately 40 days. Maternity colonies may be established in buildings or rock crevices. The newborn bats weigh slightly less than 1 g at birth but grow rapidly. By August they can fly and are difficult to distinguish from adults.

EASTERN PIPISTRELLE
Pipistrellus subflavus (F. Cuvier)

Description. A small bat with leading edge of wing and the edges of the membrane between the hind legs much paler than rest of membranes; tragus long and slender; upperparts pale yellowish brown, with grizzled effect; the individual hairs tricolored, dark basally, grayish-yellow medially, and tipped with dusky. Dental formula: I 2/3, C 1/1, Pm 2/2, M 3/3 X 2 = 34. External measurements average: total length, 85 mm; tail, 41 mm; foot, 8 mm; ear, 14 mm; forearm, 35 mm. Weight, 4-6 g.

Distribution. Eastern half of state including the Rolling Plains west to Armstrong County and central Texas as far west as Val Verde County, and a recent record from Lubbock County.

Habits. These small bats are some of the earliest to emerge in the evening from their daytime retreats in caves, crevices in cliffs, buildings, and other man-made structures offering concealment. They are relatively slow and erratic in flight and often flutter and flit along watercourses or over pastures and woodlands like large moths. They appear to favor watercourses as foraging grounds. They are much more closely associated with woodlands than is the western pipistrelle.

This species is known to spend the winter hibernating in suitable caves within its summer range. Its hibernation is more complete than that of most other American bats and they generally roost singly or in small groups. Individuals may hang in one spot for weeks on end, and their torpor is so deep that they are not easily disturbed. They emerge from hibernation early in the spring and remain active well into the fall.

Eastern Pipistrelle (*Pipistrellus subflavus*). Photo by John L. Tveten.

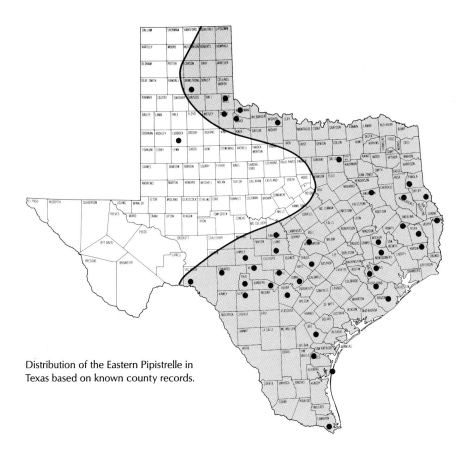

Distribution of the Eastern Pipistrelle in Texas based on known county records.

Little is known of their food habits in Texas. In Indiana they are known to eat small leafhoppers, ground beetles, flies, moths, and ants. Insects are caught by the bats in considerable quantities in a short period and within 20 minutes they are gorged. They probably feed at intervals throughout the night and hang up to digest their meals between feeding times.

Mating takes place in the fall. They have been observed copulating as late as November. Both males and females have been observed roosting together as early as August, however. During the period from March to August adult males and females usually occupy separate roosts. Data suggest that the sperm may remain viable in the vaginal tract of the female until spring, when ovulation occurs (in March or April) and fertilization of the ova takes place. However, copulation in the spring also has been observed.

The exact period of gestation is not known, but it probably does not begin until the bats have left their winter quarters. The young, usually two in number, are born from May to July. They grow rapidly and when about 3 weeks old are able to take care of themselves.

BIG BROWN BAT
Eptesicus fuscus (Palisot de Beauvois)

Description. A medium-sized bat with upperparts rich chestnut brown; ears relatively small, thick, leathery, and black; membranes blackish; under-parts paler than back; ears and membranes devoid of hair, or nearly so; wing short and broad, length of fifth metacarpal almost equal to that of third. Dental formula: I 2/3, C 1/1, Pm 1/2, M 3/3 X 2 = 32. External measurements average: total length, 114 mm; tail, 46 mm; foot, 11 mm; forearm, 47 mm. Weight, 13-20 g, rarely to 30 g.

Distribution. Widely distributed over most of the eastern and western parts of Texas, but not yet recorded in the central part of the state. The eastern and western forms are regarded as different subspecies, *E. f. fuscus* and *E. f. pallidus*, respectively, and may differ in reproductive habits as discussed below.

Habits. This species is normally a forest dweller, but it does not hesitate to utilize attics and crevices in buildings, caves, and crevices in rocks for daytime retreats. Favorite roosts are under the loose bark of dead trees and in cavities of trees. These bats emerge rather early in the evening and feed among the trees, often following a regular route from one treetop to another and back again. In contrast to red bats (*Lasiurus borealis*), big brown bats prefer to forage among the crowns of the trees rather than under the forest canopy. Their flight is relatively slow and direct.

Big brown bats are relatively ferocious when captured. They usually squeal when handled and produce a rapid ratchetlike sound; they continually try to bite and usually draw blood when they succeed in doing so. They cannot produce a serious wound, however. In the water they swim well, but they cannot take off from the surface as can some of the smaller bats (*Myotis* and *Pipistrellus*). In winter they migrate or seek hibernation quarters in caves or buildings.

Their food is entirely insects, which they capture in flight. Fecal pellets of these bats have shown that they feed on beetles, bees and their allies, flies, stone flies, May flies, true bugs, nerve-wings, scorpion flies, caddisflies, and cockroaches. Peculiarly, moths are seldom found. Food items vary, of course, from one region to another.

These bats mate in the fall, and the one or two young are born from May to August. Four embryos have been found in a female, but it is unlikely that they all would have survived because the mother has only two teats. Big brown bats in the eastern part of the United States usually produce two young per litter, whereas in the Rocky Mountains and westward only one young is produced. Since Texas spans both of these ranges, it is probable that bats in the Trans-Pecos have one young, whereas those of the Pineywoods typically produce twins. No fetal counts are available for East Texas specimens, but bats captured in the Trans-Pecos have contained only one fetus.

Big Brown Bat (*Eptesicus fuscus*). Photo by Merlin D. Tuttle, Bat Conservation International.

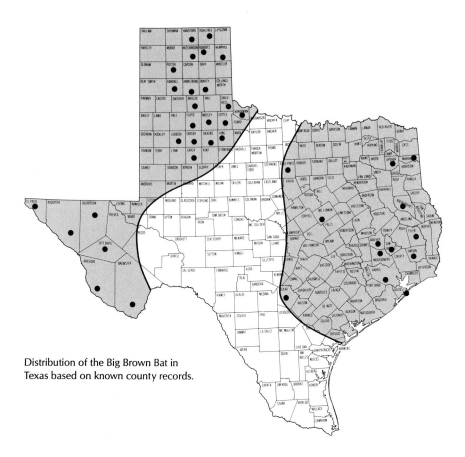

Distribution of the Big Brown Bat in
Texas based on known county records.

At birth, the young bats weigh about 3.0 g and grow quickly, gaining as much as 0.5 g per day. Maternity colonies are often located in buildings and may contain from 20 to 300 individuals. Adult males usually are not present in maternity colonies until the young mature, when they may begin using maternity colonies more frequently. At 4 weeks of age the young bats begin foraging for themselves and reach adult size approximately 2 months after birth.

Their known enemies include barn owls, horned owls, and black snakes.

WESTERN RED BAT

Lasiurus blossevillii Lesson and Garnot

Description. A medium sized bat similar in appearance to the eastern red bat (*Lasiurus borealis*). Pelage coloration is rusty red to brownish and lacks the white-tipped hairs which gives the frosted appearance so characteristic of *L. borealis*. The posterior one-third of the interfemoral membrane is bare or only sparsely haired. *L. blossevillii* is slightly smaller than *L. borealis* and most cranial measurements (greatest length of skull, zygomatic breadth, mastoid breadth, and length of maxillary toothrow) are significantly smaller. Dental formula: I 1/3, C 1/1, Pm 2/2, M 3/3 X 2 = 32. External measurements average: total length, 103 mm; tail, 49 mm; foot, 10 mm; ear from notch, 13 mm; forearm, 40 mm.

Distribution. Across the southwestern and far western areas of the United States south into Mexico and Central America. Known in Texas from only one specimen captured in the Sierra Vieja in Presidio County of the Trans-Pecos. Additional specimens are to be looked for in this region, a potential area of overlap between this bat and *L. borealis*.

Habits. Western red bats appear to prefer riparian areas where they roost in tree foliage. In New Mexico and Arizona this bat is occasionally captured in riparian habitats dominated by cottonwoods, oaks, sycamores, and walnuts and is rarely found in desert habitats. In Mexico, this bat has been captured in riparian, xeric thorn scrub and pine-oak forests of the San Carlos Mountains, only 160 km south of the Texas border. The Texas specimen was captured over permanent water in desert scrub habitat.

This bat appears to be migratory in the southwestern United States. Specimens from Arizona, New Mexico, and the Texas specimen are all from summer. A winter withdrawal from this region to Mexico is likely.

The food habits and reproductive biology of this bat are poorly known. Females pregnant with three fetuses have been captured, and pregnant bats from New Mexico have been caught from mid-May to late June. *L. blossevillii* may raise as many as three young annually with parturition occurring in mid-May through late June.

EASTERN RED BAT
Lasiurus borealis (Muller)

Description. A medium-sized, distinctly reddish bat with ears short, broad, rounded, and partly furred; membrane between hind legs densely furred above. Not easily confused with any other bat except *L. seminolus* and *L. blossevillii*. Upperparts reddish, the tips of the hairs white, producing a frosted appearance; males usually lack the white-tipped hairs and are much redder. Dental formula as in *L. blossevillii*. External measurements average: total length, 108 mm; tail, 48 mm; foot, 9 mm; ear, 12 mm; forearm, 40 mm. Weight, 10-15 g.

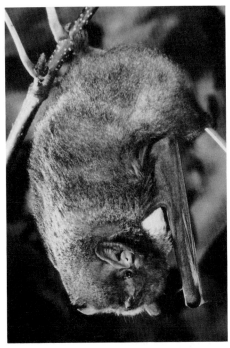

Eastern Red Bat (*Lasiurus borealis*). Photo by
Merlin D. Tuttle, Bat Conservation International.

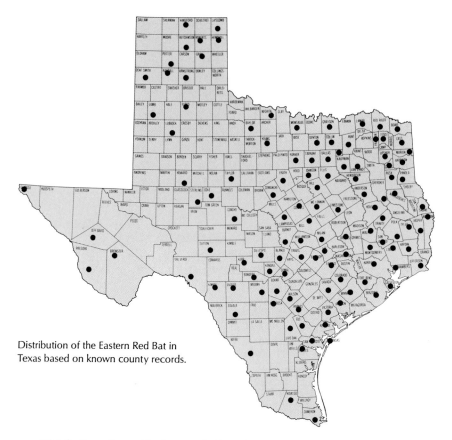

Distribution of the Eastern Red Bat in
Texas based on known county records.

Distribution. Statewide, but rare in Trans-Pecos.

Habits. Eastern red bats are forest dwelling, solitary bats and are one of the few North American species that roost in the open in trees. They do not use sites such as caves, mine tunnels, or similar sites often frequented by other species. Roosting sites are common in tree foliage or Spanish moss where the bats are concealed as they resemble dead leaves.

This bat is migratory and moves northward in spring and southward in fall. It is considered a year-round resident of eastern Texas but may only be a summer migrant in the western part of the state. These bats winter in southern United States, Mexico, Bermuda, the Antilles, and perhaps even farther south.

They appear on the wing early in the evening and forage close to the ground under the canopy of an orchard or a shaded grove. They typically follow a specific territory while feeding and generally forage near the forest canopy at or above tree-top level. They often hunt around streetlamps in towns and occasionally alight to capture insects. Twilight-flying insects such as moths, scarab beetles, planthoppers, flying ants, leafhoppers, ground beetles, and assassin beetles are among their favorite prey items.

The breeding range in western United States appears to coincide with the bats known distribution. Young bats are born in localities as far south as southern Texas and as far north as southern Canada. The young, two to four in number — usually three — are born in May, June, or July. This is one of the few bats that has more than two teats (four). The young ones remain with their mother for some time after they have learned to fly and the family group roosts together.

HOARY BAT

Lasiurus cinereus (Palisot de Beauvois)

Description. A large bat; ears short, rounded, and with black rims; dorsal surface of membrane between hind legs and feet densely furred; upperparts grayish or brownish, heavily frosted with white; membranes brownish black except along forearm where they are yellowish. Not easily confused with any other North American bat. Dental formula as in *L. blossevillii*. External measurements average: total length, 136 mm; tail, 57 mm; foot, 12 mm; ear, 18 mm; forearm, 52 mm. Weight, 20-35 g.

Distribution. Statewide migratory species.

Habits. This bat is migratory and moves northward in spring and southward in winter. Like its relative the red bat, with which it frequently associates, the hoary bat is more or less solitary and frequents wooded areas where it roosts in the open by hanging from a branch or twig. It is a strong flier, and in association with other bats it is readily recognized by its large size and swift, erratic flight. This bat usually emerges rather late in the evening, but during migration it frequently is observed in daylight hours.

The chief food is moths, although they are known to also eat beetles, flies, grasshoppers, termites, dragonflies, and wasps. Apparently, the hoary bat feeds by approaching a flying moth from the rear, engulfing the abdomen-thorax, and then biting down, allowing the sheared head and wings to drop to the ground. The usual number of young is two but ranges from one to four. In Texas, parturition occurs in mid-May into early July.

This species is a relatively rare migrant through Texas, and it has been recorded in all regions of the state.

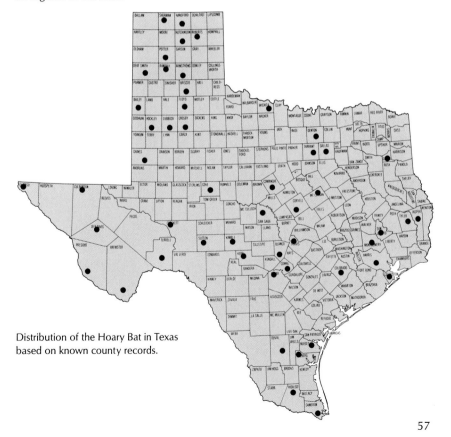

Distribution of the Hoary Bat in Texas based on known county records.

Hoary Bat (*Lasiurus cinereus*). Photo by Merlin D. Tuttle, Bat Conservation International.

SOUTHERN YELLOW BAT
Lasiurus ega (Gervais)

Description. A yellowish-brown bat similar to *Lasiurus intermedius* but smaller. Dental formula: I 1/3, C 1/1, Pm 1/2, M 3/3 X 2 = 30. External measurements average: total length, 118 mm; tail, 51 mm; foot, 9 mm; forearm, 47 mm. One of the best characters to distinguish *L. ega* from *L. intermedius* is the length of the maxillary toothrow: in *ega* it is less than 6.0 mm, in *intermedius* more than 6.0 mm.

Distribution. This is a neotropical species that reaches the United States in southern California, southern Arizona, and southern Texas where it has been recorded from Cameron, Kleberg, and Nueces Counties. Its range extends southward east of the Andes to Uruguay and northeastern Argentina.

Habits. Like other members of the genus *Lasiurus*, southern yellow bats are associated with trees which can provide them with daytime roosting sites. In the vicinity of Brownsville, numbers of them inhabit a natural grove of palm trees (*Sabal texana*). *L. ega* may be a permanent resident in that area because they have been captured there in six different months of the year, including December. These bats may be increasing their range in Texas due to the increased usage of ornamental palm trees in landscaping.

These bats feed on insects which they probably capture in flight. Bats observed in the Mexican state of San Luis Potosi started foraging about dusk. Nets stretched over ponds at which bats came to drink did not catch any *L. ega* until about 2 hours after darkness. Stomachs of those captured at that time were crammed with insect remains.

The breeding season is in late winter in the South Texas area. Six females captured in late April all carried embryos; one with two very small (3 mm crown-rump length) embryos; the other five with three embryos each, the crown-rump length of which ranged from 11 to 14 mm. Of 11 females captured on June 8, only one was pregnant. She contained four embryos whose average crown-rump length was 25 mm. Nine of the other 10 females were lactating. Three females captured in June in the neighboring Mexican state of Tamaulipas were also lactating.

Southern Yellow Bat (*Lasiurus ega*). Photo by
Merlin D. Tuttle, Bat Conservation International.

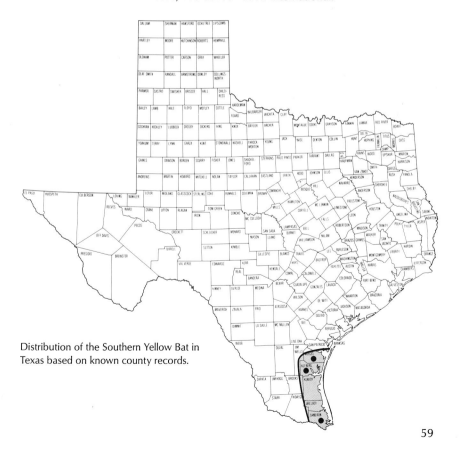

Distribution of the Southern Yellow Bat in
Texas based on known county records.

NORTHERN YELLOW BAT

Lasiurus intermedius H. Allen

Description. A large, yellowish-brown bat with short ears and long, silky fur; membranes brownish; membrane between hind legs well haired on basal third or half, the terminal half and underside are nearly naked. Dental formula as in *L. ega*. External measurements average: total length, 140 mm; tail, 51 mm; foot, 11 mm; forearm, 58 mm.

Distribution. Eastern and southern parts of state as far north as Shelby County and as far west as Bexar County.

Habits. Little is known about this uncommon bat. The distribution of this bat in the United States closely coincides with that of Spanish moss, which is its preferred roosting site. In South Texas, however, these bats roost in palm trees, where they are well concealed beneath the large, drooping fronds. A single roosting site may contain several bats and such groups are often quite noisy, especially when young are present, and their bickering gives them away from below. Migration and winter habits are poorly known.

Northern yellow bats forage over open, grassy areas such as pastures, lake edges, golf courses, and along forest edges. In Florida they often form groups while feeding. Such foraging groups are segregated by sex; males are rarely found in such groups, and they seem to be more solitary in their habits than are females. Specific prey items include leafhoppers, dragonflies, flies, diving beetles, ants, and mosquitoes.

Females carry three to four embryos in spring and litter size is believed to usually be two or three. Parturition probably occurs in late May or June in Texas.

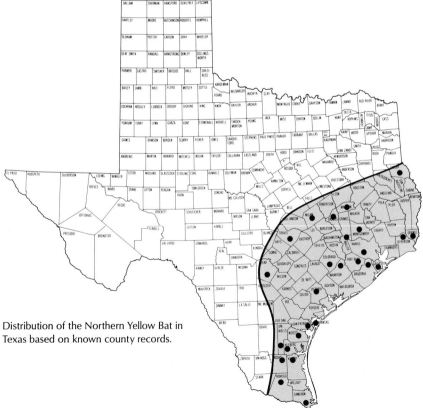

Distribution of the Northern Yellow Bat in
Texas based on known county records.

Northern Yellow Bat (*Lasiurus intermedius*). Photo by John L. Tveten.

SEMINOLE BAT

Lasiurus seminolus (Rhoades)

Description. Similar to *Lasiurus borealis* but rich mahogany brown, slightly frosted with whitish. Dental formula as in *L. blossevillii*. External measurements average: total length, 103 mm; tail, 44 mm; hind foot, 10 mm; ear, 11 mm; forearm, 39 mm.

Distribution. From East Texas (oak-hickory, pine-oak, and longleaf pine forest region) eastward along the coast to Florida and the Carolinas.

Habits. The distribution of Seminole bats seems to be closely associated with the distribution of Spanish moss, the clumps of which provide roosting sites. The adult bats are solitary and roosts are usually occupied by a single individual, or a female with young. Bat-inhabited moss clumps are usually shaded from the sun and often on the west and southwest exposures of oak trees. Bats have been observed roosting in such clumps from 1 to 5 m above the ground.

The bats emerge from their daytime roosts early in the evening and forage among or above the crowns of the trees, over watercourses, and around clearings. They may occasionally alight on vegetation to capture prey. Their food consists of true bugs, flies, beetles, and even ground-dwelling crickets.

The two to four (normally two) young are born in late May or June. The young bats grow rapidly and are thought to be capable of flight at the age of 3 or 4 weeks.

Seminole bats are thought to be resident within their range in the Deep South. They do not hibernate in the true sense, but rather are active throughout the winter when weather conditions permit. Observations indicate that on days when the ambient temperature is below 20°C the bats do not leave their daytime roosts, but whenever temperatures in the evening exceed 20°C they emerge and take wing.

Seminole Bat (*Lasiurus seminolus*). Photo by John L. Tveten.

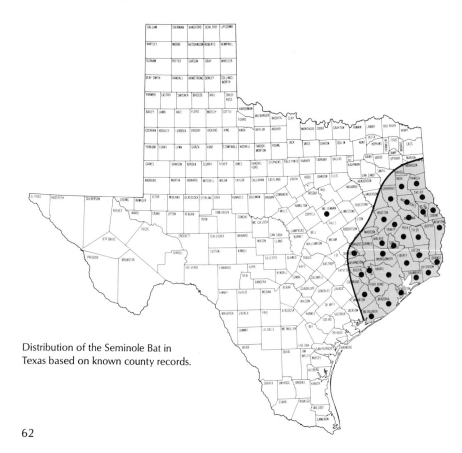

Distribution of the Seminole Bat in Texas based on known county records.

EVENING BAT
Nycticeius humeralis (Rafinesque)

Description. A small, nearly black or blackish-brown bat; ears small, blackish, thick and leathery; underparts paler. Immature individuals are darker than adults. Dental formula: I 1/3, C 1/1, Pm 1/2, M 3/3 X 2 = 30. External measurements average: total length, 93 mm; tail, 39 mm; foot, 8.5 mm; forearm, 36 mm. Weight, 5-7 g.

Distribution. Eastern one-third of state west to about Clay County in the north and Kinney County in the south.

Habits. These bats frequent forested areas and watercourses, and utilize hollow trees as roosting sites and nurseries. They use the attics of houses and other man-made structures as roosts when natural sites are not available. They have been captured in all months of the year in Texas, indicating that they are year-round residents of the state. Their winter habits are not known. In summer the adult males and females do not use the same roosts.

Evening bats seem to have two preferred times of foraging, one in the early evening hours and then again just before dawn. Specific prey items include small night-flying insects such as bugs, flying ants, spittle bugs, June beetles, pomace flies, Japanese beetles, and moths.

Copulation takes place in the fall, but it is not known where this occurs. Two young are born to the female in late May to early June. Nursery colonies may contain several hundred individuals and at this time the colonies are usually segregated by sex, with adult males rarely encountered in the nursery colonies. The young ones, at least on occasion, accompany their mother, attached to her breast. The young bats are volant at approximately 20 days of age and are nearly adult size by 1 month of age.

Evening Bat (*Nycticeius humeralis*). Photo by
Merlin D. Tuttle, Bat Conservation International.

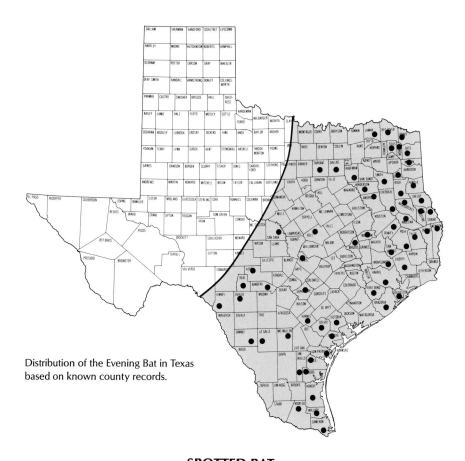

Distribution of the Evening Bat in Texas based on known county records.

SPOTTED BAT

Euderma maculatum (J. A. Allen)

Description. A moderately large bat with extremely large ears and a conspicuous dorsal color pattern of three large white spots, one on each shoulder and one on the rump, on a black background; a small white patch at the base of each ear; hairs on the underparts with white tips and blackish bases. Ears and membrane in living individuals pinkish; pale brownish in preserved specimens. Dental formula: I 2/3, C 1/1, Pm 2/2, M 3/3 X 2 = 34. External measurements average: total length, 124 mm; tail, 51 mm; ear, 42 mm; forearm, 51 mm. Weight, 16-20 g.

Distribution. The semi-arid regions of the western United States and northern Mexico from southwestern Idaho and southcentral Montana southward to the Mexican states of Durango and Queretaro. Known in Texas only from specimens captured in the Big Bend National Park, Brewster County.

Habits. Although unmistakable in appearance, the spotted bat is one of the least understood of American bats, primarily because of its relative scarcity, at least in collections. There have been scattered records of this bat throughout the western United States dating back to 1891, but it has been taken with any regularity only in California, Arizona, New Mexico, southern Utah, and southern Colorado. It was first found in Texas by David Easterla, who captured two adult females in early August, 1967 in mist nets set above a pool in a shallow, barren, hot, dry canyon in the Big Bend National Park.

The infrequency of capture of this bat has caused much confusion and speculation regarding its habitat. Several authors have reported captures in pine forests at high elevations (2400 m); others from a pinyon pine-juniper association; and still others from open scrub associations in desert areas. One worker has suggested that females give birth to their young in forested situations and later move to the lower elevations; another suggests that the bat is a cliff-dweller and roosts in cracks and crevices of canyon walls. A large number of the known specimens were captured in mist nets set over permanent streams or water holes adjacent to steep cliffs in open scrub desert country.

Little is known of the behavior of the spotted bat except that it appears to be most active well after dark. Most individuals caught in mist nets set over water, where bats come to drink, have been captured after midnight. Easterla speculated that its swoop over a water hole is made at relatively high speeds because several of the bats he has captured have been injured when they struck the nets. While in flight the bat emits a series of strident "tics" similar to, but higher pitched than, those of the Mexican big-eared bat *Idionycteris phyllotis*. Several authors have commented on the docile disposition of captive spotted bats, but occasional individuals are ill-tempered. Available data indicate that moths are highly important in their diet. In fact, these bats may feed almost exclusively on moths.

Data on reproduction are sparse. A gravid female captured by Easterla on June 11, in Big Bend National Park, gave birth a few hours later to a single male baby that weighed 4 g (one fourth of his mother's weight!). One of two females Easterla captured in the park in early August was lactating; the other was in a post-lactating condition. Two females captured June 30 and July 1 in Catron County, New Mexico, were in postpartus condition and lactating, as were three females collected in Garfield County, Utah, in mid-August. Thus, it appears that a single offspring is born to each sexually active female in June or July.

Spotted Bat (*Euderma maculatum*). Photo by Merlin D. Tuttle,
Bat Conservation International.

RAFINESQUE'S BIG-EARED BAT

Plecotus rafinesquii Lesson

Description. Similar to Townsend's big-eared bat, but hairs of the underparts have white tips that contrast sharply with the dark bases; long hairs on foot project noticeably beyond the ends of the toes; middle upper incisors with a secondary cusp; median postpalatal process triangular in shape with a broad base. Dental formula as in *P. townsendii*. External measurements average: total length, 100 mm; tail, 46 mm; foot, 12 mm; forearm, 43 mm. Weight, 7-13 g.

Distribution. A bat of the southeastern United States, Rafinesque's big-eared bat reaches the westernmost portion of its range in the pine forests of East Texas.

Habits. Unlike the closely related *P. townsendii*, Rafinesque's big-eared bat occurs in forested regions largely devoid of natural caves. Its natural roosting places are in hollow trees, crevices behind bark, and under dry leaves. It has been observed most frequently in buildings, both occupied and abandoned. Texas specimens have been captured in barns and abandoned wells. *P. rafinesquii* appears to be a solitary bat although colonies of 2-100 may be encountered in summer. Winter aggregations, usually of both sexes, are more numerous but even then solitary individuals are frequently found. The bats probably do not hibernate in East Texas, but in the northern part of their range they tend to seek out underground retreats and hibernate through the winter.

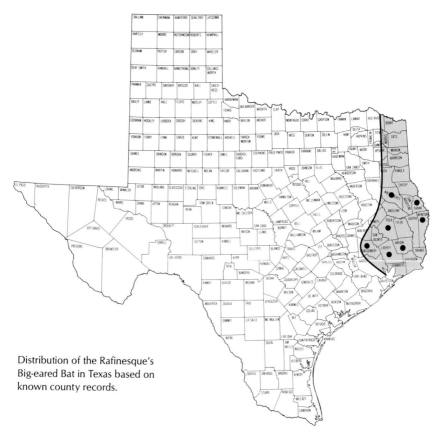

Distribution of the Rafinesque's Big-eared Bat in Texas based on known county records.

Rafinesque's Big-eared Bat (*Plecotus rafinesquii*). Photo by Merlin D. Tuttle, Bat Conservation International.

Like other *Plecotus*, *P. rafinesquii* emerges from its daytime roost well after dark to forage. Specific food items have not been recorded but small, night-flying insects, especially moths, are probably important.

The single young is born in late May or early June; they shed their milk dentition by mid-July, and reach adult size and appearance in August or September.

TOWNSEND'S BIG-EARED BAT
Plecotus townsendii Cooper

Description. A medium-sized bat with extremely long ears and a small glandular outgrowth on each side of the snout. Upperparts near clove-brown on back, wood-brown on sides, underparts slightly paler; membrane between hind legs full, wide and hairless. The combination of large flexible ears, nearly uniform color, and the lumps on the snout identify this bat. Dental formula: I 2/3, C 1/1, Pm 2/3, M 3/3 X 2 = 36. External measurements average: total length, 100 mm; tail, 46 mm; foot, 11 mm; ear, 35 mm; forearm, 44 mm. Weight, 7-12 g.

Distribution. Suitable habitat in western one-half of state.

Habits. The distribution of this bat is correlated largely with rocky situations where caves or abandoned mine tunnels are available. They do not seem to utilize crevices in such sites, and may occasionally inhabit old buildings. In the Trans-Pecos, this is probably the most characteristic bat of caves and mines.

Townsend's big-eared bats hibernate throughout their range during winter months when temperatures are between 0°C and 11.5°C. The bats hibernate in tight clusters, which may help stabilize body temperature against external changes in temperature. While torpid, the large ears are "rolled up" and laid back against the animal's neck. Males may select warmer hibernacula than do females and are more easily aroused and active in winter than are females. Their winter sleep is interrupted by frequent periods of wakefulness during which they move about in the caves or from one cave to another. They become very fat before hibernation. This fat provides them with sufficient food to maintain their lowered metabolism during the winter months when they do not eat. Males and females occupy separate roosting sites during summer. During this season, males appear to lead a solitary lifestyle while females and young form

67

Townsend's Big-eared Bat (*Plecotus townsendii*). Photo
by Merlin D. Tuttle, Bat Conservation International.

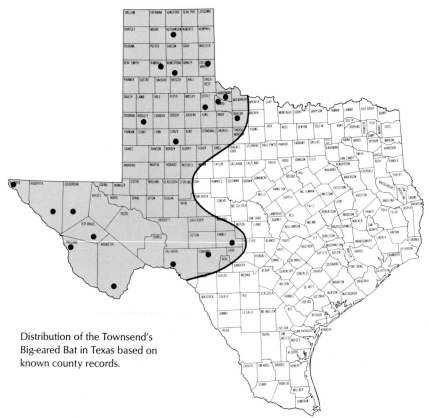

Distribution of the Townsend's
Big-eared Bat in Texas based on
known county records.

maternity colonies which may number 12-200, although in the eastern United States colonies of 1,000 or more are known.

These bats emerge late in the evening to forage and are swift, highly maneuverable fliers. Prey items include small moths, flies, lacewings, dung beetles, and sawflies.

The single young is born in late May to early June, at least in Texas. The baby bat weighs approximately 2.4 g at birth and is pink, naked, and completely helpless. At 4 days of age the newborn bat begins to display hair growth and by 1 month of age is volant and nearly adult size. At 2 months of age the juveniles are weaned and the nursery colonies begin to disperse.

PALLID BAT
Antrozous pallidus (Le Conte)

Description. A rather large, pale, yellowish-brown bat. Ears about 2.5 cm long, broad, naked, and crossed by nine or 11 transverse lines; bases of hairs light (nearly white), tips dusky; large light spot between shoulders; underparts paler and lacking dusky-tipped hairs; membranes nearly naked and brownish; nostrils surrounded by a glandular ridge producing a blunt snout; feet relatively large and strong. Dental formula: I 1/2, C 1/1, Pm 1/2, M 3/3 X 2 = 28. External measurements average: total length, 113 mm; tail, 46 mm; foot, 12 mm; ear, 28 mm; forearm, 48 mm. Weight, 12-17 g.

Distribution. A common resident of the western one-half of Texas where two distinct races are known: *A. p. bunkeri* in the northern Panhandle and *A. p. pallidus* in the west and south.

Habits. Pallid bats inhabit rocky, outcrop areas where they commonly roost in rock crevices, caves, and mine tunnels but they also roost in the attics of houses, under the eaves of barns, behind signs, in hollow trees, and in abandoned adobe buildings. Colonies are usually small and may contain 12-100 bats. Pallid bats usually appear on

Pallid Bats (*Antrozous pallidus*). Photo by Merlin D. Tuttle, Bat Conservation International.

the wing relatively late at night, well after dark. The species is probably migratory although occasional individuals have been reported from the United States in winter.

Their feeding habits are unlike those of most American bats. For years naturalists have noted the kitchen middens of discarded wings and other hard parts of insects under their "feeding roosts." Among them were remains of Jerusalem crickets, scorpions, and other flightless arthropods, although their diet also includes flying insects. To some extent though, pallid bats are terrestrial foragers. They have been observed flying, apparently at random, over an area at levels of 15-90 cm above the ground. When prey is located, presumably by sight, the bat abruptly drops to the ground, searches briefly, grabs its victim in its mouth, and takes off. Captured prey is taken to a feeding station where it is consumed. A. E. Borell described how one of these bats consumed a grasshopper. While eating, the bat hung head upward, supported by the thumbs, with the wings partly spread. The legs held the posterior part of the body well out from the timber and with the tail curved forward against it; the interfemoral membrane formed a pouch to catch parts of the large insect as they dropped.

Other than the items mentioned above, pallid bats also eat moths, froghoppers and leafhoppers, June beetles, and grasshoppers. In fact, 54 different types of prey have been documented for the pallid bat. Large, night-flying insects and ground-dwelling arthropods are most prevalent in the diet, however.

Mating occurs in fall with parturition in early summer. Females may carry one to four embryos but the birth of twins is usual. The length of gestation is 53-71 days. In

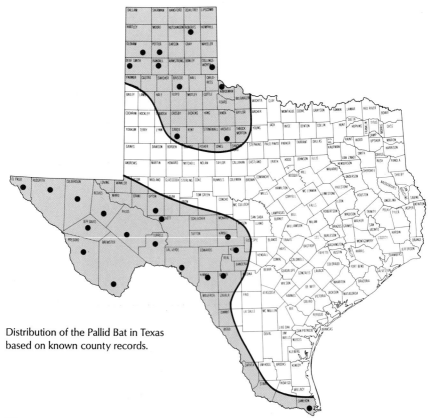

Distribution of the Pallid Bat in Texas
based on known county records.

Texas, the baby bats are born in early May to mid-June. Newborn bats weigh approximately 3 g and seem to develop more slowly than other species. The eyes open at 8-10 days of age, hair is evident at 10 days, and the young are volant by 6 weeks of age. Young bats have been found to contain both milk and insect remains in their stomachs, indicating that the young continue to nurse after becoming volant.

FAMILY MOLOSSIDAE (FREE-TAILED BATS)

BRAZILIAN FREE-TAILED BAT
Tadarida brasiliensis (I. Geof. St.-Hilaire)

Description. A medium-sized bat with broad ears, large feet, and terminal half of tail free; ears broad, extending to tip of snout when laid forward, apparently, but not actually, united across forehead, with a series of wartlike structures on anterior rim; tragus small and blunt; second joint of fourth finger 6-9 mm long; feet with distinct white bristles on sides of outer and inner toes; ratio of foot to tibia about 75; pelage short (3-4 mm) and velvety; upperparts varying from reddish to black; underparts slightly paler; membranes and ears blackish. Dental formula: I 1/2 or 1/3, C 1/1, Pm 2/2, M 3/3 X 2 = 30 or 32. The total number of lower incisors is variable, usually six, sometimes four, occasionally five. External measurements average: total length, 95 mm; tail, 38 mm; foot, 10 mm; ear, 19 mm; forearm, 42 mm. Weight, 11-14 g.

Distribution. Statewide in summer; western subspecies migrates to Mexico in autumn; eastern subspecies a year-round resident.

Habits. These bats utilize caves, mine tunnels, old wells, hollow trees, human habitations, bridges, and other buildings as daytime retreats. The prime necessity for a roost seems to be some relatively dark, dry retreat where from several dozen to several million individuals can hang up in close association and have an unobstructed space below into which they can drop when taking wing. Hollows under the roofs, spaces between downtown buildings, attics, narrow spaces between signs and buildings, and spaces in the walls of buildings all offer suitable refuge sites for these bats. Because of their frequent occurrence about and in buildings, they frequently are termed "house bats."

Brazilian free-tailed bats appear every year in Texas in multimillion numbers to inhabit a few select caves (known as "guano caves") located in the Balcones Escarpment and the adjacent Edwards Plateau. The total population of these bats that inhabit Texas caves during the summer has been estimated at 95-104 million. The largest of the caves, Bracken Cave near San Antonio, is thought to hold between 20 and 40 million bats. These same caves have been the summer homes of this animal for at least the past 100 years. Few, if any, house bats ever overwinter in the Texas guano caves. They spend the depth of winter, from early December to late February, at lower latitudes — probably in Mexico, Central America, or even South America. In East Texas, where these bats are common inhabitants of old buildings and similar structures, they are nonmigratory and are year-round residents of that part of the state.

Brazilian free-tailed bats appear on the wing several minutes before dark. The famous bat flights at Carlsbad Caverns are made up almost entirely of this species. One of us (Davis) watched these bats emerge from the attic of a house one evening. They fell from the exit, dropped nearly to the ground, then zoomed upward and, flying high, disappeared from view, each bat following the general direction of the one in front of it. In foraging, the bats fly rather high — 15 m or more as a rule — except when sweeping over some body of water to drink. Their flight is rapid and aggressive, reminding one of swifts, and the long, angular, and narrow wings, plus relatively large size, make them easy to identify.

Samples of their droppings collected at San Antonio contained remains of the following insects: moths (nearly 90% of the total number of insects eaten), ground beetles, leaf chafers, weevils, leaf beetles, flying ants, water boatmen, green blowflies, and leafhoppers. A separate food habits study showed these bats take small prey from 2-10 mm in length and listed the following food items and proportions: moths (34%), flying ants (26.2%), June beetles and leaf beetles (16.8%), leafhoppers (15%), and true bugs (6.4%). *T. brasiliensis* often feeds on swarms of insects. The huge summer colonies of these bats clearly would have a great impact on nearby insect populations; they are estimated to destroy from 6,000 to 18,000 <u>metric tons</u> of insects annually in Texas.

This bat has received considerable attention because it is a known carrier of rabies. With the exception of the eastern red bat (*Lasiurus borealis*), the Brazilian free-tailed bat has been reported to the Texas Department of Health (TDH) more often than any other species. Of 430 specimens reported to the TDH from 1984 to 1987, 105 (24%) tested positive for the rabies virus. This is the highest incidence of rabies known for any Texas bat. Although the total number of confirmed rabies cases is minuscule when compared to the population of bats as a whole, caution should be exercised when one of these bats is encountered, or any species of bat for that matter.

The major event in the life of the house bats summering in Texas is the birth and development of their young. Well over 90% of the returning females produce young each year. Most mating in the Texas population is accomplished each spring before the bats arrive at the Texas caves. Male house bats predominate at the caves for a brief period in early spring, but they are quickly outnumbered by females as populations build steadily with the approach of parturition. By mid-June, adult females outnumber adult males more than three to one.

More than 70% of the young are born within a brief span of about 10 days. More than 90% of all births occur within 15 days of the mid-June mean birth date. The newborn young are deposited together, naked and flightless, on specific areas of the ceiling in continuous colonies and are not carried by their mothers during the nocturnal feeding flights.

The sudden increase in the cave populations with the advent of the babies creates marked crowding in the cave colony clusters. In the past it was thought that adult females made no attempt to locate their own young within these masses, but nursed the first two young encountered upon their nightly return to the roost. Recent studies have shown that females do indeed recognize their own young, which is a remarkable feat given the confusion with such huge swarms of bats. The babies grow rapidly in the incubator-like climate of the caves. Within a month after birth the majority of babies are furred, of body length almost equal that of the adults, and capable of flying out to feed on their own.

The sudden increase in numbers of flying bats resulting from mass achievement of fledgling status among the babies creates an additional congestion in the caves. The congestion is relieved by the rapid disappearance of the adults as the fledglings appear. These adults presumably move rapidly south out of Texas; the missing adults have not been found elsewhere in Texas at this time. After late July, fledglings predominate in the diurnal feeding flights from the caves, and they tend to reside at the cave of their birth until the onset of cool weather in October and November drives them south out of Texas.

In Texas, the Brazilian free-tailed bat seems to be primarily a cave dweller, and its use of buildings as roosts is likely a relatively recent, possibly expanding practice. Only a small fraction of the numbers of bats found in caves is ever found in the total of all

Brazilian Free-tailed Bat (*Tadarida brasiliensis*). Photo by Merlin D. Tuttle, Bat Conservation International.

roosts in buildings. Every town in the Brazilian free-tailed bats' range in Texas is likely to have at least 15 roosts per 5,000 human population, but the occupation of buildings is especially common in eastern Texas. Most roosts in buildings house less than 100 bats at a time, but a few buildings traditionally house many hundreds each year. Overwintering in buildings occurs infrequently in the southern Gulf Coast prairies of Texas.

No particular style, size, age, state of repair, or use by man exempts a building from use by Brazilian free-tailed bats. The critical feature is whether the building has any accessible small cracks or niches into which bats can retreat into semidarkness during the day. Such openings usually are to be found even in the most modern, compact types of structure. One architectural type common in South Texas, the Spanish style building with clay tile roof, is among the most vulnerable to invasion by Brazilian free-tailed bats. The bats roost under the tiles and seldom can be driven out permanently from a roost in a building either by killing those present or by chemical treatment of the surface of the roost. The simplest, most effective method is to close the entrance to the roost. With clay tile roofs this is almost impossible unless the tile is replaced by some other kind of roofing material.

Abundance of Brazilian free-tailed bats in roosts in buildings in Texas follows an annual pattern of one peak in spring and another in fall, with general mid-summer and mid-winter lows or periods of complete absence. This pattern complements that of bat abundance in the guano caves. Brazilian free-tailed bats in buildings in Texas during spring and fall usually are itinerant between tropical latitudes and the mid-latitude guano caves of Texas, Oklahoma, Kansas, and New Mexico. Sufficient interchange of banded Brazilian free-tailed bats has occurred among the guano caves of Texas and between those in Texas and the ones in neighboring states to demonstrate that individual bats are not compelled to return each year to the cave of their birth. Rather, Brazilian free-tailed bats exhibit ability to range over great distances and find the widely separated, often well hidden, entrances to the few traditional guano caves and roosts in buildings.

The flight of Brazilian free-tailed bats on leaving and returning to a roost uniformly is accomplished in groups. It is presumed, therefore, that group flight is the norm in this animal. Yet, in the roosting clusters, where grouping is also the norm, there is strong evidence that each bat has affinity not to a specific, stable group of acquaintances but to any convenient group of its kind.

The gestation period of Brazilian free-tailed bats appears to be slightly in excess of 90 days. No more than one young is born per year by each adult female. Females in Texas are almost all pregnant the summer following birth. The left horn of the uterus does not carry an embryo. Lactation begins after delivery of the young, and two long mammae are located laterally, each with one functional pectoral teat. A vaginal plug still exists in some females arriving at the Texas caves in early spring.

Adult male Brazilian free-tailed bats arriving in Texas in spring are still sexually active, but sperm production is waning. Their sex glands decrease steadily in size in spring, and reach a resting stage size by early May. The small proportion of the male population which shows no sexual activity is composed principally of the youngest age class. In these, the testes, prostate, and hedonic glands are smaller than the resting stage sizes of the same glands in adult males. In late fall, the few adult males remaining in Texas again show some increase in size of testes and prostates, but sperm are absent. Peak production of sperm, thus, must occur during winter while the males are in lower latitudes. Since the highly disproportionate ratio of male to female Brazilian free-tailed bats in Texas cannot be explained easily as resulting from higher mortality among males, it must be that most males do not summer in Texas.

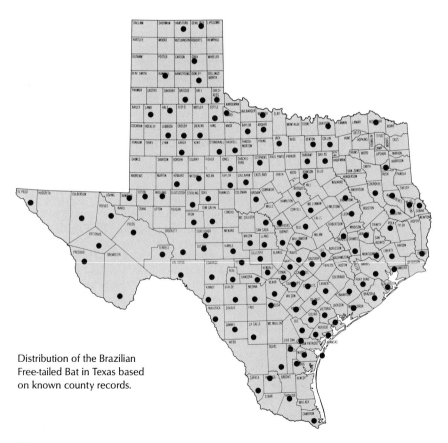

Distribution of the Brazilian
Free-tailed Bat in Texas based
on known county records.

Another colonial bat (*Myotis velifer*) is a common associate of the Brazilian free-tailed bat in the guano caves. This bat also gives birth to its young in the guano caves, but at a time about 2 weeks in advance of the Brazilian free-tailed bats. While the two kinds of bats tend to roost in separate clusters, some mixing may occur.

A number of species of snakes, birds, and mammals prey on house bats at the caves, but the total of this loss of bats is a very small proportion of the total bat population.

The annual movement of this animal between Texas and Mexico may be accomplished by most individuals in a few direct, long-distance flights between guano caves. Most adult male Brazilian free-tailed bats apparently do not leave the tropical and subtropical portion of the range and play no part in the sociology of bearing and rearing the young.

The accumulation, under crowded conditions, of millions of Brazilian free-tailed bats per guano cave each summer in Texas for the purpose of giving birth and rearing young may be an outgrowth of overpopulation, but it probably is functional in creating favorable conditions for survival of the young. Mortality among prenatal and prefledgling babies, as well as among adults, appears to be low. Longevity of adults probably is great, with an average of more than 11 years.

Remarks. The taxonomy of *T. brasiliensis* and its various subspecies has been one of confusion for many years. Two subspecies are known from Texas, according to the latest taxonomic revision of the species in the state. *T. b. cynocephala* is a nonmigratory resident of the eastern one-fourth of the state and *T. b. mexicana* is the highly migratory subspecies found throughout the remainder of Texas. Morphologically, these two subspecies are distinguished by differences in several skull characteristics (i.e. greatest length of skull, zygomatic breadth, and breadth of cranium), all of which are larger in *T. b. cynocephala*.

Most populations of the migratory subspecies, *mexicana*, have normally completed their move into Mexico prior to the onset of breeding, whereas *cynocephala* remains in the United States during the breeding season. This movement pattern would indicate that the two races are reproductively isolated and possibly separate species. However, overwintering populations of *mexicana* have been discovered in an area of contact between the two in southeastern Texas. A colony of *mexicana* was known to overwinter at the old Animal Pavilion on the Texas A&M University campus in College Station (Brazos County), which is only 160 km from colonies of *cynocephala* in extreme eastern Texas. A morphological analysis of cranial measurements from free-tailed bats captured near Navasota (Grimes County) found these bats to be intermediate between *cynocephala* and *mexicana*. Thus, it appears the two subspecies are not reproductively isolated and that they likely interbreed in this part of Texas.

These morphological data dictate that *cynocephala* and *mexicana* be regarded only as subspecies rather than as separate species, which has been the tendency in the past. Recent biochemical genetic studies of these bats have pointed strongly to specific status for each, however. Additional study will be required to finally settle the taxonomy of this most interesting bat.

POCKETED FREE-TAILED BAT
Nyctinomops femorosacca (Merriam)

Description. Similar to the Brazilian free-tailed bat, *Tadarida brasiliensis*, but the bases of the ears are joined at the midline; second phalanx of the 4th digit less (not more) than 5 mm; anterior part of hard palate narrowly, rather than broadly, excised; upper incisors placed close together, their longitudinal axes nearly parallel, not convergent, distally; the presence of a fold of skin stretching from the inner (medial) side of the femur to the middle of the tibia. This fold produces a shallow pocket on the underside of the interfemoral membrane in the vicinity of the knee, a structure to which the common name alludes. Dental formula: I 1/2, C 1/1, Pm 2/2, M 3/3 X 2 = 30. External measurements average: total length, 112 mm; tail, 46 mm; foot, 10 mm; ear, 23 mm; forearm, 46 mm. Weight, 10-14 g.

Distribution. Southwestern United States and northwestern Mexico; records from southern California, southern Arizona, southeastern New Mexico, western Texas; southward in Mexico to the state of Michoacan. Known in Texas only from Big Bend National Park, Brewster County.

Habits. This species is an inhabitant of semiarid desertlands. It has been found using day-roosts in caves, crevices in cliffs, and under the roof tiles of buildings. Nothing is known about the winter habits of these bats; apparently, they are absent from Texas during this time.

These bats leave their day roost late in the evening to forage, exhibiting swift, powerful flight. Philip Krutzsch recorded the following observations made at a colony of 50-60 of these bats he found at a daytime roost in a crevice in the face of a cliff in San Diego County, California, on March 17. The first bats left the colony at 6:15 p.m.; others followed in twos and threes for another half-hour. The bats dropped from 1 to 1.5 m before taking wing. Their flight appeared to be a rapid, complete wing beat. When first taking flight, they uttered a shrill, sharp, high-pitched, chattering call, which was repeated while the bats were in full flight. They also squeaked a great deal while in the roost. He described the odor of this bat as similar to that of the house bat, but not quite so strong. Little data on their food habits are available. The stomachs of thirteen bats captured in Big Bend National Park were found to contain moths, crickets, flying ants, stinkbugs, froghoppers and leafhoppers, lacewings, and unidentified insects.

Data on reproduction in this species are also scarce. Fifteen females captured at Big Bend National Park between June 10 and July 12 each contained a single embryo. Lactating females have been caught in this area from July 7 to August 8, suggesting that a single young is born to the female in late June to early July.

Remarks. There is some confusion about the generic name of this bat and its relative, *N. macrotis*. Patricia Freeman, in a comprehensive study of the family Molossidae world-wide, separated the New World and Old World species of *Tadarida* (exclusive of *Tadarida brasiliensis*) into two distinct genera — applying the name *Nyctinomops* to the New World species. Other mammalogists, however, have not followed this arrangement and place all of the Texas species in the genus *Tadarida*.

BIG FREE-TAILED BAT
Nyctinomops macrotis (Gray)

Description. Similar to the Brazilian free-tailed bat, *Tadarida brasiliensis*, but much larger; ratio of foot to tibia about 53; second joint of fourth finger 2.5 mm in length; ears large, and joined at their bases for a short distance over forehead; upperparts ranging from light reddish brown to rich dark brown; underparts similarly colored, but paler. Dental formula as in *Tadarida brasiliensis*. External measurements average: total length, 134 mm; tail, 51 mm; foot, 9 mm; ear, 25 mm; forearm, 61 mm. Weight (non-pregnant females in June), 22 g; of fat, October-taken, non-gravid females, 24-30 g.

Distribution. Widely, but seemingly sparingly distributed from Iowa and southwestern British Columbia, in the north, southward through Mexico and the West Indies as far as Uruguay in South America. Known in Texas from scattered localities in the Trans-Pecos, Panhandle, and southeastern portion of the state.

Big Free-tailed Bat (*Nyctinomops macrotis*). Photo by Merlin D. Tuttle,
Bat Conservation International.

Habits. This bat is rare in collections and little is known of its habits. In Texas,
these bats have been recorded primarily from the Trans-Pecos where they seem to be
seasonal inhabitants of rugged, rocky country in both lowland and highland habitats.
With the exception of a single specimen from San Patricio County, which was found
hanging on a screen door at the Welder Wildlife Refuge in December of 1959, no
winter records of this species have been recorded for Texas. In summer, a segregation
of sexes apparently occurs, as evidenced by the fact that few males have been taken in
the Trans-Pecos.

Preferred roosting sites are crevices and cracks in high canyon walls, but these
bats have also been captured in buildings. A specimen from Brazos County was
obtained when it flew down a chimney and into the owner's house. The only known
nursery colony of these bats in the United States was discovered in the Chisos Mountains of Brewster County in Big Bend National Park by A.E. Borell May 7, 1937. His
attention was attracted to a horizontal crevice in a cliff near the head of Pine Canyon
in the Chisos Mountains by the squeaking of bats. He estimated the number of adults
using the site to be about 150, and all those he collected were adult females, most of
which were pregnant. He revisited the colony on October 19, 1938 and collected
four more specimens, all females. On October 27, 1958, some 20 years later, one of
us (Davis) visited the colony with Richard D. Porter. Our notes, written the next day,
follow: "We hiked up Pine Canyon as far as the falls (a trickle of water over a cliff
about 100 feet [30 m] high). The canyon is narrow and steep-sided and has a few
large yellow pines, but most of them are dead. To the right of the falls the cliff is
overhanging, and it has several more-or-less horizontal crevices paralleling the top.
One of them, about 50 feet [15 m] above the talus and some 100 feet [30 m] north
of the falls, contained the colony. We could clearly hear the bats chattering, much
like the muted coo of doves." A considerable quantity of guano on the talus at the
base of the cliff marked the place below which the bats were roosting. None of the
bats voluntarily left the roost while we were there.

Borell found that the bats left the roost on May 7 at 8:20 p.m., when it was almost
dark, and nearly an hour after the first western canyon bat was observed. The bats left in
small groups during a period of 15 minutes. The swish of their wings was plainly audible,
and their flight was rapid. It was so dark when they emerged that he could not determine
whether they flew up or down the canyon. Possibly their habit of leaving their daytime
roosts so late is the reason they seldom are seen and rarely collected.

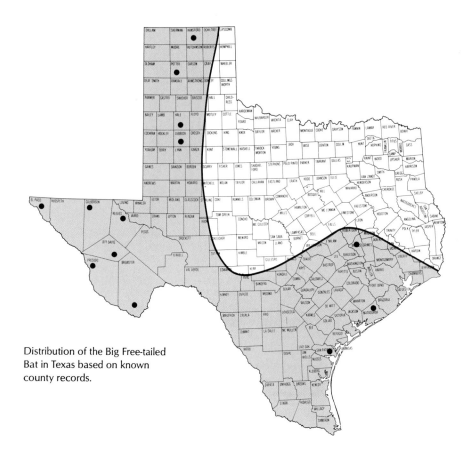

Distribution of the Big Free-tailed
Bat in Texas based on known
county records.

Another maternity colony is thought to be in McKittrick Canyon in the Guadalupe Mountains National Park. In June, 1968 and August, 1970, Richard LaVal netted 14 *N. macrotis* at a pool 8 km inside the canyon, where steep walls rise nearly 540 m above the narrow canyon floor. In this section of the canyon the bats were heard vocalizing from far above the floor. All individuals captured were females. Eight of the 12 taken in June contained a single large embryo each. One of the two females captured in August was lactating.

The winter habits of this bat are unknown, although they may possibly hibernate in the Trans-Pecos. Richard LaVal found that individuals kept in a refrigerator at 5°C for 24 hours entered a deep torpor, from which they emerged within 15 minutes after their removal. Another bit of evidence suggesting hibernation is that adult, October-taken females were very fat and weighed about 20% more than non-pregnant, June-taken females. Because they are strong fliers and prone to wander somewhat in fall, these bats often turn up far from their normal range during this season. Records from the Panhandle and southeastern Texas may represent juveniles dispersing from breeding populations in the Trans-Pecos.

David Easterla and John Whitaker, Jr. examined the stomach contents of 49 *N. macrotis* and reported that by far the most important food items found were the bodies of large moths. The only other items regularly found were the remains of crickets and longhorn grasshoppers. Other items the bats had consumed were flying ants, stink bugs, beetles, and leafhoppers. In the stomachs that contained crickets and long-horn grasshoppers, these items usually made up less than 25% of the contents, but in a few they comprised as much as 50%. One stomach contained only small flying ants and one contained only large ants. These workers speculated that while in flight the bats captured the ground-dwelling insects (crickets, longhorn grasshoppers, and large ants) by picking them from the walls of the cliffs.

Little is known about reproduction and development of the young in this bat. Seemingly, each gravid female gives birth to a single offspring in late June to early July. Development is rather rapid because by October the young-of-the-year are nearly full-grown and difficult to distinguish from adults. The females gather in nursery colonies, from which adult males are excluded, to rear their young.

Remarks. This bat was formerly included in the genus *Tadarida*. See the account of *N. femorosacca* for an explanation of the use of the generic name *Nyctinomops*.

WESTERN MASTIFF BAT
Eumops perotis (Schinz)

Description. A large free-tailed bat, similar to *Tadarida* and *Nyctinomops* in general appearance but nearly twice as large; foot large, ratio of foot to tibia about 60; ears large, united across the forehead and projecting about 10 mm beyond the snout; second joint of fourth finger about 6 mm; pelage short and velvety; upperparts brown or grayish brown, bases of hairs whitish; underparts paler. Males have a peculiar glandular pouch on the throat. Dental formula: I 1/2, C 1/1, Pm 2/2, M 3/3 X 2 = 30. External measurements average: total length, 167 mm; tail 57 mm; foot, 17 mm; ear, 40 mm; forearm, 76 mm.

Distribution. From southwestern United States (western Texas to California) southward to northern Argentina and southern Brazil, but not yet reported from Central America. In Texas, it has been taken at localities near the Rio Grande in Val Verde, Brewster, and Presidio counties.

Western Mastiff Bat (*Eumops perotis*). Photo by Merlin D. Tuttle, Bat Conservation International.

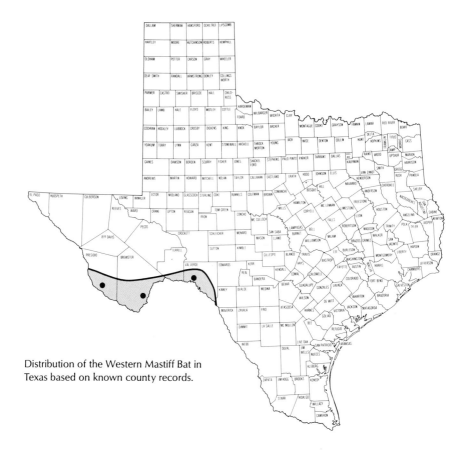

Distribution of the Western Mastiff Bat in Texas based on known county records.

Habits. Away from human habitations, this bat generally seeks diurnal refuge in crevices in rocks that form vertical or nearly vertical cliffs. The roost entrances typically are horizontally oriented, have moderately large openings, and face downward so they can be entered from below. In Capote Canyon in Presidio County, Texas, these bats were found utilizing a crevice formed by exfoliation of the nearly vertical rim rock. There are openings on both the lower and upper edges of the slab. At this site the canyon wall is about 38 m high and the rather steep slope below the cliff has no tall vegetation that might obstruct the takeoff and landing of the bats. Most authors agree that the bats choose a roost below which there is an unobstructed drop of several meters so that the emerging bats can drop and gain sufficient momentum to become airborne. Captive bats are unable to take off from the ground or from flat surfaces, and also are unable to maintain flight after launching themselves from the tops of tables. Bats tossed 4.5 m high in the air, however, are able to become airborne but those thrown half that distance cannot.

Colony size varies from two or three individuals to several dozen. Twenty individuals is a large colony of these bats although colonies of up to 70 are known. Harry Ohlendorf counted 71 individuals as they left the Capote Canyon roost about sunset on January 30. The first bats emerged about 6:45 p.m. and within 10 minutes 30 of them had taken wing. During the next 15 minutes 19 more emerged; 12 more took off during the next 10 minutes; four more in the next 15 minutes, and two more in the last 10 minutes. Thus, the exodus of the 71 bats was strung out over a period of

50 minutes. Just before launching themselves into flight, and during flight, the bats utter a series of loud, shrill, chattering calls that can be heard for a considerable distance.

These bats leave their day roosts late in the evening to forage. The stomachs of 18 bats collected in Big Bend National Park contained moths (79.9%), crickets, (16.5%), grasshoppers (2.8%), and unidentified insects (0.7%). Bees, dragonflies, leafbugs, beetles, and cicadas have also been reported in their diet. These bats are not believed to use night roosts, but instead soar at great altitudes all night long so that they can feed over wide areas. Insects carried aloft by thermal currents probably furnish an important portion of their diet. The presence of flightless insects, such as crickets, in their diet is interesting as these bats are unable to take off from the ground and therefore, cannot alight to capture such prey. These prey items could be picked from canyon walls as the bats forage.

Observations indicate that males and females of this species remain together throughout the year, even during the period when young are produced. Normally only one young is produced per pregnancy, but occasionally a female may give birth to twins. The period of parturition probably extends from June to early July and a nursery colony may contain young ranging from newborn individuals to ones that are several weeks old. At birth the young are dull black in color. The gestation period is approximately 80-90 days.

ORDER XENARTHRA
ARMADILLOS, SLOTHS, AND ALLIES

This Order seems to have developed in South America and only recently invaded North America. Its members are bizarre creatures and highly specialized in structure and habits. The toothless anteaters are provided with heavy claws to tear apart termite nests and a long, slender, protrusile, sticky tongue to capture the insects. The slow-moving, plant-eating sloths are tree dwellers, with a rudimentary tail and only two or three toes on each foot. In the large group of armadillos, the presence of a bony carapace is unique among mammals.

The Order is divided into three families, all of which are restricted to Central and South America with the exception of one species, the nine-banded armadillo, which ranges north to the United States.

FAMILY DASYPODIDAE (ARMADILLOS)

NINE-BANDED ARMADILLO
Dasypus novemcinctus Linnaeus

Description. About the size of a terrier dog, upperparts encased in a bony cara-pace with large shields on shoulders and rump and nine bands in between; front feet with four toes, middle two longest; hind foot five-toed, the middle three longest, all provided with large, strong claws; tail long, tapering and completely covered by bony rings; color brownish, the scattered hairs yellowish white. There are 30 or 32 peglike teeth. External measurements average: total length, 760 mm; tail, 345 mm; hind foot, 85 mm. Weight of adult males, 5-8 kg; females, 4-6 kg.

Distribution. Occurs throughout much of the state; absent from the western Trans-Pecos.

Habits. Soil texture exerts a definite influence upon the number of armadillos present in a given area. Those soils that are more easily dug, other factors being equal, will support a greater population density. In the sandy soils of Walker County, a popu-lation density of about one armadillo to 1 ha is common; in Brazos County, where the soils are more heavily impregnated with clay and become packed during the dry sea-sons, density averages one to 4 ha. In the rocky terrain of the Edwards Plateau, the animals tend to concentrate in the alluvial stream bottoms and den in the cracks and crevices of the numerous limestone outcroppings in that area. In the blackland section of Texas, where the soils are heavy clays, the animals are extremely rare and restricted to the vicinity of streams where they can burrow into the banks and probe for food in the relatively soft soils near water. Perhaps the most important factor contributing to the distribution of armadillos is the hardness of the soil during the dry season, because the food of the animal is obtained largely by probing for insects and other forms of animal life in the ground.

Armadillos are fond of water; where climatic conditions tend to be arid, the ani-mals concentrate in the vicinity of streams and water holes. Tracks in the mud around small ponds give evidence that the armadillos visit them not only for purposes of drink-ing and feeding, but also to take mud baths. Excess water, however, has a limiting effect on them because they avoid marshy areas.

Few animals of comparable size have so many dens per individual as the arma-dillo. The length, depth, and frequency of occurrence of their burrows depend some-what upon soil conditions. In sandy areas the animals are extremely active diggers; in addition to numerous occupied burrows, one finds many that have been abandoned or are used only occasionally as shelters. In central Texas, the majority of their dens are along creek banks whereas in the sandy soils of eastern Texas they are found almost everywhere. On the coastal prairies the sandy knolls are especially sought as den sites more because of protection from floods than because of ease of digging. In the Edwards Plateau natural caves, cracks, and crevices among the limestone outcroppings afford abundant shelter; excavated burrows are few in number and usually shallow.

Dens vary from 1 to 5 m in length and from a few centimeters below the surface to a depth of 1.3 m. Averaging between 17 and 20 cm in diameter, their plan is usually simple, with few turns except those caused by obstacles such as roots, rocks, and so forth. Many of the shallow burrows serve as food traps in which insects and other invertebrates take refuge and to which the armadillo goes on his foraging excursions. Burrows that are used for breeding purposes usually have a large nest chamber 45 cm or more in diameter and containing the rather loosely constructed nest of dried leaves, grasses, and other plant items. These materials are merely stuffed into the chamber and the animal pushes its way in and out each time the nest is used. Usually, each occupied burrow is inhabited by only one adult armadillo.

Because of their almost complete lack of hairy covering, armadillos are easily affected by climatic conditions. In the summer season they are more active in the cool of the evening and at night, but in midwinter their daily activities are reversed and the animals become active during the warmest part of the day, usually in mid-afternoon. They do not hibernate nor are they equipped to wait out long periods of inclement weather. Long periods of freezing weather effectively eliminate armadillos from an area.

Of special interest is the behavior of this animal in the water. Its specific gravity is high and the animal normally rides low in the water when swimming. Apparently, it tires easily when forced to swim for any distance. If the stream to be crossed is not

Nine-banded Armadillo (*Dasypus novemcinctus*) (5 weeks old). Photo by John L. Tveten.

wide, the armadillo may enter on one side, walk across the bottom, and emerge on the other side. If the expanse of water to be traversed is of considerable extent, the animals ingest air, inflate themselves, and thus increase their buoyancy. The physiological mechanism by which the armadillo can ingest air and retain it in its digestive tract to increase buoyancy is not known, but it appears to be under voluntary control.

Many legends have arisen concerning the food habits of armadillos. Among the rural folks in the South they are commonly called "gravediggers" and are thought to dig into human graves and dine upon the contents. Also, they have quite a reputation as a depredator of quail, chicken, and turkey eggs. A study of their food habits by examination of more than 800 stomachs revealed that no fewer than 488 different food items are eaten. Ninety-three percent (by volume) of their food is animal matter, chiefly insects and other invertebrates. Among the insects, nearly 28% were larval and adult scarab beetles — forms that are highly destructive to crops and pastures; termites and ants comprised about 14%; caterpillars nearly 8%; earthworms, millipedes, centipedes, and crayfish appeared conspicuously in their diet at times. Reptiles and amphibians comprised only a small part of their diet; these were captured usually during periods of cold weather. Birds' eggs were found in only 5 of 281 stomachs.

Observations by field workers strongly indicate that the armadillo, which usually leaves conspicuous signs of its presence, often is accused of the destruction of quail and chicken nests when the culprit is actually some other animal. More than two-thirds of the slightly less than 7% of vegetable matter in the diet was material ingested with other food items and represents nothing of economic importance. Berries and fungi made up 2.1% of the entire diet. Reports indicate that at times the armadillo may feed on such fruits as tomatoes and melons but the amount of damage done to these crops is relatively small. Carrion is readily eaten when available, and dead carcasses of animals frequently are visited not only for the carrion present but also for the maggots and pupae of flies found on or near them.

Reproduction in the nine-banded armadillo is marked by two distinct and apparently unrelated phenomena: the long period of arrested development of the blastocyst prior to implantation (delayed implantation), and the phenomenon of specific polyembryony, which results in the normal formation of identical quadruplets. In normal years about half of the females become pregnant by the end of July, which is the beginning of the breeding season. At 5-7 days the ovum forms a blastocyst and passes into the uterus. At this point development ceases, and the vesicle remains free in the uterus. Here it is constantly bathed in fluids secreted by the glandular lining of the uterus, which supplies enough nutrition and oxygen for survival. Implantation does not occur until November, about 14 weeks after fertilization. During this process, the blastocyst divides into growth centers, each of which very shortly redivides to produce four embryonic growth centers attached by a common placenta to the uterus. Development of each of the embryos then proceeds normally, and the four young are born approximately 4 months later in March, although some females have been noted with new litters as early as February and as late as the latter part of May. Young are born fully formed and with eyes open. Within a few hours they are walking, and they begin to accompany the mother on foraging expeditions within a few weeks. The nursing period is probably less than 2 months, but the young may remain with the mother even after weaning until they are several months old. Normally the young born in one year mature during the winter and mate for the first time in the early summer of the following year.

This phenomenon of delayed implantation may, in part, account for the successful invasion of the armadillo into temperate regions. Without this characteristic of the reproductive cycle, the young would be born at the beginning of winter, when their chance of survival would be greatly reduced. Apparently, the reproductive cycle is easily affected by adverse environmental conditions, particularly drought conditions. This probably is due to the shortage of ground insects or the difficulty of obtaining these in sandy or hard dried soils.

84

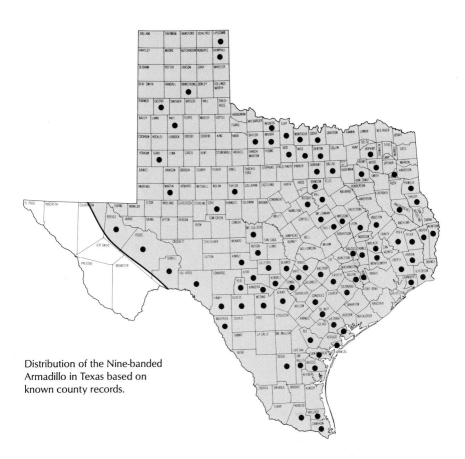

Distribution of the Nine-banded Armadillo in Texas based on known county records.

Armadillos are believed to pair for each breeding season, and a male and a female may share a burrow during the season. Because of the bony carapace and ventral position of the genitalia, copulation occurs with the female lying on her back.

Armadillos are frequently utilized as food in parts of Texas and Mexico. The meat is light-colored and when properly cooked is considered by some the equal of pork in flavor and texture.

Remarks. The common occurrence of this species in eastern Texas is a phenomenon that has developed largely since 1900. When Vernon Bailey published his *Biological Survey of Texas* in 1905, he mapped the distributional limits of the armadillo as between the Colorado and Guadalupe rivers with extralimital records from Colorado, Grimes, and Houston counties. By 1914 the armadillo had crossed the Brazos River and moved to the Trinity River, and along the coast had already reached the Louisiana line in Orange County. The northward and eastward range expansions continued over the next forty years, and by 1954 the armadillo was known from everywhere in eastern Texas except Red River and Lamar counties. By 1958 it was known from these latter two counties, and today is abundant everywhere in the region.

Apparently pioneering was most successful in a riparian habitat, and invasion was especially rapid parallel to rivers, which served as dispersal conduits. Average invasion rates have been calculated as from 4 to 10 km per year in the absence of obvious physical or climatic barriers. Possible reasons for the armadillo's northward expansion since the nineteenth century include progressive climatic changes, encroaching human civilization, overgrazing, and decimation of large carnivores.

ORDER LAGOMORPHA
HARES AND RABBITS

Mammals assigned to this Order superficially resemble rodents, but lagomorphs differ from rodents in several essential features. One of these is the peculiar tandem arrangement of the front (incisor) teeth, with a large tooth in front on each side and a small peglike tooth directly behind it. Also, the number of premolars is 2/2 or 3/2 (2/1 or 0/0 in rodents), so that the total number of teeth is 26 or 28 and never as few as the 16 to 22 found in rodents.

This group of mammals is largely diurnal or crepuscular in habit; the food is almost entirely vegetable matter — grasses, forbs, bark of trees and shrubs, and so forth. Because of their usually large size and food predilections, lagomorphs frequently come into conflict with grazing, agriculture, and forestry interests. No lagomorphs hibernate.

KEY TO THE HARES AND RABBITS OF TEXAS

1. Length of ear from notch more than 100 mm; general color grayish above, white below; tail with black dorsal stripe. *Lepus californicus* (black-tailed jackrabbit), p. 92.

   Length of ear from notch less than 100 mm 2

2. Length of hind foot usually more than 100 mm; total length (tip of snout to tip of tail) in adults near 500 mm; pelage rather harsh for a rabbit. *Sylvilagus aquaticus* (swamp rabbit), p. 86.

   Length of hind foot usually less than 100 mm; total length of adults near 400 mm 3

3. Ear 65% to 85% as long as hind foot and usually more than 58 mm in length; hind foot usually less than 90 mm; bullae relative to length of skull large. *Sylvilagus audubonii* (desert cottontail), p. 88.

   Ear 50% to 60% as long as hind foot and usually less than 58 mm in length; hind foot usually near 90 mm; bullae relative to length of skull small. *Sylvilagus floridanus* (eastern cottontail), p. 90.

FAMILY LEPORIDAE (HARES AND RABBITS)

SWAMP RABBIT
Sylvilagus aquaticus (Bachman)

Description. Largest of the "cottontails" within its range; pelage coarse and short for a rabbit; upper parts grayish brown, heavily lined with blackish; rump, upperside of tail, and back of hind legs dull ochraceous brown; sides of head and body paler than back, less suffused with blackish; underparts, including underside of tail, white except for buffy underside of neck; front legs and tops of hind feet cinnamon rufous. External measurements average: total length, 534 mm; tail, 69 mm; hind foot, 106 mm; ear, 70 mm. Weight, 1.5-3 kg.

Distribution. Found in eastern one-third of state west to Montague, Wise, and Bexar counties.

Swamp Rabbit (*Sylvilagus aquaticus*). Photo by John L. Tveten.

Habits. The swamp rabbit, as the name suggests, inhabits poorly drained river bottoms and coastal marshes. Well adapted to a semi-aquatic habitat in that its dense fur "waterproofs" its skin, the animal is at home in the water. In fact, it crosses rivers and streams on its own initiative, a habit usually not found in other rabbits in Texas. It is secretive by day and is seldom seen, except when frightened from its bed in some thicket, but its presence in an area is readily disclosed by the piles of fecal pellets deposited on stumps, down logs, or other elevations. Along the coast it is at home in cane thickets, hence the local name "cane cutter," but in inland areas it is restricted to the flood plains of rivers and streams and their associated tangles of shrubs, trees, and vines.

In southeast Texas, one swamp rabbit per 2.8 ha of poorly drained bottomland is typical. The rabbits frequent a definite local range, which they refuse to leave even when pursued by dogs. Their chief protection are thickets of briars or brush, rather than underground burrows. In this area both eastern cottontails (*S. floridanus*) and swamp rabbits occupy the creek and riverbottoms in about equal numbers, but in the uplands only cottontails are found.

Little is known of their food habits although succulent vegetation including grasses, forbs, and the new shoots of shrubs are probably important.

The breeding season extends at least from January to September, but the peak is in February and March when green vegetation is available. Possibly two or more litters of two to three young are reared annually. After a gestation period of 39-40 days, the young are born in, or transferred to, surface nests composed of vegetation and lined with rabbit fur, or nests in holes in logs and stumps. A nest found at the base of a cypress stump was composed of Spanish moss and rabbit fur; it held six small rabbits. Another found under a long, fallen branch of a tree was lined with fur and held two young rabbits. At birth the young are covered with fur, but the eyes and ears are closed. This condition is not true of other cottontails. The eyes open and the young rabbit is able to walk in 2 or 3 days.

Among their known natural enemies are gray fox, horned owl, and alligator. Doubtless, they are preyed upon by many other species. Other than man, their chief enemy is floods.

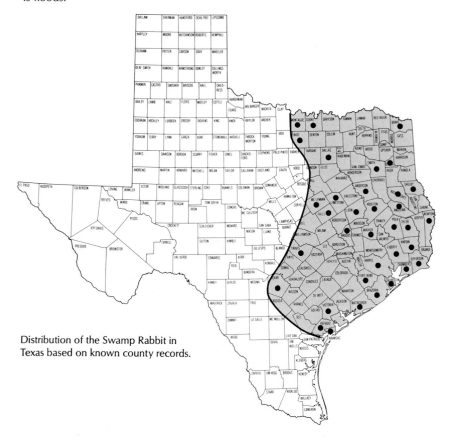

Distribution of the Swamp Rabbit in Texas based on known county records.

DESERT COTTONTAIL
Sylvilagus audubonii (Baird)

Description. Medium-sized cottontail, with relatively long ears; pelage rather harsh, but not so harsh as in the swamp rabbit; hind feet relatively slender and with relatively short pelage; auditory bullae large, with rough surface; ratio of length of ear to length of hind foot 0.66 or more; upperparts dark buffy brown, heavily lined with black; rump not conspicuously different from back; top of tail like back; nape bright rusty, almost orange rufous; front and outside of forelegs dark ochraceous buff; hind legs brownish cinnamon; underside of neck brownish buff; rest of underparts and under-surface of tail clear white. External measurements average; total length, 418 mm; tail, 73 mm; hind foot, 86 mm; ear, 60 mm. Weight, 0.5-1.4 kg.

Distribution. Occupies upland habitats in the western one-half of the state.

Habits. This species appears to be adapted to a variety of habitats, varying from grassland to creosote brush and cactus deserts. Wherever it may be, it frequents brushy areas or, where the vegetation is short, the underground burrows of prairie dogs, skunks, and so forth. In the Trans-Pecos it is often found in thickets of catclaw (*Acacia*), mesquite, allthorn, and other desert shrubs, and especially in prairie dog towns in short grass areas. In the plains regions it is so commonly associated with prairie dog towns that it is known locally as "prairie-dog rabbit."

Like other cottontails, these are more active in the twilight hours and at night, but they may be more or less active through the day. They are more or less sedentary and seldom range more than 360 m from their preferred thickets around and in which they feed, sleep, court, and rear their families. Unlike most other cottontails, they are known to climb sloping trees and thick brambles, and are not inclined to use beds when resting. However, these habits vary from one region to another.

The food is almost entirely vegetation, the kinds eaten varying with availability. In western Texas, they eat the leaves and green pods of mesquite, various grasses, forbs, bark and twigs of shrubs, and the juicy pads of prickly pear.

The breeding season is long. In Texas, onset of breeding begins in February and pregnant females, lactating females, and young in the nest have been found in every month except January, July, and October. There may be two or more litters a year. The number of young per litter varies from one to six, averaging about three. The gestation period is not known, but it is probably about 26-27 days.

As with other cottontails, the young are reared in nests which are made in pear-shaped excavations in the ground with the entrances only about 5 cm in diameter. Below, they are flared out to a width of 15-25 cm; the depth varies from 15 to 25 cm. They are lined with a layer of dried grasses, and the inside is filled entirely with rabbit fur in which the young repose. The female lies or squats over the opening to nurse her

Desert Cottontail (*Sylvilagus audubonii*). Photo by John L. Tveten.

young, which are blind and hairless at birth. By 10 days of age the eyes have opened and within another 4 days the young are able to move outside the nest, although they remain near the nest for about 3 weeks. The life span is 2 years or less.

Desert cottontails are known to be preyed upon by golden eagles, marsh hawks, Swainson's hawks, horned owls, barn owls, gray foxes, and gopher snakes. Doubtless, many other animals also feed upon them.

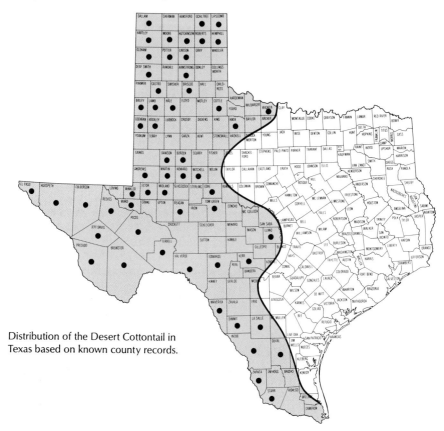

Distribution of the Desert Cottontail in Texas based on known county records.

EASTERN COTTONTAIL
Sylvilagus floridanus (Allen)

Description. A moderately large, rusty-brown cottontail with relatively short ears and large hind feet (ears 50-60% as long as hind feet). Upperparts deep ochraceous buff, heavily lined with blackish, giving a rusty or reddish-brown effect; sides paler and grayer; top of tail like back; rump dingy grayish, not conspicuously different from back; front and sides of legs deep, rich, rusty reddish; underside of neck buff or ochraceous buff, rest of underparts, including tail, white. Differs from *S. audubonii*, with which its range overlaps, in having small, smoothly rounded bullae (rather than large and rough) and relatively and actually shorter ears. External measurements average: total length, 418 mm; tail, 56 mm; hind foot, 92 mm; ear, 52 mm. Weight, 1-2 kg.

Distribution. Occurs throughout eastern three-fourths of the state and in some areas of the Trans-Pecos.

Habits. Like other cottontails, this one is a denizen of brushland and marginal areas and seldom ventures far from brushy cover. In central Texas, it commonly frequents brush-dotted pastures, the brushy edges of cultivated fields, and well-drained streamsides. Occasionally, it inhabits poorly drained bottom lands with the swamp rabbit. In many places it is common along country roads, especially where the sides are grown up to dense vegetation and adjoining areas are heavily grazed or farmed.

These cottontails are active largely in the twilight hours and at night, when they venture to open pastures, meadows, or lawns to forage. They frequently live in the edges of towns and feed in gardens and flower beds. In the daytime they rest in beds in nearby thickets or in underground burrows and small culverts. On the coastal prairies of Texas, a population density of one cottontail to 1.8 ha is not unusual.

The food is variable with the season. They feed on a variety of grasses and forbs but when such vegetation is scarce, they eat the twigs and bark of shrubs and small trees. These rabbits are not sociable and are seldom seen feeding together.

Eastern cottontails are prolific breeders. In southern Texas the breeding season is year-long, although the frequency of breeding does fluctuate throughout the year. Breeding activity is stimulated by environmental factors, such as temperature and rainfall, which affect the growth of vegetation. As many as four or five litters of one to eight young (average, four) may be reared yearly. The gestation period is 28-29 days. The young are blind and helpless at birth, but grow rapidly; when 4-5 months old they are distinguished from adults only with difficulty. Young females born early in the year may mature sexually and produce young in their first summer but ordinarily, they do not breed until their second summer.

Eastern Cottontail (*Sylvilagus floridanus*). Photo by John L. Tveten.

These cottontails are known to be preyed upon by hawks, barn owls, opossums, coyotes, foxes, and weasels. Doubtless, many others can be added to the list.

Remarks. Previously, cottontails from mountainous areas of the Trans-Pecos, including the Guadalupe and Chisos Mountains, were regarded as a distinct species (*Sylvilagus robustus*). Based on only nominal cranial differences with *S. floridanus*, these rabbits are now considered merely a subspecies of the eastern cottontail, *S. f. robustus*.

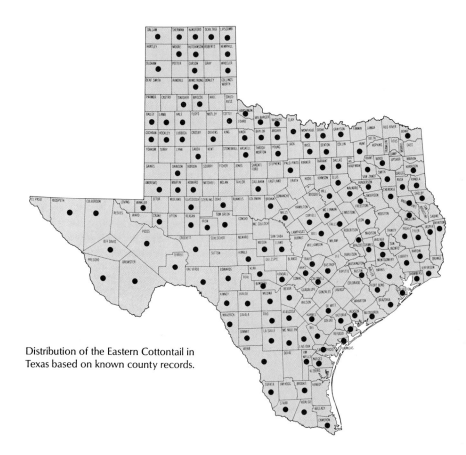

Distribution of the Eastern Cottontail in Texas based on known county records.

BLACK-TAILED JACKRABBIT
Lepus californicus Gray

Description. A large, long-eared rabbit of the open grasslands and desert scrub of the West; sides but little, if at all, differentiated from the back; ear nearly as long as the hind foot, with black patch at tip; top of tail with black stripe that extends onto rump; underparts clear, ochraceous buff, paler medially; upperparts dark buff, heavily sprinkled with blackish. External measurements average: total length, 604 mm; tail, 95 mm; hind foot, 131 mm; ear, 125 mm. Weight, 1.5-4 kg.

Distribution. Statewide, except for Big Thicket region of extreme southeastern Texas.

Habits. The black-tailed jackrabbit, so familiar to those who know the West, is a common denizen of the hot, dry, desert scrubland. It occupies a latitudinal range from sea level to well over 2,500 m on the southwest slopes of some of the desert mountains but seldom inhabits coniferous forests (pinyon pine and juniper areas excepted), although occasionally it may stray into them.

In summer, this rabbit spends the hotter part of the day dozing in a bed scratched-out at the base of some shrub, or in a clump of tall grass where the shade will protect it from the hot sun. In winter, such beds are located in vegetation that offers protection from the chilling winds. It becomes active at twilight, and forages well into the night. When molested it depends on speed and its keen senses of hearing and sight to elude its enemies.

Black-tailed Jackrabbit (*Lepus californicus*). Photo courtesy of Texas Parks and Wildlife.

The food includes forage crops, cactus, sagebrush, mesquite, and numerous grasses and herbs. Because of a preference for sparsely vegetated areas, this species often concentrates in pastures overgrazed by livestock, further depleting the vegetation. It has been estimated that 128 black-tailed jackrabbits can consume as much range vegetation as one cow or seven sheep. Thus, when these rabbits are concentrated, often as many as 154 per square kilometer, they conflict with grazing interests. Such concentrations frequently result from overgrazing, hence the wise rancher will recognize an overabundance of jackrabbits as an indication that he has been overstocking his range.

The breeding season extends throughout the year in Texas. Two to six litters of one to six young may be produced each year. The gestation period is 41-47 days. The young are precocious and active shortly after birth. They grow rather rapidly and reach adult size in about 7 or 8 months. Sexual maturity is attained at about the same time, but young females do not breed until early in the year following their birth. Usually, the expectant mother provides no nest for her young.

The natural enemies of rabbits include the larger birds of prey and such carnivores as coyotes, foxes, bobcats, badgers, and weasels. Campaigns to eliminate these predators from rangelands usually are expensive and they may lead to an increase in jackrabbits and many range rodents, which can become serious pests.

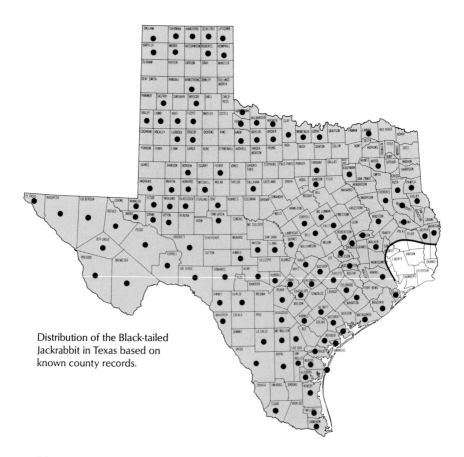

Distribution of the Black-tailed Jackrabbit in Texas based on known county records.

ORDER RODENTIA
RODENTS

The name Rodentia is derived from the Latin verb *rodere* (to gnaw), in allusion to the gnawing habits of the group. Among North American mammals, rodents are unique in that the incisors are reduced in number to one on each side above and below, in the absence of canines, and in the presence of never more than two premolars in each jaw above and one below. The dental formula varies from: I 1/1, C 0/0, Pm 0/0, M 3/3 X 2 = 16 to I 1/1, C 0/0, Pm 2/1, M 3/3 X 2 = 22. Most animals assigned to the order are small in size; some, for example the beaver, may exceed 25 kg in weight. Rodents comprise more than one-third of the known kinds of mammals, and individually they are the most abundant mammal in many sections of the world. Sixty-four species of native rodents occupy Texas, making this the most diverse group of mammals in our state.

In habits, members of this order are diverse. Most of them are nocturnal or crepuscular; ground squirrels and tree squirrels are strictly diurnal; others may be active either by day or by night. Considerable adaptive radiation occurs in the group. Some species (pocket gopher) are fossorial; others are aquatic (beaver), arboreal (tree squirrel), volant (flying squirrel), or terrestrial (cotton rat). Most rodents feed on vegetation, but a few species, notably the grasshopper mouse, feed extensively upon animal matter. Most rodents are active throughout the year, but others, notably ground squirrels, may hibernate for several months.

KEY TO THE RODENTS OF TEXAS

1. Presence of external, furlined cheek pouches 2

   Absence of external, furlined cheek pouches 15

2. Front feet much larger than hind feet; ear (pinna) short and inconspicuous; tail about half the length of head and body (pocket gophers) 3

   Front feet much smaller than hind feet; ear (pinna) conspicuous; tail as long as (or longer than) head and body (pocket mice and kangaroo rats) 5

3. Upper incisors not grooved on outer face; claws of front feet relatively small and slender. *Thomomys bottae* (Botta's pocket gopher), p. 121.

   Upper incisors distinctly grooved on outer surface; claws of front feet large and long (longest ones about 15 mm) 4

4. Upper incisors with one deep groove; feet blackish. *Cratogeomys castanops* (yellow-faced pocket gopher), p. 130.

   Upper incisor with two distinct grooves; feet whitish (species of the genus *Geomys*):
   > Seven species of the genus *Geomys* occur in Texas. These are cryptic species, identifiable primarily on the basis of geographic distribution and characters of the karyotype and genes. Only specialists working with prepared study specimens can identify them using morphological features.
   > (1) *Geomys arenarius* (desert pocket gopher) occurs in El Paso and Hudspeth counties in far western Texas, p. 123.
   > (2) *Geomys attwateri* (Attwater's pocket gopher) occurs in the south-central part of eastern Texas, p. 124.

(3) *Geomys breviceps* (Baird's pocket gopher) occurs in eastern and northeastern Texas, p. 125.

(4) *Geomys bursarius* (plains pocket gopher) occurs in northwestern and north-central Texas, p. 126.

(5) *Geomys knoxjonesi* (Jones' pocket gopher) occurs on the southwestern plains of Texas, p. 127.

(6) *Geomys personatus* (Texas pocket gopher) occurs in the southern part of Texas, p. 128.

(7) *Geomys texensis* (Llano pocket gopher) occurs in the Llano Basin region of the Hill Country in central Texas and in an isolated area on the northern border of the South Texas Plains, p. 129.

5. Hind legs more than twice as long as front legs; tail long and bushy at end; head broad, 25 mm or more in width (kangaroo rats) 6

   Hind legs less than twice as long as front legs; head about 15 mm in width (pocket mice) 10

6. Large size, total length of adults 300 mm or more; tip of tail with conspicuous white "banner" 7

   Smaller, total length of adults usually less than 250 mm; tip of tail usually dusky, not white 8

7. Hind foot (from tip of longest claw to heel) 50 mm or more in length; length of tail about 200 mm. *Dipodomys spectabilis* (banner-tailed kangaroo rat), p. 151.

   Hind foot less than 50 mm; tail normally less than 200 mm. *Dipodomys elator* (Texas kangaroo rat), p. 145.

8. Hind foot with five toes (one is very small and difficult to detect) 9

   Hind foot with only four toes. *Dipodomys merriami* (Merriam's kangaroo rat), p. 147.

9. Pelage long and silky, brownish; mastoid bullae greatly inflated, giving skull a triangular appearance; interparietal narrow and triangular in shape. *Dipodomys ordii* (Ord's kangaroo rat), p. 149.

   Pelage short and coarse, with orangish cast; mastoid bullae less inflated; interparietal broad and rectangular to roundish in shape. *Dipodomys compactus* (Gulf Coast kangaroo rat), p. 144.

10. Size small, total length 100 to 130 mm; weight 6 to 8 grams; pelage silky and soft 11

    Size larger, total length 150 mm or more; pelage harsh, often bristly, never silky 12

11. Length of tail usually 60 mm or more; total length usually 120 mm or more; length of skull usually more than 21 mm; postauricular patch inconspicuous. *Perognathus flavescens* (plains pocket mouse), p. 132.

    Length of tail usually less than 60 mm; total length usually less than 120 mm; length of skull usually less than 21 mm; postauricular patch conspicuous. Silky pocket mice:

    > Two species of silky pocket mice occur in Texas, but only specialists working with prepared study specimens can identify them.

(1) *Perognathus flavus* (silky pocket mouse) occurs in the Panhandle and Trans-Pecos portions of Texas, p. 133.

(2) *Perognathus merriami* (Merriam's pocket mouse) occurs in the Great Plains, central, and southern regions of Texas, p. 135.

12. Upper incisors plain, not grooved, on outer face; pelage spiny to touch. *Liomys irroratus* (Mexican spiny pocket mouse), p. 152.

Upper incisors distinctly grooved on outer face 13

13. Length of tail less than length of head and body (tail laid forward over back does not reach snout); weight 30 to 47 grams. *Chaetodipus hispidus* (hispid pocket mouse), p. 137.

Length of tail greater than length of head and body (tip of tail extends beyond snout when laid forward) 14

14. Rump with conspicuous black-tipped "spines"; tail sparsely haired on basal half; soles of hind feet blackish; upperparts grizzled blackish. *Chaetodipus nelsoni* (Nelson's pocket mouse), p. 140.

Rump without conspicuous, black-tipped "spines."
This category contains two species that only a specialist working with comparative material can identify with certainty.

(1) *Chaetodipus penicillatus* (desert pocket mouse) occurs in sandy soils mainly in Trans-Pecos Texas, p. 142.

(2) *Chaetodipus intermedius* (rock pocket mouse) occurs mainly in rocky situations in the Trans-Pecos section of the state, p. 139.

15. Tail paddle-shaped, naked, scaly; hind feet webbed; size large. *Castor canadensis* (American beaver), p. 154.

Tail not paddle-shaped 16

16. Pelage with intermixed sharp quills; large, 4 to 12 kg. *Erethizon dorsatum* (porcupine), p. 206.

Pelage without quills 17

17. Lower jaw with four cheek teeth on each side 18

Lower jaw with only three cheek teeth on each side 28

18. Hind feet fully webbed; adults weigh up to 12 kg; tail long, naked, and nearly circular in cross section. *Myocastor coypus* (nutria), p. 208.

Hind feet not fully webbed 19

19. "Flying" membrane between front leg and hind leg on each side; color wood brown above, white below. *Glaucomys volans* (eastern flying squirrel), p. 119.

Legs normal, no "flying" membrane 20

20. Upperparts striped or distinctly spotted or both 21

Upperparts not striped or distinctly spotted 25

21. Upperparts striped 22

Upperparts spotted 24

22. One white stripe on each side; underside of tail grayish white (held over back while animal is running); upperparts grizzled grayish. *Ammospermophilus interpres* (Texas antelope squirrel), p. 103.

Three or more white or light stripes on upperparts 23

23. Six continuous, whitish stripes alternating with seven rows of whitish spots; ground color brown. *Spermophilus tridecemlineatus* (thirteen-lined ground squirrel), p. 108.

Four whitish stripes alternating with five dark brown stripes; sides of face striped. *Tamias canipes* (gray-footed chipmunk), p. 102.

24. Spots in 10 or more distinct rows; tail narrowly bushy and about three times as long as hind foot. *Spermophilus mexicanus* (Mexican ground squirrel), p. 104.

Spots scattered, never in distinct rows; tail about twice as long as hind foot. *Spermophilus spilosoma* (spotted ground squirrel), p. 106.

25. General color yellowish brown; tail very short (1.5 times length of hind foot) and black-tipped. *Cynomys ludovicianus* (black-tailed prairie dog), p. 112.

General color gray, brown, or blackish; tail long and bushy 26

26. Belly reddish or rusty in color; upperparts grayish; hind foot 70 mm or more. *Sciurus niger* (eastern fox squirrel), p. 117.

Belly whitish or grayish; not reddish; hind foot 70 mm or less 27

27. Belly white; upperparts gray, unspotted. *Sciurus carolinensis* (eastern gray squirrel), p. 115.

Belly grayish, back grayish with faint light spots, or shoulders and head black and rump grayish or brownish. *Spermophilus variegatus* (rock squirrel), p. 110.

28. Tail flattened laterally, sparsely haired and scaly; hind toes fringed with stiff hairs; length of adults about 45 cm. *Ondatra zibethicus* (common muskrat), p. 204.

Tail round, sparingly haired or bushy 29

29. Enamel pattern of molar teeth with transverse or oblique folds or triangles 30

Enamel pattern of molar teeth with two or three rows of cusps (unworn condition) or roughly circular with slight lateral indentations (worn condition) 37

30. Mouse size, total length usually less than 150 mm; tail less than 50 mm; ears nearly hidden in the fur 31

Rat size, total length of adults 225 mm or more; tail 100 mm or more; ears conspicuous or partly hidden in the dense fur 33

31. Tail less than 25 mm in length; hind foot usually less than 18 mm; color glossy, reddish brown. *Microtus pinetorum* (woodland vole), p. 203.

Tail more than 25 mm in length; hind foot usually more than 18 mm; color brownish gray or blackish 32

32. Enamel pattern of third upper molar with no more than two closed triangles, often with no closed triangles, hence with three loops; never more than two inner re-entrant angles. *Microtus ochrogaster* (prairie vole), p. 201.

Enamel pattern of third upper molar with three closed triangles or, if with only two closed triangles, then with three inner re-entrant angles. *Microtus mexicanus* (Mexican vole), p. 200.

33. Ears conspicuous; tail in adults usually 150 mm or longer; eyes large, black, and bulging in life; fur rather soft; whiskers long, usually more than 50 mm (woodrats) 34

Ears partly hidden in dense pelage; tail 100-125 mm long; pelage rather harsh; whiskers 25 to 35 mm long (cotton rats) 35

34. First upper molar tooth with a deep antero-internal fold extending half-way across the crown. *Neotoma mexicana* (Mexican woodrat), p. 194.

First upper molar tooth without a deep antero-internal fold extending half-way across the crown:
> This category includes three species that are difficult to identify without close examination of the skull and the baculum.
> (1) *Neotoma micropus* (southern plains woodrat) occurs in the brushlands of the western and southern portions of the state. Over most of its range, this woodrat is characterized by a steel gray dorsum as compared to the brownish pelage of the other two species, p. 195.
> (2) *Neotoma albigula* (white-throated woodrat) is found in the western half of Texas, p. 190.
> (3) *Neotoma floridana* (eastern woodrat) is found in the eastern half of Texas, p. 192.

35. Underparts buffy to ochraceous; tail entirely black; top surface of feet buffy. *Sigmodon fulviventer* (tawny-bellied cotton rat), p. 186.

Underparts whitish and not buffy or ochraceous; tail bicolor, dark above and light below; top surface of feet whitish 36

36. Snout and eye rings yellowish or orangish and conspicuously different than color of backs and sides; hind foot of adults usually less than 30 mm; total length usually less than 260 mm. *Sigmodon ochrognathus* (yellow-nosed cotton rat), p. 189.

Snout and eye rings not conspicuous and same color as sides and back; hind foot usually more than 30 mm; total length usually more than 260 mm. *Sigmodon hispidus* (hispid cotton rat), p. 187.

37. Rat size, total length 230 mm or more 38

Mouse size, total length usually less than 200 mm 40

38. Cusps on upper molars in two rows; hind foot narrow and slender (rice rats). There are two species of rice rats in Texas that only a specialist can identify with certainty.
> (1) *Oryzomys palustris* (marsh rice rat), a grayish brown form characteristic of marshy areas along the coast from Brownsville northward into deep East Texas, p. 157.
> (2) *Oryzomys couesi* (Coues' rice rat), a tawny form that occurs in marshy areas in extreme South Texas (Hidalgo and Cameron counties), p. 156.

Cusps on upper molars in three rows (introduced rats) 39

39. Tail slender and as long as or longer than head and body (tail reaches to or beyond nose when laid forward); color brownish or black; weight to 225 g. *Rattus rattus* (roof rat), p. 198.

Tail chunkier and shorter than head and body; color brownish; weight to 450 g. *Rattus norvegicus* (Norway rat), p. 197.

40. Outer face of each upper incisor with deep groove (harvest mice) 41

Outer face of upper incisors not grooved 44

41. Tail much longer than head and body (projects beyond nose when laid forward along back); last lower molar with dentine in the form of an "S." *Reithrodontomys fulvescens* (fulvous harvest mouse), p. 159.

Tail shorter than or about as long as head and body; last lower molar with dentine in the form of a "C" 42

42. Color rich brown to blackish brown; a distinct labial shelf or ridge, often with distinct cusplets on first and second lower molars. *Reithrodontomys humulis* (eastern harvest mouse), p. 161.

Color mainly grayish brown or light buff; no distinct labial shelf or ridge on first and second molars 43

43. Tail shorter than head and body. Breadth of braincase not exceeding 9.6 mm. *Reithrodontomys montanus* (plains harvest mouse), p. 163.

Tail length about equal to, or slightly longer than, head and body. Breadth of braincase of adults usually over 9.5 mm. *Reithrodontomys megalotis* (western harvest mouse), p. 162.

44. Upper incisors with distinct notch at tip when viewed from the side; distinctly musky odor. *Mus musculus* (house mouse), p. 199.

Upper incisors lacking distinct notch at tip 45

45. Total length of adults 100 mm or less; tail short, 35 mm, about three times length of hind foot; color blackish or sooty. *Baiomys taylori* (northern pygmy mouse), p. 181.

Total length of adults 125 mm or more; color not blackish or sooty 46

46. Tail less than 60% of head and body; coronoid process of mandible extends high above level of condyloid process; soles of feet furred (grasshopper mice) 47

Tail more than 60% of head and body; coronoid process of mandible does not ascend above tip of condyloid process; soles of feet only slightly furred (deer mice and relatives) 48

47. Tail less than half length of head and body; crown length of maxillary toothrow 4.0 mm or more. *Onychomys leucogaster* (northern grasshopper mouse), p. 184.

Tail more than half length of head and body; crown length of maxillary toothrow 3.9 mm or less. *Onychomys arenicola* (Mearns' grasshopper mouse), p. 182.

48. General color golden yellow. *Ochrotomys nuttalli* (golden mouse), p. 179.

General color brown, buff, or gray (white-footed mice) 49

49. Tail much shorter than head and body 50

Tail as long as or longer than head and body 52

50. Hind foot (of adults) greater than 23 mm. *Peromyscus gossypinus* (cotton mouse), p. 170.

Hind foot (of adults) less than 23 mm 51

51. Tail with narrow and distinct dorsal stripe; total length of adults usually less than 170 mm; length of tail usually less than 75 mm; greatest length of skull usually less than 26 mm. *Peromyscus maniculatus* (deer mouse), p. 173.

Tail with broad dorsal stripe and not sharply bicolored; total length of adults usually more than 170 mm; length of tail usually more than 75 mm; greatest length of skull usually more than 26 mm. *Peromyscus leucopus* (white-footed mouse), p. 171.

52. Nasals decidedly exceeded by premaxillae; two principal outer angles of first and second upper molars simple, without (or at most with rudimentary) accessory cusps or enamel lophs; sole of hind foot naked to end of ankle; no pectoral mammae; inguinal mammae, 2-2. *Peromyscus eremicus* (cactus mouse), p. 168.

Nasals slightly or not at all exceeded by premaxillae; two principal outer angles of first and second upper molars with well-developed accessory tubercles or enamel lophs; sole of hind foot hairy on proximal fourth to ankle; pectoral mammae, 1-1, inguinal mammae, 2-2 53

53. Ear longer than hind foot; tail about as long as head and body (except in *P. t. comanche* in which it is longer); bullae unusually inflated. *Peromyscus truei* (piñon mouse), p. 178.

Ear equal to or shorter than hind foot; tail usually longer than head and body; bullae moderately or less inflated 54

54. Hind foot length of adults more than 24 mm. *Peromyscus attwateri* (Texas mouse), p. 165.

Hind foot length of adults less than 24 mm 55

55. Tarsal joints of ankles white like upper side of hind foot; baculum with long cartilaginous spine at its terminal end. *Peromyscus pectoralis* (white-ankled mouse), p. 176.

Dusky color of hind leg extending to end more or less over tarsal joint, baculum with a short cartilaginous spine at its terminal end 56

56. Dorsal coloration grayish black, and often like immature pelage; top of head and flanks of adults predominantly grayish; first two lower molars usually with one or more accessory lophids or stylids. *Peromyscus nasutus* (northern rock mouse), p. 175.

Dorsal coloration with considerable yellow or buff; top of head same color as back; flanks of adults predominantly bright yellowish brown; first of two lower molars usually without any accessory lophids or stylids. *Peromyscus boylii* (brush mouse), p. 167.

FAMILY SCIURIDAE (SQUIRRELS AND ALLIES)

GRAY-FOOTED CHIPMUNK
Tamias canipes V. Bailey

Description. A small, grayish-appearing squirrel, the upperparts marked with four whitish and three to five brownish stripes; the nape and shoulders usually with a distinct wash of smoke gray; dark dorsal stripes black or brownish black; inner pair of light stripes smoke gray, outer pair grayish white. External measurements average: total length, 225 mm; tail, 102 mm; hind foot, 35 mm.

Distribution. These are forest-dwelling chipmunks and occur in Texas only in the Sierra Diablo and Guadalupe Mountains in the Trans-Pecos region (Culberson County).

Habits. Favorite haunts of the gray-footed chipmunk are down logs at the edge of clearings. They occur also in dense stands of mixed timber (oaks, pines, firs) and on brushy hillsides, particularly where crevices in rocks offer retreats. When alarmed, they usually seek seclusion in crevices or underground burrows; occasionally they take to the trees.

Their food consists of a variety of items such as acorns, seeds of Douglas fir, currants, gooseberries, mushrooms, green vegetation, and insects.

Little is known of their breeding habits. The young are about half-grown in midsummer and almost full-grown in September and October, but one female taken in August in the Guadalupe Mountains contained four embryos. One litter a year is normal.

Gray-footed chipmunks (*Tamias canipes*). Photo courtesy of U.S. Fish and Wildlife Service.

TEXAS ANTELOPE SQUIRREL
Ammospermophilus interpres (Merriam)

Description. A small ground squirrel with one narrow white line on each side of back from shoulder to rump, and underside of tail grayish white, the lateral tail hairs with three black bands; upperparts vinaceous buff in summer and drab gray in winter; ears short, hardly more than a rim; tail held over back in life. External measurements average: total length, 226 mm; tail, 74 mm; hind foot, 38 mm. Weight (males), 104 (94-121) g; (females), 104 (84-115) g.

Distribution. Known in Texas east to Reagan, Crockett, and Val Verde counties.

Habits. These squirrels are characteristic of desert regions in the southwest where they live chiefly around the edges of the lower valleys and in the low hills. They seem to prefer hard-surfaced, gravelly washes or rocky hill slopes and are less common or entirely absent on level, sandy terrain.

They usually live in burrows but crevices in and among rocks may serve as den sites. They also make use of abandoned burrows of other rodents. Their burrows are usually situated at the side of a clump of bushes, a boulder, or in a cut bank. There is usually no mound of earth to mark the entrance. One burrow found in a cut bank was excavated in friable soil under a bed of hardpan about 1 m below the top of the ground and 50 cm above the roadbed. The main tunnel was 8.7 cm in diameter, 3 m long, and lay parallel to and about 30 cm back from the face of the cut. Access was by three openings. Midway in the tunnel was the nest chamber which measured 12.5 cm in width, 17.5 cm in length, and 10.0 cm in height. An accessory loop back of the nest

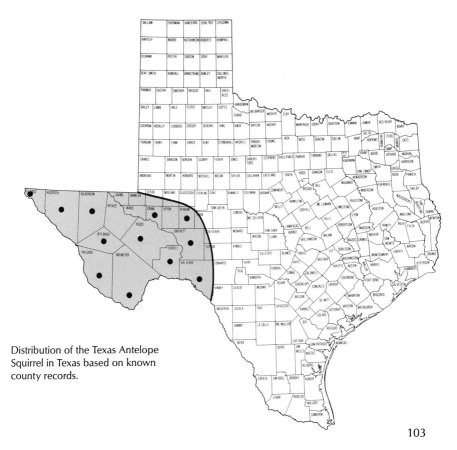

Distribution of the Texas Antelope Squirrel in Texas based on known county records.

103

Texas Antelope Squirrel (*Ammospermophilus interpres*). Photo by R.D. Porter.

and two blind pockets at one end of the main tunnel completed the system. The nest was composed of rabbit fur, shredded bark, feathers, dried grasses, and bits of cotton.

"Ammos" are fidgety, nervous creatures and seldom are still for long. They are nimble-footed and can run with surprising speed. Their peculiar habit of carrying the tail arched forward over the back, exposing to view the contrastingly colored undersurface, is a readily usable field characteristic. The nervous flickering of the tail when the animals are excited and the mellow, rolling, trill-like calls further help to identify them. They spend most of the time on the ground but they may be seen in the tops of low bushes, yuccas, and prickly pears where they also forage. Available evidence indicates that at lower elevations these ground squirrels do not hibernate.

Antelope ground squirrels are one of the few mammals that may remain active during the hottest parts of west Texas summer days. By occasionally retreating to a shady spot where they lie outstretched, with their limbs "spread eagle" and their belly in contact with the cooler terrain, excess heat accumulated during their activities is rapidly lost and the squirrels are able to maintain a safe body temperature. After such rests the squirrels once again venture into the summer sun to conduct their business.

Their food is largely a wide variety of seeds and fruits. They have been observed feeding on seeds of yucca, juniper, salt grass, ripe fruits of prickly pear and cholla cactus, seeds of mesquite, sotol, creosote bush, and insects.

Breeding begins in February. One litter of five to 14 young, based on embryo counts, is reared each year, but there is evidence that a second brood may be reared by some females. The young ones remain in the nest until they are about one-fourth grown, at which time they venture above ground and begin eating solid foods. Information on other phases of reproduction appears to be lacking.

MEXICAN GROUND SQUIRREL
Spermophilus mexicanus (Erxleben)

Description. A rather small ground squirrel with usually nine rows of squarish white spots on back; tail about two-fifths of total length, moderately bushy; ears short and rounded; upperparts wood brown or buffy brown with rows of conspicuous white spots; sides and underparts whitish or pinkish buff. External measurements average: total length, 301 mm; tail, 118 mm; hind foot, 41 mm. Weight, (males) 227-330 g; (females), 137-198 g.

Distribution. Occurs throughout much of southern and western Texas (west to Culberson, Jeff Davis, and Presidio counties in the Trans-Pecos), north almost to the Red River just east of the Panhandle.

Habits. Mexican ground squirrels inhabit brushy or grassy areas. In southern Texas, they are frequently associated with mesquite and cactus flats. In Kerr County, they are most common in pastures and along the highways; in Trans-Pecos Texas, they are frequently found in areas dominated by creosote-bush (*Larrea*).

They live in burrows, the openings to which are usually unmarked by a mound of earth. Sandy or gravelly soils are preferred, but the squirrels are by no means restricted to them. One squirrel may utilize several burrows, one of which is the homesite; the others are temporary refuges. The burrows are typically from 6 to 8 cm in diameter, enter the ground at a 30 to 50 degree angle, and range from 30 to 125 cm below the surface. The brood chamber is usually at the deepest part in a side tunnel. There are often two openings to the burrow system, possibly to facilitate escape. They also utilize burrows of pocket gophers. Although somewhat colonial, they are rather unsocial and drive away other squirrels that intrude upon their privacy. Their home range is about 45 m in radius.

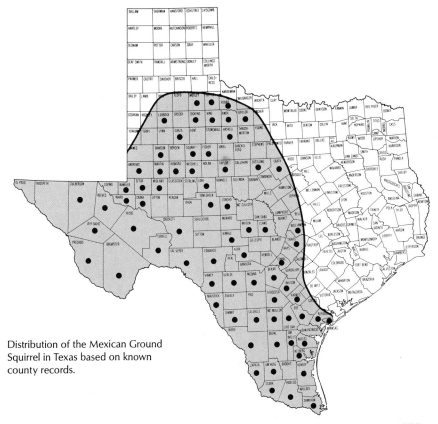

Distribution of the Mexican Ground Squirrel in Texas based on known county records.

105

Mexican Ground Squirrel (*Spermophilus mexicanus*). Photo by John L. Tveten.

Near Midland, most of the squirrels are in hibernation by November 20, although there is some activity throughout the winter. Likewise, in the Trans-Pecos they are seldom seen in winter, but in South Texas they remain active throughout the year.

Their food in early spring is chiefly green vegetation. They are known to feed on mesquite leaves and beans, agarita leaves and berries, Shasta lily, Johnson grass, pin clover, and cultivated grains. Insects also contribute importantly to their diet. In early summer about half of their diet is insects. They are fond of meat and frequently can be seen feeding upon small animals killed on the highways. In captivity they exhibit a cannibalistic tendency and kill and eat their cage mates, particularly if a strange squirrel is placed with them. Occasionally they climb into low bushes to forage, but most of their food is gathered on the ground.

Breeding begins in late March or early April and lasts for a week or two. The gestation period is probably not more than 30 days. The young, about five per litter, are born blind and almost naked and weigh from 3 to 5 g.

SPOTTED GROUND SQUIRREL
Spermophilus spilosoma Bennett

Description. A small ground squirrel with scattered, more or less squarish, light spots on back (spots not in rows as in *S. mexicana* and *S. tridecemlineatus*); ears inconspicuous; tail about one-third of total length, pinkish buff or cinnamon buff beneath; upperparts smoke gray, light drab or fawn color, the white spots small and obsolete, especially on shoulder; underparts white. External measurements average: total length, 214 mm; tail, 65 mm; hind foot, 32 mm. Weight, 100-125 g.

Distribution. Known from western one-half of state (not on Edwards Plateau) and southward on Rio Grande Plain.

Habits. Spotted ground squirrels seem to prefer dry, sandy areas, but they are also found in grassy parks, open pine forests, scattered brush, and occasionally on rocky mesas. On Mustang Island, off the coast of Texas, they live in the sand dunes and share their runways through the sparse vegetation with kangaroo rats, grasshopper mice, and other small rodents. Near Van Horn, they are rather common in the sandhills covered with yuccas and other desert shrubs, and in the southern part of the Big Bend they occur in small numbers on rather hard ground covered with creosote bushes. The opening to their burrows is usually under bushes or overhanging rocks. One excavated burrow had three openings, was about 4 m long, descended no more than 50 cm, and terminated in a nest chamber. A burrow in the Big Bend had an opening about 5 cm in diameter and was marked by a slight mound.

These squirrels are extremely shy. One can work in an area several days without seeing them. They are most active in early morning and late afternoon to avoid the midday heat. They seldom go far from their burrows and retreat to them at the slightest sign of danger. Their movements are rapid and interrupted by abrupt stops, reminding one of a lizard. In running, the body and tail are held close to the ground.

Hibernation probably is not complete in these squirrels, especially in the southern part of their range. Specimens have been taken in November, December, January, and February in Texas.

Their food is largely green vegetation and seeds. Specific items are cactus pulp, mesquite beans, saltbush seeds, sandbur, sunflower, gourd, iris, grasshoppers, and beetles.

Their breeding habits are not well-known. Females captured in mid-June, at which time half-grown young were common, contained five to seven embryos. This indicates that two litters may be reared yearly. Young, presumably about a month old, have been observed above ground as early as April 28 and as late as September 17,

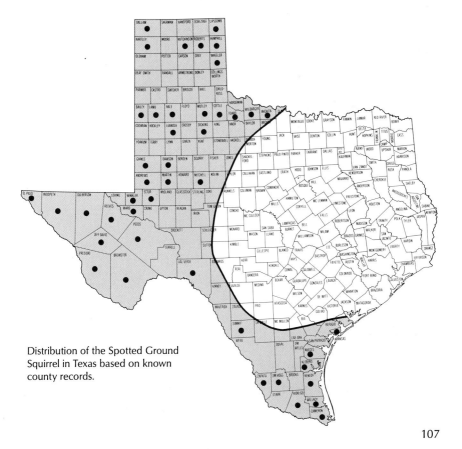

Distribution of the Spotted Ground Squirrel in Texas based on known county records.

107

Spotted Ground Squirrel (*Spermophilus spilosoma*). Photo by R.D. Porter.

which would suggest that mating begins in February and continues into mid-July. The gestation period is not known, but is probably about 30 days. Six young spotted ground squirrels reared in captivity were found to weigh an average of 17 g at 34 days of age, their eyes opened at 27-28 days, and they were weaned at about 48 days.

THIRTEEN-LINED GROUND SQUIRREL
Spermophilus tridecemlineatus (Mitchill)

Description. A small ground squirrel with usually 13 alternating dark and light stripes, the dark ones containing a series of squarish buffy spots, the light stripes occasionally broken into spots; dark dorsal stripes dark brown or black in color, the light stripes continuous and buffy white; underside of tail russet at base, shading to orange buff toward tip; lower sides cinnamon buff; belly pinkish buff; chin white; ear small. External measurements average: total length, 285 mm; tail, 105 mm; hind foot, 40 mm. Weight of males averages 154 g (up to 212 g); females, 160 g (to 220 g).

Distribution. Known from northern Texas and in a corridor extending from Tarrant and Dallas counties in north-central Texas south to Atascosa, Bee, and Calhoun counties along the Gulf Coast.

Habits. These squirrels are typically inhabitants of short-grass prairies, but they have invaded the tall-grass areas in Texas where they live principally in pastures and along fencerows. They live in burrows in the ground from which radiate well-marked paths to the feeding grounds. In tall grass the paths may become tunnels. In cultivated areas they seem to prefer fence-rows and excavate their burrows near fence posts. Occasionally, they usurp abandoned burrows of pocket gophers or even those of prairie dogs. Their own burrows are about 5 cm in diameter, have two or three openings, descend to a depth of 10-115 cm, and may be 7 m or more in length.

These squirrels are strictly diurnal but their annual cycle of activity includes a very long period of hibernation. In Texas, studies conducted by Howard McCarley revealed that the period of hibernation lasts about 240 days. Adults enter hibernation in July and young-of-the-year in August or September. They emerge from the middle of February to the first of March in the Texas Panhandle. In southern Texas they have been observed above ground as late as October 27 and as early as January.

Their food is chiefly green grasses and herbs in early spring but seeds, flower heads, and insects contribute importantly to their diet as the season advances. Grasshoppers are often conspicuous items in their stomach contents, and often more than half of the stomach contents consists of insects, including grasshoppers, crickets, caterpillars, beetles, ants, and insect eggs. They also eat mice and have been reported capturing and eating small chickens. Quantities of dry seeds stored in underground caches probably serve to carry the squirrels through the period of scarcity shortly after they emerge in the spring.

Thirteen-lined Ground Squirrel (*Spermophilus tridecemlineatus*). Photo courtesy of U.S. Fish and Wildlife Service.

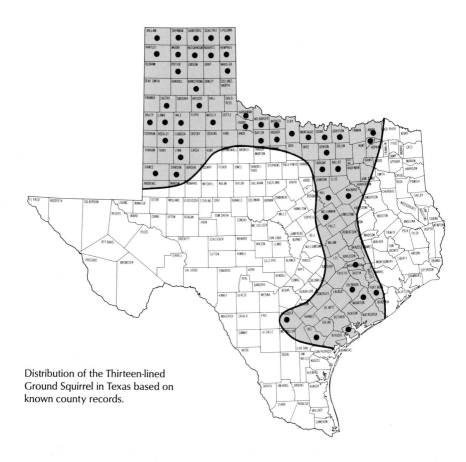

Distribution of the Thirteen-lined
Ground Squirrel in Texas based on
known county records.

Mating activities begin about 2 weeks after squirrels emerge from hibernation. The males are sexually active for only 2-3 months which of necessity restricts the length of the breeding season. Normally only one litter is produced annually, but one study found about 25% of the females observed in a marked population produced two litters. The gestation period is 27-28 days. The young vary in number from two to 13; the yearling females produce the smallest litters. The young are blind, hairless, and toothless at birth and weigh from 3 to 4 g each. By the eighth day they are dark dorsally; on the 12th the stripes begin to appear and hair sparsely covers the back; on the 26th their eyes begin to open. The female then begins to wean them and at the age of 6 weeks they are entirely dependent upon their own resources. They mature sexually at about 9 or 10 months of age.

Where concentrated in pastures and farming areas these squirrels may cause serious loss of forage and crops, but their fondness for insects partly offsets any damage they may do. On rangelands they usually do no serious damage.

ROCK SQUIRREL
Spermophilus variegatus (Erxleben)

Description. A large, moderately bushy-tailed ground squirrel; upperparts mottled grayish brown, the hind back and rump more brownish (head or head and upper back blackish in some parts of the state); tail mixed buff and brown, edged with white;

underparts buffy white or pinkish buff. External measurements average: total length, 468 mm; tail, 210 mm; hind foot, 57 mm. Weight of adults, 600-800 g.

Distribution. Known from the Trans-Pecos and central regions of the state.

Habits. Rock squirrels are nearly always found in rocky areas — cliffs, canyon walls, talus slopes, boulder piles, fills along highways, and so forth — where they seek refuge and have their dens. In the Pecos River Canyon in western Texas, where the walls are a series of alternating, nearly vertical precipices and narrow horizontal shelves, these squirrels are very much at home. They scale the steep, smooth walls with speed and assurance and never hesitate at what appear at a distance to be perfectly smooth surfaces. Closer inspection usually reveals that cracks and fissures in the rocks offer them adequate footing.

Although typical ground squirrels in most respects, they can climb trees nearly as well as tree squirrels. In the Guadalupe Mountains of western Texas, they have been observed 5 or 6 m up in the flowering stalks of agaves feeding on the flowers and buds. They also climb to the tops of junipers to forage on the berries and in mesquites to feed on the buds or beans. Occasionally, they den in tree hollows 5 or 6 m from the ground. The usual den, however, is a burrow dug under a rock; others are in crevices in rock masonry along railroads and highways, cavities in piles of boulders, or small caves and crevices in rocky outcrops. They are diurnal and most active in early morning and late afternoon, but they are rather shy and difficult to observe at close range. Their call is usually a repeated sharp, clear whistle.

They feed on a variety of plant materials depending on availability. Known items include acorns, pine nuts, walnuts, seeds of mesquite, cactus, saltbush, agave, wild gourd, cherries, sumac, spurge, serviceberry, berries of currant and juniper, and all sorts of cultivated fruits and vegetables. Insects also contribute importantly to their diet, especially grasshoppers, crickets, and caterpillars. They are fond of flesh and are known to catch and eat small wild turkeys and other birds.

Rock Squirrel (*Spermophilus variegatus*). Photo courtesy of Texas Parks and Wildlife.

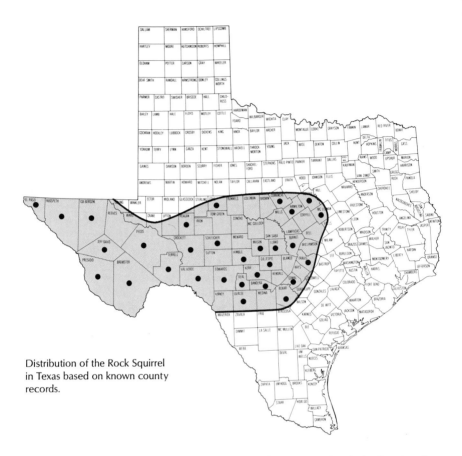

Distribution of the Rock Squirrel in Texas based on known county records.

They store quantities of food for winter use which, coupled with the fact that they are seen occasionally in winter on mild days, suggests that they either do not hibernate or that hibernation is incomplete and only for short periods. At lower elevations in the Big Bend region of Texas they are active all year.

Mating activities begin in March and continue into July, which suggests that two litters may be produced each year. Litter size ranges from two to five. Gravid females have been collected in June. Young squirrels first appear above ground at 6-8 weeks of age, and young about quarter-grown have been captured as early as June and as late as September 20. Little is known about the birth and early life of the young squirrels.

BLACK-TAILED PRAIRIE DOG
Cynomys ludovicianus (Ord)

Description. A rather large, chunky, ground-dwelling squirrel with upperparts pinkish cinnamon mixed with buff; tail sparsely haired, tipped with black, and about one-fifth of total length; eyes large; ears short and rounded. Dental formula: I 1/1, C 0/0, Pm 2/1, M 3/3 X 2 = 22. External measurements average: total length, 388 mm; tail, 86 mm; hind foot, 62 mm. Weight, 1-2 kg.

Distribution. Historically occurs in western one-half of state from north of Rio Grande Plains; easternmost records from Montague and Tarrant counties in north and Bexar County in south; now extirpated over much of its former range.

Habits. Black-tailed prairie dogs typically inhabit short-grass prairies; they usually avoid areas of heavy brush and tall grass, possibly because visibility is considerably reduced. In Trans-Pecos Texas, favored habitat sites are alluvial fans at the mouths of draws, "hard pan" flats where brush is sparse or absent, and the edges of shallow valleys.

The term "prairie dog" is an unfortunate misnomer because the animal is not even remotely related to a dog. It is a ground squirrel with a superficial resemblance to a small, fat pup. These squirrels are sociable creatures and live in colonies, or "towns," that may vary in size from a few individuals to several thousand animals. Vernon Bailey recorded that at the turn of the century an almost continuous and thickly inhabited dog town extended in a strip approximately 160 km wide and 400 km long on the high plains of Texas. This "city" had an estimated population of 400 million prairie dogs. Such large concentrations are now a thing of the past, due to the extensive use of poisoned grain to kill the animals and land conversion for agriculture.

Their homes consist of deep burrows 7-10 cm in diameter. The entrances are funnel-shaped and usually descend at a steep angle for 2-5 m before leveling off. One described burrow dropped nearly vertically for 4.5 m, then turned abruptly and became horizontal for 4 m. From the lower part extended blind side tunnels and nest chambers. The main entrances are made conspicuous by the mounds and parapets constructed around them. These craterlike "dikes" are often 30 cm or more in height and doubtless serve to keep flash floods from inundating the burrows and also as lookout points for the animals. Those who have hunted prairie dogs know how effective the craters are, both as vantage points and as retreats for the animals.

They are strictly diurnal and are most active in the morning and evening periods. The midday hours are usually spent sleeping below ground. In summer the animals store up reserves of fat to tide them over the winter months. In the northern part of Texas they begin hibernating in November. Hibernation seems to be less complete in prairie dogs than in true ground squirrels.

Black-tailed Prairie Dogs (*Cynomys ludovicianus*). Photo courtesy of U.S. Fish and Wildlife Service.

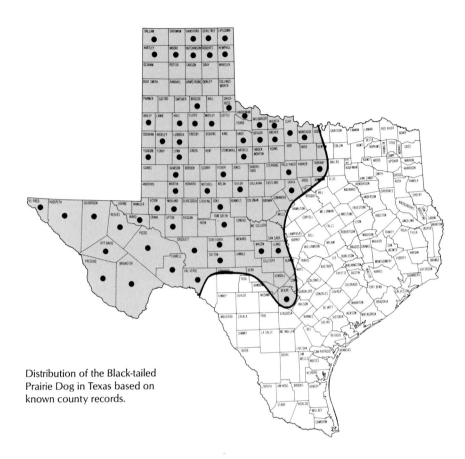

Distribution of the Black-tailed
Prairie Dog in Texas based on
known county records.

Their food is chiefly plant materials, particularly low-growing weeds and grasses. In Trans-Pecos Texas, burrow grass and purple needle grass are especially favored foods. Their year-round diet as determined by one investigator is made up about as follows: grasses (61.6%), goosefoot family (12.7%), mustard family (4.5%), prickly pear (6.0%), other plants (14.0%). Animal matter, chiefly cutworms, accounted for only 1.4% of the total diet. They are voracious eaters. According to C. Hart Merriam, 32 prairie dogs consume as much food per day as one sheep and 256 eat as much as one cow!

Prairie dog populations are comprised of several small "coteries," or harems, of two to eight females that are defended by a single dominant male. In turn, coteries are organized into larger population units called "wards," which are separated by unoccupied areas of unsuitable habitat or other such barriers. Activity and breeding are usually conducted within the coteries; however, dispersal between coteries and wards occasionally occurs, usually by young males. This complex social structure is thought to contribute to increased genetic variability between both coteries and wards.

One litter of four or five young is born in March or April. At birth the youngsters are blind and hairless and weigh about 15 g. At 13 days fine hair covers the cheeks, nose and parts of the body; the weight is then about 40 g. At 26 days, the body is well-haired and they can crawl awkwardly. Their eyes open at the age of 33-37 days, at which time the young squirrels are able to walk, run, eat green food, and "bark." They first appear above ground when about 6 weeks of age and are weaned shortly after that. The family unit remains intact for almost another month, but the ties are gradually broken and the family disperses. Sexual maturity is reached in the second year.

114

These squirrels have been displaced by livestock and farming interests for the past 50 years or more. Consequently, their former range and numbers have been considerably reduced. That large concentrations of prairie dogs can damage cultivated crops or compete seriously with livestock cannot be questioned, but the desirability of eliminating them entirely from rangelands has not been satisfactorily demonstrated. Stockmen in certain parts of Texas, for example, claim that removal of prairie dogs has had some direct association with the undesirable spread of brush. This has had detrimental effects on the livestock industry which far outweighs the damage prairie dogs might do.

EASTERN GRAY SQUIRREL
Sciurus carolinensis Gmelin

Description. A medium-sized squirrel with upperparts dark yellowish rusty, especially on head and back; legs, arms, sides of neck, and sides of rump with gray-tipped or white-tipped hairs, giving a gray tone to these parts; hairs of tail dull yellow at base, then blackish, and tipped with white; underparts white; ears with conspicuous white spot at base in winter. External measurements average: total length, 460 mm; tail, 210 mm; hind foot, 61 mm. Weight of adults, 321-590 g.

Distribution. Native distribution includes eastern one-third of state. Introduced at locations to the west of its native range.

Habits. In Texas, gray squirrels live mainly in dense hammocks of live oak and water oak and in the deep swamps of cypress, black gum, and magnolia that border the streams. Phil Goodrum found that they were most abundant in hammocks where the principal vegetation was white oak and water oak mixed with magnolia, linden,

Eastern Gray Squirrel (*Sciurus carolinensis*). Photo courtesy of Texas Parks and Wildlife.

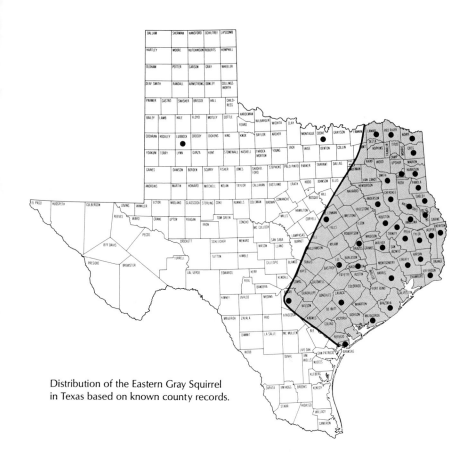

Distribution of the Eastern Gray Squirrel
in Texas based on known county records.

sweet gum, and holly. Poorly drained bottom lands with their pin, evergreen and overcup oaks, elms, bitter pecan, black gum, cypress, and ash support much smaller populations. In well-drained bottom lands with post and red oaks, hackberries, gum elastic, and pecan, the populations are still smaller, and upland forests usually are devoid of gray squirrels.

They den in hollow trees when available, but they also utilize outside leaf nests, especially in spring and summer. These serve usually as refuge, resting and feeding stations and occasionally as nurseries. Placed in trees, they are constructed of twigs, leaves, and so forth on the outside and lined with shredded bark, plant fibers, and grasses. Usually there are two openings.

Gray squirrels feed on a variety of foods, chiefly plant in origin. Goodrum lists buds and mast of oak and pecan trees, grapes, fungi, red haw buds, sedges, grasses, mulberry, larval and adult insects, and amphibians. Their mainstay, however, is mast (acorns, etc.). They begin eating acorns in the Spring and continue throughout the year if they are available. When mast crops fail in one area, the squirrels usually move en masse to other areas where food is more abundant. This accounts in large measure for the "migrations" of squirrels that are frequently reported. Normally they feed twice a day — early morning and late afternoon — and are less active at midday.

These squirrels breed throughout the year, but there are two rather distinct peaks — July, August, and September and again in December, January, and February. Mating is more or less promiscuous; several males usually attempt to mate with each receptive female. After a gestation period of 40-45 days, the two to four naked, blind, and

116

helpless young are born. They remain in the nest for about 6 weeks by which time their eyes are open and their teeth have developed so they can eat solid foods. By that time they weigh about 200 g. They remain in family groups for a month or so after they begin foraging for themselves. When 6 months old they are nearly adult in size and have left the home territory. They mature sexually in their first year and produce young of their own when about 12 months old.

These squirrels are highly prized as game. In most parts of their range they are decreasing in numbers because of overhunting and the removal of favored habitat by drainage or lumbering operations. Consequently, sound management of their habitat is becoming an increasingly important responsibility. Their future will depend upon the acreage remaining in hardwood forests, the length of timber rotations, the species composition of hardwood stands, and the abundance of mast supplies and dens. They do some damage in pecan orchards, but such depredations are local in nature and can usually be minimized by placing tin shields around the trunks which prevent the squirrels from climbing trees.

EASTERN FOX SQUIRREL
Sciurus niger Linnaeus

Description. A large tree squirrel with rusty or reddish underparts and brownish or grayish upperparts; tail usually less than half of total length, and cinnamon, mixed with black, in color; feet cinnamon. External measurements average: total length, 522 mm; tail, 245 mm; hind foot, 72 mm. Weight, 600-1,300 g.

Distribution. Occurs in suitable habitats in eastern two-thirds of state. Introduced some places outside of native range.

Habits. Fox squirrels are adaptable to a wide variety of forest habitats, but in most areas open upland forests of mixed trees support the heaviest populations. The best habitat is mature oak-hickory woodland broken into small, irregularly shaped tracts of 2-8 ha and connected by strips of woodland which serve as squirrel highways.

Eastern Fox Squirrel (*Sciurus niger*).

117

Intermixture of pine, elm, beech, pecan, maple, and other food-producing trees adds to the attractiveness of the habitat. Along the western parts of their range, fox squirrels are restricted more or less to river valleys which support pecans, walnuts, oaks, and other "required" trees.

Where hollow trees are available they are preferred as den sites and nurseries; if these are unavailable, the squirrels build outside "leaf" nests. These are composed of twigs and leaves, usually cut from the tree in which the nest is placed, and fashioned into roughly globular structures 30-50 cm in diameter surrounding an inner cavity 15-20 cm in diameter.

A fox squirrel occupies an area of at least 4 ha in extent in any one season, but during an entire year 16 or more ha may be utilized. Ranges of different fox squirrels overlap, and the animals are somewhat communal in their use of nests and probably also of winter food stores. A population of one squirrel to 1 ha is about the average carrying capacity of good, unimproved squirrel habitats.

Acorns are the natural mainstay of fox squirrels, although they are most important in fall and winter. Spring and summer foods consist of leftover mast, insects, green shoots, fruits, and seeds of such trees as elm and maple. Nuts are eaten from the time they start to develop and are buried in the fall in individual caches at the surface of the ground for winter use. The squirrels can relocate them by smell. Buds of many trees and fruits of osage orange add to the winter diet.

Mating occurs principally in two periods — January and February and again in May and June. The former period is most important. Old females usually breed twice

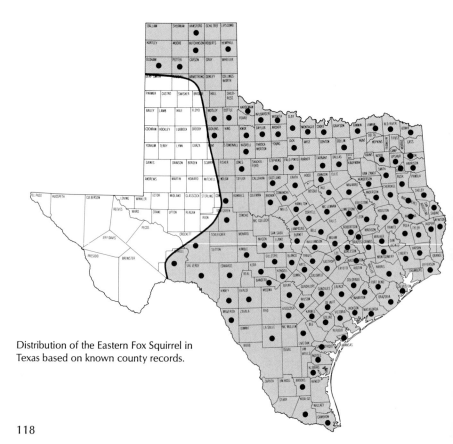

Distribution of the Eastern Fox Squirrel in Texas based on known county records.

a year and yearlings but once. The average female produces only four offspring each year. The gestation period is probably about 6 or 7 weeks, as in the gray squirrel. At birth the young are blind, nearly naked, and helpless. They develop rather slowly; their eyes open in the fifth week. They begin to climb about over the nest tree at the age of 7 or 8 weeks and to venture onto the ground at about 10 weeks. At the age of 3 months they begin to lead a more or less independent existence. Sexual maturity is reached at the age of 10-11 months.

Fox squirrels are important small game animals throughout most of their range, hence they are of decided economic value. Their fondness for green corn, however, often brings them into conflict with farming interests, as does their pilfering in nut orchards.

EASTERN FLYING SQUIRREL
Glaucomys volans (Linnaeus)

Description. A small squirrel with flattened, bushy tail; "flying" membrane connecting front and hind legs; eyes large; upperparts nearly uniform drab or pinkish cinnamon; underparts creamy white; sides often tinged with buff; toes usually strongly marked with white in winter pelage. External measurements average: total length, 225 mm; tail, 100 mm; hind feet, 29 mm. Weight, 41-67 g.

Distribution. Known from wooded areas in eastern one-third of state.

Habits. These small, nocturnal squirrels inhabit forested areas where suitable trees are present to afford den sites. In the western parts of their range, suitable habitat is restricted largely to areas along rivers and streams. In other parts of their range, they show preference for hammocks where Spanish moss is abundant. In suitable habitat they may be more abundant than most other squirrels. They are sociable and tend to live together in groups.

Holes in stumps are preferred den sites, but the squirrels will utilize almost any cavity that is dry and large enough. Woodpecker nests are ideal, particularly those of

Eastern Flying Squirrel (*Glaucomys volans*). Photo by E.P. Walker.

119

the larger species. When such sites are not available, the squirrels construct outside nests. A clump of Spanish moss is ideal.

They feed on a variety of items, but nuts and acorns are their mainstay. They also eat insect larvae, beetles, young and eggs of birds, persimmon, and cultivated corn. The frequency with which they are caught in traps set for fur animals and baited with meat indicates a decided fondness for flesh. Food is cached in holes in trees or other places for winter use.

There are two breeding seasons, the principal one in late February and March, the other in July. However, it is not known if an individual female participates in both the spring and fall breeding periods. Captive females mate only once annually. Males are in breeding condition from late January to early September. Mating is probably promiscuous because several males will chase a female in heat. The female alone assumes responsibility for rearing the young. The gestation period is about 40 days. At birth the two or three young are blind, nearly naked, and helpless and weigh about 3 g. The membrane between the wrist and ankle is well developed. The eyes open at 26-29 days, and a week later the young begin eating solid foods. At 6 weeks of age they are old enough to fend for themselves. They reach sexual maturity when about a year old.

Flying squirrels do not actually fly, but travel by gliding from one tree to another. This is accomplished by stretching the legs to extend a membrane connecting the front and hind legs. Glides are usually only about 6-9 m in length, but may extend up to 30 m.

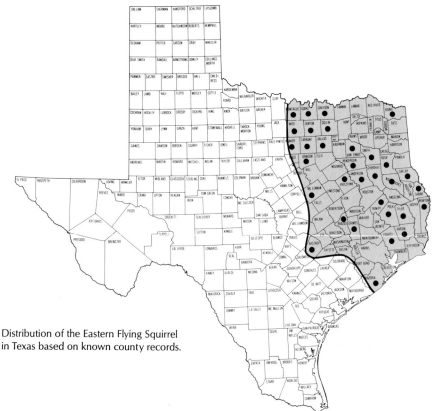

Distribution of the Eastern Flying Squirrel in Texas based on known county records.

120

FAMILY GEOMYIDAE (POCKET GOPHERS)

BOTTA'S POCKET GOPHER

Thomomys bottae (Eydoux and Gervais)

Description. A medium-sized rodent with external, furlined cheek pouches; the outer face of the upper incisors lacks conspicuous grooves; claws on front feet relatively small (less than 10 mm long); upperparts varying from pale gray to russet and blackish; underparts grayish-white, white, buffy, or mottled. External measurements average: (males), total length, 267 mm; tail, 81 mm; hind foot, 33 mm; (females), 219-69-28 mm. Weight (males), 160-250 g; (females), 120-200 g.

Distribution. Trans-Pecos Texas and eastward across the Edwards Plateau and immediately adjacent areas to Mason County.

Botta's Pocket Gopher (*Thomomys bottae*). Photo by John L. Tveten.

Habits. Pocket gophers of this species are extremely adaptable as regards habitat. They occur in soils ranging from loose sands and silts to tight clays and in vegetative zones grading from dry deserts to montane meadows. Perhaps one reason why they can tolerate such environmental extremes is that they spend fully 90% of their lives in underground burrows, secure from the elements.

Their burrow systems are often complicated structures consisting of two or more main galleries and several side chambers. A partly excavated burrow extended more than 30 m in length, had four main "forks," and averaged 6 cm beneath the surface, although the tunnel leading to the nest descended to a depth of more than 60 cm. Tunnel systems more than 150 m in length are not rare. These ramified travelways probably help the occupants to avoid predators that try to search them out; they are equally important in permitting the gopher to forage over a considerable area without exposing itself unduly to danger. Special side branches serve as storehouses for food, others as repositories for refuse and fecal pellets. In winter, when snow covers the ground, the gophers often extend their burrows into the snow and can then forage aboveground in safety.

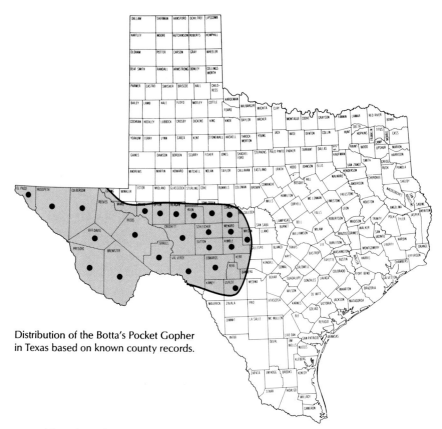

Distribution of the Botta's Pocket Gopher
in Texas based on known county records.

Although pocket gophers are active the year round, they store food to carry them over periods of scarcity, especially periods of drought when food is scarce and burrowing a difficult task. Usually, only one adult animal occupies each burrow system except for a short time in the breeding period. Associated with this solitary habit is a ferocious and seemingly fearless disposition. When two gophers encounter each other, they either fight or meticulously avoid each other. Desire for companionship seems to be completely lacking in their makeup.

They feed on a variety of foods, but fleshy roots and tubers are their main reliance. Unlike *Geomys bursarius*, Botta's pocket gophers often come to the surface to feed and clip off vegetation around the burrow as far as they can reach in all directions without losing physical contact with the opening. If molested the animals back into the burrows with amazing speed. At other times, they approach desirable plants from below and pull the entire upperparts into the burrow where they can be cut up and stored or eaten at leisure. The roots of alfalfa are especially prized, but almost any native plant is potential food.

The nest is a compact, hollow ball of dry, shredded vegetation placed in a special chamber off the main gallery, about 30-70 cm beneath the surface of the ground. Both sexes build nests as sleeping quarters.

This species breeds continuously, with three marked periods of increased fertility — spring, summer, and early winter. The main breeding season is in spring, however; summer breeding is mainly by young females, possibly those born the preceding spring.

The winter season is one of slight breeding activity and often merges with the one in early spring. Old females produce yearly an average of two litters of five young each; young females are less fecund. The young are blind, naked, unpigmented, and weigh about 4 g at birth. The ears are poorly developed, but the cheek pouches are fully formed although smaller proportionately than in adults. Growth appears to be relatively slow, but details of this phase of their life history are lacking.

In cultivated areas, pocket gophers may be destructive and require control by trapping or poisoning, but on natural lands they are of decided benefit as soil builders. They are the chief natural cultivators of soils, and the maximum thrift of wild vegetation is dependent upon their continued activity.

DESERT POCKET GOPHER
Geomys arenarius Merriam

Description. A dull, pale-brown pocket gopher, with two longitudinal grooves on outer face of each incisor; feet and underparts white. External measurements average: (males) total length, 262 mm; tail, 79 mm; hind foot, 33 mm; (females) 243-74-32 mm. Weight; males, 198-254 g; females, 165-207 g. Dental formula as in *G. bursarius*.

Distribution. Restricted in Texas to the Trans-Pecos, where it has been taken at several localities in the cottonwood-willow association along the Rio Grande in El Paso and Hudspeth counties. See map on page 124.

Habits. Near El Paso, these gophers are especially common along irrigation ditches in the sandy river-bottom area. They seemingly cannot tolerate clayey or gravelly soils, a characteristic common to all species of *Geomys*. Their mounds are large and conspicuous, and often one animal will throw up 20 to 30 of them in a relatively short time.

Their underground habits are not well-known. Seth Benson reports finding flowers and cut stems of a composite (*Baileya*) in their burrows. Doubtless, these were being eaten. Other than this plant and cultivated alfalfa, their food preferences have not been recorded.

Raymond Lee captured two gravid females near El Paso on June 28 and one on August 8. Numbers of embryos were six, four, and four, respectively. Young individuals have been captured in late June, July, and August. These data indicate a prolonged breeding season and suggest that adult females bear more than one litter a year.

Where concentrated in numbers in farming areas, they may do considerable damage. Elsewhere, their burrowing activities are largely beneficial. Frank Blair observed that the bunch grass *Andropogon* in New Mexico was intimately associated with the mounds of this pocket gopher. The grass appeared to grow more successfully on old gopher mounds than on the valley floor. The excrement of the gophers helped to fertilize the mounds.

Remarks. Using karyotypic and electrophoretic analyses, David Hafner and Kenneth Geluso found shared genetic characters in *G. arenarius* and *G. knoxjonesi*, then considered a subspecies of *G. bursarius*. These similarities were not sufficient to combine *G. arenarius* with *G. bursarius*; however, when Robert Baker *et al.* recently elevated *G. knoxjonesi* to full specific status, based on mitochondrial DNA analysis, the taxonomic status of *G. arenarius* was left in question. At this time it is uncertain whether Jones' pocket gopher and the desert pocket gopher indeed represent separate species, or if further detailed study of these taxa will show that combining the two as a single species will be warranted. It is distinctly possible that in the future *G. arenarius* will be shown to be merely an isolated population of the similar *G. knoxjonesi*.

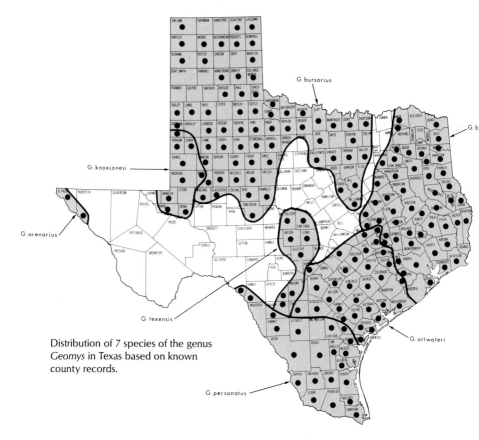

Distribution of 7 species of the genus *Geomys* in Texas based on known county records.

ATTWATER'S POCKET GOPHER

Geomys attwateri Merriam

Description. This pocket gopher closely resembles the Plains pocket gopher (*Geomys bursarius*) and Baird's pocket gopher (*G. breviceps*). Morphologically, the three are nearly identical and extremely difficult to distinguish in the field. *G. attwateri* is intermediate in size between *G. breviceps* (larger) and *G. bursarius* (smaller). A cranial feature used successfully in separating these species is the length of the jugal bone on the zygomatic arch compared with the width of the rostrum ventral to the infraorbital openings. In *G. bursarius*, the dorsal exposure of the jugal is longer than the width of the rostrum, whereas in *G. attwateri* and *G. breviceps* the dorsal exposure of the jugal is shorter than the width of the rostrum.

The best distinguishing feature is the karyotype, which in *G. attwateri* has a diploid number of 70 and a fundamental number of either 72 or 74. External measurements average: total length, 216 mm; tail, 62 mm; hind foot, 26 mm. Dental formula as in *G. bursarius*.

Distribution. From the Brazos River in eastern Texas south to southern Texas near the San Antonio River and along the coast from Matagorda to San Patricio counties. See map above.

Habits. The general habits of *G. attwateri* are similar to *G. bursarius* and *G. breviceps*. Attwater's pocket gopher is also an opportunistic herbivore, consuming a wide range of perennial and annual plant species. On the Welder Wildlife Refuge in South Texas, these gophers consume 41 of the 51 plant species available to them.

In contrast to the burrow systems of the plains pocket gopher, burrows of Attwater's pocket gopher tend to be more circuitous in nature. Their burrows are nonlinear and have few lateral or blind branches. This may be in response to a localized, or "clumped," distribution of resources, adaptations to low population densities, or their social structure.

G. attwateri is active at all hours of the day. Peaks in daily activity are not known.

Attwater's pocket gopher breeds from October through June with peaks in December-January and April-May. Little, if any, breeding occurs during the summer months of July, August, and September. Females produce an average of two or three young per litter and at least two litters per year.

Remarks. A small zone of contact between *G. breviceps* and *G. attwateri* occurs just west of the Brazos River in Burleson County. Of 42 gophers collected in this area, 31% had an apparent karyotype intermediate between the two species, indicating that hybridization may occur in the wild. In general, the range of *G. attwateri* is limited on the north by the Brazos River, although small zones of contact with *G. breviceps* (the range of which is limited on the south by the Brazos River) may occur where the Brazos River has periodically changed course in the past.

BAIRD'S POCKET GOPHER
Geomys breviceps Baird

Description. Nearly identical in appearance to *G. bursarius* and *G. attwateri*. Morphologically, this species may be distinguished from *G. bursarius* by cranial characters described in the account for *G. attwateri*, but is not readily distinguishable from *G. attwateri* without genetic testing.

The most important feature for identifying this gopher is its karyotype, which has a diploid number of 74 and a fundamental number of 72. *G. breviceps* has four more biarmed elements in the autosomal complement than does *G. attwateri*. Compared to *G. bursarius*, *G. breviceps* has two more chromosomes.

G. breviceps is smaller than both *G. attwateri* and *G. bursarius*. External measurements average: total length, 208 mm; tail, 61 mm; hind foot, 26 mm. Dental formula as in *G. bursarius*.

Distribution. This pocket gopher is found in the eastern portion of Texas. The westward limits of its range in the state are from Falls County north to Fannin County, and southeastward along the Brazos River to Brazoria County. See map on page 124.

Habits. The habits of *G. breviceps* are essentially the same as those described for *G. bursarius*.

These pocket gophers are polygamous, but breeding is restricted to immediate neighbors. The annual reproductive cycle in eastern Texas shows seven consecutive months of breeding activity, from February until August. A peak in production occurs in June and July, and a lesser peak in April; no young are produced from September through January. Litter size is from one to six, with an average of two or three. Females may produce two broods annually. The gestation period is 4-5 weeks and lactation lasts 5-6 weeks, after which the young leave the parental burrow. Young females may reach sexual maturity and produce a litter before the end of the breeding season.

Cellulose-digesting bacteria are known from the caecum and large intestine of *G. breviceps*, which may allow winter feeding on stored, underground rhizomes. Also, these pocket gophers re-ingest fecal pellets, which apparently increases the efficiency of food utilization.

PLAINS POCKET GOPHER
Geomys bursarius (Shaw)

Description. These are medium to small sized, dark brown gophers with large, furlined cheek pouches. The body is thick-set and appears heaviest anteriorly, from which it gradually tapers to the tail, widening a little at the thighs. The eyes are tiny and beadlike, and the ears are very rudimentary, represented only by a thickened ridge of skin at the base. Long curved claws are present on the front feet for digging; the claws on the hind feet are much smaller.

The dental formula is I 1/1, C 0/0, Pm 1/1, M 3/3 X 2 = 20. The upper incisors have two grooves. External measurements average: total length, 236 mm; tail, 65 mm; hind foot, 31 mm. Weight: males, 180-200 g; females, 120-160 g.

Distribution. Northwestern and north-central Texas, south to Midland and Tom Green counties in west and to McLennan County in east. Grayson and Dallas counties appear to be the eastern limit of this species in Texas. See map on page 124.

Habits. This pocket gopher typically inhabits sandy soils where the topsoil is 10 cm or more in depth. Clayey soils are usually avoided. These gophers live most of their solitary lives in underground burrows, coming to the surface only to throw out earth removed in their tunneling and to forage for some items of food. They seldom travel far overland. The average diameter of 40 burrows examined in Texas was nearly 6 cm; the average depth below the surface, 14 cm, with extremes of 10 cm and 67.5 cm. Much of their burrowing is done in search of food. The underground galleries attain labyrinthine proportions in many instances because the tunnels meander aimlessly through the feeding areas. This is particularly noticeable under oak trees that have dropped a good crop of acorns. Burrows have been examined that extend well over 100 m, excluding the numerous short side branches. Only one adult gopher normally occupies a single burrow system.

The average mound thrown up by these gophers is about 30 by 45 cm, about 8 cm in height, and crescentic in outline. The opening through which the earth is pushed is usually plugged from within. The gopher digs with its front claws and protruding teeth,

Plains Pocket Gopher (*Geomys bursarius*). Photo by L.K. Couch.

shoves the loose earth ahead of it with its chin and forefeet, and uses the hind feet for propulsion. The ceaseless energy of these subterranean miners is suggested by the size of the huge winter mounds they make in sites that have poor underground drainage. One of these was 2 m long, 1.5 m wide, 60 cm high, and weighed an estimated 360 kg. The female that occupied this mound weighed 150 g. A typical winter mound contains numerous galleries, a nest chamber, a toilet, and food storage chambers.

These rodents feed on a variety of plant items, chiefly roots and stems of weeds and grasses. Most plant food is encountered and ingested while the gopher digs, but some "grazing" of food present along burrow walls probably also occurs. The furlined cheek pouches are used to carry food and nesting material but never dirt. Captive gophers have eaten white grubs, small grasshoppers, beetle pupae, and crickets. Earthworms and raw beef were ignored.

Breeding begins in late January or early February in eastern Texas and continues for a period of some 3 or 4 months. One litter a year, or two in quick succession, appears to be the rule. The young, usually two or three in number, are born from March to July. The young are nearly naked, blind, and helpless at birth. They remain with their mother until nearly full-grown and then are evicted to lead an independent life.

As long as they remain in their burrows, pocket gophers are relatively safe from predators other than those which are specialized for digging, such as badgers and long-tailed weasels. However, when a gopher leaves its burrow it is highly vulnerable, and most predation losses probably occur on the surface. Known predators, other than those mentioned above, include coyotes, skunks, domestic cats, hawks, owls, and several kinds of snakes. As a result of the protection offered by the burrow, pocket gophers are long-lived relative to many other rodents, insectivores, and lagomorphs, living an average of 1-2 years in the wild.

In farming regions these rodents can be destructive to crops and orchards. The amount of damage is closely associated with the number of animals. The average population density in eastern Texas is about 3.2 gophers per ha. The highest population density of record is 17.6 per ha. These gophers can be controlled on small areas by trapping and on large ones by placing poisoned grain in their burrows.

Remarks. Historically, *Geomys bursarius* has been considered one wide ranging, but morphologically variable species that was distributed over most of the Great Plains and south-central United States, including the Texas Panhandle and eastern Texas. However, recent studies by specialists trained in cytological and biochemical taxonomy have revealed that in actuality there are five species of pocket gophers ranging over these regions of Texas (designated *G. bursarius, G. attwateri, G. breviceps, G. knoxjonesi,* and *G. texensis*). These are considered cryptic species, meaning that they cannot be differentiated on the basis of observed morphological characteristics although they are genetically distinct. Karyotypic, electrophoretic, and mitochondrial DNA data are required to confidently distinguish questionable specimens, although all appear to be allopatric in range.

JONES' POCKET GOPHER

Geomys knoxjonesi Baker and Genoways

Description. This is a cryptic species of the plains pocket gopher, *G. bursarius.* Morphologically, Jones' pocket gopher appears to be slightly smaller, both externally and cranially, than the plains pocket gopher but careful study of genetic characters is required before the two may be distinguished. Coloration is buff-brown dorsally, somewhat paler on the sides and ventrally, with white feet. Dental formula as in *G. bursarius.*

Distribution. Southwestern plains of Texas and southeastern plains of New Mexico. In Texas, known from Cochran, Yoakum, Terry, Gaines, Andrews, Martin, Winkler, Ward, and Crane counties at sites of deep sandy soils of aeolian origin. See map on page 124.

Habits. The habits of *G. knoxjonesi* are similar to *G. bursarius*. Although genetic evidence for hybridization with *G. bursarius* has been found, the apparent zone of contact between the two species is extremely narrow and the resultant hybrid off-spring are sterile or have a lower level of fertility, indicating that the two species rarely interact reproductively.

Remarks. Originally recognized as a new subspecies of *G. bursarius* in 1975, additional genetic analysis of this pocket gopher by Robert Baker and his students has subsequently shown that Jones' pocket gopher is essentially reproductively isolated from *G. bursarius* and therefore constitutes a separate species.

TEXAS POCKET GOPHER
Geomys personatus True

Description. A large, pale-drab or grayish-drab species with relatively long, scant-haired tail, the distal half nearly naked; upper incisors with two grooves; underparts marbled white and dusky. External measurements average: (males) total length, 321 mm; tail, 110 mm; hind foot, 41 mm; (females) 303-103-39 mm. Weight, up to 400 g. Dental formula as in *G. bursarius*.

Distribution. South Texas as far north as Val Verde County on the west and San Patricio County on the east. See map on page 124.

Habits. This species occurs in deep, sandy soils. It is entirely absent from the silt loams of the flood plains of the Rio Grande and also from gravelly, stony, or clayey soils scattered throughout its general range.

Numerous burrows of these gophers occur in the deep drift sands on Mustang and Padre Islands where the sand is moist enough to permit packing. Sometimes the tunnels are at the water table and the runways soppy with seepage, but most often they are about halfway between the surface and the water table 50 cm below. Exca-vated burrows average about 10 cm in horizontal diameter, 12.5 cm in vertical diam-eter, and 25 cm beneath the surface. In places where the sand was drier, yet still moist enough to maintain a burrow, the tunnels are about 12 to 15 cm in diameter. In the soils near Robstown, Texas, the burrows ranged from 6 to 8 cm in diameter.

Texas Pocket Gopher (*Geomys personatus*). Photo by John L. Tveten.

One partially excavated burrow system on Padre Island was more than 30 m long. There were numerous short side branches, but no food cache nor a chamber for fecal pellets, as is usual in burrows of *Geomys*, was found. Another burrow excavated on the mainland contained a food cache of Bermuda grass. The average mounds are large; a typical one might measure 45 by 60 cm in horizontal diameter and 12 cm in height. It could contain almost 6 kg of sand.

These gophers are ferocious isolationists; they resent molestation. When angry they emit a wheezy call at frequent intervals and gnash their teeth.

Their food consists largely of vegetation. Known items include roots of grasses (*Paspalum*, *Cynodon*, and *Cenchrus*) and the roots, stems, and leaves of a composite (*Helianthus*). Most of their foraging is done underground; the plants often are seized from below and pulled into the burrow. Their feces are capsule-shaped and about 19 mm in length and 7 mm in diameter. Individuals of this species, as well as other *Geomys*, have the interesting habit of ingesting their own fecal pellets. A fecal pellet is taken in the incisors directly from the anus, examined and manipulated with the aid of the forefeet, and then either discarded or thoroughly chewed and swallowed. Usually two to four pellets are produced at a time with only one or two being eaten, often none. There appears to be no pattern as to which pellet or pellets are eaten. Production of fecal pellets often occurs in the nest, in which case the rejected pellets are simply pushed out into the adjoining tunnel. Pocket gophers may also stop their travels through the burrow system to defecate, again either discarding or eating the pellets after examining each one carefully. Captive individuals have been seen to interrupt a meal of grass, potatoes, or other food to defecate and then consume one or more fecal pellets. This behavior is well-documented for many species of rabbits and rodents, and may serve to extract maximum sustenance from ingested plant foods.

Their breeding habits are not well known. Pregnant females have been captured in all months except April, June, August, and September, suggesting that breeding may occur year round. Young gophers about one-fourth grown were trapped in early April. Litter size ranges from one to five, averaging three. Probably no more than two litters are reared yearly.

In southern Texas, these gophers have little economic importance except in cultivated fields or where they become established along the highways. In the latter case, they may undermine the shoulders and initiate erosion.

LLANO POCKET GOPHER
Geomys texensis Merriam

Description. A cryptic species with *G. bursarius* and *G. knoxjonesi*. Morphologically, the Llano pocket gopher is slightly smaller than the plains pocket gopher but biochemical study is required to reliably separate the two. Dental formula as in *G. bursarius*.

Distribution. Occurs only in two isolated areas of the Texas Hill Country. Records are from McCulloch, San Saba, Mason, Llano, Gillespie, Uvalde, Zavala, and Medina counties. See map on page 124.

Habits. The natural history of *G. texensis* is undoubtedly similar to that of *G. bursarius*. The Llano pocket gopher is found in deep, brown loamy sands or gravelly sandy loams and is isolated from other species of *Geomys* by intervening shallow, stony to gravelly clayey soils.

Five specimens in the Texas Cooperative Wildlife Collection at Texas A&M University, collected in Llano County in mid-March, were reproductively active when captured. One contained three embryos, one had two embryos, one was "inseminated," one was lactating, and the fifth was pregnant with "very small embryos." A sixth specimen from this area contained no embryos and showed no signs of reproductive activity.

Remarks. Scott Block and Earl Zimmerman theorize that increasing warmer and drier periods in Texas climate beginning about 10,000 years ago may have led to the geographic isolation of this pocket gopher. As lengthy drought cycles caused accelerated soil erosion and a decrease in the former mesic vegetation of western Texas the increasingly xeric conditions may have served to help isolate *G. texensis* in the small range seen today, and contributed to its speciation.

YELLOW-FACED POCKET GOPHER
Cratogeomys castanops (Baird)

Description. A moderately large pocket gopher, dull yellowish brown in color, with one deep groove on outer face of each upper incisor; feet blackish (whitish in most other gophers). External measurements average: (males) total length, 295 mm; tail, 95 mm; hind foot, 33 mm; (females) 256-77-33 mm. Weight, (males) 216-321 g; (females) 213-330 g.

Distribution. Found in western one-third of state, from Panhandle southward to Val Verde County. Isolated populations from Maverick and Cameron counties along the Rio Grande.

Habits. These large gophers are partial to deep, mellow soils that are relatively free from rocks. Where the three genera — *Cratogeomys*, *Geomys*, and *Thomomys* — occur in the same general area, as in western Texas, *Thomomys* usually occupies the shallower, rocky soils in the mountains, *Geomys* lives in the deep sands along the rivers, and *Cratogeomys* utilizes the areas in between. However, the sandy areas in which no *Geomys* occur are likely to be occupied by *Cratogeomys*. The three genera are usually mutually exclusive in their distribution.

Their burrows are from 75 to 100 mm in diameter, depending on the texture of the soil. The tunnels and mounds are smaller in clayey than in sandy soils.

Yellow-faced Pocket Gopher (*Cratogeomys castanops*). Photo by John L. Tveten.

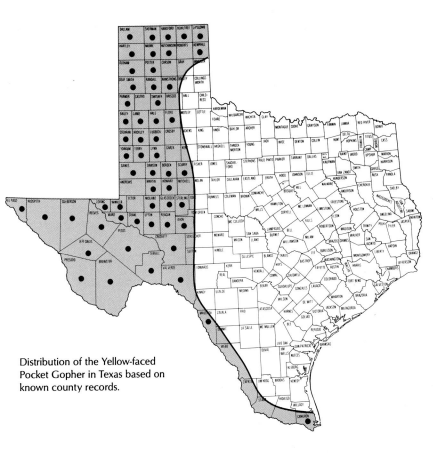

Distribution of the Yellow-faced Pocket Gopher in Texas based on known county records.

They feed chiefly on roots and stems of vegetation, including the outer bark on the roots of trees. Alfalfa, clover, and garden vegetables are also utilized.

Breeding probably begins in March or April. By mid-July nearly full-grown young in juvenile pelage are common. Lactating females have been captured in June and gravid females in early August. Litter size is two.

It appears that conditions of increasing aridity may favor the distribution of *Cratogeomys* over other gophers, such as *Thomomys*. From early 1969 to April, 1970, the Davis Mountains of the Trans-Pecos received little or no rain. As the area became drier, *Thomomys*, which once occurred from near the bed of Limpia Creek to the foot of the rock bluffs lining the canyon, moved closer to the stream and *Cratogeomys* moved into the vacated area. These changes may be linked to a decrease in soil moisture and subsequent increase in xeric-adapted plants, both conditions which would favor *Cratogeomys* over *Thomomys*.

In situations where *Cratogeomys* and *Geomys* are sympatric in the Texas Panhandle, *Geomys* are restricted to the deep sandy soils whereas *Cratogeomys* tend to occupy shallower, firmer soils. The yellow-faced pocket gopher does quite well in the deeper soils, but is apparently excluded from such sites by the presence of *Geomys*.

Remarks. In previous editions the name *Pappogeomys castanops* was used for this species. Recent genetic studies of the genus *Pappogeomys* have shown the subgenera *Pappogeomys* and *Cratogeomys* of sufficient distinction to warrant the elevation of both to generic status.

131

FAMILY HETEROMYIDAE
(POCKET MICE AND KANGAROO RATS)

PLAINS POCKET MOUSE
Perognathus flavescens Merriam

Description. A small, silky, yellowish-buff pocket mouse; upperparts more or less washed with blackish; pelage relatively short. External measurements average: total length, 130 mm; tail, 61 mm; hind foot, 17 mm. Weight of adults, 8-11 g. The dental formula, as in all heteromyids, is I 1/1, C 0/0, Pm 1/1, M 3/3 X 2 = 20.

Distribution. A mouse of the Great Plains region. Recorded in Texas from El Paso County and from High Plains and adjacent areas in northwestern part of state, south to Ward County.

Habits. This little pocket mouse is partial to sandy soils covered with sparse vegetation. In the sandhills of the Texas Panhandle its burrows are commonly excavated beneath clumps of Spanish bayonet or prickly pear, the entrances usually so distributed as to open from under the plant in all directions. Usually the main entrance is plugged with soil from within during the day, and if it is opened the mouse closes it again. The several other inconspicuous openings, hardly large enough to admit the end of one's finger, are seldom plugged and may serve as "duck-outs."

Their food is almost exclusively the seeds of grasses and weeds. Food items found in their cheek pouches include seeds of needle grass (*Stipa*), bind weed, sandbur grass, a small bean (probably *Astragulus*), and sedge (*Cyperus*). Even those caught in grain fields usually have their pouches filled with weed seeds. Seeds of two species of pigeon grass, a few other grasses, and wild buckwheat have been found in their underground food caches.

Knowledge of their breeding habits is meager. Females collected in late July and early August contained four embryos each. Two collected on July 9 and 14 contained four and five embryos. No information is available on mating, gestation, birth, growth of the young, and family life.

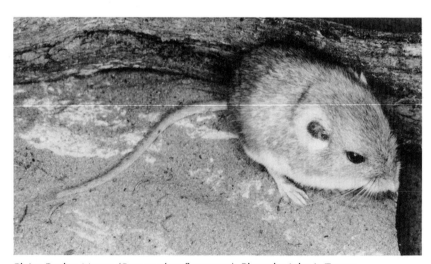

Plains Pocket Mouse (*Perognathus flavescens*). Photo by John L. Tveten.

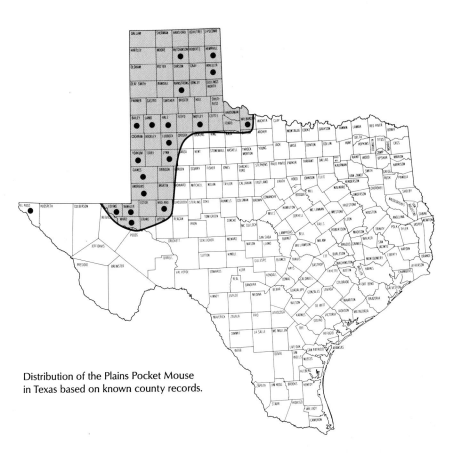

Distribution of the Plains Pocket Mouse in Texas based on known county records.

Remarks. In previous editions the Apache pocket mouse (*Perognathus apache* Merriam) was treated as a separate species; however, recent taxonomic work on these mice by Dan Williams has shown they have a karyotype identical with that of *P. flavescens* and, morphologically, are quite similar. Therefore, *P. apache* is now considered to be merely a subspecies of *P. flavescens*.

SILKY POCKET MOUSE
Perognathus flavus Baird

Description. A small pocket mouse with soft, silky fur, short ears, and short, sparsely haired tail; upperparts pinkish buff, lightly mixed with black; underparts pure white; spot behind ear clear buff and conspicuous; ears light buff on outside, blackish inside; tail pale buffy, slightly darker above. Closely resembles *Perognathus merriami*, from which it differs in minor features of the skull and the frequency of biochemical genetic markers. External measurements average: total length, 113 mm; tail, 50 mm; hind foot, 16 mm. Weight, 6-8 g. Dental formula as in *Perognathus flavescens*.

Distribution. Known from the Trans-Pecos and extreme northern Panhandle.

Habits. Silky pocket mice appear to be more tolerant of habitat conditions than some of the other species of small pocket mice. In some areas they are found in rocky situations; in others on hard, stony soils; and in still others on sands. In most localities, however, they occur on mellow soils of valley bottoms where they live among the scattered weeds and shrubs and burrow in the sand.

133

Silky Pocket Mouse (*Perognathus flavus*). Photo by John L. Tveten.

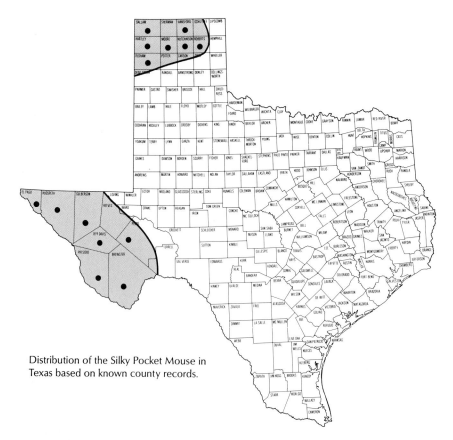

Distribution of the Silky Pocket Mouse in Texas based on known county records.

As with other species of pocket mice the burrows of *flavus* are simple in design, usually shallow and barely large enough to admit a man's finger. One excavated near Sierra Blanca, Texas was in the bank of a dike thrown up to divert water from the highway. The three openings converged to a single burrow that led along the dike for a distance of about 1 m, at no place penetrating more than 10 cm below the surface. Two side branches diverged from the main burrow, one of them sloping upward to near the surface. This branch probably was a "duck-out," because the occupant escaped from it by breaking through the thin crust of earth at the blind end of the tunnel. No nest or store of food was encountered, although this mouse is known to store food in captivity.

The diet consists wholly of seeds, so far as known. Juniper berries and seeds of grasses and weeds provide the bulk of their diet.

The breeding season extends from early spring to late fall. Half-grown young have been captured as early as April 16 and as late as September 23, and a lactating female was captured in December. Probably two or more litters of two to six young are reared each season. Nothing is known of the growth and development of the young and the family relations. An adult female lived in captivity for more than 5 years, but the age attained in the wild is probably not more than 2 or 3 years.

MERRIAM'S POCKET MOUSE
Perognathus merriami Allen

Description. A very small, silky-haired pocket mouse, similar to but smaller than *P. flavescens*; upperparts ochraceous buff mixed with black; sides brighter, less blackish; underparts clear white; spot behind ear clear buff, the one below the ears, white; eye ring light; tail slightly darker above than below; winter pelage brighter than in summer; young grayer, less ochraceous. External measurements average: total length, 116 mm; tail, 57 mm; hind foot, 16 mm. Weight, 7-9 g.

Distribution. Known from western two-thirds of state, but absent from extreme northern Panhandle and extreme western Trans-Pecos.

Habits. In southern Texas, these tiny mice are most common on sandy soils where vegetation is sparse or at least short. In Trans-Pecos Texas, they are more common on stony and gravelly soils covered with sparse vegetation. They seem to have difficulty in traveling through heavy vegetation, and if forced into grass several centi-

Merriam's Pocket Mouse (*Perognathus merriami*). Photo by R.D. Porter.

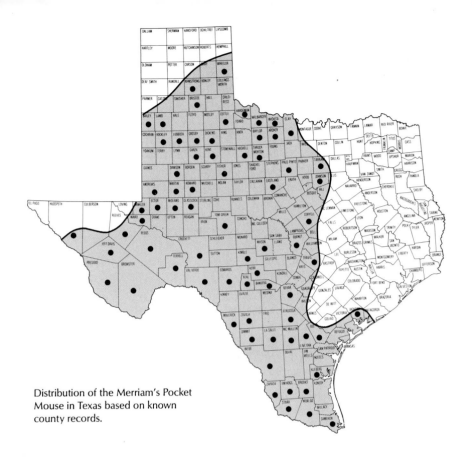

Distribution of the Merriam's Pocket Mouse in Texas based on known county records.

meters high, their progress is materially impeded. Near Oiltown, Texas, they were especially common in stands of low Bermuda grass on the shoulders of the highway where they were gathering seeds. With the aid of a lantern, it was easy to capture a dozen or more of them alive at night by hand. Their movements in the grass resembled those of large, wingless grasshoppers, but their leaps and bounds were neither so long nor so high as those of the insect. When captured they made no attempt to bite, and usually they emitted no sound, although they can produce a high, metallic squeak. When first caught they would not tolerate the company of their own kind in close quarters. Several of them placed in a cloth bag fought a battle royal, and some of them were killed; however, six were kept together in a cage for nearly a year without evidence of animosity.

Their tiny burrows are usually dug at the base of a shrub or a clump of cactus. Several were also found in the nearly vertical banks left by road graders at the sides of the highway right-of-way. One den consisted of three tunnels, 30-45 cm in length, that converged under a flat rock to a nest chamber about the size of a man's fist. Burrows were barely large enough to admit a man's index finger. These mice also make use of abandoned burrows of pocket gophers.

Their food consists largely of seeds of grasses and weeds. They also feed on juniper seeds. In captivity they are fond of millet seeds. They refuse to drink; in fact, they can live for months without water.

The breeding season appears to extend from April to November, and possibly two or more litters of three to six young are reared each season. Young in "gray" juvenile pelage have been captured in June, July, and late November. In the Big Bend region, Richard Porter found that the annual population turnover was 84%; in a study on the Black Gap Area and in the Big Bend, Keith Dixon found the turnover to be 75%. Dixon recorded a maximum life span of 33 and 22 months, respectively, for two mice on the Black Gap.

Remarks. The taxonomic status of *P. merriami* has had a confusing history. In 1973, Don Wilson presented morphological evidence indicating that *P. merriami* and *P. flavus* represented one species, and combined both under the name *P. flavus*. Subsequent study using genetic analyses has shown, however, that two species are indeed represented. Using karyology and starch gel electrophoresis, Tom Lee and Mark Engstrom have shown that, although the two taxa are highly similar morphologically, they do not appear to interbreed in areas of sympatry. Thus, in the central Trans-Pecos region and perhaps in the extreme northern panhandle region, these nearly identical species of pocket mice occur together but are reproductively isolated from each other.

HISPID POCKET MOUSE
Chaetodipus hispidus Baird

Description. A medium to large pocket mouse with harsh pelage and large hind foot, the sole of which is naked to the heel; tail less than half of total length, distinctly bicolor, sparsely haired, and lacking tuft; upperparts olive buffy, lined with black; lateral line wide and clear buff; underparts white. External measurements average: total length, 198 mm; tail, 93 mm; hind foot, 24 mm. Weight of adults, 30-47 g. Dental formula as in *Perognathus flavescens*.

Distribution. Statewide except for extreme southeastern portion of the state.

Habits. These large pocket mice prefer areas of sand or other friable soil covered with scattered to moderate stands of herbaceous vegetation. The margins of brush fields and the rank growth in fence rows offer suitable cover. Dense stands of grasses and brush usually are avoided.

Hispid Pocket Mouse (*Chaetodipus hispidus*). Photo by W.B. Davis.

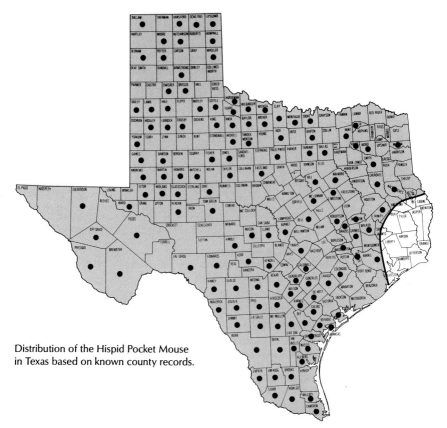

Distribution of the Hispid Pocket Mouse
in Texas based on known county records.

Their burrows are always dug in friable soil. They have been described as resembling 1-inch (25 mm) auger holes bored straight into the ground. Usually all the dirt excavated from the burrow system is piled near one opening, leaving the others inconspicuous and without mounds. The openings usually are plugged in the daytime. A burrow excavated in Brazos County had two openings, neither of which was plugged, connected by a single tunnel that descended to a depth of about 40 cm. A side branch contained food and nest chambers. Another burrow was found opening under a log which served as a roof for the nest chamber. These mice have been known to inhabit deserted burrows of Mexican ground squirrels in central Texas.

Their nest is composed of shredded dry grasses and weeds. In captivity, the mice pile the nesting material into a loose heap and then mat it down by sleeping on top of the structure. They seem to behave likewise in the wild. They appear to be active through most of the year in the southern part of their range, but they probably "hibernate," or at least hole up, in winter in north Texas.

Their food consists almost entirely of vegetation, principally seeds. Frank Blair found the seeds of gaillardia, cactus, evening primrose, and winecup most frequently in their caches; in addition, he lists 23 other species of plants that were utilized. In Texas a cache of about one-half liter of *Diodia teres* (Poor Joe) seeds was found and in another instance the store was entirely seeds of sandbur grass (*Cenchrus*). Animal matter makes up only a small part of their diet. Blair lists grasshoppers, caterpillars, and beetles.

Judging from records of capture of juveniles, one or two litters of young are produced in the northern part of the range, but breeding is practically continuous through-

138

out the year in south Texas. Young animals out of the nest (about 1 month old) have been captured as early in the year as January 8 and as late as October 14. Based on embryo counts, the litter varies from two to nine, averaging six. Nothing is known regarding the gestation period or the growth and development of the young.

In sandy-land farming areas these mice can do considerable damage by digging up and carrying away planted seeds of cantaloupe, watermelon, peas, and small grains. In range and pasture lands they perform a service by eating seeds of weeds.

Remarks. In previous editions, this mouse was included in the genus *Perognathus*; however, recent taxonomic studies have shown that it, along with all spiny-rumped pocket mice of Texas, should be included in a separate genus, *Chaetodipus*. Formerly included with *hispidus* in the *Perognathus* species group, the desert pocket mouse (*C. penicillatus*), rock pocket mouse (*C. intermedius*), and Nelson's pocket mouse (*C. nelsoni*) are all now included in the genus *Chaetodipus*.

ROCK POCKET MOUSE
Chaetodipus intermedius Merriam

Description. A medium-sized, long-tailed pocket mouse; pelage rather harsh, with weak spines on rump; sole of hind foot naked to heel; tail longer than head and body, crested and distinctly tufted; upperparts drab, with strong admixture of black on back and rump; lateral line pale fawn, narrow; tail dusky above, white below; underparts white. Similar externally to *C. penicillatus*, but hind foot usually smaller, upperparts

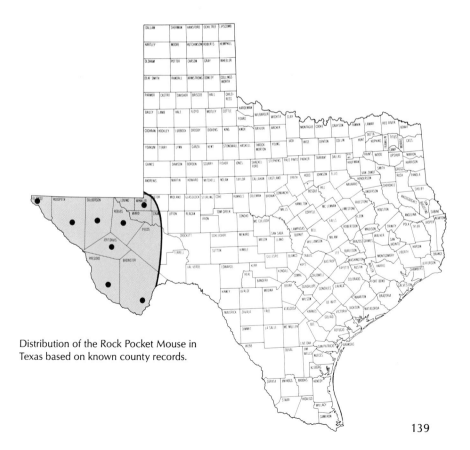

Distribution of the Rock Pocket Mouse in Texas based on known county records.

139

much darker, tail with smaller scales and narrower annulations. External measurements average: total length, 180 mm; tail, 103 mm; hind foot, 23 mm. Weight, 12-18 g. Dental formula as in *Perognathus flavescens*.

Distribution. Reported only from the Trans-Pecos region.

Habits. This species inhabits chiefly rocky situations, often where boulders are large and jumbled. At the eastern base of the Guadalupe Mountains in western Texas they have been found inhabiting rocky canyons, and in the Wylie Mountains they lived among huge boulders. Occasionally, they may be found on shrubby desert slopes on pebbly soils, rarely on silt soils. Vernon Bailey reported finding them on sandy soils among rocks. It is our impression that they rarely occur in areas of loose, alluvial, and windborne sands.

Their burrows are small, inconspicuous, and often closed during the daytime. Tiny trails lead away from them to feeding places among the plants. They choose burrow sites close to or under rocks.

They are strictly nocturnal and little is known of their habits. Their food is chiefly weed seeds, the species of plants utilized depending on availability. Judging from the meager data, breeding begins in February or March and continues for several months. Gravid females have been captured in May, June, and July. The litter varies from three to six. Nearly halfgrown young in juvenile pelage have been taken in April, May, June, and August. Their general habitat is such that they seldom conflict with man's interests.

NELSON'S POCKET MOUSE
Chaetodipus nelsoni Merriam

Description. A medium-sized pocket mouse with harsh pelage and numerous black-tipped spines on rump; tail longer than head and body, sparsely haired on basal half, the terminal half crested, penicillate, and indistinctly bicolor, darker above than below; upperparts drab gray, heavily lined with black; underparts pure white; soles of hind feet blackish. External measurements average: total length, 187 mm; tail, 104 mm; hind foot, 22 mm. Weight, 14-17 g. Dental formula as in *Perognathus flavescens*.

Distribution. A Mexican form that occurs in Texas in the southern and central Trans-Pecos region and just east of the Pecos and Rio Grande Rivers.

Habits. This is a rock-loving species. In the Big Bend section of Texas, it occurs most commonly at the base of the Chisos Mountains at altitudes ranging from 700 to 1,450 m. There it is found in rocky areas supporting sparse stands of Chino grass, sotol, bear grass (*Nolina*), and candelilla; sandy washes seem to be avoided.

In the Big Bend region, Richard Porter found that the breeding season begins in February, the peak of pregnancy among females is reached in March, and juveniles entered his live traps in April. By inference, therefore, the gestation period is about 1 month and the young leave the nest when about 4 weeks of age. Pregnant females were captured in each month from March through July. The number of embryos per litter averaged 3.2 with extremes of two and four.

The annual turnover in the population he studied was about 86%; that is, only 14 of each 100 individuals survived from one year to the next. Keith Dixon, working on the Black Gap in the Big Bend, recorded two individuals marked as juveniles that survived for at least 30 months in the wild — one other for 24 months and two others for about 20 months.

Porter reported that *nelsoni* was more active in winter (December) than either of the other two pocket mice (*Perognathus flavus* and *C. penicillatus*) on his study area. Seemingly, *nelsoni* does not hibernate.

Nelson's Pocket Mouse (*Chaetodipus nelsoni*). Photo by R.D. Porter.

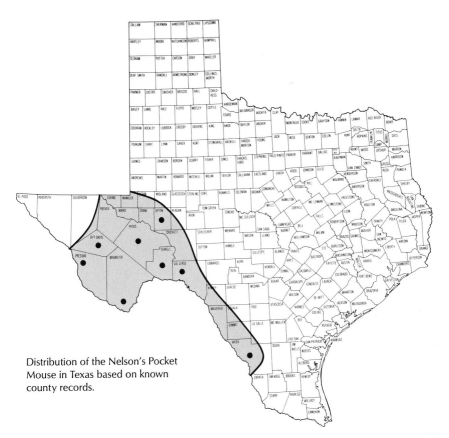

Distribution of the Nelson's Pocket Mouse in Texas based on known county records.

DESERT POCKET MOUSE
Chaetodipus penicillatus Woodhouse

Description. A medium-sized pocket mouse with long, heavily crested, and tufted tail; pelage coarse, but lacking spines on rump; sole of hind foot naked to heel; upperparts vinaceous buff finely sprinkled with black, imparting a grayish tone; sides like back; no lateral line; underparts and tail to tuft, white. External measurements average: total length, 205 mm; tail, 109 mm; hind foot, 25 mm. Weight, 15-23 g. Dental formula as in *Perognathus flavescens*.

Distribution. A southwestern pocket mouse that, in Texas, occurs mainly in the Trans-Pecos eastward to Val Verde and Crane counties.

Habits. This species in general occurs on sandy or soft alluvial soils along stream bottoms, desert washes, and valleys. In the Big Bend of Texas, large numbers of them have been trapped in loose sand along the Rio Grande where the dominant vegetation was *Baccharis* and mesquite and also in a brushy draw where the soil was hard-packed silt. We never found them on gravelly soils or among rocks, a habitat preferred by the externally similar *Chaetodipus intermedius*. Their burrows, from which the sand has been thrown well out to one side, are usually found near the bases of bushes and are closed in the daytime.

Desert Pocket Mouse (*Chaetodipus penicillatus*). Photo by R.D. Porter.

142

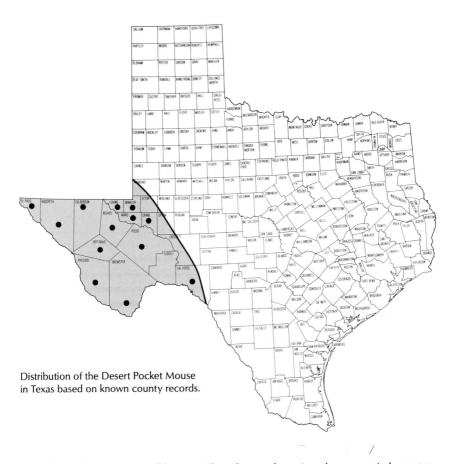

Distribution of the Desert Pocket Mouse
in Texas based on known county records.

Their habits are not well-known. Like other pocket mice, they are strictly nocturnal. Their food consists of seeds; those of mesquite, creosote bush, and broomweed
have been found in their cheek pouches.

Richard Porter found that in the Big Bend area the breeding season of this pocket
mouse began in late February, the peak of pregnancies among females was in April,
and the peak of juveniles in the population occurred in May. Lesser peaks of pregnancy occurred in June and August. The number of embryos per litter averaged 3.6
with extremes of two and six. Many of the young females reached sexual maturity
early and became pregnant while still in their juvenile pelage.

The annual population turnover in this species is high — nearly 95%, according to
Porter's studies. Consequently, only 5% of the individuals present at the season's peak
survived 12 months in the wild. Only two juveniles of the 89 live-trapped animals he
handled survived more than one year.

Remarks. Chaetodipus penicillatus is difficult to distinguish from C. intermedius
and C. nelsoni. Table 3 gives some of the external features useful in identifying these
species. In addition, the size and position of the interparietal bone in relation to the
mastoid bullae is a most useful character in separating two of the species. Note in
Figure 5 that in penicillatus the interparietal is separated from the bullae by straplike
projections of the parietals and the supraoccipital, whereas in intermedius the
interparietal is in contact with the bullae or nearly so. In addition, intermedius has a
slightly narrower rostrum and the dorsal profile of the cranium is more highly arched.

143

TABLE 3. External features used in initial identification of Trans-Pecos *Chaetodipus*.

Character	*C. nelsoni*	*C. intermedius*	*C. penicillatus*
Rump spines	numerous; prominent; well developed; distal ends usually darkly colored dorsally; entire spine lightly colored laterally	less numerous; less well developed; entire spine usually lightly colored both dorsally and laterally	absent
Thin, elongate rump hairs	absent	as in *penicillatus* but less numerous; length about same as rump spines	numerous; dark dorsally and light laterally
Total length of adults	usually greater than 180 mm	usually less than 180 mm	usually less than 180 mm
Soles of hind feet	blackish	whitish	whitish

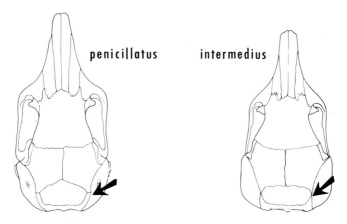

penicillatus   intermedius

Figure 5. Dorsal views of skulls of *Chaetodipus penicillatus* and *Chaetodipus intermedius* (after Hoffmeister and Lee). Arrows point to the region of the skull where the interparietal approaches or is in contact with the mastoid bullae.

GULF COAST KANGAROO RAT
Dipodomys compactus True

Description. A five-toed, medium-sized kangaroo rat; tail relatively short; pelage short and coarse; upperparts range in coloration from grayish to light ochraceous-buff intermixed with black; cheeks white and soles of feet and dorsal and ventral tail stripes brownish. Similar in appearance to *D. ordii* but with shorter tail; shorter and coarser pelage; and less brownish in coloration. *D. compactus* is smaller than *D. ordii* cranially, particularly in length of skull and size of mastoid bullae. External measurements average: total length, 223 mm; tail, 118 mm; hind foot, 36 mm. Weight, 44-60 g. Dental formula as in *Perognathus flavescens*.

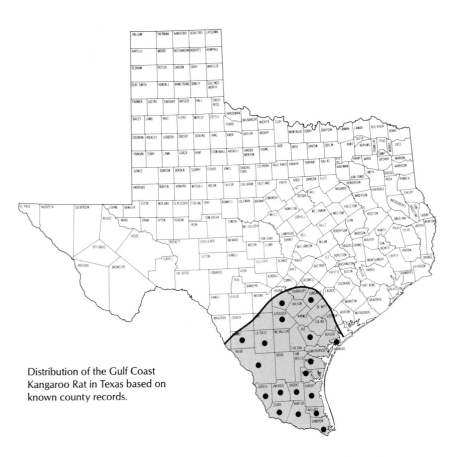

Distribution of the Gulf Coast
Kangaroo Rat in Texas based on
known county records.

Distribution. Known from most of South Texas north to Bexar and Gonzales counties; also known from Mustang and Padre Islands.

Habits. The Gulf Coast kangaroo rat inhabits sandy, sparsely vegetated soils. On Padre Island they dwell among the shifting dunes of the barrier reef and in South Texas are often found on disturbed or overgrazed areas characterized by sparse, open vegetation and deep, loose sand.

Their food consists of the seeds of grasses, annuals, and shrubs. Specific food habits are not known.

Reproductive habits are not well known. A pregnant female containing two embryos was captured on 23 August, and another female taken on 6 July displayed two placental scars.

Remarks. In previous editions this kangaroo rat has been considered conspecific with *D. ordii*; however, recent taxonomic work has produced enough evidence to identify *D. compactus* as a separate species.

TEXAS KANGAROO RAT
Dipodomys elator Merriam

Description. A rather large, four-toed kangaroo rat with conspicuous white "banner" on tip of tail; tail long, relatively thick, and about 162% of length of head and body; body large (about 121 mm in length); upperparts buffy, washed with blackish;

145

underparts white. This species superficially resembles *Dipodomys spectabilis*, but cranial differences readily separate them, and their distributions are disjunct. External measurements average: total length, 317 mm; tail, 196 mm; hind foot, 46 mm. Dental formula as in *Perognathus flavescens*.

Distribution. Occurs in north-central Texas from Cottle and Motley counties in the west to Montague County in the east.

Habits. The Texas kangaroo rat is a rare rodent with habitat preferences unusual for a kangaroo rat. It lives on clay soils supporting sparse, short grasses and small, scattered mesquite bushes. The rats make trails leading to their burrows, which invariably enter the ground at the base of a small mesquite, often in such fashion that one root of the mesquite forms the top or side of the opening. Scratching and dusting places, so characteristic of other species of kangaroo rats, are inconspicuous. The burrow is similar to that of the Ord's kangaroo rat, but usually it is shorter and the animal does not plug the entrances during the daytime. Highly nocturnal, these kangaroo rats do not become active until complete darkness and reportedly cease activity on moonlit nights.

D. elator feeds on the seeds, stems, and leaves of grasses, forbs, and some perennials. Analysis of material recovered from the cheek pouches of 52 kangaroo rats showed that the seeds of cultivated oats (*Avena*) and Johnson grass (*Sorghum*) were the most important food items, followed by annual forbs such as stork's bill (*Erodium*), broomweed (*Xanthocephalum*), and bladderpod (*Lesquerella*). Shrubs and insects were not greatly utilized for food. They store food to carry them over periods of scarcity, as do most other kangaroo rats.

D. elator may breed year round. Pregnant females have been collected in February, June, July, and September. The young appear to develop rapidly as subadult females collected in late summer have also been pregnant. Two peaks in reproductive activity —

Texas Kangaroo Rat (*Dipodomys elator*). Photo courtesy of Texas Parks and Wildlife.

146

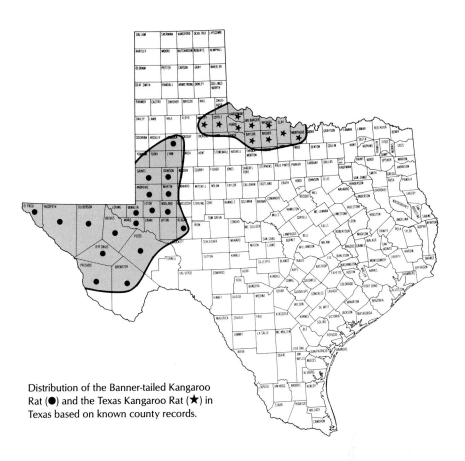

Distribution of the Banner-tailed Kangaroo Rat (●) and the Texas Kangaroo Rat (★) in Texas based on known county records.

in early spring and again in late summer — may occur as mature females give birth early in the year, and their rapidly developing young become reproductively active in late summer. Average number of embryos is three.

Remarks. The Texas kangaroo rat is listed as "threatened" by the Texas Parks and Wildlife Department. The primary threat is the clearing of the mesquite brush to which it is restricted.

MERRIAM'S KANGAROO RAT
Dipodomys merriami Mearns

Description. A small, four-toed, usually buff-colored kangaroo rat; tail rather long, usually more than 130% of length of head and body, tip dusky, and dorsal and ventral dusky stripes usually present; length of head and body usually less than 105 mm; dark facial markings rather pale; underparts white; pelage "silky." External measurements average: total length, 247 mm; tail, 144 mm; hind foot, 39 mm. Weight, 40-50 g. Dental formula as in *Perognathus flavescens*.

Distribution. A rodent of the southwest; known in Texas primarily from the Trans-Pecos eastward to Gaines County in the north and Dimmit County in the south.

Habits. In its habitat requirements this species is more tolerant than most other species of kangaroo rats. It apparently can succeed equally well on sandy soils, clays, gravels, and even among rocks. Where *merriami* occurs with *Dipodomys ordii* or

147

Merriam's Kangaroo Rat (*Dipodomys merriami*). Photo by R.D. Porter.

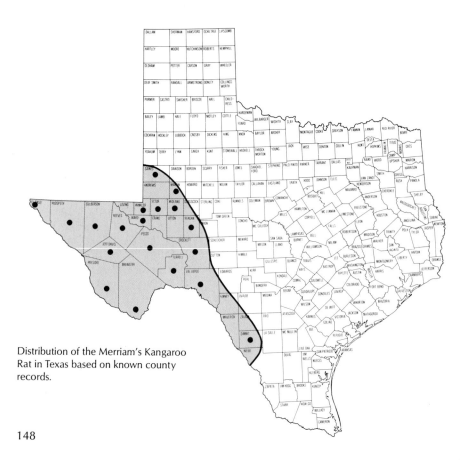

Distribution of the Merriam's Kangaroo
Rat in Texas based on known county
records.

some other less tolerant and sand-dwelling kangaroo rat, *merriami* usually inhabits the harder, stonier soils. In Trans-Pecos Texas, this is the usual relationship — *D. ordii* is found in areas of loose sands; *D. merriami* in areas of clayey or stony soils which are not suitable habitat for the other species.

Their burrows are usually simple in design, shallow and with openings near the bases of shrubs. In these, the rats live in the daytime and rear their families. Usually, only one adult occupies each burrow system.

Their food is almost entirely seeds. Seeds of mesquite, creosote bush, purslane, ocotillo, and grama grass have been found in their cheek pouches, as well as green vegetation and insects. A study of *D. merriami* in the Guadalupe Mountains showed that seeds make up 64% of the diet, with seeds of shrubs constituting 23%, those of forbs 24%, those of grasses 4.5%, and those of succulent plants 12%. The diet varies seasonally but seeds, green vegetation, and insects are eaten throughout the year. Green vegetation is most important in mid-summer, while insects are eaten in greatest abundance in winter.

Breeding begins in February and continues at least through May. The number of young per litter ranges from one to five, averaging about three.

This species is not important economically. On rangelands, the rats may do some damage by consuming seeds of grasses but, in general, losses attributable to them are negligible.

ORD'S KANGAROO RAT
Dipodomys ordii Woodhouse

Description. A five-toed kangaroo rat of medium size; tail relatively long, body actually and relatively short; tail seldom white-tipped; white patches at base of ears and above eyes usually conspicuous; upperparts pale cinnamon buff, intermixed with blackish; dark markings on face conspicuous. Juveniles similar to adults, but pelage duller and darker. External measurements of adults average: total length, 253 mm;

Ord's Kangaroo Rat (*Dipodomys ordii*). Photo by R.D. Porter.

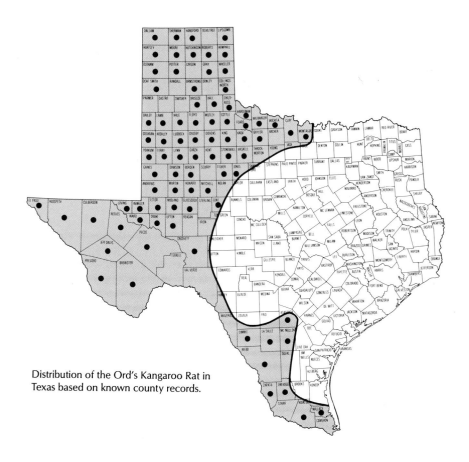

Distribution of the Ord's Kangaroo Rat in
Texas based on known county records.

tail, 159 mm; hind foot, 41 mm. Weight of adults, 60-70 g. Dental formula as in
Perognathus flavescens.

Distribution. Known from the western and southern parts of the state.

Habits. Ord's kangaroo rats, like many others of the genus, are dwellers of waste-lands where shifting sands constitute a conspicuous part of the landscape. They are one of the few pioneer mammals that move into shifting dunes and establish them-selves with pioneer plants. They rarely occur on hard and gravelly soils. Where they occur in areas with the smaller Merriam's kangaroo rat, the latter usually inhabits gravelly or hard soils; the former, the sands.

To withstand the extreme climatic conditions in their range, these rats dig deep burrows into the sand that, when plugged from the inside, permit the occupants to spend the daylight hours in comfort, and to avoid the hot, desiccating sun or the cold, wintery wind. They become active again at night, leaving their dens after sundown, and go abroad even in the dead of winter when snow is on the ground in their quest for food. They have not developed the convenient ability to hibernate.

Their food consists largely of the seeds of various desert plants which they gather and place in their cheek pouches for transport to the burrow to be consumed at leisure. Mesquite, sandbur, tumbleweed, Russian thistle, sunflowers, and countless desert annuals provide them with a wide range of choice. Surface water is not impor-tant in their economy. Like many other desert animals, they can produce their needed water physiologically from nearly dry seeds. So averse and unaccustomed to water are they that they have not learned to swim!

In a two-year study conducted in the Texas Panhandle (Hemphill County), Jack Inglis found pregnant females of *D. ordii* in the period from August through February. Young individuals first appeared in his traps in November. Litter size, based on embryo counts, averaged slightly less than three with extremes of two and four. Rate of reproduction was associated with precipitation, food supply, and population densities of kangaroo rats and other rodents. After a prolonged drought period when the food supply declined, few females became sexually active and few young were born. After a favorable growing season for food plants, most females in the population became pregnant within the first 2 months of the breeding season and most of them produced two litters; young females born early in the season produced litters themselves before the season ended. The gestation period is about 30 days. The young are born in underground nests and remain there for nearly a month. They appear aboveground when they are about three-fourths grown and weigh between 40 and 50 g.

Because of the nature of their habits, they seldom come into serious conflict with man. In sandy lands near San Antonio, Texas, however, they are reputed to do considerable damage by gathering and consuming the seeds of watermelons and other row crops at planting time. Under such conditions they can be controlled by the use of poisoned bait or by trapping, but over most of their range they do no harm.

BANNER-TAILED KANGAROO RAT
Dipodomys spectabilis Merriam

Description. A large, four-toed, long-tailed kangaroo rat; tail about 1.5 times as long as head and body, with a distinct white tuft at end; hind foot broad and usually 50 mm or more in length; upperparts dark buff; black facial markings and stripes on tail conspicuous. External measurements average: total length, 350 mm; tail, 210 mm; hind foot, 53 mm. Weight, 115 g. Dental formula as in *Perognathus flavescens*.

Banner-tailed Kangaroo Rat (*Dipodomys spectabilis*). Photo by John L. Tveten.

Distribution. Occurs in western and central Trans-Pecos region and north to Lubbock County. See map on page 147.

Habits. This large kangaroo rat appears to be limited in distribution to sparsely brush-covered slopes and low hills at elevations usually between 1,200 and 1,500 m. In Trans-Pecos Texas, it is most abundant on slopes covered with scattered, mixed stands of creosote brush and acacias on hard and moderately gravelly soil. It has never been encountered in loose soils or drift sands.

The large complex mounds of these rats are unmistakable evidence of their presence. On soils that will pack and withstand weathering, the mounds may be over 1 m in diameter and from 9 to 130 cm in height, but on sandy soils they are less pretentious. As many as a dozen openings admit the rat to the complex system of galleries and side branches, and from them lead conspicuous trails across the surrounding sparse vegetation to the feeding areas. In addition, subsidiary burrows or "duck-ins" are relied upon for protection. Usually only one rat occupies each den.

These rats are exceedingly fleet and agile, and to catch them at night by running them down is no mean feat. Once in the hand they can inflict painful wounds with their teeth unless handled carefully.

Their food is almost entirely plant materials with seeds ranking high on the list. Green vegetation is eaten on occasion. Large quantities of food are stored in the dens to carry them over the periods of scarcity. Stores from a fraction of a gram to well over 5 kg have been found. Charles Vorhies and Walter Taylor listed 13 species of grass and 29 other plants that contribute to their diet. Needle grass, grama grass, mesquite, and a composite weed (*Aplopappus*) were the most important foods. They seldom drink, even if water is present.

The breeding season begins in January and continues into August. The young begin to appear in March, sometimes as early as February, and nearly full-grown juveniles are common by April. The gestation period is not known. The young are naked at birth, and the eyes and ears are closed; the number per litter varies from one to three but usually is two. They are born in an underground nest composed of fine vegetation and chaff refuse from the food. Nest chambers vary in size from 15 by 20 cm to 20 by 25 cm.

Their known natural enemies include badger, swift fox, bobcat, and coyote. Other animals also probably prey upon them.

Banner-tails are sometimes of economic importance locally. In periods of drought they may do serious damage to rangelands by gathering and eating grass seeds. In such places, controlling their populations may be necessary.

MEXICAN SPINY POCKET MOUSE
Liomys irroratus (Gray)

Description. A medium-sized mouse with extremely harsh pelage over entire upperparts (the hairs flattened, sharp-pointed and grooved); external, furlined cheek pouches; and relatively long tail. Similar in general appearance to the spiny-haired pocket mice (*Chaetodipus*), but upper incisors lack the longitudinal groove on the outer face and the pelage is much more spiny and harsh. Tail about as long as head and body, sparsely haired and distinctly bicolor, brownish above, whitish below; upperparts dark gray, grizzled with orange; underparts pure white; sole of proximal half of hind foot hairy, blackish. External measurements average: total length, 237 mm; tail, 122 mm; hind foot, 30 mm. Weight: males, 50-60 g; females, 35-50 g. Dental formula as in *Perognathus flavescens*.

Distribution. A Mexican form reaching the United States in extreme South Texas.

Mexican Spiny Pocket Mouse (*Liomys irroratus*). Photo by John L. Tveten.

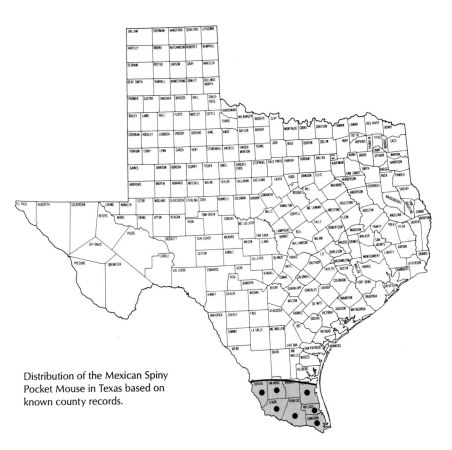

Distribution of the Mexican Spiny Pocket Mouse in Texas based on known county records.

Habits. In southern Texas they live in the densest brush on the ridges forming the old banks of the Rio Grande, along oxbows, and in the scattered remnants of the subtropical palm forests of the Rio Grande near Brownsville (Cameron County). They are often closely associated with thickets of prickly pear. In northern Mexico, they may be trapped among dense chaparral but in the valley of Mexico they occurred around stone fences and among rocks on the sides of mountain slopes. They live in burrows and sometimes throw up small mounds to close the entrances. Usually the openings are covered by vegetation or dead leaves. They are strictly nocturnal.

In southern Texas, they feed on the seeds of hackberry, mesquite, and various other shrubs. In addition, seeds of various weeds may be found in their cheek pouches.

Very little is known about their breeding habits. In Mexico, half-grown young have been found in June and nearly full-grown young in August. None of the females captured in summer was pregnant or lactating. Based on the study of a large number of Mexican records, Theodore Fleming reported immature individuals of *Liomys irroratus* from all months except May; he believed that breeding occurs throughout the year but with most of it concentrated in the winter period from November to February. Litter size is two to eight, averaging about four.

FAMILY CASTORIDAE (BEAVERS)

AMERICAN BEAVER
Castor canadensis Kuhl

Description. A large, robust, aquatic rodent with a broad, horizontally flattened, scaly tail; hind feet webbed; upperparts in fresh fall pelage dark, rich, chestnut brown

American Beaver (*Castor canadensis*). Photo by John L. Tveten.

154

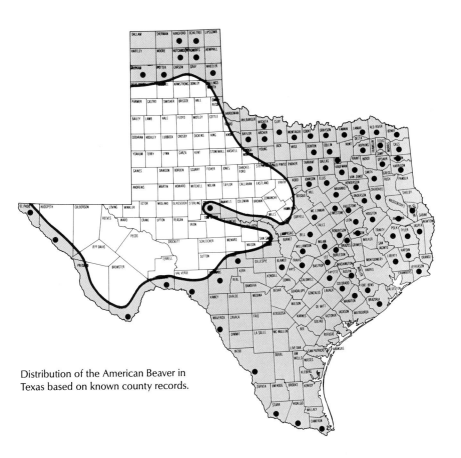

Distribution of the American Beaver in Texas based on known county records.

which fades by spring; underparts paler, often with silvery sheen. Sexes colored alike. External measurements average: total length, 1,160 mm; tail, 400 mm; hind foot, 178 mm. Weight, averages 18 kg; rarely as much as 27 kg. The dental formula is I 1/1, C 0/0, Pm 1/1, M 3/3 X 2 = 20.

Distribution. Found over most of the state where suitable aquatic habitat prevails; absent from the Llano Estacado and some adjacent areas and from much of the Trans-Pecos.

Habits. Beavers are essentially aquatic and require water in the form of a pond, stream, lake, or river for their well-being. Because of their skills in regulating water level and stream flow with dams, beavers are able to convert an otherwise unfavorable area into one that is habitable. But they must be ever alert as water engineers because their ponds tend to fill up with sediment washed off the slopes above and in time become meadows, forcing the beavers to move to new sites. Large rivers and lakes offer suitable habitat in places where natural food and den or house sites are available, but the largest populations are on small bodies of water.

In cold regions, beavers live in houses constructed of sticks and mud and enter and leave them by means of underwater tunnels or "plunge holes"; in Texas they may burrow into cut banks of streams or lakes. Burrows examined in the Rio Grande in the Big Bend section of Texas were large enough to admit a man and were 10 m or more in length. Burrows as long as 50 m have been reported. Burrows, or houses, are used for loafing, sleeping, and rearing the young.

155

The average beaver colony consists of six or seven animals, usually including parents and their young of two age classes; rarely is it as large as 12.

Beavers feed on a variety of vegetation, but the inner bark of willows and cottonwood seems to be their mainstay. In summer a number of herbaceous aquatic plants and sedges are eaten. In central Texas, where willows are absent, beavers in winter utilize as first choice such trees as button willow, juniper, and pecan and rely heavily on Bermuda grass, beard grass, ragweed, and yellow water lily in summer. Thus, the plants eaten and their order of preference depend in large measure on availability.

Breeding begins in January or February, and the young are normally born in May or June after a gestation period of about 107 days. Beavers are usually monogamous, and normally only one litter of three to four young is produced each year, but some females produce a second litter in August or September.

At birth the kits are fully furred, the eyes are open, and the incisor teeth are visible; they weigh about 450 g. The tail is broad and flat, as in adults. They grow rather slowly and attain a weight of about 10 kg the first year. They mature sexually the second year. Rarely, yearling females may breed and produce young. The young often stay with the family group through the second year.

Because of the high commercial value of their pelts, beavers figured importantly in the early exploration and settlement of western North America. Thousands of their pelts were harvested annually, and it was not many years before beavers were either exterminated entirely or reduced to very low populations over a considerable part of their former range. By 1910 their populations were so low everywhere in the United States that strict regulation of the harvest or complete protection became imperative. In the 1930s live trapping and restocking of depleted areas became a widespread practice which, when coupled with adequate protection, has made it possible for the animals to make a spectacular comeback in many sections. Their value as soil and water conservationists is well-known and, in most sections of the country, appreciated. They can be destructive to crops, trees, and irrigation systems, however, in which case they can be live-trapped and removed from the area.

FAMILY MURIDAE (MICE AND RATS)

COUES' RICE RAT
Oryzomys couesi (Alston)

Description. Similar to *O. palustris*, but pelage shorter and color ochraceous buffy or ochraceous tawny instead of grayish brown; underparts buffy instead of whitish. External measurements average: total length, 297 mm; tail, 161 mm; hind foot, 34 mm.

Distribution. A Mexican form reaching the United States in the lower Rio Grande Valley in Cameron and Hidalgo counties.

Habits. Coues' rice rats have been captured in cattail-bulrush marshes and aquatic, grassy zones near resacas (oxbow lakes) in Hidalgo County. Apparently, riparian woodland and subtropical evergreen woodland near the resacas are avoided, or at least inhabited less commonly. Likewise, brushland habitats near resacas are not frequently used.

They build their nests in cattails and small trees near or above water. Nests are constructed of leaves, twigs, small vines, and cattail, all finely shredded and woven into a globular shape. No information is available on the reproductive biology of these rats, nor are their feeding habits known.

Remarks. Due to continued and extensive land drainage practices for agricultural purposes in South Texas, these uncommon rodents may be threatened by significant losses of habitat.

Coues' Rice Rat (*Oryzomys couesi*). Photo by John L. Tveten.

MARSH RICE RAT
Oryzomys palustris (Harlan)

Description. Ratlike, with long, nearly naked, scaly tail; ears short and hairy; upperparts grizzled grayish brown, heavily lined with black, especially in winter pelage; underparts whitish. External measurements average: total length, 245 mm; tail, 116 mm; hind foot, 29 mm. Weight, 40-68 g, averaging 51 g.

Distribution. Found in eastern Texas west to Brazos County and south to Cameron County.

Habits. These rats typically inhabit marshy areas but they may be found in almost any situation where grasses and sedges offer an adequate food supply and protective cover. They are semiaquatic and do not hesitate to swim or dive to escape capture. Near Copano Bay their runways are so situated in the salt grasses and sedges that the rats have to travel in shallow water most of the time. In southeastern Texas, the rats are common on the dikes and levees thrown up in the coastal marshes. In inland areas they prefer marshes and moist meadows; occasionally they live in forested areas.

Their surface runways resemble those made by cotton rats. They are 5-8 cm in width and lead from the shallow burrows or surface nests to the feeding areas. The globular nest is composed of grasses, sedges, or weeds and frequently is placed under debris above high water in the emergent vegetation. They occasionally take over and remodel for their own use the nests of blackbirds.

The marsh rice rat is omnivorous, with about equal amounts of plant and animal matter making up the diet, although the types of food eaten varies with season and

Marsh Rice Rat (*Oryzomys palustris*). Photo by John L. Tveten, courtesy of Texas A&M University Press.

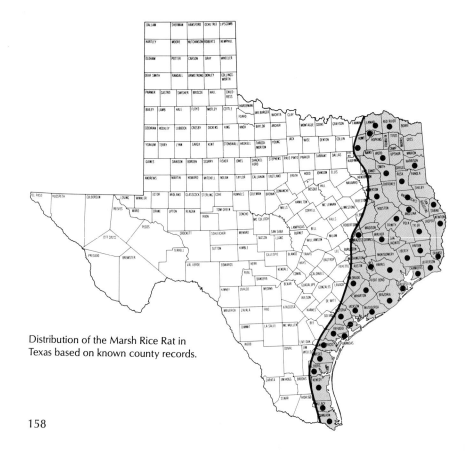

Distribution of the Marsh Rice Rat in Texas based on known county records.

availability. Plant foods include green vegetation, fungus, and the seeds of sedges, marsh grasses, and rice. Animal foods include insects, fiddler crabs, snails, fishes, and the carcasses of small rodents and birds. It is because of their fondness for cultivated rice that they were named rice rats. In most places these rats do no damage, but in rice fields they may become economically important by consuming large quantities of rice.

They are prolific. The breeding season is nearly yearlong, during which time breeding females may bear several litters. A single female may bear five to six litters per year, although suboptimal conditions may restrict reproductive output. Litter size ranges from two to seven (average, four) but may be affected by population density as crowded conditions appear to restrict the number of young produced.

The gestation period is about 25 days. A captive female produced six litters, totaling 20 young, in 1 year — an average of 3.3 young per litter. At birth the young are blind, helpless, nearly naked, and weigh about 3 g each. They grow rather rapidly. Their eyes open on the fifth or sixth day; they are weaned on the 11th day; and sexual maturity is reached between 40 and 45 days of age. These rats appear to grow continually throughout their lifetime.

FULVOUS HARVEST MOUSE
Reithrodontomys fulvescens J.A. Allen

Description. A small mouse with grooved upper incisors, tail much longer than head and body, and inside of ears covered with reddish hairs; differs from the pocket mice (*Perognathus* and *Chaetodipus*), which also have grooved upper incisors and long tail, in the absence of external cheek pouches. Upperparts ochraceous buff, sparingly mixed with blackish brown, sides nearly clear buff; underparts white or pale buff. External measurements average: total length, 165 mm; tail, 93 mm; hind foot, 20 mm. Weight 14-30 g, averaging about 18 g.

Distribution. Occurs in eastern two-thirds of state, including southern portion of Trans-Pecos. Absent from western Panhandle and central Edwards Plateau.

Habits. These largest of harvest mice occur chiefly in grassy or weedy areas dotted with shrubs, or in creek bottoms with their tangles of grasses, vines, and bushes. They are relatively rare in blackland prairies which are the home of the smaller plains harvest mouse, *R. montanus*. In favored habitat they travel from place to place on their own small trails or use those of their animal associates — cotton rats, rice rats, and white-footed mice.

In addition to living in underground burrows, many of them have penthouses in bushes above the ground. These arboreal homes may be converted birds' nests or

Fulvous Harvest Mouse (*Reithrodontomys fulvescens*).
Photo by John L. Tveten.

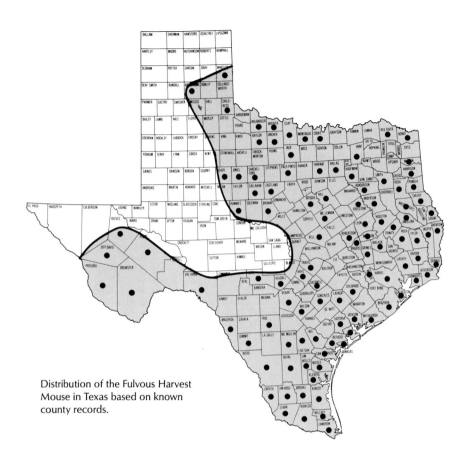

Distribution of the Fulvous Harvest
Mouse in Texas based on known
county records.

completely of the mouse's own architecture. One found in central Texas was a remodeled cardinal's nest about 1.3 m above the ground in a yaupon bush. When the nest
was disturbed, the mouse quickly left it, descended to the ground by jumping from
branch to branch and entered an underground burrow. The mouse's nest, about the
size of a baseball, neatly filled the cavity of the bird's nest. It was composed of shredded grass and weed stems and had one opening on the side. Another nest was about
7 cm above the ground, in a clump of bluestem (*Andropogon*).

Their food is nearly all vegetable matter, including seeds and the green blades of
grasses and sedges, but may include invertebrates. In coastal areas of Texas invertebrates predominate in the diet of these mice, but in regions with greater seasonal
variation in climate, vegetation dominates the diet in fall and winter, while invertebrates are more important in spring and summer. Clearly, their food habits are somewhat opportunistic and based on food availability. They readily accept dry rolled oats
as bait. In captivity, they eat about one-third of their own weight in food daily. They are
chiefly nocturnal and are active the year round.

In Texas, it appears that the breeding season extends from February to October,
although peaks in reproductive activity occur in late spring and early autumn. Litter
size may range from two to five, averaging three or four. The gestation period probably
is about 21 days. At birth, the young are naked, blind, and helpless and weigh about
1 g each. Weaning occurs at 13-16 days when the young weigh 3.0-3.5 g. By day 11
the young are well-furred and at 9-12 days the eyes open.

These mice seldom conflict with man's interests. Their known predators are barn
owls, barred owls, and red-tailed hawks but, doubtless, other animals also feed on them.

160

EASTERN HARVEST MOUSE

Reithrodontomys humulis (Audubon and Bachman)

Description. A diminutive harvest mouse like *R. montanus*, but upperparts deep brown or gray, heavily mixed with black, especially on the mid-dorsal area; ears blackish all over rather than dark at the base and light at the tip; tail about as long as head and body, the dark dorsal and light ventral stripes about equal in width. External measurements average: total length, 126 mm; tail, 61 mm; hind foot, 16 mm. Weight, 10-15 g.

Distribution. Known in the eastern part of the state, west to Fort Bend, McLennan, and Hunt counties.

Habits. The eastern harvest mouse is found mainly in habitats dominated by grasses and other herbaceous plants characteristic of early vegetational succession, including places such as abandoned fields, weed-filled ditches, and briar thickets.

Eastern harvest mice are essentially nocturnal, although at times they may be active during the daylight hours, particularly during cold weather. During periods of cold weather, these mice huddle together in the nest at night to reduce heat loss from their bodies, and they feed in the daytime when it is warmer.

R. humulis constructs nests of shredded grass and plant fibers that are placed on the ground in tangled herbage or above the ground in a clump of grass. The nest, which is about the size of a baseball, generally has a single entrance.

Although breeding may occur throughout the year, most births take place between late spring and late fall. Litter sizes range from one to eight (average, three to four), and the gestation period is 21-22 days. At birth the young weigh approximately 1.2 g. The

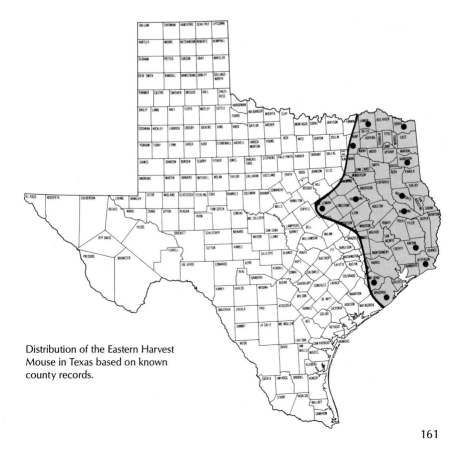

Distribution of the Eastern Harvest Mouse in Texas based on known county records.

161

Eastern Harvest Mouse (*Reithrodontomys humulis*). Photo by John L. Tveten.

eyes do not open until 7-10 days, and weaning takes place between the second and fourth weeks. The young become sexually mature and are capable of breeding at about 11-12 weeks of age.

The food habits of *R. humulis* are not well known. They appear to feed almost wholly on seeds and grain, but are known to eat grasshoppers and crickets while in captivity.

WESTERN HARVEST MOUSE
Reithrodontomys megalotis (Baird)

Description. A medium-sized harvest mouse; tail about as long as head and body; the dark dorsal and light ventral stripes about equal in width; ears pale flesh color (or buffy cinnamon); upperparts brownish buff, darkest in middle of back; underparts whitish. Differs from *R. fulvescens* in shorter tail, pale rather than blackish ears basally; from *R. montanus* in larger size, and lack of dark color at base of ears. External measurements average: total length, 140 mm; tail, 71 mm; hind foot, 18 mm. Weight, 10-16 g.

Distribution. Western Texas, from the Panhandle southward to Trans-Pecos.

Habits. These mice prefer grassy or weedy areas where adequate food and a certain degree of protective cover are available, especially in the vicinity of water. Meadows, marshes, and weed-covered banks of irrigation ditches seem to offer optimum habitat conditions. The species seldom is found in forested areas.

They utilize the runways and underground burrows of other rodents and frequently take over vacated burrows of pocket gophers. The nest usually is placed on the ground or slightly above it under some protective cover such as a board, a clump of lodged grass, or a tangle of weeds. It is a globular structure, about 7 cm in diameter, composed of plant fibers, and usually has only one opening. These mice are also known to use the nests of marsh wrens in cattail marshes. They appear to be strictly nocturnal and active throughout the year. They are almost entirely vegetarians and feed on the green parts and seeds of plants.

In Texas, the breeding season extends through most of the year. Several litters a season seem to be the rule. A captive female produced seven litters, totaling 17 young, in one year. Litter size in wild mice, based on 24 embryo counts, ranged from one to seven and averaged about four. The gestation period is about 23 days. At birth the young mice are blind, naked, and helpless and weigh from 1 to 1.5 g. By the end of the first week they are covered with pigmented hair dorsally; by the 11th or 12th day the eyes open, at which time the mice begin to eat solid food. They are weaned by the 19th day. Sexual maturity is reached in about 4 months.

These mice seldom are of economic importance. They are utilized as food by a number of flesh eaters, including weasels, foxes, owls, and snakes.

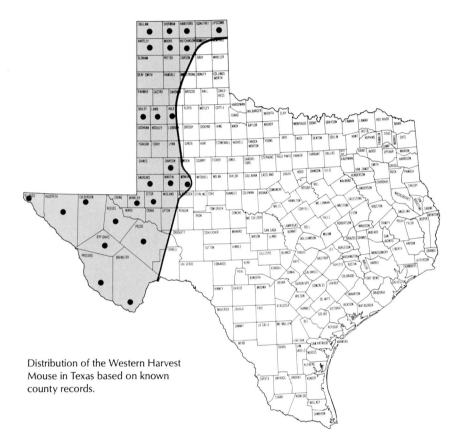

Distribution of the Western Harvest Mouse in Texas based on known county records.

PLAINS HARVEST MOUSE
Reithrodontomys montanus (Baird)

Description. A small harvest mouse about the size of *R. humulis* and considerably smaller than *R. megalotis* and *R. fulvescens*; tail usually less than half of total length and distinctly bicolor, dark above and light below; upperparts mixed brown and pale yellowish gray; outside of ears and flanks pale yellowish brown; underparts dull whitish. External measurements average: total length, 116 mm; tail, 54 mm; hind foot, 15 mm. Weight, 6-10 g.

Distribution. Found in western and central parts of state, east and southeast to Madison and Bexar counties, respectively.

Habits. These mice appear to prefer climax, or nearly climax, well-drained grassland. In Brazos County they occur most commonly in blackland prairies where the dominant vegetation is bluestem grass (*Andropogon*). Their nests are composed of fine

Plains Harvest Mouse (*Reithrodontomys montanus*). Photo by John L. Tveten, courtesy of Texas A&M University Press.

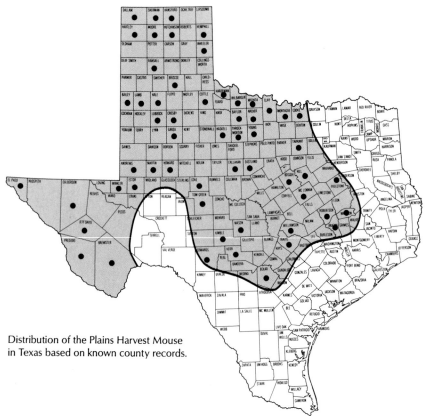

Distribution of the Plains Harvest Mouse in Texas based on known county records.

grass compacted into small balls and are either in bunch grass or just beneath the ground in their burrows.

Their food consists of green parts and seeds of a variety of plants, including small grains. In captivity they readily accept rolled oats and sunflower seeds.

Available data indicate a year-long breeding period, at least in Texas. A female captured January 13 near Bryan gave birth to four young in the trap; a gravid female was trapped in October. A captive gave birth to litters in September, October, March, and April. The gestation period is approximately 21 days; the number of young per litter ranges from two to five, averaging three. At birth the young are blind, naked, and weigh about 1 g. They are well-haired in 6 days, their eyes open in 8 days, and they are weaned in about 14 days. They are as large as adults in 5 weeks and sexually mature in about 2 months.

TEXAS MOUSE
Peromyscus attwateri J.A. Allen

Description. A medium-sized *Peromyscus* with the tail about as long as (or slightly longer than) the head and body, moderately haired, darker above than below (but not sharply bicolor) and usually with a terminal tuft; hind foot large (24-27 mm); ankles usually dark or dusky; dorsal color near sayal brown, darker and mixed with blackish along midline; sides pinkish cinnamon; ventral color pure white, the bases of the hairs plumbeous; length of maxillary tooth row 4 mm or more; each large upper and lower molar has an accessory loph (see Figure 6). External measurements average: total length, 198 mm; tail, 103 mm; hind foot, 25 mm. Weight of adults, 25-35 g.

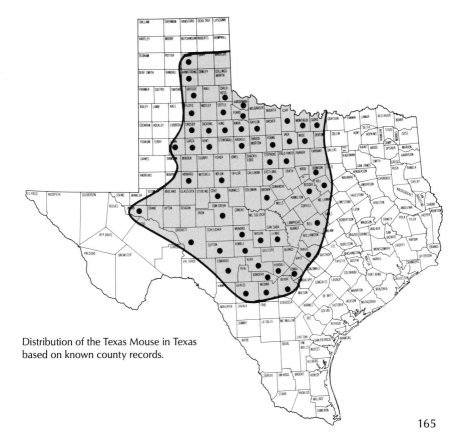

Distribution of the Texas Mouse in Texas based on known county records.

Distribution. Occurs in central part of state southward to Uvalde, Medina, and Bexar counties.

Habits. *P. attwateri* inhabits the cliffs and rocky outcrops of the Edwards Plateau, the West Cross Timbers, the Rolling Plains, and the escarpment of the Llano Estacado in Texas. Vernon Bailey recorded that in the vicinity of Kerrville he caught many of them in traps set in crevices along the cliffs, under logs in the woods, and under fallen grass and weeds on a creek bank in the bottom of a gulch, as well as under heaps of driftwood. They seem to prefer rocky areas where the dominant vegetation is juniper. They are adept at climbing. Charles Long recorded that, when compared with other species of *Peromyscus*, *P. attwateri* is a superior and more cautious climber, seldom jumps from high places when under stress, and is more capable of finding its way in darkness. Recent studies using tagged *P. attwateri* have shown that this mouse, at least in some areas, is semi-arboreal and travels frequently in trees.

Where *P. attwateri* and *P. pectoralis* co-exist, *P. pectoralis* specializes in areas of rock ledges and leaf litter, whereas *P. attwateri* is more of a habitat generalist and may be found not only in areas of rock ledges and leaf litter but also more open, grassy areas with only scattered rock cover.

Their main diet is plant material, especially seeds. In southern Missouri, Larry Brown found that about 70% (by volume) of the stomach contents he examined consisted of plant material, including fragments of seeds, berries, bulbs, and green plants. The balance consisted of insects, chiefly camel crickets and beetles.

In an ecological study of this mouse in Lynn County, Texas, Herschel Garner found that reproductive activity began in late September and continued throughout the winter. He found no evidence of their breeding during late spring and summer. The number of young per litter varies from one to six and averages about four. Based on data derived from the retrapping of marked animals, Larry Brown estimated the average lifespan to be 6.8 months with a maximum of 18 months.

Remarks. *Peromyscus attwateri* was formerly treated as a subspecies of *P. boylii* until one of us (Schmidly) removed *attwateri* and returned it to its original status as a full species. This taxonomic change was based primarily on characteristics of the karyotype (*attwateri* has six large biarmed autosomal chromosomes compared to only two in *boylii* from west Texas). In addition to chromosomal differences, the most useful morphological features available in the field, and to those not trained in cytogenetics, that separate *P. attwateri* from *P. boylii* are: (1) larger hind foot (24-27 mm in *attwateri* and 20-23 mm in Texas-taken *boylii*) and (2) the structure of the molar teeth. In *attwateri* an accessory loph is present in both the upper and lower molars, but that structure is absent from the lower molars of *boylii* (see Figure 6).

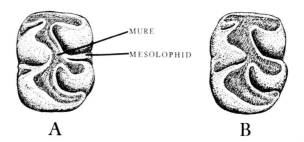

MURE

MESOLOPHID

A   B

Figure 6.   Occlusal view of the second lower molar of (A) *Peromyscus attwateri* compared with that of (B) *Peromyscus boylii*. Note that a prominent mesolophid is present in *attwateri*, but absent in *boylii*.

BRUSH MOUSE
Peromyscus boylii (Baird)

Description. A medium-sized, long-tailed, white-footed mouse; tail equal to or longer than head and body, sparsely haired, slightly tufted and indistinctly bicolor, darker above; ankles dusky, the feet white; ears moderately long (19-22 mm from notch); proximal two-fifths of sole of hind foot hairy; upperparts pale cinnamon or hair brown to sepia; sides with narrow ochraceous buff lateral line; underparts white. External measurements average: total length, 197 mm; tail, 103 mm; hind foot, 22 mm. Weight, 22-36 g. Distinguished from *P. difficilis* chiefly by smaller ears and shorter fur; from *P. pectoralis* by dusky instead of white ankles.

Distribution. Trans-Pecos region and along escarpment of Llano Estacado and in adjacent parts of Panhandle.

Habits. These mice are usually associated with brush and trees, but they have been trapped in a number of habitats including stream banks, rock walls, talus slopes, and cabins. In the Guadalupe Mountains of western Texas, they are common in the open pine-fir forest at 2,400 m where they show a decided preference for areas of down logs and brush piles. Vernon Bailey remarks that they seldom burrow into the ground but rather utilize any natural cavity that offers concealment and protection. The nest is a globular structure of dry plant fibers, mostly grasses.

They are adept at climbing. Victor Cahalane observed that several mice, upon escaping from his live traps, fled into trees in preference to running on the ground. They climbed easily, but not fast, and seemed to be at home off the ground. Without

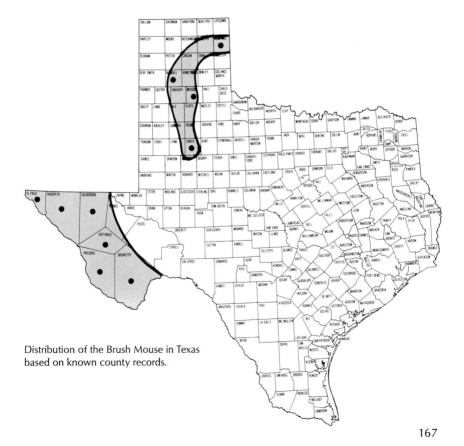

Distribution of the Brush Mouse in Texas
based on known county records.

doubt they garner much of their food in trees and utilize hollows in them for dens. They are almost entirely nocturnal in habit and are active the year round.

They feed on a variety of plant items. In the Guadalupe Mountains, they feed extensively on pine nuts and Douglas fir seeds; in the oak belt, acorns are a favorite item. They also feed on hackberries, juniper berries, and cactus fruits.

The breeding season extends through most of the year. Gravid females have been taken from May to December, but the presence of half-grown young in May indicates that breeding begins as early as March or April. Several litters of two to five (average three) young may be reared in a year, but the peak of production is in spring and early summer. The young are blind and hairless and weigh about 2 g at birth.

Usually these mice are of little or no economic importance except in instances where they occur in numbers around and in cabins and granaries in wooded areas. In such instances they can be removed readily by trapping.

CACTUS MOUSE
Peromyscus eremicus (Baird)

Description. A medium-sized, long-haired mouse; tail longer than head and body, not sharply bicolor, but darker above than below, finely annulated and covered with short hairs; ears large and almost naked; sole of hind foot naked to heel; pelage long, soft and silky; upperparts ochraceous buff, washed with dusky; lateral line pure ochraceous buff; underparts and feet white. Can readily be distinguished from other *Peromyscus* by the combination of long tail, soft pelage, and naked heels. External measurements average: total length, 185 mm; tail, 102 mm; hind foot, 20 mm; ear, 20 mm. Weight, 18-40 g, averaging about 24 g in males and 27 g in females.

Distribution. Trans-Pecos Texas, mainly in lowland desert areas, westward along the Rio Grande to Webb County.

Habits. As the name suggests, these mice are restricted almost entirely to a desert habitat, especially where rocky outcrops or cliffs offer retreats and den sites. In the Trans-Pecos region of Texas, they typically occur at the bases of cliffs or in rocky outcroppings at elevations below 1,200 m. They are expert at climbing and can scramble up stone walls

Cactus Mouse (*Peromyscus eremicus*). Photo by R.D. Porter.

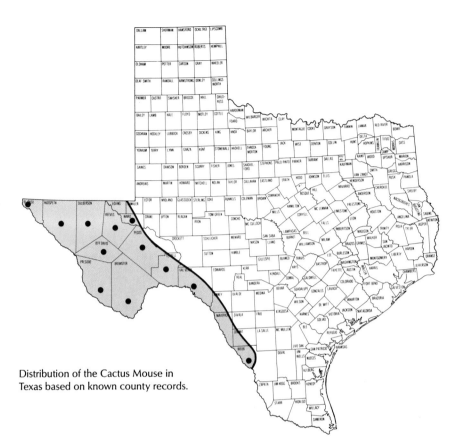

Distribution of the Cactus Mouse in
Texas based on known county records.

and cliffs with ease. They have been observed foraging in mesquite trees 1-2 m off the ground, and there is some evidence that they also climb hackberry trees and gather the seeds. Richard MacMillen and others have observed that populations of *P. eremicus* are high in numbers in midwinter and very low in numbers in midsummer. His studies, both in the field and in the laboratory, led him to conclude that cactus mice aestivate in their burrows during the summer. By employing torpor as a water-conserving device and as a means of prolonging food stores, the mice escape the most rigorous annual period of the desert. By virtue of the ability to aestivate, cactus mice are probably able to successfully inhabit severe desert situations in which they otherwise would be unable to survive.

Their food is largely seeds of various desert annuals, mesquite beans, hackberry nutlets, insects, and green vegetation. They are also fond of such trap bait as rolled oats, sunflower seeds, and various whole grains. In captivity, they relish water but in the wild they probably supply this need by feeding on succulent vegetation since they occur in areas that are waterless except for infrequent rains.

The breeding season extends at least from January to October and possibly throughout the year. The number of young per litter varies from one to four, averaging about three, and two or more litters may be reared each year. A captive female is known to have produced three litters in a year. The cactus mouse has only two pairs of milk glands, so only four young can be nursed at one time. Most white-footed mice (*Peromyscus*) have three pairs. The gestation period is 21 days. At birth the young are blind, pigmented dorsally, and not pink. They weigh about 2.5 g. They develop quite rapidly; the ears unfold in less than 24 hours, and the eyes open in 15-17 days. Because the litters are never produced in quick succession, the young may be nursed for as long as 30-40 days.

COTTON MOUSE
Peromyscus gossypinus (Le Conte)

Description. A medium-sized, heavy bodied, white-footed mouse; tail much shorter than head and body, between three and four times the length of hind foot and not sharply bicolor, but darker above than below; ears small (16-18 mm from notch); upperparts mummy brown, the mid-dorsal area suffused with black; sides bright russet; underparts creamy white; feet white, but tarsal joint of heel dark like leg. External measurements average: total length, 180 mm; tail, 78 mm; hind foot, 23 mm. Weight, 34-51 g.

This mouse is most easily confused with the white-footed mouse (*Peromyscus leucopus*), from which it can be distinguished by larger size (weight usually over 30 g in adults as opposed to 15-25 g in *leucopus*) and longer skull (27 mm or more in *gossypinus* and less than that in *leucopus*).

Distribution. Found in woodlands in eastern one-fourth of state.

Habits. Cotton mice are typically woodland dwellers and occur along water courses where stumps, down logs, and tangles of brush and vines offer suitable retreats; frequently they occur in woodland areas bordering open fields. They have been trapped in eastern Texas in canebrakes, under logs, and around and in old, tumbledown buildings in wooded areas. That they are adept at climbing and may live off the ground in hollows in trees as indicated by the capture of individuals in live traps set on platforms in trees.

Their other habits are not well-known. Nothing specific is known of their natural foods, although cotton mice are omnivorous. Over one-half of their diet may be made up of animal matter and food availability probably determines the dietary composition.

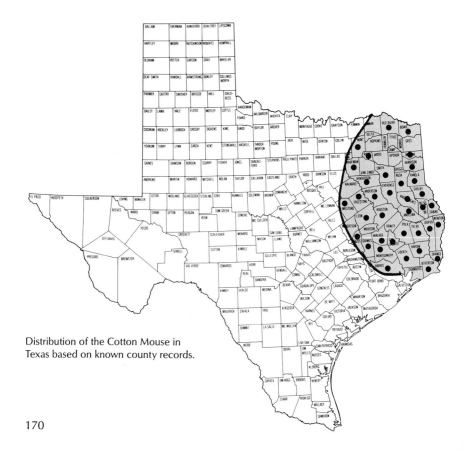

Distribution of the Cotton Mouse in Texas based on known county records.

Captive mice seemed to relish rolled oats, wheat, corn, and bread. Green foods were eaten sparingly.

Breeding may occur throughout the year although there is a decline in reproductive activity during the summer months. In Texas, most breeding commences in late August, reaches a peak in November, December, and January and subsides by early May. The gestation period is about 23 days in non-nursing females and about 30 days in females which are nursing a previous litter. Adult females may produce four or more litters a year. The litter size ranges from one to seven and averages three or four. The young are naked and blind at birth. Their ears open in 5 or 6 days at which age their incisor teeth erupt. Their eyes open in about 13 days and shortly after that they begin to eat solid foods. They are completely weaned at an age of 20-25 days. They become sexually mature at about 60-70 days of age.

The name cotton mouse was applied to the species by Le Conte, who found that the mice often used cotton for nest construction. Ordinarily, however, they do little or no damage to cotton or foodstuffs.

WHITE-FOOTED MOUSE
Peromyscus leucopus (Rafinesque)

Description. A medium-sized, short-tailed, white-footed mouse; tail about 43% of total length, sparsely haired, darker above than below but usually not sharply bicolor; upperparts cinnamon rufous mixed with blackish; sides paler, with less admixture of black; underparts and feet white, the "ankle" slightly brownish. External measurements average: total length, 173 mm; tail, 78 mm; hind foot, 21 mm. Weight, 18-32 g, averaging about 22 g. Most easily confused with *P. gossypinus* and *P. maniculatus; P. leucopus* differs from the former in smaller size, shorter body, lighter weight, and brighter colors; from the latter in less hairy and not sharply bicolor tail, usually shorter pelage, and lack of whitish tufts at base of ears.

Distribution. Statewide.

Habits. In the main, these mice are woodland dwellers, a fact that is best illustrated along the western border of their range where they are restricted almost entirely to creek and river bottoms. As one progresses eastward, the mice are found in a

White-footed Mouse (*Peromyscus leucopus*). Photo by John L. Tveten, courtesy of Texas A&M University Press.

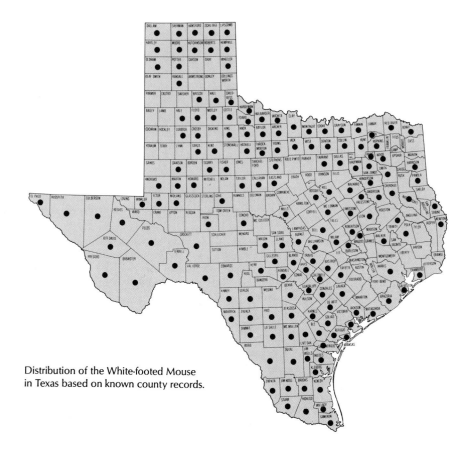

Distribution of the White-footed Mouse
in Texas based on known county records.

progressively greater variety of habitats. In east-central Texas, they are most abundant in bottom lands, less so in post oak uplands and almost completely absent from prairie lands. They are adept at climbing and often den in hollow trees out of danger from overflow waters. In areas not subject to inundation, they live in dens under logs, in stumps, brush piles, burrows, or buildings.

In much of its range, this mouse is one of the commonest of small mammals. In Brazos County, the population of this mouse is exceeded only by that of the cotton rat. In 3,483 trap-nights, 161 cotton rats and 121 white-footed mice were captured; a ratio, respectively, of 21.6 and 28.7 trap-nights per animal. The maximum home range of adult males is about 0.2 ha, that of adult females about 0.15 ha. The mice seldom travel more than 50 m once they are established in suitable quarters. The dispersal of the population generally is accomplished by movements of the unestablished young mice.

The food of white-footed mice is varied, but their chief reliance is seeds and such nuts as acorns and pecans. When food is abundant, they store it in and about their nests for winter use. Caches of "several quarts" have been reported. Like squirrels, these mice have internal cheek pouches in which they can place food for transport to caches. In spring and summer they feed to some extent on fruits and on insects, snails, and other invertebrates.

In east-central Texas, gravid females have been captured in nearly every month of the year. Litter size varies from one to six, averaging about four. Captive females have produced as many as 10 litters and 45 offspring in 1 year, but in the wild the number of litters appears to be four or five. The gestation period is from 22 to 25 days in nonlactating females and 23 to 37 days in those that are lactating. At birth the young are blind, pink, and weigh about 2 g. They become pigmented dorsally in the first 24 hours, their eyes open in about 13 days, and they are weaned at the age of 22 or 23 days if the mother is expecting a new family; if otherwise, they may nurse as long as 37 days. Young females mature sexually at the age of 10 or 11 weeks and may bear their first litters at the age of 13 or 14 weeks. Usually, females born in the spring rear one or two litters themselves before winter sets in. They seldom live to be more than 18 months old in the wild.

Where numerous in an area, they can become destructive of stored and shocked grains and consequently need to be controlled. But in most places they are of little or no economic significance if such natural predators as owls, snakes, and weasels are not destroyed.

DEER MOUSE
Peromyscus maniculatus (Wagner)

Description. A small, white-footed mouse with sharply bicolor tail, white beneath and dark above; ears usually shorter than hind foot, prominent and leaflike; upperparts bright fulvous or brownish, intermixed with dusky; underparts and feet white. External measurements average: total length, 170 mm; tail, 81 mm; hind foot, 20 mm; ear, 18 (12-20) mm. Weight, 15-32 g.

This species is most easily confused with *Peromyscus leucopus*, from which it differs in (1) sharply bicolor tail, (2) more hairy and often shorter tail, (3) frequently whitish tufts of hair at base of ears, and (4) usually longer pelage.

Distribution. Statewide but uncommon in the eastern, coastal, and southern parts of the state.

Habits. These mice occupy a variety of habitats, ranging from mixed forests to grasslands to open, sparsely vegetated deserts. In Texas, they usually inhabit grasslands or areas of open brush, especially where weeds and grasses offer concealment and a source of food. Weed-choked fence rows and washes offer almost ideal habitat. Mice of this group seem to be poor climbers and live close to or on the ground.

Deer Mouse (*Peromyscus maniculatus*). Photo by R.M. Bond.

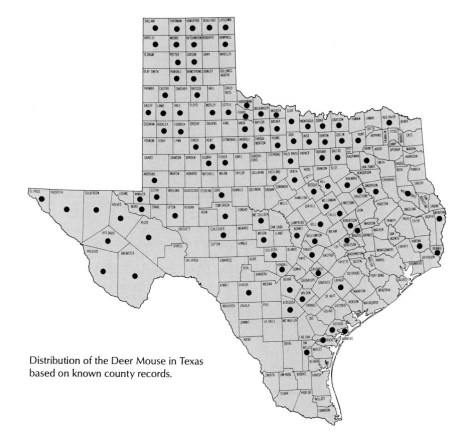

Distribution of the Deer Mouse in Texas based on known county records.

They are almost strictly nocturnal. Trapping records indicate that they leave their daytime retreats early in the evening and remain abroad until shortly after sun up. They live in underground burrows, in brush piles, or in crevices among rocks. The burrow is simple in design and usually consists of two or three short branches converging from as many surface openings to a single tunnel that slopes steeply to the globular nest chamber which is 7-10 cm in diameter. The nests are hollow balls of dry grass, shredded weed stems, and other available material including rabbit fur and bird feathers.

Deer mice do not hibernate. Their winter activities may include taking up quarters in a pile of logs, from which they venture nightly in search of food. The tracks of one mouse led from the logs to one bush after another in a wandering fashion to the edge of a bare field some 100 m distant and then back to the log pile. The others traveled less than 50 m from their headquarters. Bits of bark, leaves, and seed coats scattered on the snow beneath many of the bushes indicated that they had climbed into them in quest of food. Their food consists of a variety of items, chiefly seeds. In season fruits, bark, roots, and herbage are also consumed and, judging from the behavior of these mice about camps, nearly everything edible is sampled.

Deer mice breed in every month of the year, with peaks in the periods from January through April and from June through November. Litters seem to be born in rapid succession — one captive female produced 11 litters with 42 young in a year. The gestation period varies from 22 to 27 days, averaging about 24 days. Litter size ranges from one to nine, averaging about four. At birth the young are blind, pink, and hairless and weigh from 1.1 to 2.3 g. They become pigmented dorsally in about 24 hours, the pinna of the ear unfolds on the third day, the eyes open in 12-17 days,

174

and they are weaned when about 4 weeks old. The longest observed time of suckling is 37 days. Sexual maturity is reached before the young lose their "blue" juvenile pelage, and females born early in the year may themselves produce young by late summer or early fall.

These mice are often abundant in favorable habitats and then, as with other animals that overpopulate an area, they may become troublesome. Because of their tolerance to a wide variety of habitat conditions and their often large population they are difficult and expensive to control. Since they are an important source of food for many small carnivores, owls, and snakes, the assistance of these animals should be enlisted in keeping the populations of mice within bounds.

NORTHERN ROCK MOUSE
Peromyscus nasutus (J.A. Allen)

Description. A rather large, long-tailed, grayish buff mouse; tail sharply bicolor, brownish to blackish above and white below, slightly tufted, more than 100 mm in length and longer than the combined length of head and body; tops of front and hind feet (including ankles) white; ears about as long as hind feet. External measurements average: total length, 193 mm; tail, 104 mm; hind feet, 22.5 mm. Resembles both *P. boylii* and *P. pectoralis*, but differs from the former in having white ankles like *pectoralis*. Differs from *pectoralis* in having a noticeably longer tail and heavier molars (length of maxillary toothrow 4.5 mm as opposed to less than 4.0 mm). Differs from *P. truei* in grayish buff rather than ochraceous buff upperparts and with smaller ears; differs from

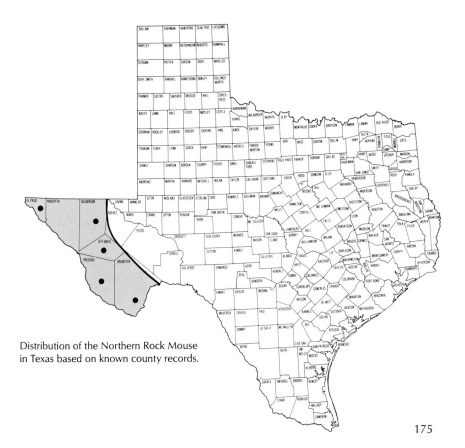

Distribution of the Northern Rock Mouse in Texas based on known county records.

P. attwateri in shorter hind feet (less than 24 mm) and in white rather than dusky ankles.

Distribution. Known in Texas only from the Trans-Pecos, where it has been recorded from mountainous regions of Brewster, Culberson, El Paso, Jeff Davis, and Presidio counties.

Habits. This species is found among boulders on rocky mountain slopes and in rockpiles in Texas madrone and oak associations where the crevices and cracks are covered with a thick layer of leaves. In the Franklin Mountains (El Paso County), the rock mouse is common in rocky areas and talus slopes. *P. boylii* is absent from rocky areas where *nasutus* is abundant, but *boylii* is abundant in adjacent areas with fewer rocks and more vegetation. It appears that *nasutus* prefers rugged, rocky habitat with sparse vegetation.

In captivity the rock mouse is docile and easily handled. It is highly gregarious, and a dozen or more individuals of young and adults of both sexes often crowd into one nest without apparent conflict.

Little information is available on its breeding habits. Pregnant females have been taken in June, July, and August. Vernon Bailey reported capture in New Mexico of a female containing four large fetuses in late July and another in late August with six fetuses. Individuals captured alive in the Franklin Mountains readily bred in captivity and produced several litters of two to six young. The gestation period is about 30 days.

WHITE-ANKLED MOUSE
Peromyscus pectoralis Osgood

Description. A small-eared, long-tailed, white-footed mouse with tarsal joint of hind foot white; pelage moderately long and lax; tail longer than head and body, scantily haired, not sharply bicolor, but darker above than below, and annulations 20-24 per cm; upperparts grayish to wood brown; underparts and feet white; young, bluish gray. External measurements average: total length, 187 mm; tail, 95 mm; hind foot, 22 mm; ear, 16 mm. Weight, 24-39 g. Most easily confused with *P. eremicus*, *P. attwateri*, and *P. boylii*. Distinguished from *P. eremicus* by having proximal part of sole of hind foot hairy rather than naked; mammae in three pairs rather than in two. Differs from *P. boylii* and *P. attwateri* in smaller scales on the tail, and in white, rather than dusky, tarsal joints and in shorter maxillary tooth row (often less than 4 mm).

Distribution. Recorded from most of Trans-Pecos region and northeastward through central part of state to Oklahoma (eastern limits of range along Balcones Escarpment from Bexar County northward to McLennan County).

White-ankled Mouse (*Peromyscus pectoralis*). Photo by John L. Tveten.

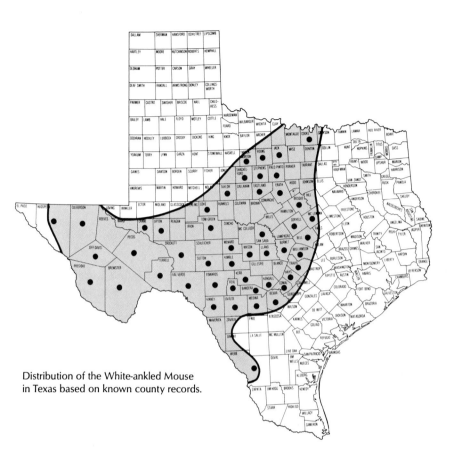

Distribution of the White-ankled Mouse in Texas based on known county records.

Habits. This is another rock-dwelling species, and it often is taken in the same habitat occupied by *P. boylii*. In the Chisos Mountains and again in the Delaware Mountains in Trans-Pecos Texas, they have been caught in the oak-juniper belt in traps set among jumbled boulders, near rock walls, in talus slopes, along rocky outcroppings, and in buildings. Near Austin, white-ankled mice are common in the rocky outcropping where the Colorado River cuts through the Balcones Escarpment; in Kerr County they prefer rocky bluffs along the rivers and creeks. In the Davis Mountains region of Trans-Pecos Texas, they usually are found in the grama-bluestem association. Elsewhere, in our experience, they are associated with rocks in oak-juniper woodlands.

They feed on a variety of seeds, including juniper berries, acorns, and hackberries. Although their diet has not been studied in detail, other seeds, some fruits, and insects probably are taken when available. They readily come to traps baited with rolled oats.

Their breeding habits are not well-known, but the breeding season extends at least from March to October. Pregnant females have been captured in March, April, May, July, August, September, and October, which suggests that several litters may be reared each year. The average litter size is three, ranging from two to five. The gestation period has not been determined, but it is probably about 23 days as in closely related species. Growth and development of the young is not well known.

These mice are abundant in certain localities and may become troublesome in cabins and ranch buildings. They usually can be controlled easily by the use of traps or poisoned grains.

PIÑON MOUSE
Peromyscus truei (Shufeldt)

Description. A moderately large, large-eared, white-footed mouse; tail as long as, or slightly longer than, head and body and scantily haired; upper parts ochraceous buff mixed with dusky giving an overall effect of cinnamon or tawny olive in unworn pelage and wood brown in worn pelage; the pronounced lateral line is ochraceous buff; sides of face and nose grayish; ears dusky; feet and underparts white; tail dark above, white below. External measurements average: total length, 204 mm; tail, 100 mm; hind foot, 22.5 mm; ear, 22.2 mm.

Distribution. In Texas, known from the caprock at the eastern edge of the high plains in Armstrong, Briscoe, and Randall counties and in the Trans-Pecos from the Guadalupe Mountains in Culberson County.

Habits. This species is restricted to rocky situations in cedar forests on the canyon slopes and floors in the Palo Duro Canyon region. Areas in the juniper-mesquite association that have large, massive boulders seem to support the highest populations. Even so, intensive trapping produces few mice. James Tamsitt reported that in 1,803 trap-nights he captured only 25 specimens — a success ratio of 72 trap-nights per mouse caught. In Guadalupe Mountains National Park, the species is rarely found in the juniper and pinyon woodlands.

The food habits of these mice are not well known. In California, specimens examined in midsummer had been eating primarily insects and spiders although by late summer their diet was predominantly acorn mast. In Colorado, the winter diet is primarily juniper berries.

Breeding habits are likewise poorly known. In southwest Colorado, breeding occurs from April through September and in Arizona, from February through November. One specimen captured July 24 in the Guadalupe Mountains of the Trans-Pecos was an adult female pregnant with four embryos. Litter size ranges from three to six, average

Piñon Mouse (*Peromyscus truei*). Photo by John L. Tveten.

four. At birth, the young are hairless and the eyes and ears are closed. Between 2 and 3 weeks of age the eyes and ears open. The body is haired by 2 weeks of age.

Remarks. The Texas population of *P. truei* has had a rather confusing taxonomic history. Frank Blair recognized it as a new species in the *P. truei* group of mice and in 1943 gave it the name *Peromyscus comanche*. Donald Hoffmeister in 1951 placed *comanche* as a subspecies of *Peromyscus nasutus* and 10 years later he and Luis de la Torre transferred both *nasutus* and *comanche* to the largely Mexican species *Peromyscus difficilis*. In 1972 Raymond Lee and associates examined the karyotypes of *comanche* and found them to be identical with those of *Peromyscus truei* and markedly different from those of *Peromyscus difficilis*. Finally, in 1973 one of us (Schmidly) reviewed its systematic status and placed *comanche* as a subspecies of *Peromyscus truei*.

GOLDEN MOUSE
Ochrotomys nuttalli (Harlan)

Description. A medium-sized, golden-colored (rich ochraceous tawny), white-footed mouse with soft, thick pelage; larger than *Reithrodontomys fulvescens* and without grooves on upper incisors; feet white; underparts pale cinnamon buff; tail brownish, darker above than below. External measurements average: total length, 176 mm; tail, 78 mm; hind foot, 19 mm. Weight, 15-25 g.

Distribution. Woodlands of extreme eastern Texas.

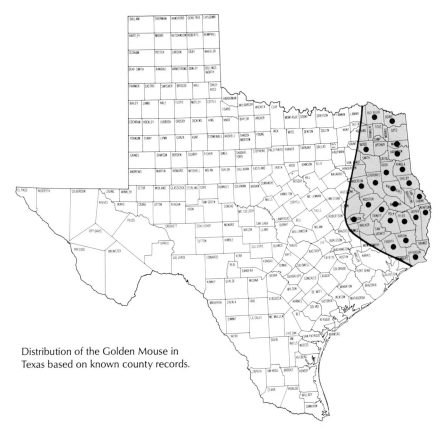

Distribution of the Golden Mouse in Texas based on known county records.

Golden Mouse (*Ochrotomys nuttalli*). Photo by John L. Tveten, courtesy of Texas A&M University Press.

Habits. These small, arboreal mice are adapted to, and occur chiefly in, forested areas. Tangles of trees, vines, and brush seem to be a preferred habitat. Specimens have been trapped on dark, wooded slopes where the mice lived in nests in tangles of grapevines; others were taken in an old pasture overgrown with blackberry, wild grape and a few small trees. Near Bowie, a pair of mice was taken in a hollow, fallen tree in river bottom lands, while near Lufkin, one specimen was trapped in a pile of brush in hammock territory near the edge of the Angelina River bottom.

Their nests are constructed of grasses, Spanish moss, or leaves; lined with shredded plant fibers, or occasionally feathers; and vary in size from the small brood nest about the size of a baseball to the large "communal" nests as big as 20 by 30 cm that may house a half-dozen or more mice. One such nest housed eight mice, all males. Usually the nests are placed in trees or bushes from a few centimeters to 3 m above the ground; occasionally they are on the ground under some protective cover such as a log, a stump, a pile of brush, or they may be in cavities in standing trees.

Invertebrates make up about 50% of their diet. They also eat a variety of seeds including sumac, wild cherry, dogwood, greenbriar, poison ivy, and blackberry.

The breeding season begins in September and extends through winter and spring, with little reproductive activity during summer. The peak breeding season is in winter. Adult females may produce up to three litters annually. The young, ranging in number from two to five (average, three), are born following a gestation period of 25-30 days.

Newborn golden mice weigh about 2.7 g and are reddish with relatively smooth skin. The eyes and ears are closed at birth, but open between 11 and 14 days of age. Weaning is completed at 3 weeks and adult size is attained between the eighth and tenth weeks. The young mice are sexually mature 1-2 months after birth.

NORTHERN PYGMY MOUSE
Baiomys taylori (Thomas)

Description. Smallest of the muroid mice in Texas, with the exception of two harvest mice, *Reithrodontomys humulis* and *Reithrodontomys montanus*, both of which differ in having grooved upper incisors and longer tail. Upperparts grizzled grayish in adults, blackish in juveniles; underparts smoke gray; tail about three times as long as hind foot, sparsely haired and decidedly shorter than head and body. They have a strong, musky odor similar to that of house mice, *Mus musculus*. External measurements average: total length, 98 mm; tail, 38 mm; hind foot, 14.5 mm. Weight, 7-10 g, averaging 8 g.

Distribution. Distributed over the central portions of the state; range excludes Trans-Pecos and eastern Texas. This species is extending its range northward and westward.

Habits. This is a southern species, characteristic of the tropical lowlands of Mexico, that reaches its northern distributional limits in Texas. Early records indicate that *B. taylori* was restricted to the coastal region of eastern Texas and the mesquite-chaparral regions of southern Texas. Since the early twentieth century, the species has consistently extended its range northward and eastward by invading the oak-hickory association, the blackland prairies, the cross-timbers, rolling plains, and the high plains.

These mice have a preference for grassy areas, and they are commonly found in old fields, pastures, and along railroad and highway rights-of-way, where they usually live in close association with cotton rats (*Sigmodon hispidus*) and harvest mice

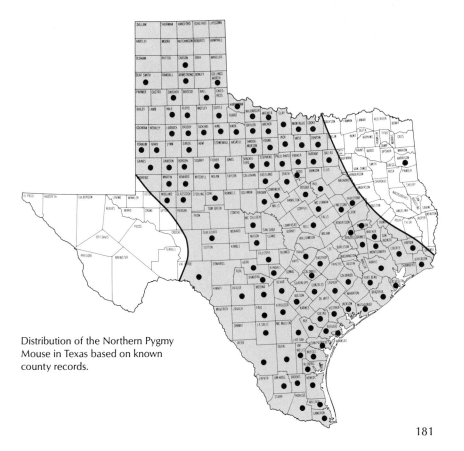

Distribution of the Northern Pygmy Mouse in Texas based on known county records.

181

Northern Pygmy Mouse (*Baiomys taylori*). Photo by R.D. Porter.

(*Reithrodontomys* spp.). If other types of ground cover such as rocks, cactus, and fallen logs are available, the pygmy mouse may be found in areas where grass is relatively sparse.

Pygmy mice live in nests placed in burrows in the ground, beneath fallen logs, among cactus pads, or in thick clumps of grass. The nest is typically a ball of finely shredded grass or cactus fibers with a central cavity and one or two openings. A network of runways or beaten paths leads away from the nest sites beneath the thick mat of dead grass.

The mice feed chiefly on vegetation; seeds are especially well-liked. They are active the year round and do not hibernate; neither do they store food for winter use. Although they are chiefly nocturnal, they have been caught in traps on several occasions in the daytime. They can swim well when necessary, but water is avoided whenever possible because their short fur is easily water-soaked.

The breeding season is nearly year-long — gravid females have been taken from January to October. In captivity, one female gave birth to nine litters in 195 days; another, to eight litters in 221 days. The gestation period is about 20 days. The litters vary in size from one to five, averaging about three. At birth the young are naked, blind, and helpless and weigh about 1 g each. The eyes open in 12-15 days; the mice are weaned in 18-22 days; and sexual maturity is attained at the age of about 60 days.

MEARNS' GRASSHOPPER MOUSE
Onychomys arenicola (Mearns)

Description. A small, "fat-tailed" mouse with pinkish-cinnamon or grayish-buff upperparts and pure white underparts; usually a conspicuous white or grayish tuft at anterior base of ear; nose, cheeks and sides white; tail sparsely haired, more than 30% of total length, from two to 2¹/₂ times as long as hind foot and distinctly bicolor, dark above and white below. Similar to *Onychomys leucogaster*, but smaller, with relatively longer tail, and smaller teeth. Juveniles similar to adults, but upperparts bluish gray. External measurements average: total length, 146 mm; tail, 52 mm; hind foot, 21 mm. Weight of males, 26.5 (24-30) g; females, 25 (22-28) g.

Mearns' Grasshopper Mouse (*Onychomys arenicola*). Photo courtesy of University Calif. Mus. Vert. Zool.

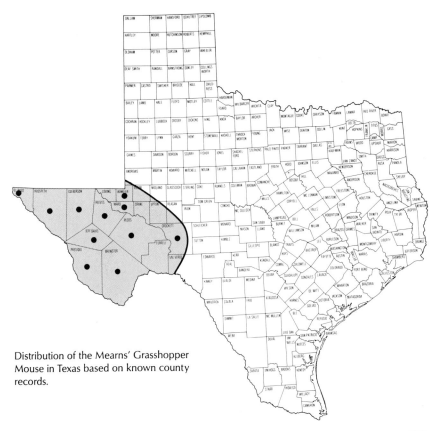

Distribution of the Mearns' Grasshopper Mouse in Texas based on known county records.

Distribution. Throughout the Trans-Pecos (except for the southeastern part) and a few counties east of the Pecos River.

Habits. This mouse chiefly inhabits the low, arid, sandy or gravelly desert areas where vegetation in the form of creosote bush, mesquite, yucca, lechuguilla, condalia, and so forth is sparse and scattered. It lives in burrows of its own or in those it usurps from other small rodents. Like the northern grasshopper mouse, it is relatively rare in most localities.

Its behavior and feeding habits are similar to those outlined for *O. leucogaster*. Breeding begins in late January or early February and continues into September. Gravid females have been captured as early as February 27 and as late as September 5. The litters vary in size from two to seven; average 4.2. Half-grown young have been captured in April, June, July, and August, suggesting that two, or even three, litters are produced each year. The young grow rapidly and females become sexually mature when 7 or 8 weeks of age. A young female can give birth to her first litter at the age of 4 months. The gestation period is 26-35 days.

Remarks. In previous editions, the scientific name for this rodent was reported as *Onychomys torridus*; however, recent genetic work on the species has indicated that formerly, two species have been included under that name. Consequently, the species occurring in Texas has been renamed *O. arenicola*, with *O. torridus* occupying southwestern New Mexico and westward.

NORTHERN GRASSHOPPER MOUSE
Onychomys leucogaster (Wied)

Description. A stout-bodied, short-tailed mouse similar to *O. arenicola* but larger, heavier, and shorter-tailed; upperparts drab brown; the nose, sides, cheeks, and underparts white; tuft at anterior base of ear white and conspicuous; tail usually less than 30% of total length and usually from $1\frac{1}{2}$ to two times as long as hind foot. External measurements average: total length, 164 mm; tail, 42 mm; hind foot, 22 mm. Weight, 27-46 g, occasionally as much as 52 g.

Northern Grasshopper Mouse (*Onychomys leucogaster*). Photo by R.D. Porter.

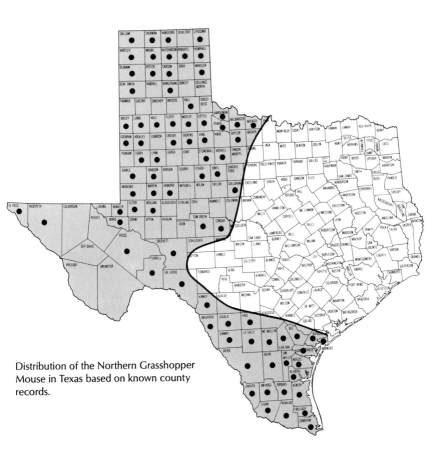

Distribution of the Northern Grasshopper Mouse in Texas based on known county records.

Distribution. Throughout most of western Texas (except the central part of the Trans-Pecos) and the Rio Grande Plains of South Texas.

Habits. These "predatory" mice occur chiefly in association with sandy or powdery soils in grasslands or open brushlands, but they are never very common as compared with other small mammals.

They are wanderers and do not live long in one place. They are reputed to usurp the burrows of other small mammals rather than take the time to construct their own. This is in keeping with their pugnacious disposition. Vernon Bailey attributes to them many of the habits of the weasel and compares one of their calls with the howl of a wolf which "is made with raised nose and open mouth in perfect wolf form." Because of their short legs and chunky body they are not fleet-footed, but they are expert at dodging, twisting, and turning and in close quarters can easily capture and overpower other mice their own size or even larger.

As the name implies, one of their chief food items in season is grasshoppers. In addition, numerous other kinds of insects, scorpions, small mice, and a variety of plants contribute to their diet. Captives are especially fond of raw liver and newborn mice. Vernon Bailey and Charles Sperry report that animal matter makes up nearly 89% of their natural food; plant material comprises only 11%.

The breeding season extends at least from May to October, as judged from pregnancy records. The capture of half-grown young in the dark juvenile pelage from

185

February to September indicates that some breeding occurs throughout much of the year. The bulk of the young are born in May and June, however. The litter varies from two to six; average about four.

The gestation period varies from 32 to 47 days, with the longer periods in lactating females. At birth the young are pink and hairless (except for the prominent vibrissae), and weigh about 2 g each. The eyes and ears are closed, and the tail is characteristically short and thick. Within 3 days the ears unfold, but the eyes remain closed until the 19th or 20th day, at which time the young mice are almost weaned. They are probably evicted from the nest shortly after. Sexual maturity is reached in about 3 months when the mice are still in the soft, gray juvenile pelage.

Because of their fondness for insects and small mice their economic status is either neutral or beneficial.

TAWNY-BELLIED COTTON RAT
Sigmodon fulviventer J.A. Allen

Description. A small to medium sized cotton rat with brownish, buff brown, or fulvous underparts from throat to anus. Dorsal coloration is light brown heavily speckled with dark brown to black, giving a "salt-and-pepper" or "hispid" appearance. The tail is uniformly blackish and the tops of the feet are buff brown.

The tawny-bellied cotton rat is similar in appearance to two other cotton rats that occur in Texas. From the yellow-nosed cotton rat (*S. ochrognathus*), *S. fulviventer* differs in having a rich buffy ventral coloration rather than whitish, a more heavily speckled dorsal coloration, buff-colored tops to the feet rather than grayish, and a uniformly dark colored tail. Also, *S. fulviventer* lacks the tawny colored nose of *S. ochrognathus*. The hispid cotton rat (*S. hispidus*) differs from *S. fulviventer* in having gray or whitish underparts, a bicolored tail that is lighter below than above, grayish tops of the feet, and slightly larger ears and hind feet.

External measurements reported for the holotype of *S. f. dalquesti* from Fort Davis, Texas were: total length, 242 mm; length of tail, 90 mm; hind foot, 28 mm; ear, 18 mm.

Distribution. In the United States known from grassland habitats in southeastern Arizona and southwestern New Mexico to middle Rio Grande valley. In Texas known only from an isolated population near Fort Davis in Jeff Davis County.

Habits. The tawny-bellied cotton rat inhabits grassy areas interspersed with shrubby growth that affords cover and allows dense growth of grasses. In Mexico these rats are associated with bunch grasses in the mesquite-grassland vegetation type. Over their limited range in Arizona and New Mexico, tawny-bellied cotton rats are found in weedy and grassy places in pinyon-juniper-live oak woodland, Mexican oak-pine woodland, and mesquite-yucca-grassland vegetation types, where their runways are hidden in the thick, grassy cover.

In Texas, tawny-bellied cotton rats have been taken in similar habitat at one site near Fort Davis. Within a general area described as a "heavily grazed, level valley plain" with "small, scattered mesquite, catclaw, and a fence line" that protected against livestock grazing, tawny-bellied cotton rats were caught in dense grasses along fencerows and in adjacent grassy areas protected by clumps of mesquite and catclaw. Hispid cotton rats were also caught in these areas.

Of 20 Texas specimens captured in late March, eight were juveniles. Both adult males were in reproductive condition and of the 10 mature females, one was lactating and four were pregnant. Embryo counts revealed litter sizes of three, four, four, and four.

Remarks. Previously unknown in the state, the tawny-bellied cotton rat was first recorded in Texas in the spring of 1991 near Fort Davis by Fred Stangl of Midwestern

State University. This isolated population represents not only a new species of mammal for Texas, but appears to be a new subspecies as well — *S. f. dalquesti*. The extent of this rat's range and population numbers in Texas remain unknown. The brief life history notes available on the Texas specimens are taken from Stangl's paper published in the *Southwestern Naturalist*.

HISPID COTTON RAT
Sigmodon hispidus Say and Ord

Description. A moderately large, robust rat with pattern of last two lower molars S-shaped; tail shorter than head and body, sparsely haired, the annulations and scales clearly visible; ears relatively small and blackish or grayish; pelage coarse and grizzled, the black guard hairs rather stiff (hispid); hind foot with six plantar tubercles and with three middle toes longer than outer two; upperparts grizzled brown; underparts grayish white or buff. External measurements average: total length, 270 mm; tail, 110 mm; hind foot, 31 mm. Weight, 80-150 g.

Distribution. Statewide.

Habits. Normally this rat inhabits tall-grass areas where such grasses as bluestem (*Andropogon*), cordgrass (*Spartina*), or sedges (*Carex*) offer both freedom of movement under a protective canopy and an adequate food supply. In such situations, their runways form a network of interconnecting travelways about 5-8 cm wide. In western Texas, where grassy ground cover is not available, the rats live in dens at the bases of small, low clumps of mesquite in otherwise nearly barren terrain, much after the fashion of white-throated wood rats. Between these two extremes are several types of habitat that may support small populations of cotton rats. Preferred sites are old fields, natural prairie, unmolested rights-of-way for roads and railroads, and other places not subject to flooding and where the vegetation grows rank and tall.

The rats place their nests either in chambers off underground burrows or above ground in dense clumps of grass, piles of brush, or other situations that offer some concealment and protection. The nests are globular, about 12 cm in diameter and composed of shredded grasses and weeds. Underground burrows are from 3-5 cm in

Hispid Cotton Rat (*Sigmodon hispidus*).

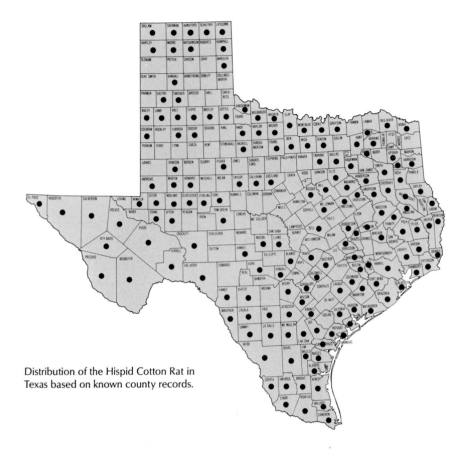

Distribution of the Hispid Cotton Rat in Texas based on known county records.

diameter, simple in design, and seldom longer than 8 m. Occasionally, the rats take over and use the discarded burrows of pocket gophers and moles.

Their food is almost exclusively plant material, but there is some evidence that they feed also on the eggs of ground-nesting birds such as bobwhite and meadow lark. The telltale piles of grasses, sedges, and herbs cut into lengths of 5-8 cm and piled at their feeding stations along the runways give a good clue to their natural foods. In captivity, they are fond of most greens, rolled oats, corn, apples, potatoes, dog biscuits, and so forth. They are active the year round and do not store food for winter use.

Cotton rats are prolific and produce several litters of two to 10 young, averaging about five, a year. Captive females have given birth to as many as nine litters a year; data from wild-caught rats likewise indicate a nearly yearlong breeding season at least in the warmer parts of their range. The gestation period is approximately 27 days. Females frequently breed again immediately after partus. At birth the young are hairless, for the most part, pink, blind, and weigh about 5 g. They develop rapidly. The eyes open in about 36 hours, the incisors erupt on the fifth or sixth day, and the young rats are usually weaned when 15 or 20 days old. They can be successfully weaned, however, as soon as the teeth have erupted (5-6 days). Sexual maturity is reached in about 40 days when the animals are still in juvenile pelage; 6-month-old rats are indistinguishable externally from adults.

Cotton rats are subject to violent fluctuations in numbers. The last serious outbreak in Texas occurred in 1958 when millions of these rodents seemed to appear from nowhere and caused serious losses to farm crops, particularly peas, peanuts, watermelons, and cauliflower — as much as 90% loss in some instances.

Normally, cotton rats occur in moderate to low populations in all parts of the state where ground cover is present. The size of the population is correlated with the amount of suitable habitat, and suitable habitat in turn is correlated with the amount of rainfall. Thus, in the marginal parts of its range this rat is attuned to climatic changes and the population is subject to violent fluctuations. In fact, peak populations are recorded about every 10 years in central Texas. Records reveal a severe outbreak in 1919. Lesser peaks were reported in the late 1930s and again in the late 1940s. During the 7-year drought that began about 1950, cotton rat populations in central Texas were low because there were few places where they could live in numbers. Ground cover was sparse or even absent over most of their range west of a line drawn from Fort Worth to San Antonio and Corpus Christi.

When the rains came in 1957 they were a blessing, not only to the ranchers, but also to the cotton rat. Ground cover increased, providing better cover and more nutritious green food, and the cotton rat population took off. More of the youngsters in each litter could survive and produce young of their own. Because green food was available in quantity during most of 1957 and well into 1958, females were able to produce more and larger litters than normally. By late May 1958, they were found in unbelievable numbers in especially favorable areas. Estimates were as high as several hundred rats per hectare.

This rate of increase sounds fantastic, but is not difficult to comprehend when one is aware of the reproductive potential of these rats. Let's repeat some data for emphasis. An adult female may breed throughout the year in Texas when conditions are favorable. She may produce as many as nine litters of 10 young each (normally less). The gestation period is only 4 weeks, and the female breeds again within a few hours after giving birth. Young females are sexually mature in 40 days and can be mothers at the tender age of 68 days and grandmothers at 136 days! Thus, if we assume a new generation of cotton rats every 68 days, a female could be a great-great-great-grandmother at the age of 1 year and be the ancestor of about 15,500 cotton rats. If this same rate of reproduction were extended for only three more generations and all survived, the grand total of offspring from the original female would be more than $3^1/_2$ million!

Although this potential is always present in cotton rats, it is seldom realized because of death due to predators, disease, lack of suitable or sufficient food, accidents, smaller litters, fewer litters a year, and so on. But when conditions are just right, the population "explodes," and we are hip deep in cotton rats before we know it.

Fortunately, every eruption is followed by a crash in the population that is brought on by a combination of factors, principally disease. Predators such as coyotes, bobcats, hawks, owls, and certain snakes take their toll, but the main killer is disease. As the rats increase in numbers, the animals become more and more crowded and provide more contacts for the rapid spread of disease. At the same time, the virulence of the disease increases until finally the crash occurs and the population is low once again.

YELLOW-NOSED COTTON RAT
Sigmodon ochrognathus Bailey

Description. Similar to *S. hispidus* but paler, and with the snout distinctly orange or rusty; tail hairier and distinctly bicolor, nearly black above, grayish buff below; underparts grayish white. External measurements average: total length, 259 mm; tail, 114 mm; hind foot, 28 mm. Weight, 50-80 g, occasionally as much as 112 g.

Yellow-nosed Cotton Rat (*Sigmodon ochrognathus*). Photo by John L. Tveten.

Distribution. Isolated at higher elevations in the Chisos Mountains, Big Bend National Park region, Brewster County; Davis Mountains, Jeff Davis County; and the Sierra Vieja, Presidio County.

Habits. Yellow-nosed cotton rats live primarily on rocky slopes with scattered bunches of grass. In the Chisos Mountains their runways have been located in lodged needle grass in Laguna Meadow at the foot of Emory Peak. There, the rats occupied an area of about 40 ha. Their runways radiated from underground dens, some of which were under clumps of agaves; others were among the roots of large junipers. A surface nest under a pile of dead blades of agaves was composed of dry grasses and long fibers from the agave plants. It was about 12 cm in outside diameter. Other nests have been found beneath the dead lower leaves of sotol.

These rats seem to be active mainly in the daytime, as confirmed by trapping records from 1944. In spite of the fact that the vegetation appeared to be too sparse to offer concealment by day, no individuals were captured in night trapping.

The breeding season appears to extend from March to October. Young about 3 weeks old have been captured in early May, late June, and early November which suggests that several litters may be reared each season. The gestation period is approximately 35 days.

At birth, young cotton rats weigh 4.5-6.6 g and are haired. They gain about 2 g in weight each day and reach sexual maturity by 45 days. Captive females have produced offspring at 71 days of age.

WHITE-THROATED WOODRAT
Neotoma albigula Hartley

Description. A medium-sized woodrat with large ears, bulging black eyes and relatively short, distinctly bicolor tail (grayish brown above, white below), densely covered with short hairs; throat, and usually breast and chin, with hairs white to base; upperparts dull pinkish buff, brightest along sides, thinly suffused with blackish; underparts and feet white. External measurements average: total length, 328 mm; tail, 152 mm; hind foot, 34 mm. Weight, 136-294 g.

Distribution. Found in Panhandle and broken country south of Red River to Bexar and Uvalde counties, and westward throughout much of the southwestern part of state.

Habits. This woodrat is characteristic of the brush lands of the southwestern deserts. The availability of such desert shrub vegetation as prickly pear, cholla cactus, mesquite, sotol, lechuguilla, and creosote bush which afford shelter for their houses, seems to affect their abundance more than the nature of the terrain. Cholla cactus and prickly pear offer preferred home sites because they supply not only protection but also food and water. Occasionally, their houses are built in the open or in sparse vegetation. In rocky situations the associated cracks and crevices afford the usual den site.

The house is a crude cone of sticks, cactus joints, and other rubbish which surrounds the nest proper — a compact, cup-shaped structure composed of shredded dry leaves, blades of grass, and weed stems. Access to the house is by means of openings near the base to which well-worn trails lead. Frequently, especially in localities where building materials are scarce, the house is supplemented by a system of underground burrows.

Although several houses may occupy a small, desirable patch of cacti, the rats are not social creatures. Only one animal or a female and her young occupy each house. Their home range or feeding territories overlap considerably, but to each rat his house is a personal affair and thus is not shared.

The menu of these rats consists of a variety of desert plants, but the cactus family led the list of more than 30 items found in the stomachs of 360 rats examined. Mesquite and forbs were next in preference. Grasses constituted less than 5% of their fare, but small quantities were regularly consumed. The amount of animal material consumed (ants, birds, beetles, and grasshoppers) was less than 1% of the total diet. The habit of storing food is not well developed in these rats, but small quantities of food are usually found at each house. Drinking water is not required because of the high water content in their choice of foods.

The breeding season is restricted largely to the period from January to September. At least two and possibly three or more litters of two or three young each may be

White-throated Woodrat (*Neotoma albigula*). Photo by R.D. Porter.

191

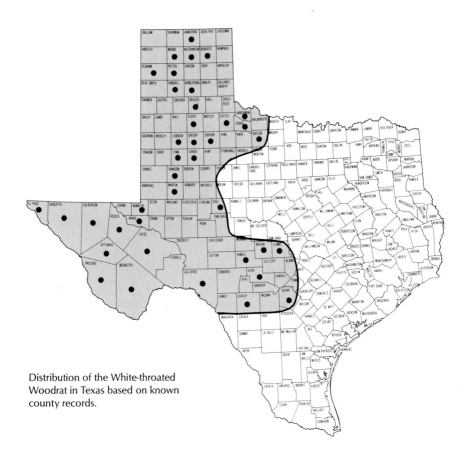

Distribution of the White-throated Woodrat in Texas based on known county records.

reared during this period. The period of gestation is approximately 38 days. At birth the young are helpless, weigh about 11 g, and are about twice the size of newborn house rats. As is the case with other woodrats and many related species of mice, the young ones have specially developed front teeth that permit them to grasp the nipples of the mother and to be dragged along behind her, skidding and bouncing along on their backs, when she leaves the nest. They grow rapidly; the ears open on the 13th to 15th day, the eyes open on the 15th to 19th day, and they are weaned when 62-72 days old. When about 6 months old they are almost indistinguishable from their elders.

The spiny fortress in which the house is located, coupled with the nocturnal habits of the rats, makes them relatively safe from most predators. Owls catch a few individuals, as do coyotes, bobcats, ringtails, and weasels but their chief natural enemies appear to be the large desert gopher snake and the rattlesnake, both of which can enter the houses of the rats with impunity.

EASTERN WOODRAT
Neotoma floridana (Ord)

Description. Large rat with long, round, tapering, scantily haired tail, large ears, and bulging, black eyes. Upperparts creamy buff to buffy gray, clearest along sides; underparts and feet white; tail distinctly bicolor, white below and brownish above. External measurements average: total length, 369 mm; tail, 160 mm; hind foot, 40 mm. Weight, 200-350 g.

192

Distribution. Eastern one-third of Texas west to Wichita, Bell, and Edwards counties; south to Victoria County.

Habits. The wide range occupied by the eastern woodrat, encompassing habitats ranging from swamplands along the lower Mississippi River, through forested uplands, to the arid plains of eastern Colorado, is reflected in its geographic variation and in the correlated differences in habits. In the mixed hammock and river bottom associations in eastern Texas, these rats do not construct surface nests but rather, live in burrows at the bases of trees. In the upland post oak association in east-central Texas, they normally use underground burrows but occasionally resort to a combination surface house and underground burrow or a large surface house built at the base of a tree or against a fallen log with no associated burrow. In central Texas (Kerr County) they frequently live in rocky canyon walls.

In localities where underground dens are the fashion, the rats do not hesitate to take over burrows dug by other and larger animals. In one such den in Brazos County the large nest, located about a meter from the entrance, was composed of dried broom sedge grasses, leaves, and small twigs.

The diet of eastern woodrats consists almost exclusively of vegetable matter which provides both food and water. In east-central Texas they feed on acorns, yaupon berries, and the leaves of oaks, yaupon, French mulberry, green briar, peppervine, rattan, and hackberry. Many of these items were garnered by the rats well above ground, which indicates that most of their foraging is done in the crowns of the trees and shrubs.

The breeding season extends from January to September in Texas. Litter size ranges from one to five (average, two) and up to three litters may be produced annually. The gestation period is about 33 days. Newborn woodrats are blind, deaf, naked, and weigh only 15 g. The eyes open at about 15 days of age, and weaning takes

Eastern Woodrat (*Neotoma floridana*). Photo by John L. Tveten.

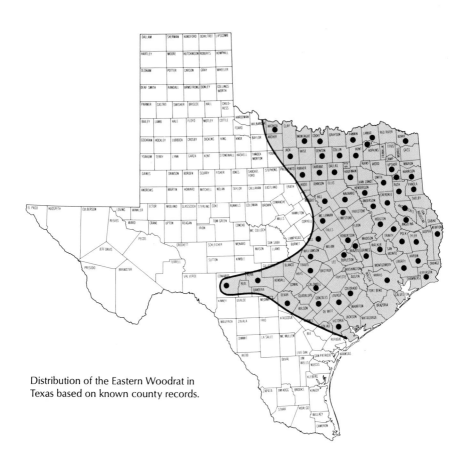

Distribution of the Eastern Woodrat in
Texas based on known county records.

place around the twentieth day. Woodrats do not reach adult size until they are
about 8-9 months of age, and most females do not breed until they are about
1 year old.

The home range is rather limited; the animals usually stay close to the home den.
Studies suggest that 85 m is an exceptional distance for them to travel in their foraging
activities. Also, they are more or less colonial to the extent that several rats will establish themselves in a relatively restricted locality. In one instance 35 to 50 rats lived in a
180 m distance along a favorable gully.

Since these rats usually inhabit wooded or brushy lands, they seldom come into
close contact with man and conflict but little, if at all, with his economy. They are
preyed upon by owls, skunks, foxes, and other flesh-eaters.

MEXICAN WOODRAT

Neotoma mexicana Baird

Description. Medium-sized, about as large as the white-throated woodrat but
white hairs of entire underparts usually buffy basally, not white to roots; first upper
molar with deep anterointernal re-entrant angle; upperparts grayish buff, moderately
darkened over back by blackish hairs; tail brownish above, white below. External measurements average: total length, 300 mm; tail, 125 mm; hind foot, 28 mm. Weight,
140-185 g.

194

Distribution. Known only from Trans-Pecos Texas, where it occurs in mountainous regions of Brewster, Culberson, Hudspeth, Jeff Davis, and Presidio counties.

Habits. These rats frequent rimrocks, canyon walls, and other rocky areas where they establish themselves in cracks and crevices. Into these retreats they carry considerable quantities of rubbish with which to build their nests. Preferring to construct their dens among the cracks and crevices of boulders and other rocky situations, these woodrats do not build elaborate, above ground nests as do other woodrats. Where rocky retreats are not available they construct houses about the roots of trees, in hollow logs, and in piles of logs, or they may take up residence in deserted or little-used cabins. Where they occupy dens among the rocks, their presence is usually evidenced not only by the piles of rubbish at the entrances but also by copious deposits of elongated, capsule-shaped fecal pellets on rocky shelves or in niches in the rocks. Seemingly, they establish regularly used sites for defecation.

Their food consists of a variety of plants, including green vegetation, nuts, berries, acorns, and fungi. Much of their range is above the limits of growth of cactus, so these plants do not figure importantly in their diet although, if available, they are eaten with relish.

The breeding season of this species extends from early spring through summer in the Trans-Pecos. In Colorado, nearly all adult females produce two litters in quick succession. Litter size for adult females is two to five (average 3.4); that for young females averages 2.4. The gestation period ranges from 31 to 34 days. At birth the young rats weigh 9-12 g. Growth is rapid and young females reach sexual maturity in about a month. Females born in April and May often produce litters of their own in June and July while they are still partly or wholly in the gray, juvenile pelage. Young males, however, do not become sexually mature until the following year when they are 8 or 9 months old.

Since the range of these rats is confined largely to mountainous areas, the rats ordinarily do not conflict seriously with man's economy but they may rifle mountain cabins and the camps of vacationers.

SOUTHERN PLAINS WOODRAT
Neotoma micropus Baird

Description. A large, gray-colored rat with large ears and relatively short, heavy, sparsely-haired tail. Differs from *Neotoma floridana*, to which it is most closely related and which may occur in the same area, in gray, often bluish-gray, dorsal coloration. Upperparts pale drab, mixed with blackish hairs along the back; tail blackish above, grayish below; underparts and feet white. External measurements average: total length, 351 mm; tail, 163 mm; hind foot, 41 mm. Weight, (males) 272-310 g; (females) 204-243 g.

Distribution. Found in western two-thirds of state eastward to Johnson County in north and Gulf Coast in south.

Habits. This rat is characteristic of the brushlands in the semi-arid region between the timberlands and the arid deserts to the west. Unlike other woodrats, it is rarely associated with rocks or cliffs; rather, it is usually found associated with cactus or some of the thorny desert shrubs. It is at home in thickets of cacti, mesquite, or thorn bush where it constructs a house of sticks, joints of cactus, thorns, and other readily available material. Frequently, an underground burrow system is added, particularly in localities where building materials are not abundant. These houses may be a meter or more high with two or more openings near the base to which well-worn trails lead through and over the spiny vegetation. So well protected are these rats by their spiny fortresses that, when at home, they seldom are molested by larger animals.

Southern Plains Woodrat (*Neotoma micropus*). Photo by John L. Tveten.

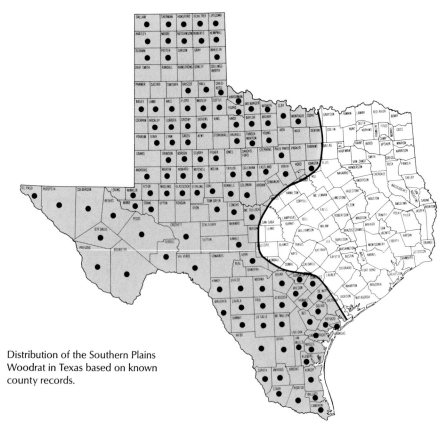

Distribution of the Southern Plains
Woodrat in Texas based on known
county records.

Their food consists almost entirely of vegetation; the thick blades of the prickly pear and the juicy fruits of many species of cactus are favored items. Specific items include the thick basal parts of the leaves of sotol, blades of agaves, beans and pods of mesquite, and acorns. Their food also supplies the necessary water.

The breeding season is restricted to early spring and there is some evidence that the species is monestrous and produces only one litter a year. The usual number of young per litter is three, but ranges from two to four. The gestation period is about 33 days. At birth the young weigh about 10 g, but growth is rapid. They are weaned when about 30 days old and at the age of 3 months are nearly full-grown and weigh about 85% as much as adults. At the age of 300 days they are sexually mature.

Under suitable conditions the population density may become high, at which times the rats may compete seriously with livestock and big game animals for forage. However, they ordinarily are not serious pests.

NORWAY RAT*
Rattus norvegicus (Berkenhout)

Description. Similar to the roof rat but larger and chunkier; tail shorter than length of head and body. External measurements average: total length, 440 mm; tail, 205 mm; hind foot, 46 mm. Weight, 400-500 g.

Distribution. Widespread in Texas but not so common in the southern half of the state as the roof rat.

Habits. The Norway, or brown, rat lives both as a commensal in close association with man and in the feral state, chiefly where vegetation is tall and rank and affords adequate protection. For example, the marshy lands on Galveston Island off the coast of Texas offer ideal habitat for them. As a commensal this rat lives principally in basements, on the ground floor, or in burrows under sidewalks or outbuildings. They appear to be most common about feed stores, chicken houses, and garbage dumps. Although more at home on the ground, these rats are adept at climbing and have been

Norway Rat (*Rattus norvegicus*). Photo courtesy of U.S. Fish and Wildlife Service.

observed traveling along telephone wires from one building to another. In places they become exceedingly numerous and destructive.

They feed on a variety of items including both plant and animal materials. All sorts of garbage appear to be welcome, but their main stay is plant material. Grains of various sorts are highly prized. When established around poultry houses, they feed extensively on eggs and young chickens. They even have been known to kill lambs and young pigs!

These rats are prolific breeders. The gestation period varies from 21 to 23 days and the number of young from two to 14, averaging seven or eight. At birth they are blind, naked, and helpless. They grow rapidly; their eyes open in 14-17 days and they are weaned when 3 or 4 weeks old. There is no delimited breeding season, but there is a tendency for a slow-up in reproduction during fall and winter. The life span is reported to be 2-3 years.

Although these rats are preyed upon by a number of animals including the spotted skunk and the barn owl, as well as house cats, these predators often are not able to keep the rat population in check. Considerable destruction of property and foodstuffs can take place where rats are abundant. In addition, they constitute a menace to public health. They are known to be reservoirs of bubonic plague (transmitted to man by the bite of a flea or other insect), endemic typhus fever, ratbite fever, and a few other dreaded diseases. Because of this it is commonly said that Norway and roof rats are more dangerous than lions or tigers! Every effort should be made to exterminate them when they are found on your premises, and it is advisable to ratproof garbage cans and all buildings to prevent their entrance.

ROOF RAT*
Rattus rattus (Linnaeus)

Description. A blackish (or brownish), medium-sized, slender rat with long, naked, scaly tail; tail usually longer than head and body but not always so. External measurements average: total length, 370 mm; tail, 190 mm; hind foot, 36 mm. Weight, up to 200 g.

Distribution. Common over most of Texas, especially in towns.

Habits. Roof rats are largely commensals and live in close association with man. They seldom become established as feral animals as do the Norway rats; however, in Lavaca County they have been found throughout the county, in the towns, and on the farms. They inhabited grocery and drug stores, warehouses, feed stores, and poultry houses and were very common in cotton gins and associated grain warehouses. On the farms they lived in barns and corncribs. They may live near the ground, but usually they frequent the attics, rafters, and crossbeams of the buildings. They make typical runways along pipes, beams or wires, up and down the studding, or along the horizontal ceiling joists, often leaving a dark-colored layer of grease and dirt to mark their travelways. Like the Norway rat, the roof rat is largely nocturnal and only where populations are relatively high does one see them frequently in the daytime. There is some indication that the larger and more aggressive Norway rat is supplanting the roof rat in many parts of the United States. In the southern United States, however, the roof rat is by far the more common of the two.

They accept a wide variety of food items, including grains, meats, and almost any item that has nutritive value.

Roof rats breed throughout the year, with two peaks of production — in February and March and again in May and June. The period of least activity is in July and August.

The gestation period is approximately 21 days, and the number of young per litter averages almost seven. The young rats at birth are naked, blind, and nearly helpless. They mature rather rapidly, are weaned when about 3 weeks old, and are able to reproduce when approximately 3 months old. In Texas, young females with a head and body length of 125 mm were sexually mature. Like the Norway rat, the roof rat is destructive to property and foodstuffs. Also, it plays an important part in the transmission of such human diseases as endemic typhus, ratbite fever, and bubonic plague.

HOUSE MOUSE*
Mus musculus Linnaeus

Description. A small, scaly-tailed mouse with a distinct notch in the cutting surface of upper incisors (seen best in side view); hair short; ears moderately large and naked; upperparts ochraceous, suffused with black; belly buffy white, or buffy, usually without speckling and with slaty underfur; yellowish flank line usually present; tail brownish with black tip, not distinctly bicolor, but paler on underside; ears pale brown, feet drab or buffy, tips of toes white. Mammae in four or five pairs. External measurements average: total length, 169 mm; tail, 93 mm; hind foot, 18 mm. Weight of adults, 17-25 g.

Distribution. Widely distributed over Texas, particularly in human dwellings and outbuildings.

Habits. Although not native to North America the house mouse, since its early accidental introduction at most of our seaport towns, has become widespread throughout the United States and occurs either as a commensal or feral animal in practically all parts of the United States. As commensal animals, house mice live in close association with man — in his houses, outbuildings, stores, and other structures. Where conditions permit, feral mice may be found in fields, along watercourses, and in other places where vegetation is dense enough to afford concealment. These feral animals make runways through the grass similar to those of *Microtus* or *Baiomys*, or they may utilize runways made by cotton rats and other meadow-inhabiting species. In the agricultural regions where irrigation is practiced house mice often are found in the vegetation along irrigation ditches, sometimes sharing common runways with native mice. Along the Rio Grande in Texas the patches of cane often are honeycombed with the runways of these mice. At

House Mouse (*Mus musculus*). Photo by John L. Tveten, courtesy of Texas A&M University Press.

one locality along this river several hundred trap-nights yielded only house mice which suggested that these animals had evicted the native mice from the area.

Although largely nocturnal, house mice are moderately active during the day, chiefly in their quest for food. In the wild they feed on a variety of plant material, including seeds, green stems, and leaves. Alfalfa hay, either in shocks or in stacks, affords an ideal source of food supply and, consequently, it is frequently infested with these mice. As commensals, house mice feed on practically any type of food suitable for the use of man or beast. They are particularly obnoxious around granaries, feed houses, and stores and may do considerable damage in destroying or contaminating food supplies intended for human consumption. In addition they will feed on such animal matter as insects and meat when available.

These mice are exceedingly prolific breeders; as many as 13 litters can be produced in one year. The number of young per litter averages about six. The gestation period is approximately 19 days, varying from 18 to 20. At birth the young mice are nearly naked with their eyes and ears closed. They develop rapidly; at the age of 3 weeks they are fully weaned and at the age of 4 weeks some of the young females are ready to assume family duties, although the average age of sexual maturity is about 35 days in females and 60 days in males. With commensals, breeding occurs throughout the year although it is somewhat curtailed in the colder months. In the wild state breeding appears to be restricted to the period from early June to late fall.

Although these mice are destructive when allowed to run free, they are widely used in laboratories as subjects for biological, genetic, and medical studies. When ranging free, however, they do a considerable amount of damage although they are not nearly so troublesome as the introduced rat. Mice can be controlled in houses relatively easily with snap traps.

MEXICAN VOLE
Microtus mexicanus (Saussure)

Description. A small mouse with short tail, brown color, and only four mammary glands; tail usually less than 35 mm in length, less than twice as long as hind foot; pelage long and fluffy; upperparts dull umber brown, underparts buffy gray, feet and tail brownish gray. External measurements average: total length, 141 mm; tail, 32 mm; hind foot, 21 mm. Weight, 29-48 g.

Distribution. Restricted in Texas to the higher parts of the Guadalupe Mountains in Culberson County.

Habits. In the Guadalupe Mountains of western Texas these mice live in colonies in the grassy openings of the yellow pine forest, especially in the vicinity of old logs that are partly decayed and well-bedded in the soil. Their numerous, well-defined runways meander through the tall grass, radiating chiefly from the logs under which the mice live and rear their families. They also occur on open ridges where their runways wind about among stones, under shinnery oaks, and even into the edge of dry woods.

Their globular nests of dried grasses and herbs are placed in dense clumps of vegetation above ground, in hollowed-out places under logs, or in special underground chambers off their burrows. One located under a log was cup-shaped, rather than globular, about 10 cm in diameter, and contained four small mice.

Trapping records indicate that these mice are more active in the daytime than are most small mammals, especially in places where adequate ground cover offers concealment. More than 90% of a series trapped in the Guadalupe Mountains were caught in the daytime although the traps were kept set day and night.

Mexican Vole (*Microtus mexicanus*). Photo by John L. Tveten.

Their food is almost entirely vegetation — the green parts of grasses and herbs in summer and the basal portions, roots, bulbs, and bark in winter. There is no evidence that they store food other than the small piles of cut vegetation seen along their trails and at their feeding stations.

Breeding probably continues through most of the year with an interval of about 30-40 days between litters. Gravid females have been trapped in every month from May to October, inclusive. The size of litters, based on embryo counts, ranges from two to five, averaging three. At birth the young are nearly naked, blind, and helpless. They develop rapidly as indicated by the records of young females in the "black" juvenile pelage, weighing slightly more than 20 g, that were sexually mature and gravid. Such mice were probably not more than 6 weeks old.

In Texas, these mice are restricted to the high parts of the Guadalupe Mountains and are of no economic importance except as for food for fur-bearers and other flesh-eaters. Their remains have been identified in droppings of gray fox, bobcat, badger, coyote, and skunk.

PRAIRIE VOLE

Microtus ochrogaster (Wagner)

Description. A dark (brownish or blackish) mouse with tail less than twice as long as hind foot, ears almost hidden in long, lax fur, and only five plantar tubercles; underparts tinged with buff. External measurements average: total length, 146 mm; tail, 34 mm; hind foot, 20 mm. Weight, 30-50 g.

Distribution. Known in Texas only from Hardin County in southeastern Texas, and Hansford and Lipscomb counties in the extreme northern Panhandle.

Habits. Prairie voles for the most part inhabit tall-grass prairies. They live in colonies, utilizing underground burrows and surface runways under lodged vegetation for concealment and protection. Their burrows are said to be shallow but complex in their ramifications and to contain large storage chambers. In farming regions they frequently take up winter quarters in shocks of corn and other small grains which offer both food and protection. Their nests are rather large structures, averaging about 20 by 10 by 10 cm in length, width, and height and may be placed either above ground or in underground chambers about 12 cm below the surface. Small hillocks of earth and pieces of grass at the entrances of burrows often indicate the presence of underground nests.

Their food is almost entirely vegetable matter including green parts of plants, seeds, bulbs, and bark, much of which they store for winter use. They also seem to relish flesh and feed on their own kind caught and killed by traps.

Their breeding habits are not well-known. They probably breed throughout the year. Gravid females have been captured in the winter months of November, January, and February. The main season, however, is in spring and summer. Apparently each breeding female produces several litters a year, the size of which varies from two to six and averages about four. At birth the young are blind, nearly naked, and helpless. They mature rather rapidly and are capable of reproducing in their first year.

Remarks. Previously, this vole was known in Texas on the basis of a single specimen captured at Sour Lake (Hardin County) in 1902. No additional specimens have since been encountered at this locality; however, eight specimens recently were recorded by the late J. Knox Jones, Jr., and his students at Texas Tech University from two counties (Hansford and Lipscomb) in the northern Panhandle. It is probable that this species is extirpated from southeastern Texas but a small, relic population still survives in the northern Texas Panhandle.

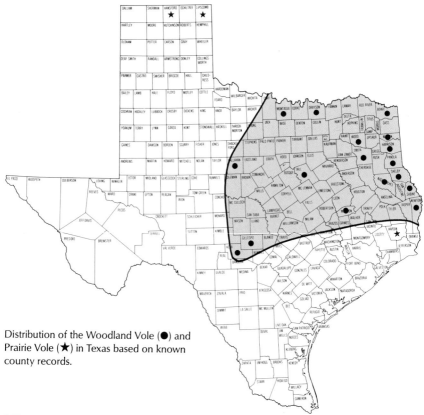

Distribution of the Woodland Vole (●) and Prairie Vole (★) in Texas based on known county records.

WOODLAND VOLE
Microtus pinetorum (Le Conte)

Description. A small mouse with short, dense, glossy fur and short tail; five tubercles on sole of hind foot; two pairs of mammary glands, inguinal in position; upperparts dull chestnut tinged with black; underparts tinged with cinnamon; tail slightly darker above than below. Juveniles plumbeous gray, tinged with chestnut. External measurements average: total length, 135 mm; tail, 25 mm; hind foot, 18 mm. Weight, 25-45 g.

Distribution. Found in eastern and central parts of state west to Callahan, Kerr, and Gillespie counties.

Habits. These mice occur largely in woodland areas where ground cover in the form of leaf litter and lodged grasses offers suitable protection. They are rarely, if ever, found westward in the zone of sparse rainfall. This fact seems to correlate well with their fondness for burrowing just under the surface of the ground, much after the fashion of moles. Although they sometimes use surface runways in grassy areas, they are more inclined to spend their time in underground galleries that they dig for themselves or usurp from moles, short-tailed shrews, or other small mammals. Their burrows are about 4 cm in diameter and seldom more than 7-10 cm beneath the surface of the ground. The normal home range of individuals appears to be about one-tenth of a hectare.

The nest is globular in shape, constructed mainly of dead grasses, leaves, and other vegetation and usually placed in a special chamber in the ground. Occasionally, it is located under a partly buried log or among the roots of a stump. Two or more passages usually lead from it to the surface, thereby providing avenues of escape should the occupants be molested.

The food of these mice is largely roots and tubers. Specific items include peanuts, tuberous roots of violets, berries of red haw, bark from the roots of several kinds of trees, and shrubs and roots of several grasses. In their stores have been found acorns,

Woodland Vole (*Microtus pinetorum*). Photo by John L. Tveten.

nuts of various kinds, and tuberous roots of several species of herbs and grasses. Due to their subterranean habits, these mice rarely sit up to eat. Instead, the food is held pressed against the floor of the burrow and eaten at leisure.

The breeding season extends at least from February to October, and may continue through the winter. During the breeding period an adult female may give birth to as many as four litters of two to four young each. At birth the young ones are blind and naked and weigh slightly more than 2 g. In about 1 week they are well-furred; the eyes open in 9-12 days; and they are weaned when about 17 days old. They begin to acquire adult pelage at about 4 weeks of age. The gestation period is reported as 24 days.

In orchards these mice may become so abundant as to cause considerable damage by girdling the roots and killing the trees, but otherwise they are not of much economic importance. Predators include barn owls, hawks, rat snakes, gray foxes, opossums, mink, and weasels.

COMMON MUSKRAT
Ondatra zibethicus (Linnaeus)

Description. A large, brownish, aquatic, scaly-tailed rodent; feet and toes fringed with short, stiff hairs and toes of hind feet partly webbed; tail about as long as head and body, nearly naked, scaly, and compressed laterally; fur dense; eyes and ears small; upperparts brown to black, sides chestnut to hazel; underparts tawny brown, usually

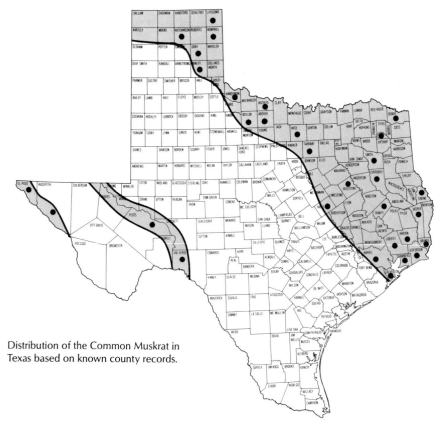

Distribution of the Common Muskrat in Texas based on known county records.

Common Muskrat (*Ondatra zibethicus*). Photo by John L. Tveten.

with a white area on chin. External measurements average: total length, 516 mm; tail, 240 mm; hind foot, 74 mm. Weight, (males) 923 g; (females) 839 g.

Distribution. Occurs only in suitable aquatic habitats in northern, southeastern, and southwestern parts of the state.

Habits. Muskrats are principally marsh inhabitants; creeks, rivers, lakes, drainage ditches, and canals support small populations in places where requisite food and shelter are available. In the interior areas shallow, freshwater marshes with clumps of cattails interspersed among bulrushes, sedges, and other marsh vegetation support the heaviest populations; in coastal areas, the brackish marshes that support good stands of three-square grass (a sedge, *Scirpus*) are most attractive. Such marshes with a stabilized water depth of 15-60 cm seem to offer optimum living conditions.

In marshes, the muskrats live in dome-shaped houses or lodges constructed of marsh vegetation. Access to the inner chamber usually is gained by means of two or more underwater openings, the "plunge holes" of trapper parlance. Such houses are usually 60 cm or more in diameter at water level, and project 50-60 cm above the water. They seem to be of two types: (1) those used for feeding only, in which case the floor may be submerged in water, and (2) those used for dens or resting places. Frequently, several animals — usually members of one family — occupy one lodge. Conspicuous travelways radiate from the houses and lead to the forage areas. In canals, creeks, rivers, and so forth, where house construction would be out of the question, the muskrats burrow into the banks and live below ground. Entrance to such burrows also is usually by means of underwater openings. Dens that have been excavated were about 10 cm in diameter and 2-3 m in length and usually terminated in an enlarged nest chamber.

The food of muskrats is varied, principally vegetation. Where available the tender basal parts of cattails and rushes are the main reliance. In the brackish marshes of Texas and Louisiana a sedge is the chief item on their menu. Normally, the animals have well-established feeding stations at the edges of travel lanes or in feeding lodges to which pieces of food are brought to be consumed at leisure. The animals are active throughout the year and store no food for winter use. At that season, when nutritious food is scarce or made unavailable by freezing weather, the rats will eat almost anything, including parts of their lodges and nests, dead fish, frogs, wood, and so forth, or they may turn cannibalistic and prey upon their own kind.

In southeastern Texas, the animals breed throughout the year. Breeding females produce two or more litters a year, ranging in size from one to 11 and averaging about six. The gestation period is from 22 to 30 days. At birth the young are blind, almost naked, and helpless and weigh about 21 g. The pelage develops rapidly and by the end of the first week the young are covered with a good coat of gray-brown fur. Their eyes are open in 14-16 days, at which time they can dive and swim with alacrity. When 4 weeks old they are generally weaned. Sexual maturity is reached in 10-12 months, at which time the rats have attained the size and characteristics of adults.

Muskrats are the victims of many predators. Marsh hawks, large owls, raccoons, foxes, minks, water snakes, and large turtles are known to plague them.

Muskrats were, at one time, the most economically important furbearing mammal in eastern Texas, but this is no longer true. The decline in importance of the muskrat as a furbearing mammal is a reflection of a loss of habitat as a result of marsh deterioration and resultant population decline, variations in market demand, and the increasing importance of the nutria as an important furbearing mammal.

FAMILY ERETHIZONTIDAE (NEW WORLD PORCUPINES)

PORCUPINE

Erethizon dorsatum (Linnaeus)

Description. A large rodent with distinct, barbed quills on back, sides, and tail; long guard hairs usually yellowish, impart a yellowish or yellowish-brown appearance to the animal. External measurements average: (males) total length, 808 mm; tail, 235 mm; hind foot, 98 mm; (females) 737-230-81 mm. Weight, 5-11 kg.

Distribution. Known from western one-half of state, east to Bosque County.

Habits. The porcupine is adapted to a variety of habitats. It is largely an inhabitant of forested areas in the West and prefers rocky areas, ridges, and slopes. It is less common in flats, valleys, and gulches. Porcupines wander about a great deal and may be found irregularly in areas that appear wholly unsuited to them. In recent years, it has expanded its range into southern Texas.

They are expert at climbing trees, although their movements are slow, methodical, and seemingly awkward. They apparently are aware of their limitations and they take few chances. Porcupines seem to be as much at home in the rocks as on the ground or

Porcupine (*Erethizon dorsatum*). Photo courtesy of U.S. Fish and Wildlife Service.

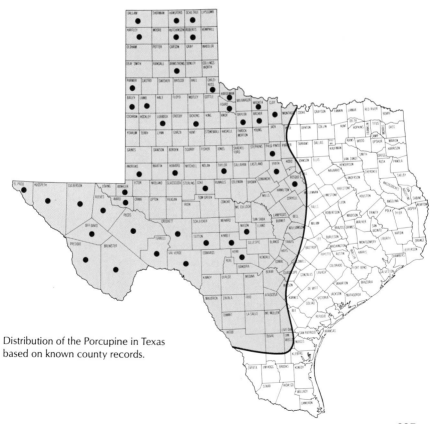

Distribution of the Porcupine in Texas based on known county records.

in trees. The more massive and broken the rocks the better they serve the animals for the numerous crevices and caves can be used as den sites and the large boulders as resting places. Where rocky dens are accessible, they are visited at intervals by many porcupines from the surrounding region and are used from year to year. Where such dens are unavailable a hollow log, a windfall, or an upturned or loosened tree root system may serve the purpose.

In winter when snow covers the ground, porcupines seldom travel far from their dens, especially in freezing weather. As warm weather approaches, the amount of travel increases.

Herbaceous ground vegetation makes up 85% of the food of both old and young in summer. In fall only 27% of their food is herbaceous; 73% is tree-gathered and includes mistletoe, the inner bark of a variety of trees, and pine needles. In winter the food is wholly from trees, and pine needles and inner bark are consumed at their peak during this season. In spring they again return to herbaceous ground vegetation which then makes up nearly 40% of their diet. Throughout the year the porcupine is more of a browser than a grazer and subsists in large measure on the inner bark of trees and shrubs; grass is of no importance at any time of the year. Porcupines are especially fond of salt and are easily attracted to it, a fact which is useful in their control.

Breeding takes place in late summer and early fall, with the peak of activity in September and early October. The young, usually one, rarely two, are born about 7 months later in April and May. The gestation period is 209-217 days. At birth the young porcupine weighs about 450 g and is larger than a newborn black bear. It is covered with a good coat of blackish hair, the quills are well-developed, the eyes and ears are functional, and the incisors and some of the cheek teeth have erupted. It is usually suckled for only a short period, begins to feed on vegetation shortly after birth, and soon becomes entirely dependent upon its own resources. The young porcupines grow slowly as compared with most rodents, and females do not mature sexually until their second fall when they weigh about 4 kg. Porcupines have a relatively long lifespan. One marked female is known to have lived more than 10 years under natural conditions.

FAMILY MYOCASTORIDAE (MYOCASTORIDS)

NUTRIA*

Myocastor coypus (Molina)

Description. A large rodent, nearly as large as a beaver but with long, rounded, scaly, ratlike tail; hind feet webbed; incisors orange-colored; female with mammae along each side of back, not on belly; upperparts reddish brown; the underfur dark slaty; tip of muzzle and chin white. External measurements of adults average: total length, 800-900 mm; tail, 350-400 mm; hind foot, 130-140 mm. Total length may reach 1.4 m. Weight, normally 8-10 kg.

Distribution. Known from aquatic habitats in eastern two-thirds of state.

Habits. Throughout much of their natural range in South America, nutria prefer a semiaquatic existence in swamps, marshes, and along the shores of rivers and lakes. In southern Chile and Tierra del Fuego they are found mainly in the channels and bays separating the various islands off the coast. Here, their habitat seems to be mostly in the estuaries of glacier-fed streams, and colonies of nutria are often seen swimming among the floating ice blocks in the vicinity of glaciers. Apparently, the nutria is equally at home in salt and fresh water.

Nutria (*Myocastor coypus*). Photo courtesy of Texas Parks and Wildlife.

They are docile creatures, much like the beaver in this respect, and can be handled easily in captivity. They are almost entirely nocturnal, consequently their presence in an area usually is revealed only by their trails, feces, and lengths of cut vegetation that have been left in their trails. They are not extensive burrowers. Burrows that have been examined were approximately 20 cm in diameter and extended into the bank for a distance of over 1 m. Often they were open at both ends, with the entrance toward the river usually above water level. Some of the burrows are under roots of trees that are exposed along the banks of the river or stream. Their nests are made of reeds and sedges built up in large piles somewhat after the fashion of a swan's nest. These are built on land among the marsh vegetation and close to the water's edge.

Their natural food consists almost entirely of aquatic and semiaquatic vegetation, but when these animals live along the coast they also feed upon shellfish. Cattails, reeds, and sedges appear to be especially prized items of food. When established near gardens, they take cabbage readily; they are also fond of carrots and sweet potatoes.

These animals appear to breed throughout the year. Each adult female produces two or three litters a year. The gestation period is from 127 to 132 days. The number of young per litter ranges from two to 11 and averages about five. At birth the young are fully furred, and their eyes are open; they are able to move about and feed upon green vegetation within a few hours. At that time they weigh approximately 200 g. They mature rapidly, increasing at the rate of about 400 g per month during the first year, and reach sexual maturity at the age of 4 or 5 months. Females sometimes give birth to their first litter when they themselves are 8 or 9 months old. The maximum length of life for nutria kept in captivity is 12 years, but the life span in the wild probably is considerably less.

These animals are important fur producers in their native range. They are reared extensively on fur farms in South America and most of their pelts are sold on the

European market. On the American market, nutria pelts have at times been of some value, but currently there is no market for nutria pelts. Because of their known competition with muskrats, which are well-established and valuable fur-producing animals in this country, it appears that muskrats may be driven out and replaced by the much less desirable nutria.

They have been widely introduced in Texas as a "cure-all" for ponds choked with vegetation. They do reduce many kinds of aquatic plants, but they will not eat "moss" (algae) and many of the submerged plants. At times they do the job too well. The trouble is that once nutrias get established in a lake, their high reproductive capacity soon results in overpopulation. There are so many nutrias that the available food supply will not satisfy them, and then trouble begins. The animals move into places where they are not wanted or where they destroy vegetation that is valuable for such wildlife as waterfowl and muskrats. A case in point is Eagle Lake in Colorado County. There, a stocking of nutrias increased to the point where the animals seriously damaged the waterfowl values of the lake. Hundreds of dollars were spent in attempts to eradicate the pests.

Currently, nutria populations in Texas are moderately high and on the increase. Unless the market for nutria improves, a serious and costly overpopulation problem is likely in the very near future.

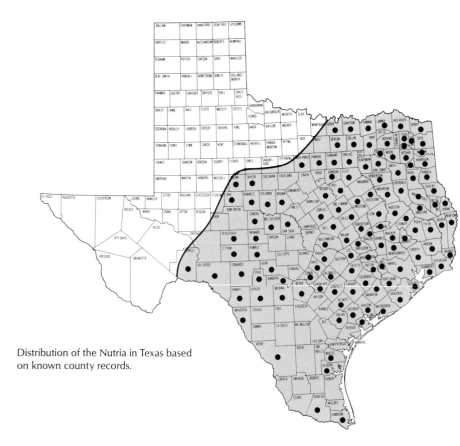

Distribution of the Nutria in Texas based on known county records.

ORDER CARNIVORA
CARNIVORES

To this group belong some of our most common and best-known wild mammals — dogs, cats, bears, weasels, skunks, raccoons, and so forth.

The carnivores are nearly worldwide in distribution and occur in the native wild state on all the continents. They are absent, except for introduced domesticated kinds, from all the oceanic islands and are represented in Australia only by the dingo, a wild dog.

The habits of the group are diverse. Coyotes and wolves are terrestrial and adapted for running; martens, fishers, and cats are expert at climbing trees; the badger is adept at digging in the ground; otters are expert swimmers and spend much of their time in the water. Most forms subsist on flesh either as carrion or that freshly killed. Bears, raccoons, ringtails, coyotes, and foxes, however, feed on a variety of foods, including insects, fruits, nuts, grain, and other plant materials, as well as flesh.

Texas has a varied carnivore fauna, including 27 native and one introduced species in five families. However, at least six of these species are now extinct in the state and several others are in danger of the same fate.

KEY TO THE CARNIVORES OF TEXAS

1. Catlike; total number of teeth 30 or less; claws retractile 2

   Not catlike; total number of teeth 34 to 42; claws usually not retractile 7

2. Tail 10 to 15 cm, shorter than hind foot; total number of teeth 28; upperparts reddish or grayish brown streaked with black. *Lynx rufus* (bobcat), p. 261.

   Tail 30 to 100 cm, much longer than hind foot; total number of teeth, 30 3

3. Upperparts concolor in adults, not spotted 4

   Upperparts spotted with black rosettes with light centers at all ages 5

4. Total length of adults up to 3 m; tail about 1 m; weight usually more than 45 kg; color tawny. *Felis concolor* (mountain lion), p. 255.

   Total length of adults up to 1 m; tail about 45 cm; weight up to 7 kg; upperparts reddish or grayish. *Felis yagouaroundi* (jaguarundi), p. 259.

5. Total length of adults 2 m or more; weight more than 45 kg. *Panthera onca* (jaguar), p. 260.

   Total length usually less than 1.2 m; weight usually less than 18 kg 6

6. Length of hind feet more than 120 mm; length of head and body alone about 75 cm; weight 7 to 16 kg. *Felis pardalis* (ocelot), p. 257.

   Length of hind foot less than 120 mm; length of head and body about 50 to 55 cm; weight 2 to 3 kg. *Felis wiedii* (margay), p. 258.

7. Doglike; total number of teeth, 42 8

   Not doglike; total number of teeth less than 42 (except in bears) 13

8. Hind foot usually less than 170 mm; weight less than 9 kg (foxes) 9

Hind foot usually more than 170 mm; weight more than 9 kg (coyotes, wolves) 11

9. Tip of tail white; upperparts yellowish or reddish; feet and lower part of legs black; hind foot near 160 mm. *Vulpes vulpes* (red fox), p. 223.

Tip of tail black; hind foot usually less than 150 mm 10

10. General color of body grizzled grayish; legs reddish brown; tail with black stripe on upperside and black tip; hind foot usually more than 140 mm. *Urocyon cinereoargenteus* (common gray fox), p. 225.

General color of body grayish-tan; hind foot usually less than 140 mm. *Vulpes velox* (swift or kit fox), p. 220.

11. Hind foot less than 200 mm; nose pad less than 25 mm in width; weight usually less than 18 kg. *Canis latrans* (coyote), p. 214.

Hind foot more than 200 mm; nose pad more than 25 mm in width; weight usually more than 18 kg 12

12. Hind foot more than 250 mm; general color grayish. *Canis lupus* (gray wolf), p. 216.

Hind foot less than 250 mm; general color tawny or reddish mixed with black. *Canis rufus* (red wolf), p. 217.

13. Tail considerably shorter than hind foot; total number of teeth, 42; weight of adults usually more than 100 kg; color black or brown (bears) 14

Not as above 15

14. Claws of front feet 7 to 12 cm long; face distinctly "dished in"; ruff or mane present between shoulders; last upper molar nearly twice as large as the one in front of it. *Ursus arctos* (grizzly or brown bear), p. 228.

Claws on front feet seldom as long as 75 mm; face slightly arched or nearly straight in profile; no ruff or mane; last upper molar about 1.5 times as large as the one in front of it. *Ursus americanus* (black bear), p. 227.

15. Total number of teeth, 40; tail usually with indications of alternating dark and light rings 16

Total number of teeth, 32 to 36; tail lacking dark and light rings 18

16. Tail as long as, or longer than head and body with 14 to 16 alternating black and white rings and a black tip; hind foot less than 80 mm; weight 1 to 2 kg. *Bassariscus astutus* (ringtail), p. 229.

Tail shorter than head and body and with six to seven alternating dark and light rings or rings inconspicuous; hind foot of adults 85 mm or more 17

17. Snout extending conspicuously beyond mouth and highly flexible; tail about five times as long as hind foot; alternating rings obscured in adults. *Nasua narica* (white-nosed coati), p. 234.

Snout not extending conspicuously beyond mouth; tail two to three times as long as hind foot, rings conspicuous at all ages. *Procyon lotor* (common raccoon), p. 232.

18. Upperparts black with longitudinal white stripe or stripes (skunks) 19

Upperparts not black and white striped 24

19. Total number of teeth, 32; back with single, broad white stripe from head to tail; nose pad large and flexible (hog-nosed skunks) 20

Total number of teeth, 34; back normally with two or more white stripes; nose pad normal 21

20. Total length of adults 700 mm or more; hind foot, 75 mm or more. *Conepatus leuconotus* (eastern hog-nosed skunk), p. 250.

Total length of adults usually less than 600 mm; length of hind foot usually less than 70 mm. *Conepatus mesoleucus* (common hog-nosed skunk), p. 250.

21. Six distinct broken or continuous white stripes on anterior part of body; white spot in center of forehead; hind foot seldom more than 50 mm 22

Not as above 23

22. Black and white stripes on back nearly equal in width; white spot on forehead large, covering more than half of the area between the eyes; white stripes beginning between the ears or just behind them. *Spilogale gracilis* (western spotted skunk), p. 243.

Black stripes on back wider than the white ones; white spot on forehead small, seldom more than 15 mm in diameter; white stripes on back begin about 25 mm behind the ears. *Spilogale putorius* (eastern spotted skunk), p. 245.

23. Dorsal white stripe bifurcate; sides black. *Mephitis mephitis* (striped skunk), p. 248.

Dorsal stripe white or black but never bifurcate; sides usually with narrow white stripe beginning at ear. *Mephitis macroura* (hooded skunk), p. 247.

24. Total number of teeth, 36; feet webbed; tail long, heavy, tapering; ears short; color chocolate brown; total length 1 m or more. *Lutra canadensis* (river otter), p. 252.

Total number of teeth, 34; feet not webbed; total length less than 1 m 25

25. Tail about as long as hind foot; claws on front feet about 25 mm in length and much longer than those on hind foot; body thick-set, heavy; fur lax and long. *Taxidea taxus* (American badger), p. 241.

Tail noticeably longer than hind foot; body long and slender; fur relatively short 26

26. Color chocolate brown to black; midline of belly white. *Mustela vison* (mink), p. 239.

Color yellowish brown; head usually with black and white markings; tip of tail black and contrasting markedly with rest of tail 27

27. Feet brown or tan; hind foot 50 mm or less; weight 500 g or less. *Mustela frenata* (long-tailed weasel), p. 236.

Feet black; hind foot more than 50 mm; weight 500 to 1,500 g. *Mustela nigripes* (black-footed ferret), p. 238.

FAMILY CANIDAE (CANIDS)

COYOTE
Canis latrans Say

Description. A medium-sized, slender, doglike carnivore, similar in appearance to the red wolf but usually smaller, more slender, with smaller feet, narrower muzzle, and relatively longer tail; colors usually paler, less rufous, rarely blackish; differs from gray wolves in much smaller size, smaller feet and skull; upperparts grizzled buffy and grayish overlaid with black; muzzle, ears and outersides of legs yellowish buff; tail with black tip, and with upperpart colored like back. Dental formula: I 3/3, C 1/1, Pm 4/4, M usually 2/2, occasionally 3/3, 3/2, or 2/3 X 2 = 40, 42, or 44. External measurements average: total length, 1,219 mm; tail, 394 mm; hind foot, 179 mm. Weight, 14-20 kg.

Distribution. Statewide.

Habits. Although often called "prairie wolf," the extensive range of the coyote includes from sea level to well over 3,000 m and habitats ranging from desert scrub through grassland into the timbered sections of the West. Around the turn of the century, coyotes were not known in eastern Texas, where red wolves were common. Land use in this area, including intensive lumbering and agriculture, as well as intensive predator control, eradicated the wolves and now coyotes have expanded their range to also include that part of the state.

The basic social unit is the family group, comprised of a mated pair and their offspring. Nonfamily coyotes include bachelor males, nonreproductive females, and

Coyote (*Canis latrans*). Photo by John L. Tveten.

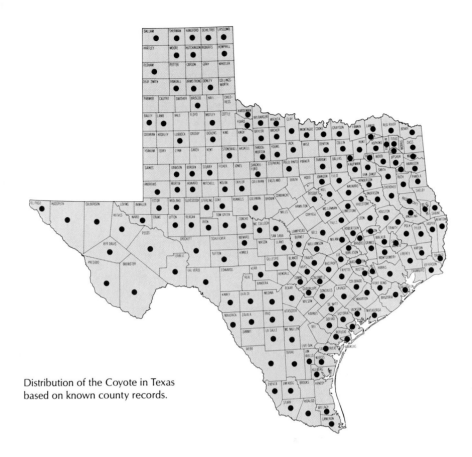

Distribution of the Coyote in Texas
based on known county records.

near-mature young. They may live alone or form loose associations of two to six animals. One animal in such "packs" usually is dominant, but the interaction among pack members is only temporary.

Coyotes may be active throughout the day, but they tend to be more active during the early morning and around sunset. Their movements include travel within a territory or home range, dispersal from the den, and long migrations. The home range size of coyotes varies geographically, seasonally, and individually within populations.

The food habits of coyotes are varied. They are opportunists and make use of anything that can be eaten — garbage, carrion, fresh meat in the form of both wild and domestic animals, insects, frogs, snakes, fruits, melons, and so forth. Although coyotes prey on poultry and the smaller livestock, their natural foods consist largely of rabbits, rodents, and carrion. Charles Sperry analyzed 8,339 stomachs of coyotes from the western United States with the following results (expressed in percentages): rabbits, 33; carrion, 25; rodents, 18; domestic livestock (chiefly sheep and goats), 13.5; deer, 3.5; birds, 3; insects, 1; other animal matter (skunks, weasels, shrews, moles, snakes, and lizards), 1; vegetable matter, 2.

Nursery dens are usually located in brush covered slopes, steep banks, thickets, hollow logs, or rock ledges. One den was in a hollow cottonwood tree with the entrance 5 m above the ground. Access to this unusual den was gained by means of a large limb that sloped to the ground. They are also known to den in crevices and shallow caves in rocky bluffs. Rarely is no den provided for the young.

The breeding season begins in January, reaches its peak in late February or early March, and terminates by the middle of May. Coyote mates maintain a close social bond throughout the year, although when the female is in late pregnancy the male often hunts alone and brings food to his mate. One litter a year is the rule. Normal litter size is two to 12, averaging about six. The gestation period is approximately 63 days. At birth, the young are blind and helpless. The eyes open at about 9 days of age and by October or November the young are difficult to distinguish from their parents.

Few coyotes live more than 6-8 years in the wild. Losses are due mainly to predation, parasites and disease, and man. Mortality is particularly high for pups, who are vulnerable to hawks, owls, eagles, mountain lions, and even other coyotes. Hunting and trapping account for many adult deaths. In terms of economic importance, the coyote is the second most important furbearing animal in the state, exceeded only by the raccoon.

GRAY WOLF
Canis lupus Linnaeus

Description. A large, doglike carnivore with heavy, broad skull and muzzle; height at shoulder slightly greater than at rump, imparting a suggestion that the animal is partly crouched; legs relatively long (as compared with a coyote); tail relatively short; upperparts grayish, usually heavily washed with blackish, occasionally predominately blackish; head more or less tinged with cinnamon; underparts whitish or buffy; tail black-tipped. Dental formula as in the coyote. External measurements of a male: total length, 1,626 mm; tail, 419 mm; hind foot, 267 mm; a female, 1,473-360-269. Weight: males, 30-80 kg; females, 20-60 kg.

Distribution. The gray wolf formerly ranged over the western two-thirds of the state, but now is extirpated over all of the west, including Texas. The last authenticated reports of gray wolves in Texas are of two males, the skulls of which were donated to Sul Ross State University. According to James Scuddy, one wolf was shot December 5, 1970, on the Cathedral Mountain Ranch, 27 km south of Alpine, Brewster County. The

Gray Wolf (*Canis lupus*). Photo courtesy of U.S. Fish and Wildlife Service.

216

other was trapped several days before December 28, 1970, on the Joe Neal Brown Ranch located at about the point where Brewster, Pecos, and Terrell counties meet.

Habits. The gray wolf inhabits forests, brushlands, or grasslands, preferring broken, open country in which suitable cover and denning sites are available. Formerly, wolves occurred commonly in the grassland plains of the buffalo on which they relied for their chief food supply.

Wolves have marvelous stamina and endurance and can travel for hours without apparent fatigue. They usually travel and hunt in packs, occasionally in pairs or singly, depending on their own endurance or numbers to "wear down" the intended large prey. The family group constitutes the nucleus of the pack, to which bachelor friends or members of another family may be added. The usual pack consists of six to 10 individuals, but packs twice this size are not uncommon. Packs of as many as 50 individuals are rare.

Under natural conditions, the food of wolves consists of the larger herbivores — deer and pronghorns. But when such game is scarce they turn their attention to mice, ground squirrels, and rabbits. The young pups normally spend considerable time in stalking and capturing small mice. Where natural foods are scarce and domesticated livestock available, wolves soon learn that such items are satisfactory substitutes.

The extirpation of the wolf over most of its former range released predator pressure on such big game as deer, which in part created a serious problem of overpopulation of this game animal in several localities in Texas. That wolves play a valuable role in the economy of big game animals is frequently overlooked.

Wolves mate for life. The young, usually four to six in number, are whelped in late winter or early spring in a den dug into a hillside, cut bank, or in a crevice in a rocky bluff. The breeding season begins in late December and continues through February; the gestation period is about 63 days. At first, the young are blind, naked, and helpless but they grow rapidly. At about 9 days of age their eyes open, at which time they are covered by wooly, juvenile fur. By October they are nearly full-grown. Females are sexually mature when 2 years old; males mature about a year later.

RED WOLF
Canis rufus Audubon and Bachman

Description. A rather small, slender, long-legged wolf resembling the coyote in color but often blackish; typically larger, with wider nose pad, larger feet and coarser pelage; smaller and more tawny than the gray wolf. Dental formula as in the coyote. External measurements of an adult male: total length, 1,473 mm; tail, 362 mm; hind foot, 235 mm; a female, 1,448-355-216 mm. Large males weigh 30-40 kg; large females 20-30 kg.

Distribution. Formerly, red wolves ranged throughout the eastern half of Texas but their numbers and range quickly declined under pressure of intensive land use in the region. Also, early lumbering and farming practices allowed the coyote to expand its range into East Texas; hybrid offspring of interbreeding red wolves and coyotes more closely resembled coyotes and the genetic identity of the red wolf was gradually suppressed.

In 1962 Howard McCarley, who had assiduously searched for them in East Texas for several years, held the opinion that they no longer occurred there. John Paradiso reported in 1965, however, that seven specimens taken near Anahuac (Chambers County) in 1963-1964, and one specimen from Armstrong (Kenedy County) taken in 1961, were definitely red wolves. All of the recent, so-called red wolves we have examined from eastern Texas have proven to be large coyotes. It appears that in Texas, red wolves are now extinct.

217

The following comparisons are derived mainly from a review of the status and knowledge of the red wolf prepared by G.A. Riley and R.T. McBride.

	RED WOLF	COYOTE
Weight (in kg): means and extremes	22.7 (17.3-34.5) Male 20.0 (16.3-24.5) Female	15.0 (10.0-16.0) Male 13.1 (9.5-15.9) Female
Total length (m)	1.42 (1.32-1.60) Male 1.34 (1.22-1.42) Female	1.27 (1.21-1.35) Male 1.20 (1.12-1.30) Female
Hind foot (cm)	23.1 (21.0-24.9) Male 22.1 (20.3-24.1) Female	20.5 (19.0-21.3) Male 19.8 (17.8-21.6) Female
Ear length (cm)	12.7 (11.4-14.0) Male 12.2 (11.4-12.7) Female	11.6 (10.7-12.2) Male 10.9 (8.6-12.2) Female
Width of nose pad (mm)	More than 25	Less than 25
Length of skull (mm)	More than 215; usually more than 220	Less than 215; usually less than 210
Tracks (back of heel pad to end of longest claw, in millimeters)	102.0 (89.0-127.0)	66.0 (57.2-72.4)
Stride (cm)	65.8 (55.8-76.2)	41.4 (32.4-48.3)
Muzzle and head	Normally broad	Normally narrow
Muzzle coloration	White area around lips may extend well up on sides of muzzle	White area around lips thin and sharply demarcated
Threat behavior (when trapped or cornered)	Tail held upright; snarl exposes only the canines and a few front teeth; ruff on neck and back raised	Tail held between legs; mouth opened wide and all teeth exposed; back arched and ruff may or or may not be raised

Habits. Red wolves inhabited brushy and forested areas, as well as the coastal prairies. They are more sociable than coyotes. Three or more may maintain a group structure throughout the year. Riley and McBride, on the basis of systematic tracking, estimated that the home range is approximately 40-80 km², averaging 56 km².

They are known to feed on cottontails and other rabbits, deer, native rats and mice, prairie chickens, fish and crabs (along the Gulf Coast), as well as upon domestic livestock, especially free-ranging pigs. Riley and McBride list nutria (which they consider an important buffer between red wolves and domestic livestock), swamp rabbit, cottontail, rice rat, cotton rat, and muskrat as specific food items.

Breeding occurs in January and February, and the three or four pups are born in March and April. The nursery den normally is dug in the slope or crest of a low, sandy mound or hill, or in the bank of an irrigation or drainage ditch. Man-made culverts and drain pipes occasionally are utilized. The dens average about 2.4 m in length and normally are no deeper than 1 m. Den entrances vary from 60 to 75 cm in diameter and normally are well-concealed. Both sexes take part in rearing the young. Frequently, young of the previous year occur in the vicinity of a nursery den, but they do not appear to participate in guarding, feeding, or training of the pups of the year. When about 6 weeks old the pups may forsake the nursery den.

Red wolf (top) and Coyote (bottom). Notice the facial markings, the length of the ears and the width of the nose pad and muzzle. Photos courtesy of U.S. Fish and Wildlife Service.

Remarks. The red wolf was apparently extinct in the wild by 1980. However, captive breeding colonies of red wolves have been established at several locations throughout the country. Beginning in 1987, red wolves were re-introduced to the Alligator River National Wildlife Refuge (ARNWR), located on an island off the coast of North Carolina. Between 1987 and 1992, 42 wolves were released in ARNWR and at least 23 wolves

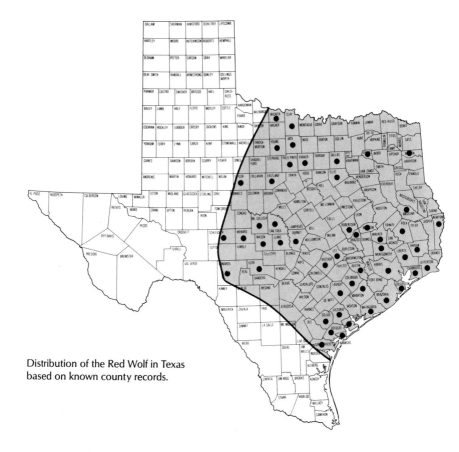

Distribution of the Red Wolf in Texas based on known county records.

were born in the wild. As of August 1992, the ARNWR population numbered at least 24 wolves. Additionally, red wolf pairs have been released on Bull's Island, South Carolina, St. Vincent Island, Florida, and Horn Island, Mississippi, but breeding and survival on these islands have been limited. Most recently, red wolves have been re-introduced to the Great Smoky Mountains National Park. It is doubtful red wolves can be re-introduced in Texas because of human population pressures where they formerly occurred.

SWIFT OR KIT FOX
Vulpes velox (Say)

Description. Smallest of the American foxes; upperparts pale buffy yellow, frosted with white and lightly washed with blackish; back of ears yellowish brown; tail buffy gray with black tip and black spot at base on upperside; underparts whitish. Dental formula: I 3/3, C 1/1, Pm 4/4, M 2/3 x 2 = 42. External measurements average: total length, 840 mm; tail, 330 mm; hind foot, 135 mm; ear, 75 mm. Weight, 1-3 kg.

Distribution. Known from western one-third of state east to Menard County.

Habits. These small foxes, not much larger than a good-sized house cat, generally live in the open desert or grasslands where they often have dens and hunt mesa country along the borders of valleys, sparsely vegetated habitats on sloping plains, hilltops, and other well-drained areas. Also, they have adapted to pasture, plowed fields, and fencerows. They rely on speed and nearness to their dens for safety.

Swift or kit foxes are primarily nocturnal, although they may occasionally be seen in the daylight hours. Usually, they emerge from their dens shortly after sunset for hunting, which occurs sporadically throughout the night. Foxes may cover several kilometers while systematically hunting for prey but seldom venture more than 3 km from their dens. Home ranges may overlap broadly, and foxes from different family groups hunt the same areas, although not at the same time.

The diet of these foxes consists largely of small mammals, particularly rodents, but also includes insects, small passerine birds, lizards, amphibians, and fish. Known food items are kangaroo rats, jackrabbits, cottontails, small birds, grasshoppers, Jerusalem crickets, and other insects. W. L. Cutter examined 12 stomachs and 250 scats (droppings), collected mainly in late spring, summer and early fall, to determine the food habits of these foxes. Rabbit remains, both cottontails and jackrabbits, were found almost as frequently (60 times) as all other vertebrates combined (68 times). Small rodents occurred 26 times; passerine birds, 33 times; lizards, four times; and fish, three times.

No remains of gallinaceous birds, either game birds or poultry, were found although two of the dens were no more than 170 m from a farmyard where poultry was raised. Insect remains (11 families represented) comprised approximately 29% of the bulk of the stomach contents and 55% of the bulk of the scats. Shorthorned grasshoppers occurred most frequently, followed by beetles of three families. Grass was found in 43 scats and 10 stomachs. Thus, it appears that this fox is not in conflict with man's interests insofar as its feeding habits are concerned.

Male and female foxes establish pair bonds during October and November, during which time large family dens are used. These foxes are monogamous for a breeding season but the pairs are not necessarily the same from year to year. Breeding occurs from December to February, and most litters are born in March or early April. Litter size varies from three to six and the swift or kit fox is monestrous. W. L. Cutter observed

Swift or Kit Fox (*Vulpes velox*). Photo by John L. Tveten.

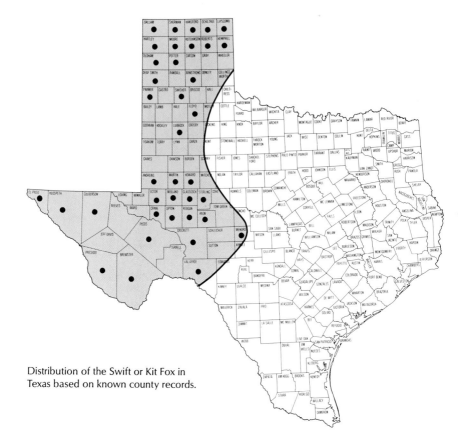

Distribution of the Swift or Kit Fox in
Texas based on known county records.

that in the Texas Panhandle (Hansford County) these foxes usually den in open, overgrazed pastures. Of 25 occupied dens that he observed, 19 were so located; two were in plowed fields and four were along north-south fence rows. The den is a simple structure with one or more openings. One that Cutter excavated had a circular entrance 20 cm in diameter and a total of 378 cm of open, underground tunnel. The main chamber was 30 cm wide, 22 cm high, and 80 cm below the surface of the ground. Three dens were as close as 85 m to human habitation. These foxes spend most of the daytime in their dens; when they do come out in daylight, they remain close to the den into which they retreat when molested.

Swift foxes are relatively unafraid of man and are far less cunning than most other foxes. They are so unsuspicious that they are easily trapped, and even more easily poisoned. Consequently, wherever trappers are active, and especially wherever control campaigns involving the use of poison have been carried out against predatory animals on areas inhabited by swift foxes, the foxes have been greatly reduced in number or entirely eliminated.

Remarks. In previous editions, arid-land foxes have been regarded as comprising two similar but separate species, the swift fox (*Vulpes velox*) and the kit fox (*Vulpes macrotis*). However, in a recent taxonomic study of these foxes using advanced morphometric and protein-electrophoretic methods, Dragoo and colleagues concluded that these taxa are not sufficiently distinct to warrant separate specific status. Thus, the two foxes are now grouped into a single species, *Vulpes velox*, comprised of two subspecies, *V. v. velox* and *V. v. macrotis*.

RED FOX*
Vulpes vulpes (Linnaeus)

Description. Similar in size to the gray fox but conspicuously different in color and in cranial characters. Considerably larger and more reddish than the swift fox. Tail a thick "bush," circular in cross section, and white-tipped; face rusty fulvous, grizzled with white; upperparts bright golden yellow, darkest along middle of back; chin, throat and mid-line of belly white; forefeet and legs to elbow black; black of hind feet extends as a narrow band along outer side of leg to thigh; backs of ears black. Several color phases — cross, black, silver, Sampson, and the normal red. Young duller in color than adults. Dental formula: I 3/3, C 1/1, Pm 4/4, M 2/3 X 2 = 42. External measurements average: total length, 972 mm; tail, 371 mm; hind foot, 163 mm; females average slightly smaller than males. Weight, 3-5 kg.

Distribution. Introduced in eastern and central parts of state. Now ranges across central Texas from eastern part of the state to central Trans-Pecos region.

Habits. Red foxes are not native to Texas, having been introduced for purposes of sport around 1895. Today, red foxes occur throughout central and eastern Texas, but they do not seem to be common anywhere. Their favored habitat is mixed woodland uplands interspersed with farms and pastures. Although usually active at night, the red fox moves about considerably in daylight hours and occasionally may be observed then, especially if the observer is alert and still. The den is usually an underground burrow, a crevice in a rocky outcrop, or a cavity under boulders. Occasionally, the burrow of some other animal, such as the badger, is taken over and remodeled to suit the new occupants.

Red foxes are opportunistic feeders and will take any acceptable food in proportion to its availability. The major food items are small rodents, rabbits, wild fruits and berries, and insects. Small mammals evidently constitute staple foods during the greater

Red Fox (*Vulpes vulpes*). Photo by John L. Tveten.

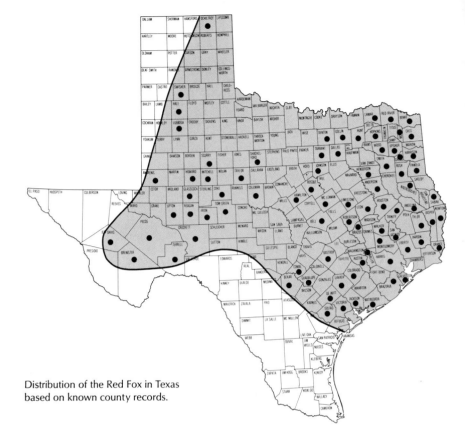

Distribution of the Red Fox in Texas
based on known county records.

part of the year. Other kinds of prey fluctuate according to season, weather conditions, abundance, and vulnerability of prey populations, and with the experience of the fox. Young animals learning to hunt have to take what they can get.

Female red foxes have a single estrous each year and reputedly remain mated for life. Males and females pair off and mate from late December to January or February. Females have a very short period of heat that lasts only 2-4 days. The young, which may number anywhere from one to 10 (average, four to six), are born in March or April following a gestation period of about 53 days.

The female establishes the den site for the young in late winter, but both parents live together while raising the young. Foxes either dig their own dens or utilize those of other burrowing animals. Sometimes two litters may occupy one den.

The young at birth are dark brown or black in color, but the tip of the tail is white. They are blind and helpless; the eyes open at the age of 8 or 9 days. They seldom venture out of the den until they are a month old, and the den may also be their refuge for the next 2 months or longer. The parents are solicitous of the pups, bringing them food and guarding the den. The family remains together until autumn, by which time the young have attained almost adult proportions.

Few foxes live beyond the age of 3 or 4 years, particularly in areas where they are hunted and trapped heavily. Man and domestic dogs are their major predators, although pups may be lost to great horned owls and other predators. Red foxes are susceptible to a variety of diseases, including rabies, distemper, and infectious canine hepatitis.

224

COMMON GRAY FOX

Urocyon cinereoargenteus (Schreber)

Description. A medium-sized fox with grayish upperparts, reddish brown legs, tawny sides, and whitish throat, cheeks and mid-line of belly; sides of muzzle and lower jaw with distinct blackish patch; tail with distinct blackish stripe on upperside and black tip (no white on end of tail as in the red fox); tail roughly triangular, not round, in cross section; skull with distinct lyrate temporal ridges, which meet only at hind part of skull. Dental formula as in the red fox. External measurements average: total length, 970 mm; tail, 347 mm; hind foot, 143 mm. Weight, ordinarily 3-5 kg, occasionally as much as 9 kg.

Distribution. Statewide.

Habits. The gray fox is essentially an inhabitant of wooded areas, particularly mixed hardwood forests. It is common throughout the wooded sections east of the shortgrass plains and in the pinyon-juniper community above the low lying deserts.

This fox is adept at climbing trees, particularly if they are leaning or have branches within 3 m of the ground, and it is not unusual for it to use this escape device when pursued by hounds. Contrary to common belief, gray foxes are not strictly animals of the night, but they are much more active then. They have been observed on many occasions in the daytime under conditions that suggested they were foraging. When so encountered, they often move to one side behind a protecting screen of vegetation and wait for the intruder to pass.

Gray foxes usually den in crevices in the rocks, in underground burrows, under rocks, in hollow logs, or in hollow trees. In eastern Texas, one was found denning about 10 m above the ground in a large hollow oak. In central Texas, a den was found in a hollow live oak with the entrance about 1 m above the ground. Two unusual den sites which have been documented include a pile of wood and a field of sorghum into which a fox had "tunneled."

The gray fox is omnivorous; the food varies with season and availability. Based upon the stomach contents of 42 foxes from Texas, the winter food consisted chiefly of

Common Gray Fox (*Urocyon cinereoargenteus*). Photo courtesy of U.S. Fish and Wildlife Service.

225

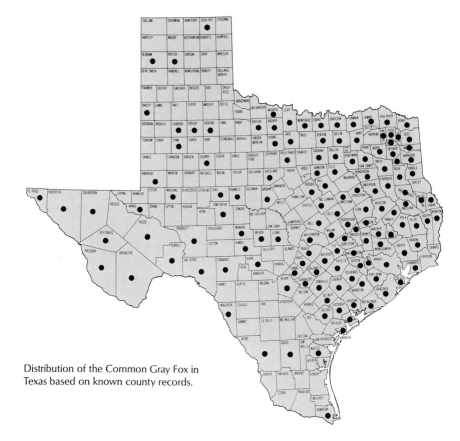

Distribution of the Common Gray Fox in
Texas based on known county records.

small mammals (cottontails, cotton rats, pocket gophers, pocket mice), 56%; followed by insects, largely grasshoppers, 23%; and birds (doves, quail, sparrows, blackbirds, towhees), 21%. In the spring the diet was but slightly changed — small mammals, 68%; insects, 25%; small birds, 17%. In late summer and fall, persimmons and acorns led with 30%; insects, 26%; small mammals, 16%; birds, 14%; crayfish, 14%. In these 42 stomachs, chicken and quail occurred once each, and mourning doves twice. Consequently, as judged from these analyses, the usual food habits of the gray fox do not conflict much with man's economy.

In Texas, the breeding season begins in December and continues on into March. Most females captured in March and April are gravid. The three to six pups are born in April or May after a gestation period of about 53 days. At first they are blind and helpless, but they grow rapidly and soon leave the home nest, possibly because of the heavy infestation of fleas characteristic of such nests. Then they seek shelter in rock piles, under rocks, in piles of brush, or in other sites that offer concealment and protection.

Of some interest is the possible relationship between gray foxes and coyotes. In sections of Texas where coyotes formerly were numerous, the gray fox was scarce; now, after elimination of the coyote, the gray fox has become abundant. Perhaps the coyote tends to hold this fox in check under conditions where they both occupy the same area.

Gray foxes are thought to live six to 10 years in the wild. Major factors causing mortality include predation, parasites, diseases, and man. The gray fox is among the most important of Texas' fur-bearing animals.

FAMILY URSIDAE (BEARS)

BLACK BEAR

Ursus americanus Pallas

Description. A medium-sized bear, black or brown in color; snout brownish in the black color phase; front claws slightly longer than the hind claws, curved, adapted for climbing; profile of face nearly straight, not "dished-in" as in the grizzly; fur long and rather coarse. Dental formula: I 3/3, C 1/1, Pm 4/4, M 2/3 X 2 = 42. External measurements average: total length, 1,500 mm; tail, 125 mm; hind foot, 175 mm; height at shoulder about 625 mm. Weight, 100-150 kg; occasionally as much as 225 kg.

Distribution. Formerly widespread throughout the state; now restricted to remnant populations in mountainous areas of the Trans-Pecos region.

Habits. Black bears have been restricted by the inroads of "civilization" to the more remote, less accessible mountainous areas or to the nearly impenetrable thickets along watercourses. Only in places that have a low human population or an enlightened public have black bears been able to cope successfully with humans.

Largely creatures of woodland and forested areas, black bears are more at home on the ground than they are in the trees. They are expert climbers, however, and, especially when young, often seek refuge in trees. Ordinarily they are shy and retiring and seldom are seen. They appear to use definite travelways or runs, a habit that is frequently taken advantage of by hunters.

In spite of their large size and reputed clumsiness, bears are fleet-footed. One of us (Davis) once surprised a bear feeding in a berry patch. After the initial shock of meeting each other at close range, the bear regained its presence of mind first and bolted along a trail through the underbrush. It ran with amazing speed, resembling a big hog as it noisily left the thicket.

Black Bear (*Ursus americanus*). Photo courtesy of U.S. Fish and Wildlife Service.

In the colder parts of their range, black bears "hole up" in a windfall, at the base of a tree, under a shelving rock, or in some other suitable site, and are inactive for a part of the winter. They do not exhibit the characteristics of true hibernation; their temperature does not drop markedly nor are the heartbeat and respiratory rate materially reduced. Often the bears are nearly fully exposed to the winter weather during their prolonged sleep. They may awaken and become active during a warm spell in midwinter and return to the nest to sleep again when the temperature drops.

Their food is extremely varied as reflected by the crushing type of molar teeth. They are known to feed upon nest contents of wild bees, carpenter ants and other insects, manzanita berries, coffee berries, wild cherry, poison oak, apples, pine nuts, acorns, clover, grass, roots, fish, carrion, and garbage about camps. Occasional animals become killers of livestock and young deer.

The breeding season is in June or July. The one to four young (usually two) are born in January or February, while the mother is "hibernating," after a gestation period of 210-217 days. At birth the young are blind, covered with a sparse growth of fine hair, and almost helpless. They weigh less than 500 g and are about 15 cm long. They grow rather slowly at first; their eyes open in about 6 weeks. By the time the mother is ready to leave her winter den they are strong enough to follow. The cubs remain with her until the fall of their second year when they venture forth on their own. By that time, the female is preparing for her next family. Normally, old females mate every other year, and young females do not mate until 2 years or more of age.

Bears have few enemies other than man. They make interesting pets when small, but they become dangerous as they grow older. Their chief economic value is as a game animal. Their pelts have little value on the fur market, but they are prized as trophies.

Remarks. There have been many recent sightings of black bear in the Chisos Mountains of Big Bend National Park. Studies by Eric Hellgren of Texas A&M – Kingsville University suggest that black bears dispersing from the mountains of Mexico are recolonizing their historical habitat in the Trans-Pecos. A resident, breeding population of perhaps 20 individuals is thought to occur in the Chisos Mountains.

GRIZZLY OR BROWN BEAR
Ursus arctos Linnaeus

Description. Largest of the carnivores in western United States; head large with face distinctly "dished in"; body robust; legs strong, massive, and relatively short; tail much shorter than hind foot; last upper molar about as large as the two teeth in front of it combined; front claws 7-12 cm in length; upperparts brownish or yellowish brown, often with inter-mixture of white-tipped hairs; underparts similar to upperparts but lacking white-tipped hairs. Dental formula as in the black bear. External measurements of adult male: total length, 1,982 mm; length of tail, 76 mm; hind foot, 280 mm; height at shoulder, 1,017 mm. Females smaller. Weight of males, 180-360 kg, seldom as much as 500 kg; females, 130-180 kg, seldom as much as 360 kg.

Distribution. Only two specimens of grizzly bears are available from Texas. According to Vernon Bailey, who wrote of this bear in his "Biological Survey of Texas," a large and very old male grizzly was killed in the Davis Mountains in October, 1890 by C. O. Finley and John Z. Means. Measurements of the skull are: greatest length, 370 mm; basal length, 310 mm; zygomatic breadth, 220 mm; mastoid breadth, 157 mm; interorbital breadth, 71 mm; postorbital breadth, 69 mm. Mr. Finley reported that the claws on the front feet were about 3$\frac{1}{2}$ inches (9 cm) long, and the color of the bear was brown with gray tips to the hairs. Its weight was estimated at 1,100 pounds (500 kg) "if it had been fat." Mr. Finley found that this bear had killed a cow and eaten most of it in a gulch near the head of Limpia Creek, where the dogs took the trail. Out of a pack of 52 hounds, only a few would follow the trail, although most of them were used to hunting black bear. These few followed rather reluctantly, and after a run of about 8 km over rough country stopped the bear, which killed one of them before it was quieted by the rifles of Finley and Means. It took four men to put the skin, with head and feet attached, upon a horse for the return to camp.

Walter Dalquest reported examining the partial skull of a grizzly bear that had washed out on the banks of the Red River (Montague County) about 1950. This specimen has since been lost.

Habits. The grizzly is essentially an inhabitant of rough, mountainous country today, but considerable evidence points to the fact that 100 years ago it was also very much at home in the plains of the West. The impact of contact with the white man has forced the grizzly to make his last stand in rough, wilderness terrain.

The home range of grizzlies is estimated to be about 40 km in diameter in regions where food is plentiful. On the Sun River Game Preserve in Montana, on which no hunting has been permitted since 1912, the population averages one grizzly to 28 km^2 of range. This figure probably is close to the maximum population density attained before the white man settled the West. Outside the preserve, the population density is about one-third as great, because of hunting pressure, and in many sections of the state the grizzly has long been extinct.

Like the black bear, the grizzly holes up and sleeps through the severe part of the winter, subsisting on fat stored in the body. It does not hibernate in the true sense of the word. The young are born while the mother is in her winter den.

The natural food of grizzlies is extremely varied. Results of a study made in Montana revealed the following: early spring: winter-killed animals, green grasses, and weeds; middle and late spring: bulbs and roots, increasing use of grasses and sedges, few rodents, occasional young elk calves; summer: continued use of green vegetation, ants, beetles, and other insects, fruits and berries, few rodents; fall: largely pine nuts, few rodents. In certain sections they feed extensively on salmon during the spring run; occasional individuals turn renegade and become killers of livestock.

The breeding season is in June and July, and from one to four cubs (usually two) are born 6 or 7 months later. Seton gives the gestation period as 180-187 days; Brown, 236 days. The young cubs weigh about 750 g at birth, are about 20 cm long, and their eyes and ears are closed. Their eyes open in 8 or 9 days, in contrast to 6 weeks in the black bear.

FAMILY PROCYONIDAE (PROCYONIDS)

RINGTAIL

Bassariscus astutus (Lichtenstein)

Description. A cat-sized carnivore resembling a small fox with a long raccoon-like tail; tail flattened, about as long as head and body, banded with 14 to 16 alternating black and white rings (black rings incomplete on underside), and with a black tip; five toes on each foot, armed with sharp, curved, non-retractile claws; upperparts fulvous, heavily overcast with blackish; face sooty gray with large, distinct, whitish area above and below each eye, and one at anterior base of each ear; eye ring black; back of ears whitish toward tip, grayish basally; underparts whitish, tinged with buff; underfur all over plumbeous. Dental formula as in raccoons. External measurements average: (males), total length, 802 mm; tail, 410 mm; hind foot, 78 mm; ear, 55 mm; (a female), 714-350-65 mm. Weight, 1-1.5 kg.

Distribution. Statewide, but uncommon in lower Rio Grande and Coastal Plains of southern Texas.

Habits. Ringtails live in a variety of habitats within their range, but they have a decided preference for rocky areas such as rock piles, stone fences, canyon walls, and talus slopes. They occur less commonly in woodland areas where they live in hollow trees and logs, and they are also known to live in buildings. They are expert climbers, capable of ascending vertical walls, so they have little difficulty in searching out and denning in well-protected crevices, crannies, and hollows.

These "cats" are almost wholly nocturnal and spend the greater part of the day asleep in their dens and venture forth at night to feed. Resting dens seem to differ in no essentials from nursery dens. One nursery den found in Mason County was in a crevice near the bottom of a rocky bluff. It was about 12.5 cm in diameter at the entrance and tapered to a narrow crack about 75 cm beyond. A female and her four young were occupying it at the time. No nest was constructed for the young. In this section of Texas, rock fences seemed to be favored denning sites. Another nursery den found in

Ringtail (*Bassariscus astutus*). Photo courtesy of Texas Parks and Wildlife.

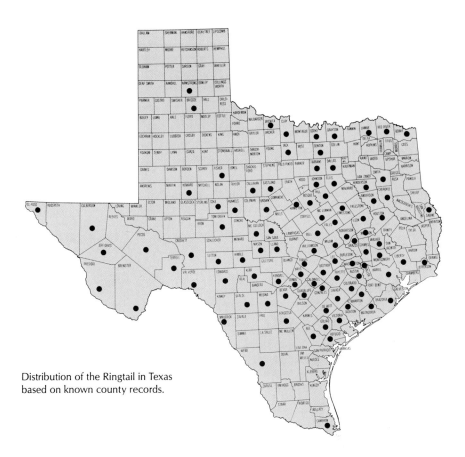

Distribution of the Ringtail in Texas based on known county records.

McCulloch County was in an old hollow stump on the side of a rocky bluff. A nest consisting of a few dry leaves was in the bottom of the cavity.

Ringtails eat a wide variety of foods. In central Texas, as judged by the examination of the digestive tracts of more than 100 ringtails, their diet consists of small passerine birds (9.9%); small mammals (rats, mice, squirrels, cottontails), including carrion (24.4%); snakes and lizards (3.9%); toads and frogs (0.2%); insects, mostly grasshoppers and crickets (31.2%); spiders, scorpions and centipedes (11.1%); and fruits of native plants, principally persimmon, hackberry, and mistletoe (19.3%). The diet varies with the season: largely birds, mammals, and fruits of hackberry and mistletoe in winter; mammals, insects, and juniper berries in spring; insects, spiders, scorpions, centipedes, and persimmon fruit in summer. Insufficient data are available to determine the food in autumn.

The breeding season appears to be restricted to a relatively short period of the year. In central Texas, the females appear to come into heat about April 1. Most females examined between April 15 and May 18 were pregnant. The exact gestation period is unknown, but it is probably about 45-50 days. In 10 females examined, the number of embryos ranged from two to four, averaging 3.3. At birth, the young are covered with short, whitish hair; they are blind, the ears are closed, and they are nearly helpless. The eyes open about 31-34 days after birth; the ears about a week earlier. The juvenile pelage, which is similar to that of the adult but paler and fuzzy, has replaced the natal pelage by this time. At the age of 4 months the young are indistinguishable from adults, except for their smaller size.

COMMON RACCOON
Procyon lotor (Linnaeus)

Description. A robust, medium-sized carnivore with distinctive, blackish facial mask outlined with white, and with alternating black and buff (or whitish) rings on the bushy tail; tip of tail black; general color of upperparts grayish, suffused with orange, and heavily sprinkled with blackish buff; top of head mixed gray and brownish black, giving a grizzled effect; throat patch brownish black; rest of underparts brownish, thinly overlaid with light orange buff; limbs similar to underparts, but becoming whitish on feet except for dusky marking near heels; the complete hind foot touches the ground when the animal walks; five toes on each foot, claws non-retractile; soles naked; pelage coarse, long, and full. Young like adults, but fur "woolly." Molar teeth "flat"-crowned and adapted for crushing, not for cutting as in dogs and cats. Dental formula: I 3/3, C 1/1, Pm 4/4, M 2/2 X 2 = 40. External measurements of adult male: total length, 880 mm; tail, 265 mm; hind foot, 125 mm; a female 834-243-123 mm. Weight, 4-13 kg.

Distribution. Statewide.

Habits. Raccoons are primarily inhabitants of broadleaf woodlands, although they are rather common in the mixed-pine forests of southeastern Texas. They seldom occur far from water, which seems to have more influence on their distribution than does any particular type of vegetation. Still, they are one of the most abundant carnivores in the semi-desert areas of West Texas.

They are strictly nocturnal and seldom are seen except when hunted with dogs or caught in traps. Their fondness for water is well-known and, except in seasons when fruits, nuts, and corn are maturing, they do most of their foraging near or in bodies of water. They often make well-worn trails at the water's edge where they have been searching for food.

The den is usually a large hollow tree or hollow log in which the animal spends the daylight hours sleeping and in which it also rears its young. In the western part of the range, dens usually are in crevices and crannies in rocky bluffs, but hollow trees are used when available. Several unusual nesting sites have been reported in the literature. In eastern Texas, a female and her three newborn young were found in a nail keg that had been fashioned as a nest site for wood ducks and wired 5 m up in a tree standing

Common Raccoon (*Procyon lotor*). Photo by John L. Tveten.

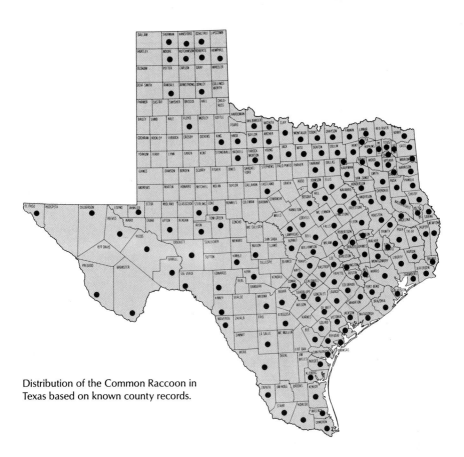

Distribution of the Common Raccoon in Texas based on known county records.

in water some 6 m from shore. A young raccoon was seen using a crow's nest some 6 m up in a willow tree as a daytime bed. Near Parker, Colorado, a raccoon and her naked and blind young occupied a large magpie nest located about 4 m above the ground in a scrub oak.

In the colder parts of their range, raccoons are said to "hibernate" during periods of inclement weather. This appears to be mere "holing up and sleeping," and not true hibernation. Raccoons do not exhibit the marked physiological changes — reduced temperature, reduced rate of respiration and heart beat, insensibility to pain — that characterize true hibernation.

The crushing type of molars indicates that raccoons are not specialized feeders. Stomach and fecal analyses bear out this assumption. In eastern Texas, acorns and crayfish constitute more than half their yearly diet and both are consumed in considerable quantities at all seasons. Grapes and persimmons are utilized when available and other fruits in smaller amounts. Insects and other invertebrates form an important part of the diet. Fish, birds, and snakes are taken occasionally. In summer and early autumn raccoons develop a fondness for adult and larval wasps and their stored foods. In winter they concentrate in the river bottoms and subsist largely on acorns and crayfish.

The breeding season begins in February and continues through August. The single litter of one to seven (average three or four) young usually is born in April or May after a gestation period varying from 60 to 73 days (average, 63 days). Raccoons are promiscuous in their sexual relations.

At birth, young raccoons are well-furred and have dark skins, no rings on the tail, and the eyes and ears are closed. The eyes open between the 18th and 23rd day. The mother alone tends her youngsters, and when they have grown large enough to leave the den site they follow her about, seeking shelter when necessary in tangles of roots or vines, in crevices, or under rocks. The family group remains intact long after the young ones have been weaned. The young do not reach adult size until their second year but females, at least, reach sexual maturity when 9 or 10 months old; males appear to mature sexually when about 2 years old.

WHITE-NOSED COATI

Nasua narica (Linnaeus)

Description. A raccoon-like carnivore, but more slender and with longer tail; snout long, slender, and projecting well beyond lower lip; five toes on each foot; tail with six or seven indistinct light bands; ears short; general color of upperparts grizzled yellowish brown, fulvous on top of head; snout and areas around eyes white, as is inside of ears; dark brown facial band across snout between eyes and whiskers, interrupted on top of snout by extensions of white from stripe above eye; lower legs and tops of feet blackish brown; underparts pale buff, lightest, nearly white on chin. Young like adults, but bands on tail more conspicuous. Molars adapted for crushing, not shearing as in most carnivores; upper canines flattened laterally, broad basally, shaped like a spear point; lower canines with a deep groove on inner face. Dental formula as in the raccoon. External measurements of adult male: total length, 1,130 mm; tail, 500 mm; hind foot, 91 mm; ear from notch, 30 mm. Weight, 4-5 kg.

Distribution. Coatis inhabit woodland areas of the warmer parts of Central America, Mexico, and the extreme southern United States including southern Texas. In Texas, they are only rarely known from Brownsville to the Big Bend region of the Trans-

White-nosed Coati (*Nasua narica*). Photo by Alfred M. Bailey.

234

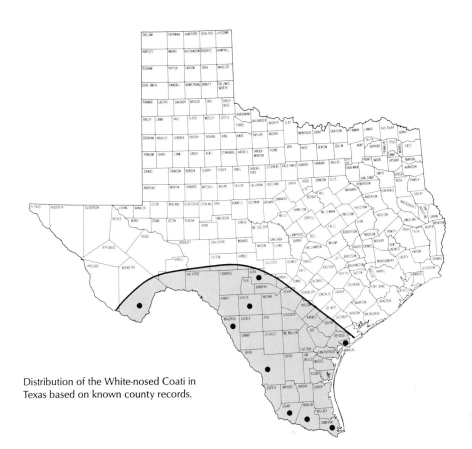

Distribution of the White-nosed Coati in
Texas based on known county records.

Pecos. They have been reported from Aransas, Brewster, Cameron, Hidalgo, Kerr, Maverick, Starr, Uvalde, and Webb counties.

Habits. Coatis spend considerable time on the ground, but they climb trees as easily as a squirrel. When in trees, their long tail seems to function, as does that of a squirrel, largely in maintaining balance. They also occur in some of the rocky canyons that enter the mountains from the lowlands. Except for old males, which are largely solitary in habit, coatis are sociable creatures and travel in packs or troops.

Unlike their relatives, the raccoons and ringtails, coatis are largely active by day, particularly in the early morning and late afternoon. They are omnivorous and consume a wide variety of available food including insects and other ground-dwelling arthropods, lizards, snakes, carrion, rodents, nuts and fruits of native trees, and prickly pear. Captives have eaten bananas, milk, and bread.

Their breeding habits are not well-known. One of us (Davis) purchased a young coati near Mante, Tamaulipas, Mexico in mid-June of 1941 that was estimated to have been 6 weeks old, indicating that it was born about May 1. The man from whom it was purchased reported that four were in the litter. He was of the opinion that all the young are born in the spring of the year. In Arizona, mating takes place in April and young are born in June. The animals are thought to be polygamous. The female alone rears and provides for her offspring.

Remarks. Previous editions have listed the coati under the scientific name *Nasua nasua*. However, we follow Decker in treating the white-nosed coati as specifically distinct from *N. nasua* of South America.

FAMILY MUSTELIDAE (MUSTELIDS)

LONG-TAILED WEASEL
Mustela frenata Lichtenstein

Description. A slender, long-bodied carnivore with small head, long neck, short legs, and relatively long, slender tail; upperparts yellowish-brown; head blackish; spot between eyes, broad band (confluent with color of underparts) on each side of head between ear and eye, chin and upper lip white; tip of tail black, remainder colored like back; underparts, except for chin, orange buff, which color extends down back of front legs over forefeet and on inside of hind legs to foot and sometimes onto toes. Dental formula: I 3/3, C 1/1, Pm 3/3, M 1/2 X 2 = 34. External measurements average: (males), total length, 488 mm; tail, 192 mm; hind foot, 51 mm; (females), 438-187-42 mm. Weight of adult males, about 300-500 g; females slightly less.

Distribution. Statewide, except for extreme northern Panhandle, but scarce in western Texas.

Habits. Long-tailed weasels occupy a variety of habitats in Texas. In general, they occupy a range nearly coextensive with the ranges of pocket gophers and ground squirrels on which they prey in large measure. At one time they occurred throughout the state save for the extreme northern Panhandle.

Although largely terrestrial, these weasels are adept at climbing trees. They are strong swimmers and do not hesitate to cross swift streams. On the ground they frequent areas occupied by small rodents and often live in the burrows of ground squirrels and pocket gophers or in rotten logs, hollow stumps, and under tree roots. Their nest is made of grass and leaves and is lined with rodent and rabbit fur. They may have more than one home. Weasels are active both in the daytime and at night, but more so after dark. They are active year round and show no tendency to "hole up" or hibernate during winter.

They are apparently unafraid of man and have a strong sense of curiosity. Davis once observed one watching him with only its head projecting from the burrow of a pocket gopher. When he approached, it withdrew and reappeared at another opening about 7 m farther on. His closer approach again caused it to retreat and reappear at a third opening. This "game" continued for several minutes, the weasel always exposing itself to watch him but allowing him to approach no closer than about 5 m. By imitating the distress call of a bird, Davis was able to attract weasels to within 10 m of him.

Long-tailed Weasel (*Mustela frenata*). Photo by Robert J. Baker, Texas Tech University.

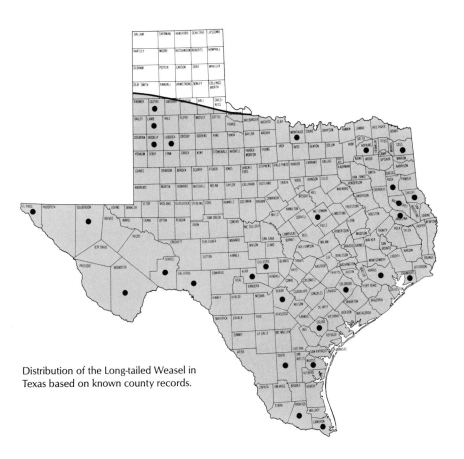

Distribution of the Long-tailed Weasel in Texas based on known county records.

They are vicious and aggressive when cornered and a bundle of fury in the hand. Charles Oehler reported that one he captured by hand could not be released because the weasel would not cooperate.

The food of long-tailed weasels consists almost entirely of small mammals — ground squirrels, pocket gophers, wood rats, cotton rats, small cottontails, and so forth; insects make up a small percentage of the total diet. Birds are rarely taken when other foods are available.

This weasel is polygamous and breeds mainly in July, with implantation and development of the embryos delayed until about 27 days before the young are born. The three to eight young are born about the first week in April in southern Texas. The young are blind, covered with a growth of fine white hair, nearly helpless, and weigh about 3 g at birth. Their eyes open at the age of 36 days, at which time they are already weaned and feeding on solid food. Shortly thereafter they begin to follow their mother on hunting excursions and remain with her until nearly full-grown. Sexual maturity and adult size are reached in females in about 3 months, but not in males until the age of about 12 months.

King snakes, gopher snakes, foxes, bobcats, house cats, large hawks, and owls are known to prey on them.

In general they are desirable residents of a community, but on occasion they enter poultry houses and wantonly kill chickens. Their destruction of mice, ground squirrels, and pocket gophers certainly benefits the agriculturist.

BLACK-FOOTED FERRET

Mustela nigripes (Audubon and Bachman)

Description. A large edition of the common long-tailed weasel; upperparts pale buffy yellow, overcast with brown hairs on head and back; underparts buffy or cream-colored; feet and tip of tail blackish; broad, black mask across face and eyes. External measurements average: (males), total length, 570 mm; tail, 133 mm; hind foot, 60 mm; (females), 500-120-55 mm. Weight, probably 850-1,400 g in males, 450-850 g in females.

Distribution. Originally the same as that of the black-tailed prairie dog, roughly the northwestern third of Texas including the Panhandle, much of the Trans-Pecos, and a considerable part of the Rolling Plains east and southeast of these areas. Now extirpated from Texas. The last Texas records were from Dallam County (1953) and Bailey County (1963).

Habits. Black-footed ferrets are associated primarily with prairie dogs and prairie dog towns. Although individuals have been seen under haystacks, in alfalfa fields, and in buildings, most of these sightings were made during the fall dispersal of the young. Historically, the range of the ferret has coincided closely with that of the various species of prairie dogs which are the main source of the ferret's food. In addition, prairie dog burrows provide the ferrets with shelter and nursery sites for rearing their young.

Both the young and the adults are primarily nocturnal. Young ferrets rarely appear above ground during daylight hours until about mid-August. Adults, however, occasionally leave their burrows during the day to sunbathe or to forage. When a ferret is active in daylight, the prairie dogs stay above ground, keep the intruder under surveillance, and appear to be highly nervous and agitated. This behavior of the prairie dogs is one of the clues one can rely on that a ferret is present in the dog town. A better clue, however, is the presence of a peculiar, shallow trench leading from a prairie dog burrow. When a ferret alters a prairie dog burrow or digs one of its own, it backs out with the dirt held against its chest and drags the dirt farther from the burrow entrance each time. The result is a trench 8-12 cm wide and up to 3.5 m long. These trenches are formed mostly at night and, if fresh, are a sure sign of the presence of a ferret. No other species of animal living in a dog town leaves this type of structure.

Black-footed Ferret (*Mustela nigripes*). Photo courtesy of U.S. Fish and Wildlife Service.

As mentioned above, the mainstay of black-footed ferrets is prairie dogs which the ferrets capture and kill in their burrows at night. Analyses of 56 scats revealed that remains of prairie dogs occurred in 51 of them and comprised 82% of the identifiable animal material. Mouse remains occurred in 19 scats and made up the remaining 18%. Ferrets have also been seen chasing birds and catching moths. Determining their food habits by scat analyses can become quite a chore because the ferrets deposit most of their feces in the burrows they occupy. Only a few scats have ever been found aboveground by investigators diligently searching for them.

Mating is believed to occur in April or May. One female killed on May 16 appeared to be in heat; a female trapped May 3 was pregnant; a nursing female was captured on June 20. The female alone cares for her litter of four or five young even though the male may stay in the same dog town. As soon as the young are able to travel the female coaxes them out of the nest burrow and leads them as she carefully checks several other burrows and finally selects one for her litter and a separate one for herself. As they grow older, the young readily follow their mother and from June to mid-July they may be seen regularly at night as the family extends its activities. By mid-July the young are half-grown and readily eat prey which the female kills. By early August the young ferrets are usually occupying separate burrows in the dog town and by mid-August they are often out during the early morning, playing, and following their mother. By early September the young are nearly full-grown and begin to disperse from their birth place. It is during the period of dispersal that the young are exposed to the greatest danger. More than 40% of the dead ferrets found outside prairie dog towns were recorded from mid-August to mid-October. Ferrets do not hibernate and during late fall, winter, and spring they are usually found singly.

Remarks. The black-footed ferret is an endangered species and is now offered full protection by Federal regulations and cannot be killed or captured legally without a special permit. Although all of the western states have conducted intensive surveys in recent years for black-footed ferrets, only one colony at Meteetsee, Wyoming, was found. These ferrets, numbering about 130 in 1984, subsequently suffered an epidemic of canine distemper that left the species on the brink of extinction. Beginning in 1986, the remaining 18 ferrets known to have survived at the Meteetsee site were captured and put into a captive breeding program with the hope that successful matings would one day allow for the return of this species to its natural habitat. By late 1992, the captive breeding population totaled 225. In the fall of 1991, 49 ferrets were released in the Shirley Basin area of Wyoming. By the spring of 1992, four of these original 49 remained, and two litters of two and four young had been born in the wild. An additional 83 captive-born ferrets were released in Shirley Basin during the fall of 1992.

MINK
Mustela vison Schreber

Description. A weasel-like carnivore about the size of a house cat and semiaquatic in habit; general color dark chocolate brown, darkest on back, and nearly black on feet and end of tail; underparts paler than back, with considerable white on midline from chin to vent; neck long, head hardly larger around than neck; tail long and moderately bushy; eyes and ears small; legs short; pelage soft and dense, overlaid with longer, blackish guard hairs. Dental formula as in the weasel. External measurements of an adult male: total length, 560 mm; tail, 190 mm; hind foot, 67 mm; of a female, 540-180-60 mm. Weight (males), 680-1,300 g; (females), 450-700 g.

Distribution. Known from eastern one-half of state westward to northern Panhandle in habitats near permanent water.

Habits. Mink are closely associated with the waterways and lakes of North America, but the smaller streams are preferred to the large, broad rivers. Along the coast they frequent the brackish marshes and, on occasion, the littoral area adjacent to the ocean. They are most common along streams partly choked by windfalls and other debris

Mink (*Mustela vison*). Photo by Donald F. Hoffmeister, courtesy of Museum of Natural History, University of Illinois.

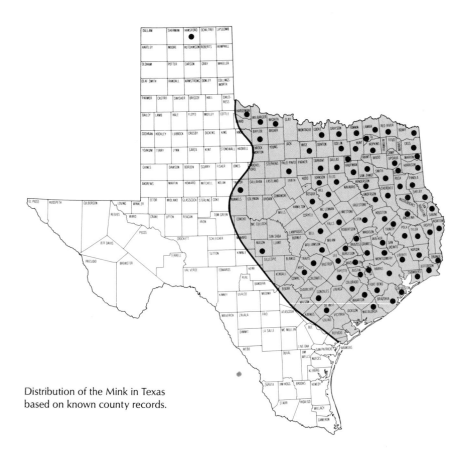

Distribution of the Mink in Texas based on known county records.

which create numerous water holes and at the same time offer concealment for the mink. Lake and marsh-dwelling mink are usually larger than those that live along streams.

Mink are active throughout the year. They are tireless wanderers and may travel several kilometers in their search for food.

The den is usually a retreat under the roots of a tree near the water, in a hole in the bank of a stream, in a pile of debris choking a stream, or in the houses of muskrats, which they kill or otherwise evict from their dens.

Their food consists of a wide variety of animals which they usually capture and kill. The fact that they are attracted to traps by carcasses of birds and other animals suggests that they also feed on carrion. Fish, frogs, clams, freshwater mussels, snakes, rats and mice, ground squirrels, muskrats, and birds constitute their main diet.

Mink are polygamous. The mating season is in January, February, and March and the four to eight young are born after a gestation period of from 39 to 76 days. At birth the young are blind, helpless, and covered with a coat of fine, short, silvery-white hair. They weigh about 6 g. When they are about 2 weeks old, the whitish hair is replaced by a dull, fluffy, reddish brown coat which, late in the year, is replaced by the adult pelage. Their eyes open at about 37 days of age and they leave the nest for the first time when about 7 weeks old. They are weaned when 8 or 9 weeks of age, at which time they weigh about 350 g. When about 5 months old, they are as large as adults.

The mink is one of the principal fur-bearing animals in the eastern United States and is one of the few animals that can be reared economically on fur farms. This is not the case in Texas, however, where mink ranked only thirteenth in numbers of individuals harvested and ninth in economic value to trappers during the 1988-89 trapping season, as determined in a survey conducted by the Texas Parks and Wildlife Department.

AMERICAN BADGER
Taxidea taxus (Schreber)

Description. A rather large, robust, short-legged "weasel"; body broad and squat; tail short, thick and bushy, usually shorter than the outstretched hind legs; pelage long and shaggy, especially on back and sides; upperparts grizzled grayish-yellow in color; a distinct white stripe from near tip of nose back over top of head to shoulder area, also a white crescent on each side of face just back of eye and another at anterior base of ear, enclosing or outlining a large blackish area; snout and rest of head grayish or blackish; underparts yellowish-white; feet blackish; five toes on each foot; front feet large, with claws 25 mm or more in length; hind feet smaller, claws much shorter; skin loose on the body; eyes and ears small; neck short. Dental formula: I 3/3, C 1/1, Pm 3/3, M 1/2 X 2 = 34. Young similar to adults in color and color pattern. External measurements of adult male: total length, 788 mm; tail, 133 mm; hind foot, 120 mm; female, 730-150-114 mm. Weight of adults, 4-10 kg, averaging about 7 kg.

Distribution. Found across state except in extreme eastern part; may be extending its range eastward in connection with changing land-use patterns.

Habits. Badgers occupy a variety of habitats. It ranges over most of Texas except for the extreme eastern part of the state, and recent records suggest it is expanding eastward as a result of land-clearing operations. Badgers are most common in the prairie and desert sections of the West, but limited numbers venture into the mountains where individuals have been seen or captured at elevations well above 3,000 m. In general, they occupy the entire range inhabited by ground squirrels and prairie dogs on which they rely in large measure for food. In Texas, they range from sea level, as on Padre Island, to at least 1,500 m in the Davis Mountains.

As suggested by the disproportionally long front claws, badgers are expert diggers and their short, powerful front legs can move earth with amazing speed. A badger was encountered on Padre Island as it sought refuge in a shallow burrow in a sandbank. Three people, working frantically with shovels for more than an hour, were so outdistanced in their race to capture the animal that they gave up.

It is a common belief that badgers hibernate in winter, but such is not the case. They may sleep through several days of inclement weather, as do skunks and bears, subsisting on fat stored in the body but they do not experience the physiological changes characteristic of true hibernation; namely, considerably reduced rate of respiration and heart beat, lowered body temperature, and insensibility. They are frequently encountered in winter, particularly on mild days, and in the southern parts of their range they are active throughout the entire year.

As indicated above, the chief food of badgers is ground squirrels. In addition, pocket gophers, kangaroo rats, other burrowing rodents, and cottontails are dug out, caught, and eaten. They also eat lizards, birds, eggs, insects, and occasionally carrion.

Badgers are ordinarily solitary except during the mating season. They breed in summer and early autumn. Males are probably polygamous and mate with more than one female. Implantation is delayed until between December and February, and the young are not born until March or April. Litter size ranges from one to five, averaging about three. The young are born in an underground nest and are lightly furred and blind at birth. The eyes open at 4 weeks, and weaning occurs at about 8 weeks of age, when the young are half grown. The young remain with their mother until late fall, when the family scatters.

Badgers have few natural enemies other than man. They are ferocious fighters and are usually more than a match for any dog. In one recorded instance a badger successfully defended itself in a fight with two coyotes.

American Badger (*Taxidea taxus*). Photo by R.D. Porter.

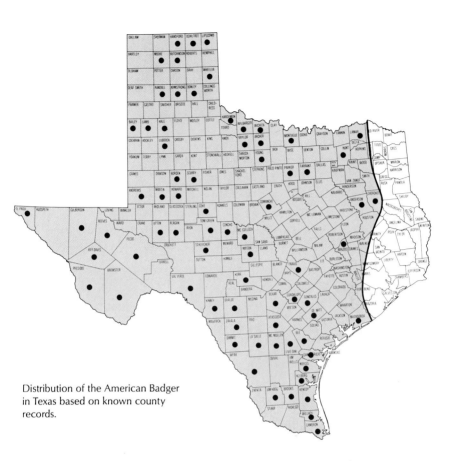

Distribution of the American Badger in Texas based on known county records.

The fur of the badger ordinarily does not command a high price and, because of this, relatively few are trapped. Data indicate that the population is now increasing except in those parts of the animal's range where poison is used ostensibly to reduce the population of coyotes. The badger's chief value lies in helping to keep down excessive populations of rodents.

WESTERN SPOTTED SKUNK

Spilogale gracilis Merriam

Description. Color pattern resembles that of the eastern spotted skunk, *Spilogale putorius*, but white marking is more extensive, the black and white stripes on upper back nearly equal in width (in *putorius* the black areas are much more extensive than the white); dorsal pair of white stripes begin between the ears or just posterior to them (on back of head in *putorius*); white area on face large, extending nearly from nose pad to a line back of eyes and covering more than half of area between eyes; underside of tail white for nearly half its length, the tip extensively white. External measurements average: (males), total length, 423 mm; tail, 134 mm; hind foot, 43 mm; (females), 360-129-40 mm. Weight of males, 565 g; of females, 368 g.

Distribution. Recorded from southwestern part of state as far north as Garza and Howard counties and eastward to Bexar and Duval counties.

Habits. This skunk occupies a variety of habitats and often occurs in close association with man. In Texas, most records of capture indicate that it is most often

243

associated with rocky bluffs, cliffs, and brush-bordered canyon streams or stream beds. In the Edwards Plateau, rock fences seem to be especially attractive, possibly because they also provide denning sites and serve as refuges for many kinds of animals on which the spotted skunks feed. They also have been reported denning in hollow logs and, since they are adept at climbing, in the attics of houses.

Their natural foods are not well documented, but they are known to feed on turkey eggs, young rabbits, mice, and such arthropods as grasshoppers and scorpions.

Sexually mature females come into heat in September and most of them are bred by the first week in October. The blastula stage of the embryo spends 180-200 days floating free in the uterus of the female before it becomes implanted. The two to five (average, four) young are born in late April and May after a total gestation period of from 210 to 230 days. Young females become sexually mature when only 4 or 5 months of age. Testes of both adult and young males begin to enlarge in March, are producing quantities of sperm by May, and reach their largest size during the height of the breeding season in September. In October, the testes begin to regress in size and the forma-

Western Spotted Skunk (*Spilogale gracilis*). Photo by R.D. Porter.

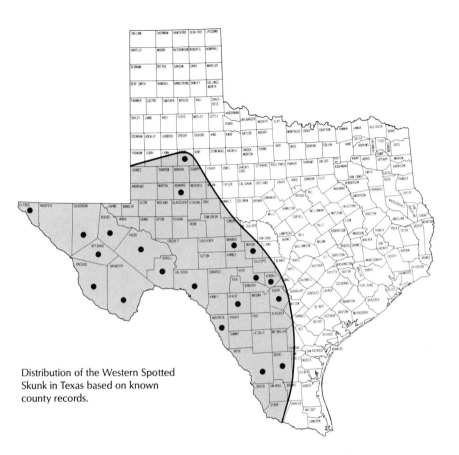

Distribution of the Western Spotted Skunk in Texas based on known county records.

tion of sperm is halted. Thus, the males are incapable of fertilizing the females during the period from November through March. Even though the males are capable of breeding several months before the females come into heat, no breeding takes place until the females are receptive.

Remarks. The previous editions of this book followed Richard Van Gelder in placing all of the spotted skunks in Texas in the species *Spilogale putorius*. Subsequent studies conducted in the Pacific Northwest by Rodney Mead and in Texas by Robert Patton clearly indicate that we have two species. In addition to certain differences in color pattern and cranial features, the most striking differences between the two are found in their reproductive physiology and the period of the year when breeding takes place.

EASTERN SPOTTED SKUNK
Spilogale putorius (Linnaeus)

Description. A small, relatively slender skunk with small white spot on forehead and another in front of each ear, the latter often confluent with dorsolateral white stripe; six distinct white stripes on anterior part of body, the ventrolateral pair beginning on back of foreleg, the lateral pair at back of ears, the narrow dorsolateral pair on back of head; posterior part of body with two interrupted white bands; one white spot on each side of rump and two more at base of tail; tail black except for a small terminal tuft of white; rest of body black; ears short and low on side of head; five toes on each foot, the front claws more than twice as long as hind claws, sharp and recurved. Dental

245

formula: I 3/3, C 1/1, Pm 3/3, M 1/2 X 2 = 34. External measurements average: (males), total length, 515 mm; tail, 210 mm; hind foot, 49 mm; (females), 473-170-43 mm. Males weigh about 680 g; females, about 450 g.

Distribution. Occurs in eastern one-half of state east of the Balcones Escarpment, westward through north-central Texas, to the Panhandle as far south as Garza County.

Habits. Spotted skunks are much more active and alert than any of the other skunks. They occur largely in wooded areas and tall-grass prairies, preferring rocky canyons and outcrops when such sites are available. They are less common in the short-grass plains. In areas where common, they have a tendency to live around farmyards and often den under or in buildings.

Their den sites are varied. In rocky areas they prefer cracks and crevices in the rocks or a burrow under a large rock. Since they are expert climbers, they occasionally den in hollow trees or in the attics of buildings. In settled communities they frequently live under buildings, in underground tile drains and in underground burrows. They are almost entirely nocturnal and seldom are seen in the daytime.

Their food habits are largely beneficial to the agriculturist although they can do considerable damage to poultry if they develop a taste for such food. Their seasonal natural foods consist of: winter — cottontails and corn; spring — native field mice and insects; summer — predominantly insects, with smaller amounts of small mammals, fruits, birds, and birds' eggs; fall — predominantly insects, with small amounts of mice, fruits, and birds. They are excellent rat-catchers and can soon rid a barn of these pests.

Mating occurs in March and April. Some females possibly mate again in July and August and produce a second litter. The gestation period is estimated to be 50-65 days, and no known period of delayed implantation exists. The number of young in a litter may range from two to nine, but the usual litter consists of four or five young.

At birth the young are blind, helpless, and weigh about 9 g each; the body is covered with fine hair. The black and white markings are distinct. Their eyes open at the age of 30-32 days; they can walk and play when 36 days old; emit musk when 46 days old; and are weaned when about 54 days old. When 3 months old they are almost as large as adults. Sexual maturity is reached at the age of 9-10 months in both sexes.

Eastern Spotted Skunk (*Spilogale putorius*). Photo by John L. Tveten.

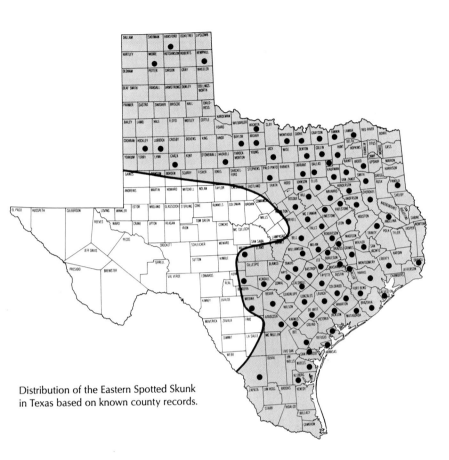

Distribution of the Eastern Spotted Skunk
in Texas based on known county records.

Their enemies, other than man, include dogs, coyotes, foxes, cats, bobcats, and owls. Their defensive behavior consists of a rapid series of handstands, which serve as a warning device to aggressors. If approached too closely, they drop to all fours in a horseshoe-shaped stance, lift their tail, and direct their anus and head toward the potential aggressor. The foul-smelling musk can be accurately discharged for a distance of 4-5 m.

HOODED SKUNK
Mephitis macroura Lichtenstein

Description. Superficially similar to the striped skunk, *Mephitis mephitis*, but differs in having longer, softer fur and a distinct ruff of longer hair on the upper neck. Two color patterns: a white-backed phase with upperparts chiefly white, frequently with two narrow, short white stripes on each side behind shoulder, and underparts black or mottled with white; and a black-backed phase with upperparts black, except for two narrow lateral white stripes, and underside of tail frequently white (occasionally tail wholly black, but bases of hairs always white). In the white-backed phase, a broad white band begins between the eyes and covers most of the back and upper surface of the tail; the white stripe never bifurcates as in the striped skunk. Differs from the hog-nosed skunk in much finer fur, small snout, smaller size, and much longer tail. Dental formula as in the spotted skunk. External measurements of an adult male: total length, 700 mm; tail, 377 mm; hind foot, 69 mm; of adult female, 650-370-60 mm. Weight of males, 800-900 g; of females, 400-700 g.

247

Distribution. Mainly a Mexican species. Occurs in Texas in the Big Bend region and adjacent parts of the central Trans-Pecos. Recorded definitely only from Brewster, Pecos, Presidio, Jeff Davis, Ward, and Reeves counties.

Habits. These slender, "white-sided" skunks occur along stream courses where they resort to rocky ledges or tangles of streamside vegetation for safety. Occasionally they resort to burrows in the banks of washes. One captured in Brewster County, Texas, was trapped in a heavy stand of willows along the sandy banks of Tornillo Creek. It had been feeding in that vicinity in company with hog-nosed skunks.

Little is known of the natural history of hooded skunks, which are the rarest of the skunks in Trans-Pecos Texas. Males and females are in breeding condition from the middle of February to the last of March. Two litters, each consisting of three individuals, have been recorded. Hooded skunks are primarily insectivorous, although they also eat some vertebrates (shrews and rodents) as well as plant materials (prickly pear fruit).

The fur of this animal is much longer and softer than that of any other skunk, but it does not command a high price on the fur market.

STRIPED SKUNK
Mephitis mephitis (Schreber)

Description. A medium-sized, stout-bodied skunk with two white stripes on sides of back that join each other in the neck region and extend onto the head anteriorly and onto each side of the tail posteriorly; tip of tail black; two large scent glands, one on each side of the anus, produce the characteristic skunk musk; ears short, rounded; eyes small; five toes on each foot, front ones armed with long claws; hind feet with heel almost in contact with ground; tail long and bushy; pelage long, coarse and oily. Dental formula as in the spotted skunk. Sexes colored alike, but males usually larger than females. External measurements average: (males), total length, 680 mm; tail, 250 mm; hind foot, 90 mm; (females), 610-225-65 mm. Weight, 1.4-6.6 kg, depending on age and amount of fat.

Distribution. Statewide.

Habits. Striped skunks are inhabitants of wooded or brushy areas and their associated farmlands. Rocky defiles and outcrops are favored refuge sites, but when these are absent the skunks seek out the burrows of armadillos, foxes, and other animals. In central Texas, favored refuge sites are under large boulders.

These skunks are largely nocturnal and seldom venture forth until late in the day; they retire to their hideouts early in the morning. One of us (Davis) has seen striped skunks abroad in midday only twice, and in each instance a female was trailing her family of third-grown youngsters in single file across a meadow to a patch of woodland beyond.

Striped Skunks (*Mephitis mephitis*). Note varying patterns. Photo by D.W. Lay.

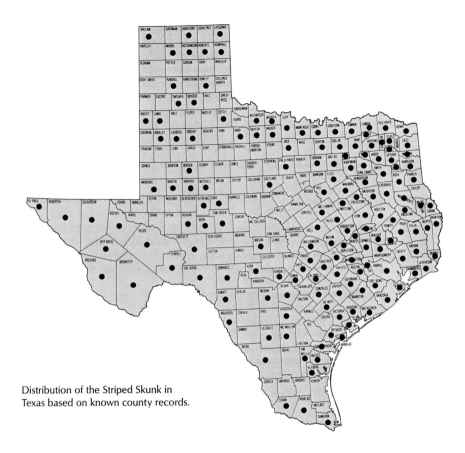

Distribution of the Striped Skunk in Texas based on known county records.

In late fall they become exceedingly fat. In Texas, they are abroad throughout the year and seemingly more active in winter than in the heat of summer. They are social creatures; often several individuals occupy a well-situated winter den. J.D. Bankston of Mason, Texas informed us that he removed as many as seven striped skunks from one winter den and that one of his neighbors found 10 in one den in December. These may have constituted family groups.

Striped skunks are not choosy in their food habits. In Texas, their seasonal food, as judged from the analyses of 79 viscera, is as follows (expressed in percentages): Fall — insects, 76; arachnids, 24. Winter — insects, 52.3; arachnids, 5.3; reptiles, 1.6; small mammals, 18.3; vegetation, 22; birds and millipedes making up the balance. Spring — insects, 96; reptiles, 1.6; small mammals, 2; vegetation and small birds making up the balance. Summer — insects, 88; arachnids, 4; reptiles, 1.5; small birds, 3.5; centipedes, small mammals, and vegetation making up the balance.

Breeding begins in February or March. After a gestation period of about 63 days, the three to seven (average, five) young are born. In Texas, most of the young appear in the first half of May. There is some evidence that two litters may be born to certain females, but one litter seems to be the general rule. The nursery is a cavity under a rock, a burrow, or a thicket of cactus or other protective vegetation. Usually the mother builds a nest of dried grasses and weed stems for the blind, helpless young. The young remain in the nest until their eyes are open and they are strong enough to follow their mother.

Striped skunks have few natural enemies. Owl, hawks, coyotes, bobcats, foxes, and dogs may occasionally take one, but most predators are repulsed by the odor of their musk. Striped skunks are highly susceptible to being struck by vehicles, and road-killed animals are commonly seen along highways throughout Texas. Individuals seldom live more than two years in the wild.

When disturbed or startled, skunks utter a peculiar purring sound and often growl when attacked by man. They typically express their anger by rising upon their hind feet, lurching forward, stamping both front feet, and at the same time clicking their teeth. The expelling of musk generally follows this behavior.

Their fur is the most valuable of all the skunks. They are easily reared on fur farms, but the relatively low value of their pelts does not make such a practice economically worthwhile.

EASTERN HOG-NOSED SKUNK

Conepatus leuconotus (Lichtenstein)

Description. Largest of the North American skunks; superficially resembling the inland species, *Conepatus mesoleucus*, but larger; white stripe on back much narrower, wedge-shaped rather than truncate at anterior end and reduced or absent on the rump; upperside of tail white, underside blackish basally, but white toward tip. Dental formula as in *C. mesoleucus*. External measurements average: (males), total length, 825 mm; tail, 362 mm; hind foot, 85 mm; (females), 700-295-75 mm.

Distribution. Restricted to the Gulf coastal plains of South Texas and northeastern Mexico south to central Veracruz. Specimens are available from the following Texas counties: Aransas, Brooks, Cameron, Kleberg, Nueces, San Patricio, and Webb.

Habits. Little is known about the habitat or habits of this skunk, but it is presumed they are similar to those of the common hog-nosed skunk, *C. mesoleucus*. The species has been collected or observed in the following habitat types in South Texas: live oak brush, mesquite brushland, and improved pasture within semi-open native grassland. The stomachs of three specimens collected in Veracruz, Mexico, were filled with insect remains, but the skunks are also thought to eat small vertebrates and fruit.

Remarks. All evidence suggests this skunk is extremely rare and in need of protection. Most records are from biological surveys of the mid-1800s to the mid-1900s, and there is a growing consensus among professional mammalogists that the population level of this species in Texas has declined drastically during the past few decades. Out of 27,446 steel trap-days from a study of predator control in Kleberg County over a two-year period, Sam Beasom only captured two of these skunks. The reasons for the population decline are unknown at this time, but the species has been afforded category 2 status (in need of careful watching) on the U.S. Fish and Wildlife Service endangered species list.

The taxonomic status of the eastern hog-nosed skunk is also uncertain. Many well known mammalogists have speculated that it is merely a subspecific variant of the common hog-nosed skunk, *C. mesoleucus*.

COMMON HOG-NOSED SKUNK

Conepatus mesoleucus (Lichtenstein)

Description. A rather large skunk with a single, broad white stripe from top of head to base of tail; long, bushy tail white all over with a few scattered black hairs beneath; rest of body blackish brown or black; white stripe on head truncate; snout relatively long, the naked pad about 20 mm broad and 25 mm long; nostrils ventral in position, opening downward; ears and eyes small; five toes on each foot; claws of forefeet much larger than on rear feet, strong and adapted for digging; pelage relatively long and coarse; underfur thin. Young colored like adults; sexes alike in coloration. Dental formula: I 3/3, C 1/1, Pm 2/3, M 1/2 X 2 = 32. External measurements average: (males), total length, 577 mm; tail, 248 mm; hind foot, 65 mm; (females), 542-202-68 mm. Weight, 1.1-2.7 kg, rarely to 4.5 kg. Females are smaller than males.

Distribution. Ranges across southwestern, central, and southern Texas, north at least to Collin and Lubbock counties; former isolated population in Big Thicket region probably extirpated.

Habits. These white-backed skunks inhabit mainly the foothills and partly timbered or brushy sections of their general range. They usually avoid hot desert areas and heavy stands of timber. The largest populations occur in rocky, sparsely timbered areas such as the Edwards Plateau of central Texas and the Chisos, Davis, and Guadalupe mountains of Trans-Pecos Texas. A few have been reported from the Big Thicket area of East Texas, but these are apparently extirpated now. Their presence in an area usually can be detected by the characteristically "plowed" patches of ground where the skunks have rooted and overturned rocks and bits of debris in their search for food. This hog-like habit of rooting has led to the adoption of the term "rooter skunk." Most Texans know the skunk by this name.

Although largely nocturnal, they are not strictly so. In midwinter in central Texas, many of them prefer to feed during the heat of the day. In this respect they remind one of the habits of the armadillo at that season. They seldom are as abundant in any part of their range as the striped skunk, *Mephitis*. Like other skunks, they are relatively unafraid of man or beast and do not hesitate to defend themselves with their powerful musk if unduly molested. In the Guadalupe Mountains of western Texas, one of us (Davis) watched one at close range at night with the aid of a flashlight for nearly 30 minutes as it rooted about in search of food. When approached too closely, fair warning was given as the skunk elevated its tail and maneuvered to place the observer in the line of fire.

As mentioned previously, these skunks prefer rocky situations when available because the numerous cracks and hollows can serve as den sites. Not only do they winter in such dens, but they also use them as nurseries. Unlike the striped skunk, this species is more or less unsocial. Usually only one individual lives in a den, but a trapper in central Texas reported that he once found a winter den occupied by two of them.

Their food habits make them valuable assets in most areas. Based on analysis of stomachs and other viscera of 83 "rooters" from central Texas, their seasonal food

Common Hog-nosed Skunk (*Conepatus mesoleucus*).

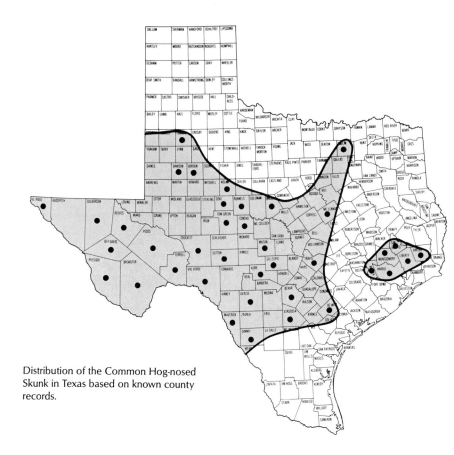

Distribution of the Common Hog-nosed
Skunk in Texas based on known county
records.

(expressed in percentages) consists of: Fall — insects, 52; arachnids, 4; vegetation, 38; reptiles, 6. Winter — insects, 76; arachnids, 12; small mammals, 9; vegetation, 3; with reptiles and mollusks making up the balance. Spring — insects, 82; arachnids, 12; reptiles, 6. Summer — insects, 50; arachnids, 9; small mammals, 3; vegetation, 31; snails, 5; reptiles, 2.

The breeding season begins in February, and most females of breeding age are with young in March. The fact that the female has only six teats, as compared with 12-14 in the striped skunk, suggests small litters of young. Robert Patton found that females generally produce two litters, each consisting of three individuals. The late J. D. Bankston of Mason, Texas reported that he had never seen more than four young with a female. The young are born in late April or early May. The gestation period is approximately 2 months. Nothing has been recorded on the growth and development of the young, but we do know that they can crawl about in the nest before their eyes are open and that at that tender age they can emit a drop or two of musk. By the middle of June they are about the size of kittens and weigh about 450 g. By August most of them are weaned and are "rooting" for their living.

RIVER OTTER

Lutra canadensis (Schreber)

Description. A large, dark brown "weasel" with long, slender body; long, thick, tapering tail; webbed feet; head broad and flat; neck very short; body streamlined; legs short, adapted for life in the water; five toes on each foot, soles more or less

252

hairy; pelage short and dense; upperparts rich, glossy, dark brown, grayish on lips and cheeks; underparts paler, tinged with grayish. Dental formula: I 3/3, C 1/1, Pm 4/3, M 1/2 X 2 = 36. External measurements average: total length, 1,168 mm; tail, 457 mm; hind foot, 124 mm. Weight, 6-7 kg, occasionally as much as 10 kg.

Distribution. Presently known only from eastern one-fourth of state in major watersheds; probably extirpated from the Panhandle, north-central, and southern Texas.

Habits. River otters are largely aquatic and frequent lakes and the larger streams. In the Gulf Coast region, marshes, bayous, and brackish inlets afford suitable range. They are expert swimmers and divers and can remain underwater for several minutes if necessary. They are not bound to water, however, and when occasion demands they do not hesitate to travel overland from one body of water to another. Their movements on land appear awkward. The long body is arched and supported by four short legs and reminds one somewhat of a "measuring" worm.

The slides and apparent playfulness of otters are well-known. The slide, situated on some steep clayey bank, seems to be used chiefly for "recreational" purposes. The otters play "follow the leader" in tobogganing, with front legs folded back, from the top of the slide into the water below.

Otters are notorious wanderers in their chosen habitat and an animal may range over several kilometers of a waterway. For this reason they are never abundant in any locality. They are ordinarily shy, unobtrusive creatures that are seldom seen even though they are active throughout the year.

The den varies with the locality and availability of sites. Most otters locate their dens in excavations close to water under tree roots, rock piles, logs, or thickets. The

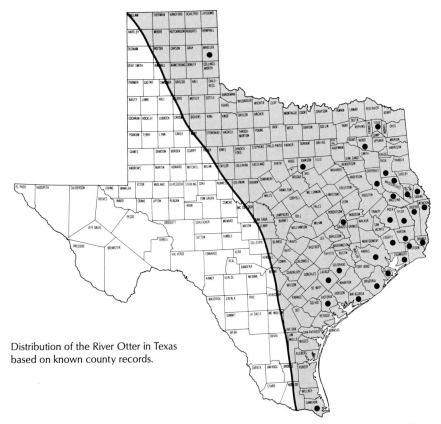

Distribution of the River Otter in Texas based on known county records.

River Otter (*Lutra canadensis*). Photo by John L. Tveten.

hollow bases of cypress trees and tupelo gums are especially popular. Occasionally, they will take over beaver lodges or muskrat dens for their own use after killing the occupants. A typical den consists of a hole leading into a bank, with the entrance below water level. Otters may occupy two dens, one as a temporary resting den and the other as a permanent nesting den.

Otters are not specific in their food habits. Their main diet consists of fish, crustaceans, mollusks, amphibians, reptiles, invertebrates, birds, and mammals. One of their choicest morsels is crayfish, and where they are abundant, an otter will consume a tremendous number annually. The fish they eat are primarily rough fish.

Virtually nothing is known about their reproduction in Texas. They probably breed in fall, but males do not generally mate until they are four years of age, and females rarely breed before two years. Males typically engage in fierce combat during the mating season, and they are believed to be solitary except when accompanying estrous females. Estrous lasts 40-45 days, and the female is receptive to the male at about six-day intervals. Mating usually occurs in the water. Delayed implantation results in the gestation period extending to as much as 270 days. Litter size varies from one to five, with two about average. Females may mate again as soon as 20 days following birth, which means that otters may remain continuously pregnant once they reach sexual maturity.

Newborns are about 275 mm in total length and weigh about 130 g. They are fully furred, but the eyes are closed and none of the teeth are erupted. Their eyes open at 22-35 days, and they are weaned at 18 weeks. The adult waterproof pelage appears after about 3 months.

254

FAMILY FELIDAE (CATS)

MOUNTAIN LION
Felis concolor Linnaeus

Description. A large, long-tailed, unspotted cat; body long and lithe; tail more than half the length of head and body, rounded in cross section, and black-tipped; claws long, sharp, and curved; soles haired, but pads naked; ears small, rounded, without tufts; upperparts and sides dull tawny, darkest on middle of back and tail; face from nose to eyes grayish brown; a pale patch above each eye; back of ear blackish; chin, lips, throat, and underparts whitish; underside of tail grayish white. Dental formula: I 3/3, C 1/1, Pm 3/2, M 1/1 X 2 = 30; upper molar very small, sometimes absent. External measurements of a large adult male: total length, 2.6 m; tail, 927 mm; hind foot, 259 mm. Total length of three males averaged 2.3 m; of females, 2.0 m. Weight of three males, 160-227 kg; of six females, 105-133 kg.

Distribution. Once statewide; now known with certainty, except for occasional occurrences northward, only in desert mountain ranges of the Trans-Pecos region, especially in Big Bend National Park, and in the dense brushlands of the Rio Grande Plain.

Habits. Mountain lions, frequently called pumas or cougars, formerly occurred in almost every kind of habitat within their range in which their chief prey species, deer, occurred. Now, because of continued persecution, they are nowhere common except in the most remote, thinly populated areas.

Retiring and shy by nature and nocturnal by habit, they are seldom seen in their native haunts. In more than 30 years of field work in areas known to be inhabited, we have seen only one of these large cats. In this instance, the animal was accidentally flushed from its daytime lair in a thicket.

These cats spend most of their time on the ground, but they are adept at climbing trees and often do so when pursued by dogs. Their chief range preferences are rocky, precipitous canyons, escarpments, rimrocks or, in the absence of these, dense brush. Heavily timbered areas usually are avoided. The presence of a mountain lion in an area can usually be detected by looking for scrapes, the signpost of the male, which consist of

Mountain Lion (*Felis concolor*). Photo by John L. Tveten.

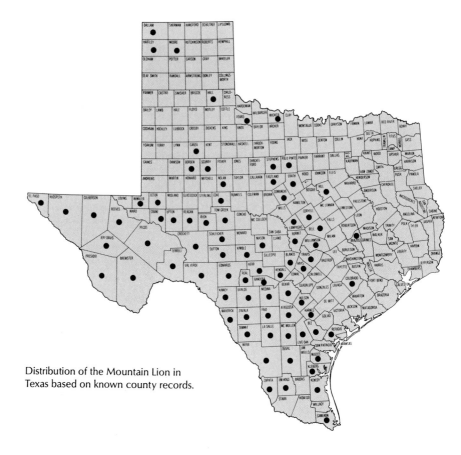

Distribution of the Mountain Lion in
Texas based on known county records.

small piles of leaves, grasses, and so forth that he scrapes together and on which he urinates. These are best found on their travel routes along the ridges and rimrocks.

Contrary to popular opinion, mountain lions seldom use caves as dens. An area under an overhanging ledge, a crevice in a cliff, a dry cavity in a jumbled pile of rocks, an enlarged badger burrow, a cavity under the roots of a tree, or a dense thicket seem to be more desirable.

Their food is almost entirely animal matter but, as with domestic cats, grasses may be eaten occasionally. The chief item of diet is deer. Analyses of stomachs revealed that in the southwest, the mule deer accounted for 54% of the total food (by frequency of occurrence); white-tailed deer, 28%; porcupines, 5.8%; cottontails, 3.9%; jackrabbits, 2%; domestic cows, 1.6%; miscellaneous (including sheep, goats, skunks, foxes, coyotes, beavers, prairie dogs, and grasses), 4.7%. In certain areas they are known to kill and feed upon horses, particularly colts. In general, the mountain lion's food habits are of neutral or beneficial character. The high percentage of predation on deer probably is beneficial from a game management view in most instances because the mountain lion tends to prevent overpopulation of deer, which is the bane of the game manager in many areas where this cat has been exterminated.

Mountain lions are solitary except for a short breeding period of up to two weeks duration, when the female is in estrous. The gestation period is about 3 months. The number of young ranges from two to five, averaging three. At birth, the kittens are woolly, spotted, have short tails, and weigh about 450 g each. They develop teeth when about a month old, are weaned when about 2 or 3 months old, and may remain with their mother until more than 1 year old. Adult females usually breed for the first time between two and three years of age, and breed once every two or three years afterwards.

At present, mountain lions usually are considered as unwanted predators. Their value as game animals has received little attention, but those who have hunted them with trained dogs vouch that the sport is thrilling and exciting. Some day we may see this animal recognized as a game animal, hunted in season, and under license — a position it should have now.

OCELOT
Felis pardalis Linnaeus

Description. A medium-sized, spotted and blotched cat with a moderately long tail; about the size of a bobcat but spots much larger, tail much longer, and pelage shorter; differs from the jaguar in much smaller size and in presence of parallel black stripes on nape and oblique stripes near shoulder; upperparts grayish or buffy, heavily marked with blackish spots, small rings, blotches, and short bars; underparts white, spotted with black; tail spotted, and ringed with black; both sexes colored alike. Dental formula as in the mountain lion. External measurements average: (males), total length, 1,135 mm; tail, 355 mm; hind foot, 157 mm; (females), 930-285-135 mm. Weight, 10-15 kg.

Distribution. Once ranged over southern part of Texas with occasional records from north and central Texas; now restricted to several isolated patches of suitable habitat in three or four counties of Rio Grande Plains.

Habits. The ocelot is a neotropical felid that once inhabited the dense, almost impenetrable chaparral thickets of South Texas, the Gulf coast, and the Big Thicket of eastern Texas. Today, it is found only in several small, isolated patches of suitable habitat remaining in South Texas and is on the verge of completely disappearing from the state. It is listed as "endangered" by the U.S. Fish and Wildlife Service.

In Kerr County, Texas, where ocelots occurred as late as 1902, Howard Lacey reported that he found them in the roughest, rockiest part of the dense cedar brakes. He was of the opinion that they travel in pairs and that they often rest in the trees and so escape the dogs.

Ocelots feed on a variety of small mammals and birds, as well as some reptiles, amphibians, and fish. Lacey reported that they are fond of young pigs, kids, and lambs; E.W. Nelson says that birds, including domestic poultry, are captured on their roosts, and rabbits, wood rats, and mice of many kinds, as well as snakes and other reptiles, are important items in their diet.

The den is a cave in a rocky bluff, a hollow tree, or the densest part of a thorny thicket. The two young are born in September, October, or November. Like other

Ocelot (*Felis pardalis*).

257

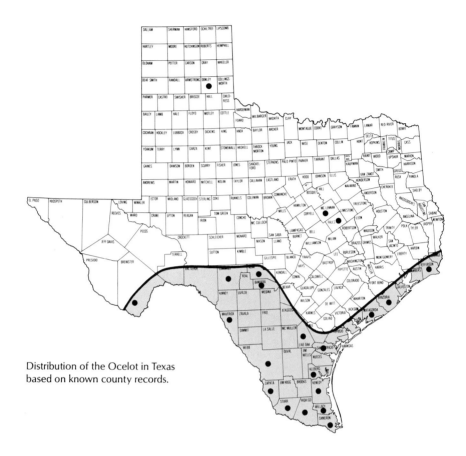

Distribution of the Ocelot in Texas
based on known county records.

young of the cat family, they are covered with a scanty growth of hair, and the eyes are closed at birth. Gestation has been estimated to last 70-80 days and captive kittens opened their eyes 15-18 days after birth.

Remarks. Mike Tewes, of the Caesar Kleberg Research Foundation in Kingsville, Texas, has been studying the ecology and conservation of the ocelot in Texas. He has documented aspects of their biology and natural history and is developing a habitat conservation plan to preserve this species in Texas.

MARGAY
Felis wiedii Schinz

Description. A small, spotted cat similar to the ocelot in color and color pattern but smaller, more slender, and usually with longer tail; skull seldom exceeding 110 mm in greatest length. Dental formula as in the mountain lion. External measurements: total length, 862 mm; tail, 331 mm; hind foot, 112 mm. Weight, 2-3 kg.

Distribution. The margay is a neotropical felid that ranges from northern Mexico to northern Argentina. It is recorded from Texas on the basis of a specimen taken near Eagle Pass in the 1850s. Eddleman and Akersten found remains of this cat in Pleistocene deposits along the Sabine River in Orange County, so a few thousand years ago it ranged over a considerable part of southern Texas.

Habits. The margay inhabits the forested areas of tropical America. It is not a common animal and its habits are not well-known. It is expert at climbing trees, in which it is likely to be found resting during the day. The margay spends some of its time foraging in trees catching birds and small mammals, but also captures prey on the ground. Very little is known about its food habits except that the opossum is known to be included in its diet.

Virtually nothing is known about reproduction in wild margays. In the wild, gestation is estimated to be about 70 days, but in captivity it has been measured at 81 days. Litter size is one or two.

JAGUARUNDI
Felis yagouaroundi Geoffroy

Description. Small, slender-bodied, long-tailed, unspotted, weasel-like cat; size somewhat larger than the ordinary alley cat; legs short for a cat; two color phases. Grayish phase: upperparts grizzled, salt-and-pepper gray; underparts slightly paler; more black in winter pelage. Red phase: upperparts reddish, intermixed with blackish; head and legs more brownish; lips and throat usually whitish. Dental formula as in the mountain lion. External measurements of an adult male: total length, 1,070 mm; tail, 572 mm; hind foot, 137 mm; females usually smaller.

Distribution. Brush country of extreme southern Texas in Cameron, Hidalgo, Starr, and Willacy counties — where it is rare.

Habits. Jaguarundis are denizens of the dense, thorny thickets of southern Texas where cacti, mesquite, cat claw, granjeno, and other spine-studded vegetation abounds. There, these cats live a life of relative safety because such thickets are almost impenetrable to both dogs and man which are their chief enemies. They spend most of their time on the ground, but they are expert climbers and garner part of their food in the trees and bushes. They are largely active at night but move about a good deal in the daytime, often going to water to drink at midday. One of us (Davis) saw an individual cross the highway early one afternoon near the city of Victoria, Tamaulipas, Mexico, using a graceful gait somewhat like that of a disjointed lope. The cat disappeared immediately in the "wall" of brush and could not be followed.

Their food consists of rats, mice, birds, and rabbits. They also are reputed to make inroads on poultry. Robert Snow has stated that their chief food is birds and that the

Jaguarundi (*Felis yagouaroundi*). Photo by John L. Tveten.

young in the dens are fed a similar diet. He reported seeing one old cat spring about 1.5 m into the air and knock feathers out of a low-flying dove. An analysis of stomach contents from 13 Venezuelan jaguarundis revealed the remains of lizards, rodents, small birds, cottontail rabbits, and grass.

Their breeding habits are not well-known. F. B. Armstrong was of the opinion that they have no regular breeding season. He found young in both summer and winter, born probably in March and August. This suggests two litters of two young each year. Snow has found their dens under fallen trees grown over with grass and shrubs and in thickets. They were merely "forms" in this protective cover. He has found young in the den only in March, the number always being three. The young of a litter may all be slate blue, all chocolate brown, or some of them may be blue and the others brown. He reported finding several litters in the vicinity of Raymondville, Willacy County. No information is available on their home life, growth, and development.

This cat is too rare in the United States to be of economic importance. Its pelt is of little value on the fur market. The clearing of brushlands in the Rio Grande Valley threatens to destroy its habitat in Texas, and it is now regarded as endangered by the U.S. Fish and Wildlife Service.

JAGUAR
Panthera onca Linnaeus

Description. Largest of the spotted American cats; form robust; tail relatively short and tapering; ears small, short, and rounded, without tufts; pelage short and rather bristly; upperparts spotted at all ages; ground color buffy to tan, spots blackish, often with light-colored centers; underparts and inner surfaces of legs white, heavily spotted with black; tail with irregular black markings. Dental formula as in the mountain lion, but canines relatively smaller. External measurements of an adult male: total length, 1,933 mm; tail, 533 mm; female, 1,574-432 mm; height at shoulder of a large male, 712 mm. Weight, up to 90 kg; one male from Texas weighed 63.6 kg; another, 42 kg.

Distribution. The jaguar inhabits the dense chaparral and timbered sections of the New World tropics and seldom ventures into the high, cooler inland areas. Apparently, it was once fairly common over southern Texas and nearly the whole of the eastern part of the state to Louisiana and north to the Red River. The last verified records of the jaguar in Texas are from near the turn of the century and this beautiful cat is now extirpated from the state. The jaguar is listed as "endangered" by the U.S. Fish and Wildlife Service.

Habits. Jaguars are the third largest cat of the world, ranking behind the tiger and African lion. In spite of their large size and powerful build, however, jaguars (el tigre of the Mexicans) are shy and retiring. They seldom, if ever, attack man unless cornered or at bay. They are thought to roam over a large territory, much as does the mountain lion, and nowhere are they abundant.

Their food habits are not well-known. In Mexico, they are known to prey on peccaries; many of the Mexicans believe that each large herd of peccaries is trailed by a jaguar so that he can feed on the stragglers. They probably prey also on deer and large ground-dwelling birds. Jaguars are reputed to be so destructive of cattle and horses that the larger Mexican ranches retain a "tiger hunter" to kill them or at least to drive them away. Jaguars are also fond of sea turtle eggs and they roam the beaches on spring nights to dig up and eat the eggs that are buried in the sand.

The den is a rocky cave or the security of a dense, thorny thicket. The mating season is in December and January, and the two to four young are born in April or May

Jaguar (*Panthera onca*). Photo by Lowell Nash.

after a gestation period varying from 93 to 110 days. The kittens are covered with woolly fur, are heavily spotted at birth, and have their eyes closed. When about 6 weeks old they are as large as house cats and begin to follow their parents about. The parents mate at least for the season of parenthood, and both cooperate in rearing the young, although most of the burden falls on the mother. The family unit is maintained until the kittens are nearly a year old, at which time they begin to fend for themselves.

BOBCAT
Lynx rufus (Schreber)

Description. A medium-sized, short-tailed, reddish brown or grayish cat about the size of a chow dog; upperparts reddish brown, streaked with black; underparts whitish, spotted with black; back of ears black-rimmed, with white in center; ears usually slightly tufted; hair on sides of head long, producing a ruff; pelage elsewhere rather short; tail usually shorter than hind foot; the tip black above and white below, with three or four blackish bars above just in front of tip; legs relatively long; feet large, with five toes in front, four behind. Dental formula: I 3/3, C 1/1, Pm 2/2, M 1/1 X 2 = 28. External measurements average: (males); total length, 870 mm; tail, 146 mm; hind foot, 171 mm; females, 772-144-158 mm. Weight of adults, 5-9 kg, occasionally as much as 16 kg in old animals.

Distribution. Statewide.

Habits. Bobcats occupy a variety of habitats, but they have a decided preference for rocky canyons or outcrops when such are available. In rockless areas they resort to thickets for protection and den sites. They are associated more commonly with pinyon pines, junipers, oak, or chaparral in Texas but they also occur in small numbers in open pine forests. These cats are highly adaptable and in most places have been able to cope with the inroads of human settlement.

Shy and retiring, they are active largely at night although they frequently leave cover and begin hunting long before sundown. In hilly country, their presence can often be detected by their habit of dropping their feces on large rocks on promontories or ridges. Also, like the mountain lion, the males make scrapes — small piles of leaves, sticks, and so forth on which they urinate — along their travel routes, but these scrapes are smaller. They den in crevices in canyon walls, in boulder piles, or in thickets. The dens can be readily recognized by the strong odor emanating from them. Expert at climbing trees, bobcats seek refuge in them when available.

Bobcat (*Lynx rufus*). Photo courtesy of Texas Parks and Wildlife.

Distribution of the Bobcat in Texas
based on known county records.

Their food consists mainly of small mammals and birds. The stomachs of 118 bobcats contained the following (expressed in percentages): mammals, 65.8 (44.5 of which were harmful species, 20.5 beneficial, 1.1 neutral); birds (bait), 3.1; fish (bait), 0.6; unidentified foods, 3.1; miscellaneous material (not food), 27.1. Among the mammals, wood rats, ground squirrels, mice, and rabbits supply the bulk of the diet. Although deer occasionally are killed and eaten, most of the deer meat found in bobcat stomachs has been carrion. They also prey upon domestic sheep, goats, and poultry but the damage done is rarely great.

The breeding season begins usually in February, and after a gestation period of about 60 days the two to seven young are born. Average litter size is three. The young are well-furred and spotted at birth; their eyes open in about 9 days. The kittens are weaned when about 2 months old. They remain with their mother until early fall, at which time they begin to fend for themselves. Females do not breed during their first year, but they may mate between their first and second years and breed annually afterwards until 8-9 years of age.

ORDER PINNIPEDIA
SEALS, WALRUSES, AND ALLIES

The Pinnipedia ("fin foot") includes the so-called aquatic carnivores. In fact, some mammalogists consider pinnipeds to be merely a subgroup of the order Carnivora, and do not recognize the ordinal classification of Pinnipedia.

In contrast to some aquatic true Carnivora (i.e. otters), swimming in pinnipeds is accomplished almost entirely by means of the front limbs. The hands and feet are elongated, and the digits are bound together by webs of skin. The tail is rudimentary. Its function as a steering apparatus is taken over by the backward-directed hind feet and the flipperlike front feet. The dentition is of simple, peglike teeth.

The entire group is adapted to feeding on fish, molluscs, and other aquatic animal life. The order is worldwide in distribution, restricted largely, of course, to the oceans and their borders. One species has been recorded from Texas, but it is now extinct.

FAMILY PHOCIDAE (SEALS)

CARIBBEAN MONK SEAL
Monachus tropicalis (Gray)

Description. The Caribbean monk seal was a relatively small seal, the upperparts nearly uniform brown, tinged with gray; sides paler; underparts pale yellow or yellowish white; soles and palms naked; pelage very short and stiff; nails on anterior digits well developed, on posterior digits rudimentary. Dental formula: I 2/2, C 1/1, Pm 4/4, M 1/1 X 2 = 32. Total length of males about 2.25 m; females slightly smaller. Weight, 70-140 kg.

Distribution. Now extinct, the Caribbean monk seal was the only seal native to the Gulf of Mexico. They were tropically distributed but limited to the Gulf of Mexico coast, Yucatan Peninsula, western Caribbean Sea, the Greater and Lesser Antilles, the Bahamas, and the Florida Keys. Records from Texas include one sighting in 1932 and several instances of remains recovered from coastal archaeological sites. *M. tropicalis* probably became extinct by the mid-1950's.

Habits. Notwithstanding the fact that this seal has been known from the time of Columbus, no specimens reached museums until the middle of the last century when its numbers were already so depleted that it had become rather rare. Likewise, very little life history information is at hand.

Caribbean Monk Seal (*Monachus topicalis*). Illustration by Pieter A. Folkens.

These seals preferred sandy beaches for hauling-out grounds, such as the low, sandy islets making up the Triangle Keys west of Yucatan. While on land they were sluggish and had no fear of man, a trait that permitted their slaughter to the point of extinction. In former years they were used extensively as a source of oil.

Virtually nothing was learned about the life history of the Caribbean monk seal before its extinction. Apparently, the young were born in early December because several females killed in the Triangle Keys during this time had well-developed fetuses.

No information is available on their food habits but they probably ate fish and molluscs.

ORDER ARTIODACTYLA
EVEN-TOED UNGULATES

This Order is characterized by either two or four (usually) hoofed toes on each foot, with the exception of the peccary which has four toes on each forefoot, but only three on the hind. The American forms of the order are readily divisible into two groups on the basis of structure of the teeth, presence or absence of horns, and structure of the stomach and feet. The pig group has crushing cheek teeth, upper incisors, a simple stomach, no horns, four hoofed toes, and includes the peccaries. The cow group has rasping cheek teeth, no upper incisors, two or four hoofed toes on each foot, complex stomach, and horns or antlers in most species. It includes the deer, elk and allies; cows and allies; and the pronghorn.

Seven species of artiodactyls are native to Texas although three of these — the mountain sheep, bison, and American elk have been extirpated. Recent reintroductions of these big game animals account for their current presence in the state. In addition, 123 species of ungulates not native to Texas have been imported into the state since 1930. For the most part, these "exotic" animals have been confined on private ranches; however, seven species have escaped, reproduced, and now exist in parts of Texas as free-ranging, feral populations that comprise a part of the local fauna. As the possibility of sighting, or for finding the remains of, these unusual animals mounts yearly in Texas, accounts for the most common exotics have been included in this revision. Accounts of exotics are adapted from the book, *Texotics*, by Elizabeth Cary Mungall and William J. Sheffield, Texas A&M University Press, College Station, Texas.

KEY TO THE EVEN-TOED UNGULATES OF TEXAS

1. Medium size; body form stocky and barrellike; head long and pointed with very short neck; legs short; snout with terminal nasal disc (piglike); upper incisors present 2

    Large size; body form slender or cowlike; head with well developed neck; legs long; snout never piglike; upper incisors absent 3

2. Sparsely covered with coarse bristly hair; some individuals with a scantily haired dorsal mane; tail approximately 300 mm in length; each foot with four toes (the middle two are flattened and have hooves, whereas the lateral toes are higher up on the limb and do not normally touch the ground); adult weight up to 350 kg. *Sus scrofa* (feral pig), p. 268.

    Pelage thick and bristly; well developed dorsal mane of long, stiff hairs extending along back from crown to rump; tail length 15-55 mm; front feet with four toes, hind feet with three toes; adult weight 14-30 kg. *Tayassu tajacu* (collared peccary), p. 268.

3. Two toes on each foot; males with prominent, forked horns; horn sheaths shed annually; females usually with smaller horns that do not shed annually. *Antilocapra americana* (pronghorn), p. 284.

    Four toes on each foot; horns or antlers present 4

4. Males (rarely females) with branching antlers that are shed annually. Family Cervidae 5

    Males and females (except in nilgai) with backward curving, unbranched horns no part of which is shed 10

5. Adults with reddish, brown, or dark brown pelage generally heavily speckled with white spots 6

   Adults with unspotted pelage (juveniles often spotted) 8

6. Antlers flattened, palmate, and with numerous points. *Cervus dama* (fallow deer), p. 272.

   Antlers not palmate 7

7. Antlers 75-100 cm in length along outer curve; normally with only three tines; brow tines project outward to form a nearly 90° angle with main beam. *Cervus axis* (axis deer), p. 271.

   Antlers 28-48 cm in length; normally with 3 or 4 tines branching from main beam. *Cervus nippon* (sika deer), p. 276.

8. Large size (cow size); conspicuous white or cream colored rump patch; upper canine teeth normally present. *Cervus elaphus* (wapiti or elk), p. 274.

   Medium size; white rump patch reduced; upper canine teeth absent 9

9. Antlers usually equally branched (dichotomous) and normally with five or more tines per side, including brow tine; metatarsal gland on hind leg narrow and elongate, 75-125 mm long, and situated above mid point of shank; tail narrow at base. *Odocoileus hemionus* (mule deer), p. 278.

   Antlers with all tines branching off the main beam in a nearly vertical position; metatarsal gland on hind leg nearly circular and about 25 mm or less in diameter; tail broad at base, when alarmed held erect to show conspicuous white "flag." *Odocoileus virginianus* (white-tailed deer), p. 281.

10. Large size; body form stocky and compact ("cowlike"); conspicuous hump dorsally over shoulder. *Bos bison* (bison), p. 288.

    Medium size; body form slender and "deerlike"; dorsal hump absent 11

11. Horns short and smooth; or tall, marked with strong transverse wrinkles, and twisted in a "corkscrew" pattern; but in all cases rise straight above head in a V-shaped pattern 12

    Horns massive (in males), curve out and back from head and then inward to form a "curl" at side of head; females with smaller horns that do not curl, but horns in both sexes marked with strong transverse wrinkles 13

12. Large size; height at shoulder greater than height at rump, giving a backward sloping appearance to profile; males with short, straight horns seldom exceeding 18 cm in length; coloration uniform light brown to iron gray. *Boselaphus tragocamelus* (nilgai), p. 287.

    Medium size; height at shoulder equal to height at rump, no backward slope to profile; males with long, twisted horns up to 79 cm in length; coloration tan to black dorsally with striking white eye rings, chin, chest, belly, and inner legs. *Antilope cervicapra* (blackbuck), p. 294.

13. Conspicuous ventral mane of long hairs hanging from throat and chest; coloration light rufous-brown; whitish rump patch small and inconspicuous. *Ammotragus lervia* (Barbary sheep), p. 292.

    Ventral mane absent; coloration light brown to gray; white rump patch large and prominent. *Ovis canadensis* (mountain sheep), p. 290.

FAMILY SUIDAE (PIGS)

FERAL PIG*
Sus scrofa Linnaeus

Description. Feral pigs in Texas are descended from introductions of European wild hogs for sporting purposes, and from escaped domestic swine that have established feral populations. European wild hogs have several distinguishing characteristics that set them apart from domestic or feral hogs. Among these are brown to blackish brown color, with grizzled guard hairs, a mane of hair (8-16 cm long) running dorsally from the neck to the rump, a straight heavily tufted tail, and ears covered with hair. Characteristics of feral hogs are varied, depending upon the breed of the ancestral stock. European wild hogs and feral hogs interbreed readily, with traits of European wild hogs apparently being dominant.

Distribution. Feral pigs have established sizeable, free-ranging populations in various places on the Rio Grande and Coastal Plains, as well as the wooded country of eastern Texas.

Habits. Good feral hog habitat in timbered areas consists of diverse forests with some openings. The presence of a good litter layer to support soil invertebrates and/or the presence of ground vegetation affording green forage, roots, and tubers is desirable. Hogs are also fond of marsh and grass-sedge flats in coastal areas, particularly if wild grapes are common. During hot summer months, "wallows," or depressions dug in the mud by feral hogs, are much in evidence near marshes or standing water, such as along roadside ditches.

On the Texas coast, feral pigs eat a variety of items, including fruits, roots, mushrooms, and invertebrates, depending on the season. The major foods in spring are herbage, roots, invertebrates, and vertebrates. Fruit, invertebrates, and herbage are most common in fall and winter diets. Herbage eaten by feral pigs includes water hyssop, pennywort, frog fruit, spadeleaf, onion, and various grasses while important roots used for food include bulrush, cattail, flatsedges, and spikesedges. Fruits and seeds such as grapes, acorns, and cultivated sorghum are important, and animal matter ingested by feral pigs includes earthworms, marsh fly larvae, leopard frogs, snakes, and rodents.

Feral pigs can have detectable influences on wildlife and plant communities as well as domestic crops and livestock. Extensive disturbance of vegetation and soil occurs as a result of their rooting habits. The disturbed area may cause a shift in plant succession on the immediate site. Feral pigs also compete, to some degree, with several species of wildlife for certain foods, particularly mast.

Feral pigs generally breed year round; litters range from one to seven, averaging two per sow. An average of one to three suckling pigs usually accompanies brood sows. The heat period is only about 48 hours in duration and the average gestation period is 115 days.

FAMILY DICOTYLIDAE (PECCARIES)

COLLARED PECCARY
Tayassu tajacu (Linnaeus)

Description. These piglike creatures are characterized by presence of four-hoofed toes on the front feet, but only three on the hind feet (outer dewclaw absent); short, piglike snout; crushing molars; nearly straight and daggerlike canines (tusks); harsh pelage with distinct "mane" from crown to rump; distinct musk gland on rump; two pairs of mammae, inguinal in position; distinct whitish collar across shoulder in adults,

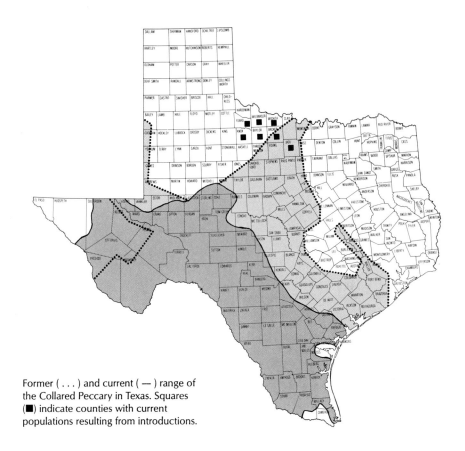

Former (. . .) and current (—) range of the Collared Peccary in Texas. Squares (■) indicate counties with current populations resulting from introductions.

rest of upperparts grizzled black and grayish, with dark dorsal stripe; young reddish to yellowish brown, with black stripe down back. External measurements average: total length, 870-1,016 mm; tail, 12 mm; hind foot, 210 mm; height at shoulder, 816 mm. Dental formula: I 2/3, C 1/1, Pm 3/3, M 3/3 X 2 = 38. Weight, 13-25 kg.

Distribution. Formerly north to the Red River and east at least to the Brazos River Valley. Now restricted to western Texas and the brush country south of San Antonio.

Habits. In Texas, collared peccaries (often called "javelinas") occupy the brushy semidesert where prickly pear is a conspicuous part of the flora. They are commonly found in dense thickets of prickly pear, chaparral, scrub oak, or guajillo; also in rocky canyons where caverns and hollows afford protection and in barren wastelands. Peccaries are active mainly in early morning and late afternoon and often bed down in dense brush or prickly pear thickets during the heat of midday.

They travel in bands ranging from a few animals to several dozen and have a rather limited home range. In the brush country of South Texas, for example, marked individuals moved within home ranges varying in size from 73 to 225 ha. Home ranges of adjacent peccary herds may overlap slightly, but usually only one herd at a time is found in this "border." The boundaries of the home range are marked by scent emitted from the conspicuous musk gland on the animal's rump, which also serves the individual in keeping contact within the herd.

Legendary tales of the peccary have caused inexperienced hunters to kill them through fear rather than for either sport or food. Through exaggerated tales of the

Collared Peccary (*Tayassu tajacu*). Photo by John L. Tveten.

peccary's ferociousness, it has been charged that peccaries will kill or injure dogs and that they are a menace to deer hunters in the dense brush. It is true that encounters between peccaries and untrained dogs usually end with dead or crippled dogs, but it is also true that in these battles the dog is always the aggressor, and any animal will defend its life to the best of its ability when attacked. The peccary is absolutely harmless to the range, to livestock, and to people.

Peccaries are chiefly herbivorous and feed on various cacti, especially prickly pear, mesquite beans, sotol, lechuguilla, and other succulent vegetation. In areas where prickly pear is abundant, peccaries seldom frequent water holes because these plants provide both food and water. Contrary to the habits of the common pig, peccaries rarely root in the ground but rather, push around on the surface — even where the soil is very sandy and loose — turning up chunks of wood and cactus. Mast, fruits, and terrestrial insects also are eaten.

The collared peccary is the only wild ungulate of the western hemisphere with a year-round breeding season. The number of young is usually two, but litters range in size from one to five. The gestation period is 142-149 days (5 months). At birth the young are reddish or yellowish in color and weigh about 500 g. They are able to follow the mother within a few days, at which time the family joins with the rest of the herd. Young females attain sexual maturity in 33-34 weeks; young males, in 46-47 weeks.

In Texas, the peccary was hunted commercially for its hide until 1939 when it was given the status of a game animal. Perhaps a far greater value is in its relationship to range vegetation as peccaries are able to control (by eating) certain undesirable cacti present on overstocked rangeland.

FAMILY CERVIDAE (CERVIDS)

AXIS DEER*
Cervus axis (Erxleben)

Description. A moderately large, spotted deer with three tines on each antler; the brow tine forms nearly a right angle with the beam and the front (or outer) tine of the terminal fork is much longer than the hind (or inner) tine; a gland-bearing cleft is present on the front of the pastern of the hind foot; upperparts yellowish brown to rufous brown, profusely dappled with white spots; abdomen, rump, throat, insides of legs and ears, and underside of tail white; dark stripe from nape to near tip of tail. Dental formula as in *Cervus elaphus*, but upper canines (the so-called elk teeth) usually lacking. External measurements average: (males) total length, 1.7 m; tail, 200 mm; height at shoulder, 90 cm; females smaller and usually without antlers. Weight, 30-75 kg in males; 25-45 kg in females.

Distribution. Native to India, where it is known as the "chital," the axis deer was introduced into Texas about 1932. In 1988, free-ranging herds were established in 27 counties of central and southern Texas. At this time, it also occurs as a confined animal on ranches in 67 other counties. Axis deer are the most abundant exotic ungulate in Texas.

Habits. Axis deer are inhabitants of secondary forest lands broken here and there by glades, with an understory of grasses, forbs, and tender shoots which supply adequate drinking water and shade. They tend to avoid rugged terrain. Their food consists largely of grasses at all seasons, augmented with browse. Green grasses less than 10 cm high seem to be preferred. In Texas, they graze on grasses such as paspalum,

Axis Deer (*Cervus axis*). Photo by Martin T. Fulfer, courtesy of Texas Parks and Wildlife.

switchgrass, and little bluestem. Sedges are favorite spring foods. Browse species include live oak, hackberry, and sumac.

These animals are gregarious and usually are found in herds ranging from a few animals to 100 or more. In each herd the leader is usually an old, experienced doe. Unlike our native deer, adult male axis deer normally are found living with herds of young and old animals of both sexes. Anatomically, axis deer are more closely allied to the North American elk than to our native deer. Like our elk, rutting male axis deer emit buglelike bellows, and both sexes have alarm calls or barks.

The reproductive pattern in axis deer is similar to that in domestic cattle. In the wild, bucks with hardened antlers and in rutting condition may be found throughout the year. Each buck seems to have a reproductive cycle of its own which may not be synchronized with that of other bucks in the herd. Consequently, when some bucks are coming into rut, others are going out or are in a non-breeding condition, with no antlers and with their testes quiescent. Likewise, females experience estrous cycles throughout the year with each cycle lasting about 3 weeks. Gravid females may be found throughout the year, but the major breeding season lasts from mid-May through August with a June-July peak in activity. The bucks make no attempt to collect or retain harems of does, but instead they seek out and service the does in each herd as they become receptive.

Normally, only one fawn is produced per pregnancy after a gestation period of 210-238 days. Reflecting the summer peak in rutting activity, nearly 80% of Texas fawns are born in early January to mid-April, although fawns may arrive in all seasons. Following parturition, females again mate during the subsequent breeding period, so that adult females tend to produce one fawn each year. Twins are rare.

Fawns begin eating green forage by $5^1/_2$ weeks of age, but weaning is delayed until 4-6 months. Permanent dentition is acquired when $2^1/_2$-3 years of age and adult size is reached at 6 years for females and 4-5 years for males. Possibly, does may breed in the breeding season following birth, but most do not breed until the following season, when 14-17 months of age. Lifespan is 9-13 years, although zoo animals may reach 18-22 years of age.

FALLOW DEER*

Cervus dama Linnaeus

Description. A medium sized, "rangy" deer; adult males with large palmate antlers. Bucks develop "spike" antlers beginning in their first year and until 3-4 years old, grow and cast only antlers comprised of beams and simple points. At 3-4 years of age males may develop antlers with broad, palmate areas that measure 8-25 cm in width; total length of antlers is up to 39 cm.

Coloration is highly variable, but four color forms predominate: 1) common — rust color with white rump patch and belly, white spots on back and sides merging into a white line along the lower side and near the rump on the haunches; a black line runs down the back and often connects with the black upper surface of the tail; in winter, spots become indistinct; 2) menil — contrasts with common color form in that ground coloration is tan rather than rust and dorsal lines are brown rather than black; white spotting remains distinct in winter coat; 3) white — coloration is white, with dark eyes; not true albinism; and 4) black — very dark (but not truly black); spotting barely visible; in winter appears as dull brown. In Texas, black, white, and menil color forms predominate.

Fallow deer stand 91-97 cm at the shoulder and appear thin. Males weigh 79-102 kg but may lose 9-23 kg during rut. Females weigh 36-41 kg.

Distribution. Native to the Mediterranean region of Europe and Asia Minor, fallow deer are the most widely kept of the world's deer and have been introduced to all inhabited continents. This deer has been introduced to 93 Texas counties, primarily in the Edwards Plateau region. In 1988, the Texas population was estimated to be 14,163, both free-ranging and confined animals combined.

Habits. Fallow deer do much of their feeding in open, grassy areas but require tree cover and undergrowth for shelter and winter food. Deciduous or mixed woodlands on gently rolling terrain are best, but conifer forests may be suitable in some places. The Edwards Plateau region, with its mosaic of oak mottes, juniper brushland, and grassy areas is well-suited for fallow deer.

Food availability appears to determine whether fallow deer in an area are predominantly grazers or browsers. On the Kerr Wildlife Management Area (Kerr County), fallow deer ate 54% browse, 30% grass, 12% forbs, and 5% other, although these figures varied as the degree of competition with domestic livestock and white-tailed deer varied. Live oak, shin oak, hackberry, and Spanish oak were the dominant browse species taken while Texas wintergrass, fall witchgrass, and common curlymesquite were the predominant grasses eaten. Increased competition for browse with white-tailed deer caused fallow deer to increase their dependence on grasses, while increased livestock competition for grasses led fallow to increase their use of browse.

Fallow Deer (*Cervus dama*). Photo by John L. Tveten.

Rutting may begin in mid-September and continue into November but peak breeding activity takes place in October. During rut, bucks mark off and defend a small area, known as a "stand," from which other rutting males are excluded; females and young remain within the male territories and as each doe comes into heat, she is followed until mating is accomplished. After the rut, males gradually cease defending their territories and form "bachelor groups," while females and young remain segregated from males and in their own groups.

The gestation period is approximately $7^1/_2$ months, with most fawning occurring from late May through June. Generally, only a single fawn is born, although twins are not uncommon.

Females reach sexual maturity at 16 months and can bear their first fawns by 2 years of age. Bucks mature sexually at 14 months but rarely compete successfully in rutting until several years later. Bucks attain physical maturity at 6 years of age. Lifespan is about 11-15 years, with a maximum record of 25 years.

WAPITI OR ELK
Cervus elaphus Erxleben

Description. Large, deerlike, the males with large, usually six-pointed antlers that are shed annually; hair on neck long and shaggy; upperparts buffy fawn, the head, neck, legs and belly dull rusty brown to blackish; large rump patch creamy buff to whitish; metatarsal gland oval, about 75 mm long, the center white; tail a mere rudiment. Dental formula: I 0/3, C 1/1, Pm 3/3, M 3/3 X 2 = 34. External measurements average: (males) total length, about 2 m; tail, 160 mm; hind foot, 670 mm. Weight, up to 300 kg, averaging about 275 kg. Females are smaller and usually without antlers.

Distribution. Formerly present only in the Guadalupe Mountains (Culberson County) but presently, free-ranging elk exist in Texas in five small herds in the Guadalupe Mountains, Glass Mountains (Brewster County), Wylie Mountains (Culberson County), Davis Mountains (Jeff Davis County), and Eagle Mountains (Hudspeth County). Others are kept in deer-proof pastures on scattered ranches over the state. Total statewide population in 1984 was estimated to be 1,600.

Habits. Elk formerly inhabited the plains region of the western United States in winter and open, forested areas in summer. They migrated from one to the other seasonally. Now, they are forced by land-use practices into yearlong use of the mountainous regions. Lack of adequate winter range is one of the big obstacles to the increase or even maintenance of elk on much of their former range.

Elk are gregarious at all seasons, but in spring and summer the old bulls usually are solitary or in bachelor herds. Except during the period of rut, the herd invariably is in charge of a cow and it is she who leads them to water, to the feeding grounds, and so forth. When bedded for the night, for the noonday siesta, or when feeding a sentinel is posted (again a cow) to stand guard and give the alarm if danger threatens. On sensing danger the sentinel or any other cow gives warning by an explosive "bark" that instantly alerts the entire herd. When elk are traveling or feeding, the rear stragglers are usually immature animals.

The normal gait of elk is a saunter, but they can trot or gallop, depending upon the mood of the individual. After a really bad scare, the animals may gallop at top speed for a kilometer or so, then stop and reconnoiter; if the alarm has proven serious, the herd may resume flight at a dogtrot, often in single file — a pace that can be maintained for several hours. In spite of their large size, elk are rather agile and can readily jump over fences and corrals as high as 2 m.

Although their senses of sight and hearing are well developed, it seems that elk depend largely upon the sense of smell to detect danger. One can easily stalk them upwind as long as the animals do not scent the stalker. The calls of elk are described as of three kinds: (1) the bark of the cow, usually a danger signal, (2) the bugling of the bull during the period of rut, and (3) the bleating of calves and yearlings.

The antlers usually are shed between February 15 and April 15, and new growth starts soon after the old scars are healed. Between the time of shedding and the latter part of August or early September, the adult bull grows a new set of antlers weighing as much as 15-20 kg. During this period, W. B. Sheppard found that animals kept in confinement consumed seven times the ration customarily eaten during other times of the year. The normal number of points per antler in old males is six, very often five, and rarely as many as nine.

Elk are both grazers and browsers. Palatability studies in northern Idaho revealed that the "key forage species" on the summer range are willow, maple, broom grass, rye grass, and elk sedge. Serviceberry, mountain ash, and bitter cherry also were heavily utilized browse species. There is limited information about their food habits in Texas. In the Guadalupe Mountains, they feed on mountain mahogany, agaves, and several species of grasses.

Bugling, which marks the onset of the breeding season, usually starts in the latter part of August, shortly after the velvet has been shed from the antlers. Breeding activities increase until mid-September and close by November. Not all cows come

Wapiti or Elk (*Cervus elaphus*). Photo courtesy of National Parks Bureau of Canada.

into heat at the same time. Shortly after bugling starts, the herds break up and bulls collect their harems of five to 15 adult females. Sheppard maintains that the bulls do not actively seek out the cows, but rather the cows gravitate toward the larger, more virile bulls. Usually, the younger, unattached bulls remain near a harem and, although the leader tries to keep them at a distance, he finds it difficult to do so. Adult bulls start into the rut excessively fat, but they usually emerge in poor physical condition. This emaciation is due to the fact that for the 6 week rutting season the larger bulls have little time to eat or even sleep because they are constantly on the alert to ward off the younger bulls. Old bulls do not ordinarily stay with the same harems throughout the breeding period but move from one herd to another. It frequently happens that the larger bulls become so exhausted that they retire from the herd for a time to recuperate. Toward the close of the rutting season the larger bulls desert the cows for good and seek seclusion.

The average gestation period of elk is about $8^1/_2$ months (249-262 days). The main caving period extends from about the middle of May to the middle of June; the number of young is almost invariably one. At birth the calf is long-legged and reddish-brown in color, with interspersed white spots on the back and sides. The rump patch is poorly defined. For the first few days the calves are rather helpless and, except for the feeding periods, remain hidden beside logs, under bushes, or in other places. When about 2 weeks old they are able to follow the females; soon after that the mother and her young one rejoin the main herd. At the age of 1 month elk calves eat grass and other vegetation, and when 2 or 3 months old they graze regularly with the adults. Weaning evidently does not take place until October or even after the rutting season. Sexual maturity in females ordinarily is not reached until the second year. Bulls do not enter actively into the rut until they are about 3 years old.

Remarks. Although there are no museum specimens to document their presence, the only native elk in Texas were in the southern part of the Guadalupe Mountains. Those elk belonged to the species *Cervus merriami*, which became extinct around the turn of the century. In 1928, Judge J. C. Hunter and his associates imported 44 elk (*Cervus elaphus*) from the Black Hills of North Dakota and released them at McKittrick Canyon in the Guadalupes. They multiplied rapidly and expanded their range to nearly all parts of the mountains. The estimated population size in 1938 was 400. In 1959, elk were added to the list of game that could be hunted, and the population was estimated to number about 300. The most recent estimates place the Guadalupe Mountain herd size at no more than 40 individuals. In 1992, the Eagle, Davis, and Wylie Mountain herds each were estimated to number 15-40 individuals, while the Glass Mountain herd numbered 150-180 elk.

SIKA DEER*

Cervus nippon Temminck

Description. A small to medium sized deer that, due to extensive hybridization in Texas, is highly variable in size and coloration. In general, sika are all "compact" in form; appear "dainty-legged"; and have a short, trim, wedge-shaped head. Males carry antlers that average 28-48 cm in length, although exceptional racks may be up to 74 cm in length. Sika antlers have 3-4 points branching from a main beam; there is no palmate growth as in the fallow deer. Females have a pair of black bumps on the forehead, their placement corresponding to that of the males's antlers.

Coloration is drab brown to a deep, mahogany brown mottled with numerous white spots. The degree of spotting is highly variable, however, and in some individuals spotting may be absent. The head, as well as the hair tuft over each metatarsal gland, tends to be lighter than the body. A distinctive, white rump patch is evident, especially when the animal is alerted.

Texas sika range in size from 76-89 cm shoulder height and 45-80 kg for the smaller Japanese and Formosan varieties to 89-109 cm shoulder height and 68-109 kg

Sika Deer (*Cervus nippon*). Photo by John L. Tveten.

for the larger Dybowski's variety. Female Dybowski's sika stand about 81 cm in height and weigh 45-50 kg.

Distribution. Formerly, sika were native from southern Siberia and the adjacent Japanese island of Hokkaido south, along both the mainland and islands, to southeastern China and Formosa. Sika have rapidly disappeared from much of their range due to habitat loss. Sika have been introduced in 77 counties of central and southern Texas, with free-ranging populations known from 12 of these counties. In 1988, the total statewide population was estimated to be 11,879.

Habits. Sika are woodland deer characteristic of broad-leaved and mixed forests where snowfall does not exceed 10-20 cm and snow-free sites are also available. Large forest tracts with dense understory and occasional clearings are ideal; the patchwork of brush cover and open grassland found in the Edwards Plateau and South Texas regions are well-suited to these deer.

Sika feed on grasses, leaves, twigs, and tender shoots of woody plants depending on seasonal availability. In Texas, the spring preference is for grasses, although browse may also be consumed regularly, and browse use increases after the flush of spring growth has passed. The most important food for sika in Texas is live oak, with hackberry, wild plum, mustang grape, Texas sotol, and greenbriar also serving as important browse species. Favored grasses include Texas wintergrass, fall witchgrass, and meadow dropseed. Forb use generally increases in summer, and is lowest in winter.

Sika males are territorial and keep harems of females during the rut, which peaks from early September through October but may last well into the winter months. Territory size varies with type of habitat and size of the buck; strong, prime bucks may hold up to 2 ha. Territories are marked with a series of shallow pits, called "scrapes," into which the males urinate and from which emanates a strong, musky odor. Fights between rival males are sometimes fierce, long, and may even be fatal.

The time of fawning is primarily May through August. After a $7^{1}/_{2}$ - 8 month gestation period a single fawn is born; twins are rare. Zoo longevity records typically range from 15-18 years, although an exceptionally long lifespan of 25 years, 5 months is known for one animal.

MULE DEER
Odocoileus hemionus (Rafinesque)

Description. A moderately large deer with large ears; antlers typically dichotomously branched and restricted almost entirely to males; metatarsal gland 8-12 cm long, narrow, and situated above midpoint of shank; upperparts in winter cinnamon buff suffused with blackish, more reddish in summer; brow patch whitish; ear grayish on outside, whitish on inside; tail usually with black tip and white basal portion; underparts white. Dental formula: I 0/3, C 0/1, Pm 3/3, M 3/3 X 2 = 32. External measurements average: (males) total length, 1,755 mm; tail, 152 mm; hind foot, 555 mm; metatarsal gland, 129 mm; (females) 1,453-175-475 mm. Weight, 57-102 kg.

Distribution. Occurs over most of the Trans-Pecos and Panhandle regions of Texas and in some areas immediately east thereof, partly as a result of introductions.

Habits. Mule deer occupy to some extent almost all types of habitat within their range but, in general, they seem to prefer the more arid, open situations in which sagebrush, juniper, pinyon pine, yellow pine, bitter brush, mountain mahogany, and such plants predominate. In western Texas, rocky hillsides covered with lechuguilla, sotol, juniper, and pinyon pine provide the essentials.

The mule deer is noted for its peculiar, high-bouncing gait. Estimates of their speed vary, but Donald McLean was able to force one to a speed of 58 km an hour on a dry lake flat in California. After the first short burst of speed, the animal dropped to about 35 km an hour and was badly winded after a chase of less than 1.5 km. When allowed to choose their own gait, they are able to travel at about 30 km an hour for a considerable period of time. In rough, broken country they are at their best. There, the long, high bounds send them over the rocks and brush much faster than the average running animal can go through or around the obstructions. The longest bounds are generally made when the animals are going downhill or leaping across gullies. McLean measured two flat jumps that were 5.9 and 7.1 m, respectively. A downhill bound on a 7% slope measured 8.7 m. They can easily clear a fence 2 m high.

Although equipped with acute senses of sight and hearing, these deer rely largely upon the sense of smell in detecting danger. Stationary objects are easily overlooked by them, but they readily detect any that are in motion.

Mule deer of both sexes normally do most of their feeding in early morning before sunrise or in late afternoon and evening after sundown. They spend the middle of the day bedded down in cool, secluded places. In summer, the bucks retire as soon as the sun shines where they are feeding and go to the dense shade of some grove to bed down for the day. In general, mature bucks prefer rocky ridges for bedding grounds because there they seem to feel more secure from the approach of danger. Does and fawns are more likely to bed down in the open. In winter, however, they often seek out sunny places well screened on at least three sides by vegetation. At night, they usually bed down in the open away from trees and bushes.

The food of the mule deer is quite varied. In Trans-Pecos Texas, the flowering stalks of lechuguilla, the basal parts of sotol, mesquite, juniper, and a number of forbs contribute to their diet. Feeding time varies with the weather, the phase of the moon,

Mule Deer (*Odocoileus hemionus*). Photo by Frank Aguilar, courtesy of Texas Parks and Wildlife.

the time of the year, and type of country. During cold, snowy, winter months when food is difficult to obtain and a considerable amount is required to maintain body heat and energy, deer feed at all times of day and night. During the rutting season, feeding is often erratic, especially with bucks. During the hunting season, when many hunters are on the range, bucks do the major part of their feeding at night. Deer are more prone to feed on dark nights and are relatively quiet and bedded down when the moonlight is intense. In spring and summer, mule deer tend to feed to a greater extent upon green leaves, green herbs, weeds, and grasses than they do upon browse species; the reverse is true in fall and winter.

The rut begins in the fall, usually in November or December, but varies with locality and climatic conditions and continues until the latter part of January or even into February. During this period, the bucks have terrific battles in which the antlers are used almost exclusively. Bucks that are evenly matched in size and strength may fight until almost exhausted before one or the other is the victor. The animals are polygamous. The stronger, more virile bucks attract females to them and attempt to defend them against the attentions of the younger bucks. Small, persistent bucks can lead a large buck a miserable life, leaving him little time to take care of family duties or even to eat, because of his continued attempts to drive them away. In this period the necks of bucks become swollen, a development that is closely associated with reproduction.

The gestation period is approximately 210 days, and the fawning period extends over several weeks in June, July, and August. The female sequesters herself and drops her fawn in a protected locality where it remains for a period of a week or 10 days before it is strong enough to follow her. At birth fawns are spotted and weigh approximately 2.5 kg. They are nursed at regular intervals by the female, 10 minutes of nursing usually sufficing for a full meal. The young ones are weaned at about the age of 60 or 75 days, at which time they begin to lose their spots. The weaning time is a critical one because if green forage is not available, the fawns seldom make their transfer from milk to a diet of vegetation. If the fawn is not weaned, both mother and fawn are likely to experience difficulty in surviving a severe winter. Sexual maturity is attained at the age of about 18 months in does but ordinarily, young bucks are not allowed to participate actively in the rut until they are 3 or 4 years old.

Antlers are shed after the breeding season, from mid-January to about mid-April. Most mature bucks in good condition have lost theirs by the end of February; immature bucks generally lose them a little later. New antler growth begins immediately following the shedding of the old. Growth is extremely rapid, and massive antlers develop fully in about 150 days. While the antlers are growing, the bucks remain on the open slopes and benches where the brush is short or scattered to avoid injuring the soft, new growth. Mature bucks normally have four main points on each antler, but beyond the third year there is little or no correlation between the number of points and the age of the deer. Beyond the prime of life, the so-called "Pacific buck" type may develop, which consists of only two points, or a spike, on each side of a large set of antlers.

The age of mule deer can be determined fairly accurately up to about 24 months. At birth the fawn is equipped with upper premolars, the third and fourth lower

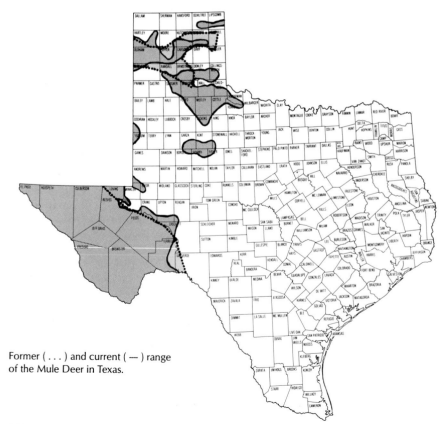

Former (. . .) and current (—) range
of the Mule Deer in Texas.

280

premolars, the lower canines, and the entire lower incisor series. The second lower premolar may erupt shortly after birth or within the first 60 days. By the age of 3½ months, the first upper molar is functional. At the age of approximately 1 year, the middle lower incisor is shed and replaced by a permanent one. Each permanent incisor is wider than its predecessor. At the age of 15-18 months, the molars erupt and take their place in the series, and at the age of 24-25 months, the premolars are replaced by the permanent dentition.

Mule deer are of considerable economic importance as a big game mammal. Statewide, the population was estimated to be about 198,000 in 1991 and the harvest by hunters that year was estimated at 7,900. On the other side of the ledger, there is some competition between mule deer and livestock on the range, particularly in spring and early summer. Furthermore, such maladies as hoof-and-mouth disease can be transmitted from deer to livestock, and vice versa, so that once the disease is established in wild animals drastic measures must be taken to curb it. Anthrax is also said to be propagated and spread by deer, and these animals are also capable of harboring the causative agents of tularemia or rabbit fever.

Remarks. Sympatric populations of mule deer and white-tailed deer (*Odocoileus virginianus*) in western Texas have been found to interbreed and produce hybrid offspring. Genetic analyses indicate that these hybrids are more characteristic of white-tailed deer than of mule deer; thus, it appears that hybridization may be one factor contributing to the displacement of mule deer by white-tailed deer in this region.

WHITE-TAILED DEER
Odocoileus virginianus (Boddaert)

Description. A relatively small deer with relatively short ears; all major points of the antlers come off the main beam; tail relatively long, broad basally, and white underneath; metatarsal gland small and circular; females usually antlerless; upperparts reddish brown in summer, bright grayish fawn sprinkled with black in winter; face and tail usually lack blackish markings; underparts white. Dental formula as in the mule deer. External measurements average: (males) total length, 1,800 mm; tail, 300 mm; hind foot, 450 mm; females slightly smaller. Weight of males, 30-70 kg.

Distribution. Suitable brushy or wooded country throughout the state.

Habits. White-tailed deer occur almost entirely in the hardwood areas within their general range except for the southeastern section of Texas where the principal vegetation is a mixture of pines and hardwoods or nearly pure stands of pines. In the Chisos Mountains of Texas they occur in the mountains, whereas the mule deer occupies the lower foothills and broken deserts; in most other places this habitat relationship is reversed. For example, in the Guadalupe Mountains the whitetail occurs almost entirely in the foothills; the mule deer, in the higher mountains.

White-tailed deer have a relatively small home range and cruising radius. Normally, when food conditions are adequate, the deer tend to stay in one locality for long periods. For example, in the Edwards Plateau region, where deer were belled in an experimental study, many of the marked deer remained on an area of 259 ha for at least 3 years. A few of them were found as far away as 8 km.

Deer are most active just before sunset and again shortly after sunrise. It has been found in experimental trials that they are most easily observed in the hour just before dark. During the middle part of the day they are generally bedded down in some thicket or on some promontory where they are more or less protected. Under cover of darkness it is not uncommon for them to feed well into the night, but there is usually a period of resting and cud chewing during the middle part of the night. In regions heavily populated with deer their trails and beds, the latter usually scraped out places

White-tailed deer (*Odocoileus virginianus*).

under the protection of overhanging boughs or at the bases of trees, are readily seen and give some clue to the density of the population.

As with most other mammals, the feeding habits of whitetails vary from place to place and from season to season. E. L. Atwood listed more than 500 different plants utilized by whitetails in the United States. Availability determines in large measure what the animals will eat but if adequate food is available, the deer are dainty eaters and exercise considerable choice in the items taken. In the Chisos Mountains of Trans-Pecos Texas, whitetails feed extensively on mountain mahogany and other low shrubs. In the Edwards Plateau region the deer graze twice as much as they browse. There, 67% of their total feeding time was spent in grazing on forbs and grasses, 26% in eating fruits and mast, and only 7% in browsing. In South Texas, however, browse species make up the bulk of the diet.

The 10 most favored foods as observed in the Edwards Plateau of Texas are grasses and weeds, Mexican persimmon, live oak acorns, live oak leaves, mesquite beans, oats or other grain, Spanish oak acorns, spike rush, *Foresteria* or elbow bush, and turkey pear. On the basis of food consumed, seven deer will eat about as much as one medium-sized cow.

White-tailed deer are polygamous. The rut begins in early fall and continues through early winter. The onset of breeding varies considerably from one section of the country to another. In coastal Texas, for example, it is not uncommon for breeding to begin as early as September. In the Edwards Plateau, not more than 300 km distant, the peak of the breeding season is in November, whereas in the southern "brush country" section of Texas the peak is in late November and December.

The fawns, usually one or two in number, are dropped after a gestation period of approximately 7 months and hidden by the female for 10 days to 2 weeks. She goes several times daily to nurse them but as soon as they are strong enough to follow her about they do so. The spots are retained until the fawns molt in early fall by which time they are usually weaned. Normally, sexual maturity is not reached in females until the second year but occasionally, when food conditions are excellent, female fawns mate the first fall and produce offspring the following spring when they themselves are only 1 year old. This appears to be unusual throughout most of their range, however.

There is a relationship between testicular activity and the growth and shedding of antlers. The antlers begin their annual growth when the testes and accessory organs are inactive, harden and lose their velvet when these glands are enlarging, and are shed when they begin to decline. Castration following loss of the velvet results in shedding within 30 days. New growth, which occurs at the normal time, is abnormal in shape and the velvet is not lost. Growth ceases at the usual time and part of the growth, being somewhat fragile, may be lost by accident. Renewed growth activity follows in the spring. Eventually, an aggravated burr is produced. These events have been interpreted as indicating that antler growth is under the influence of a nontesticular hormone, possibly from the anterior pituitary, and antler hardening and subsequent loss of the antler is due to the action of a testicular hormone.

One can estimate the age of whitetails by examination of the teeth. At 9 months of age the fawn will be acquiring the middle pair of permanent incisors while the remainder of the incisors as well as the premolars will be milk teeth. At this age one molar on either side of each jaw is well developed while the second is barely breaking through the gum. At the age of 1½ years all milk incisors have been replaced by permanent teeth. At least two molars are fully developed while the third may be in any condition from barely emerging from the mandible to fully emerged. At the age of 2 years the full set of permanent teeth is acquired. Beyond 2 years age determination is somewhat uncertain but can be roughly estimated by the wearing of the teeth. Wear of the teeth is gradual until at 5 years the ridges of enamel are no longer sharp, but rise slightly and gradually above the dentine. At still later ages the crowns of the premolars and molars rise only a short distance above the gums, and the grinding surfaces are worn practically smooth.

Contrary to popular opinion, it is almost impossible to determine accurately the age of deer by the number of points on the antlers. For example, the shed antlers collected from one buck in Texas over a period of 5 years had each year either four or five points on each side. There is some correlation between age and diameter of the beam of the antler, however. The older bucks tend to have heavier antlers, but antler development is also so closely associated with nutrition that it is hazardous to make generalizations concerning age and diameter of the beam. Also, a certain amount of geographic variation is seen in antler development.

White-tailed deer are the most important big game animals in Texas. In the face of an expanding human population this species has done remarkably well. It is estimated that our 1991 white-tailed deer population numbered more than 3.1 million in spite of heavy hunting pressure and approximately 474,000 were harvested by hunters in that year.

On some ranges there is considerable competition for forage between white-tailed deer and domestic livestock. This is particularly true between deer and domestic goats. Competition between deer and cattle is not so severe. Where abundant in farming areas, deer often become pests and destroy such crops as peas, peanuts, wheat, oats, and other small grains.

FAMILY ANTILOCAPRIDAE (PRONGHORN)

PRONGHORN

Antilocapra americana (Ord)

Description. A small, deerlike mammal with black, pronged horns that reach beyond the tip of the ears in males; in females they are shorter and seldom pronged; only two toes on each foot (no dewclaws); rump patch, sides, breast, belly, side of jaw, crown, and band across throat white; chin and markings on neck black or dark brown; black patch at angle of jaw in males (absent in females). Dental formula: I 0/3, C 0/1, Pm 3/3, M 3/3 X 2 = 32. External measurements of males average: total length, 1,470 mm; tail, 135 mm; hind foot, 425 mm; females, 1,250-135-400 mm. Weight of males, 40-60 kg; females somewhat smaller, averaging about 40 kg.

Distribution. Formerly distributed over the western two-thirds of Texas, as far east as Robertson County in the north, and Kenedy County in South Texas. Now restricted to limited areas from the Panhandle to the Trans-Pecos.

Habits. The fleet-footed, large-eyed pronghorn is an animal of the plains. Adapted for speed and for seeing long distances, it inhabits areas where both its sight and its running will be unimpaired by woodland vegetation. Water in the immediate vicinity is

Pronghorn (*Antilocapra americana*).

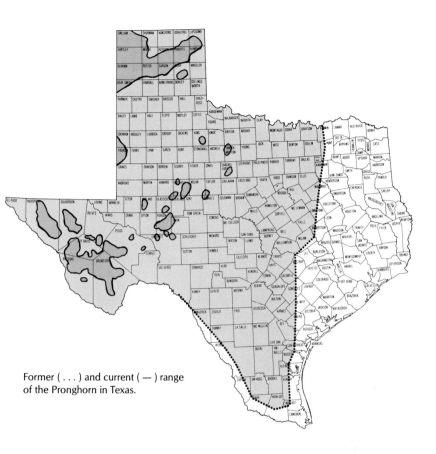

Former (. . .) and current (—) range of the Pronghorn in Texas.

not a requisite because the pronghorn is so adapted physiologically that it can go for long periods without drinking. Apparently, it has the ability to conserve body water and to produce metabolic water.

Among North American mammals, pronghorns are the most fleet-footed. The top speed at which they can run probably does not exceed 70 km an hour, and certainly it varies with individuals. An interesting trait of pronghorns is their highly developed sense of curiosity. They insist on examining at close range any unrecognized object, particularly one that is in motion. Because of this, it is possible for man to lure the animals within close range by hiding behind a bush and waving a handkerchief or other object slowly back and forth. Indians, and sometimes our present-day hunters, have utilized this ruse in bagging them. Another peculiar trait is their disinclination to jump over fences or other objects. A low brush fence no more than a meter high will ordinarily turn the animals, and it is not uncommon for small bands to be reduced almost to the point of starvation within a fenced enclosure while plenty of food is available on the outside. They can jump over moderately high obstructions, however, when hardpressed. Ordinarily, they crawl under or between the wires of barbed-wire fences.

The pattern of daily activities in Trans-Pecos Texas varies considerably with the season, daily weather, and interruptions from enemies or man's activities. Usually, the animals rise shortly after daybreak and begin a period of intensive feeding lasting from 1 to 3 hours, followed by a period of lying down to rest. Resting for about 1 hour is followed by a long period of feeding through most of the morning. Near midday, another extended period of lying down occurs, succeeded by one or two feeding periods during the afternoon. When the heat of the day is intense in spring and summer, little activity takes place. After about 5 p.m., pronghorns feed steadily until nightfall, at which time they recline for a long period of rest. The alternation of feeding and resting is repeated at night, with longer periods of lying down than during the day.

Pronghorns feed entirely upon vegetation, chiefly shrubs and forbs. In Trans-Pecos Texas, Helmut Buechner found that their summer forage consists of about 62% forbs, 23% browse, and 15% grasses. All parts of the plants were consumed including leaves, stems, flowers, and fruits.

Pronghorns have a particular fondness for flowers and fruits. The flowers of cutleaf daisy, white daisy, stickleaf, paper flower, and woolly senecio are consumed in large amounts. Although paper flower is poisonous to sheep and woolly senecio is poisonous to cattle, pronghorns apparently suffer no ill effects from either and consume large quantities of both. They do suffer from locoweed (*Astragalus mollissimus*), although few eat enough of it to die from its poisonous effects.

Autumn forage consists of about 59% forbs, 34% browse, and 7% grasses. More browsing is done in fall than in summer. Winter forage is the same as that in late autumn, with some variation when snow covers the ground, during which time pronghorns consume larger quantities of green woolly senecio; the dried stems and old flower parts of broom weed, stickleaf, and groundswell; old heads of grama grasses; dried leaves of goatweed; and browse species such as javelina bush, Mexican tea, and sacahuiste. Little attempt is made to paw away the snow to get these plants. Cedar is used throughout the winter where available in large quantities. Four of the most important winter foods are cutleaf daisy, paper flower, fleabane, and wild buckwheat. In late February, early annuals become available. Early spring flowers, which appear about the middle of March, are eagerly sought. More grass is taken when new green growth appears in spring.

The breeding season of the pronghorn in Trans-Pecos Texas extends from the last week in August to the first week in October. The most vigorous bucks gather small harems of two to 14 does. Young bucks frequently linger at the outskirts of the harem herd and at times attempt to steal a doe or even to interfere with a mature buck in his mating activities. The master of the harem has an endless task in keeping his does together and warding off intruding bucks. The gestation period is between 7 and 7$^1/_2$ months. The young (usually two) weigh from 2 to 4 kg each and appear in May or June. The female hides her young ones, and at first the fawns are active only a small part of the day. The female goes to them three or more times a day so they can nurse. When about a week old, they are able to walk and run well and begin nipping at vegetation. When a month old, they graze readily on green vegetation. When the fawns are a month to 6 weeks old, does and fawns gather together in small herds which are maintained well into and sometimes throughout the winter season. Nursing continues until the fawns are about 4 months old, so that most of them are weaned about the time of the onset of mating activities.

Sexual maturity is reached at the age of about 1 year in both sexes. There is some indication, however, that young does may breed late in the year in which they are born, as is the case in white-tailed deer. The covering of the horns is shed shortly after the breeding season, beginning about the middle of October and ending in early November. New horn growth is rapid but the prong is not evident until about the first week in December.

An apparently satisfactory method of judging the age of pronghorns is one also used for domestic sheep. Fawns are born with only two lower incisors and develop four teeth (three incisors and a canine) on each side of the lower jaw by fall. At the age of about 15 months, the first middle incisors are being replaced by permanent teeth; at

2¹/₂ years the second incisors are replaced; at 3¹/₂ years the third incisors are replaced; and at about 4 years the pronghorn has a full set of permanent front teeth. After 4 years, age must be judged on the spread of the two middle incisors and the amount of wear on all of the teeth. The life-span under natural conditions may be as much as 12-14 years, but the average age attained is probably considerably less.

The pronghorn is one of our more desirable game species, but despite extensive management efforts it has been decreasing in numbers in recent years. The estimated statewide population in 1990 was 13,920 and the 1989 harvest by hunters was 543.

It is commonly believed that these animals compete seriously with livestock for available forage on the range. According to Buechner, the total amount of competition between cattle and pronghorns is approximately 25%. Competition with sheep is much more severe, reaching at least 40%, as determined by studies in Trans-Pecos Texas. Pronghorns are far more dependent upon weeds than are sheep, and where sheep have eliminated these plants on heavily stocked ranges pronghorns cannot successfully maintain themselves.

FAMILY BOVIDAE (BOVIDS)

NILGAI*
Boselaphus tragocamelus (Pallas)

Description. A large antelope with short, smooth horns in males. Horns average only 18 cm in length, with lengths of only 23-30 cm the maximum. Females usually do not grow horns, but may occasionally.

Nilgai stand 119-150 cm at the shoulder, with prominent withers giving them a backline that slopes to the rump. In bulls, powerful shoulders and a thick neck tend to accentuate this sloping profile.

Nilgai (*Boselaphus tragocamelus*). Photo courtesy of Texas Parks and Wildlife.

Overall coloration is gray to brownish gray in males; females and young are brown to orangish brown. Patches of white on the face and below the chin, extending into a broad, white "bib" on the throat, break up the ground coloration. A narrow white band along the brisket area broadens over the abdomen and spreads between the hind legs to form a narrow rump patch that is edged with darker hair. Below the white bib hangs a tuft of hair, or "beard," which may be as long as 13 cm in males.

Bulls weigh 109-288 kg, with the maximum about 306 kg. Females weigh 109-213 kg.

Distribution. Nilgai are native to India and Pakistan, where they are the largest species of antelope. Nilgai were imported into Texas as game animals and have readily reproduced and established free-ranging populations. They are the most abundant free-ranging exotic ungulate in Texas and have done especially well in South Texas. The majority of Texas nilgai are found in free-ranging populations on several large ranches in Kenedy and Willacy counties.

Habits. Avoiding densely wooded areas, nilgai inhabit relatively dry areas of flat to rolling country with a moderate cover of thin forest or scrub. The South Texas brush country is ideally suited to these animals.

Forage preference is based primarily on availability. Nilgai both graze and browse, with grasses constituting the bulk of the diet. In Texas, mesquite, oak, partridge pea, croton, nightshade, and a variety of grasses are eaten.

Nilgai typically herd in small groups of about 10 animals although larger groups of 20-70 are occasionally seen. Males and females remain segregated for most of the year, with bulls joining the cow-calf groups only for breeding. In Texas, most mating activity occurs from December through March; however, breeding can occur throughout the year. The period of gestation is 240-258 days and nilgai commonly bear twins. In favorable conditions females only 18 months of age can conceive, but few females mate before 3 years of age. Males become sexually mature by $2^{1}/_{2}$ years of age but usually cannot compete successfully with other males until about 4 years old.

In South Texas the life expectancy of nilgai is about 10 years, providing they survive the most vulnerable period — from birth to about 3 years of age, when adult proportions are attained. In Texas, coyotes are the primary predator of nilgai calves but are not of sufficient size to take full grown animals. In addition to people and coyotes, cold weather can cause significant mortality among nilgai in South Texas. Nilgai have a thin coat and store only a meager winter fat reserve. Although rare in South Texas, prolonged periods of cold temperatures will dramatically reduce nilgai populations. During the severe winter of 1972-73, 1,400 of 3,300 nilgai were killed by the weather in South Texas. This die-off was exacerbated by previous brush clearing, which resulted in forage loss and increased competition with livestock and other wildlife.

BISON

Bos bison (Linnaeus)

Description. A large, cowlike mammal with distinct hump in the shoulder region; head, neck, shoulders, and forelegs with long, shaggy hair; hind part of body with short hair; head heavy with short, curved, black horns; tail short and ending in tuft of hair; color brownish black anteriorly, brownish posteriorly. Dental formula: I 0/3, C 0/1, Pm 3/3, M 3/3 X 2 = 32. External measurements approach: (males) total length, 3,400 mm; tail, 610 mm; hind foot, 610 mm; height at shoulders, 1,800 mm; females somewhat smaller. Weight of bulls, 700-1,000 kg; females, 300-400 kg.

Distribution. Formerly widespread in the western two-thirds of Texas; now extirpated or confined in captivity. It is no longer considered a game animal in Texas.

Habits. In early days the bison was found in great numbers over a vast range in North America. With the westward expansion of the white settlers, it became an

Bison (*Bos bison*). Photo courtesy of the U.S. Fish and Wildlife Service.

object of exploitation on a tremendous scale that resulted in its total disappearance from the East and its almost complete extermination over much of its western range. By 1825 it had become practically extinct east of the Mississippi River. The building of the transcontinental railways after 1830 hastened the slaughter of the vast herds west of the river. In the 1870s hundreds of thousands were recklessly killed for their hides and tongues. In 1877-78 the last great slaughter of the "southern herd" took place south of the main transcontinental railroads. In the north their numbers likewise rapidly decreased.

When protection of the buffalo was under consideration by the Texas Legislature, General Phil Sheridan opposed it, pointing out that the sooner the buffalo was eliminated the sooner the Indian would be starved into submission. Sure enough, before 1880 both the buffalo and the Indian had all but passed away.

The big slaughter took place about 1877-78 when there were reported to be 1,500 hunting outfits working out of Fort Griffin (Shackelford County) alone. More than 100,000 hides were taken in the months of December and January of that winter. From 1881 to about 1891 there were shipments of buffalo bones from Texas totaling $3 million in value.

In the late 1880s it was realized that the bison was approaching extinction. By then, there were left in the United States only a few privately owned herds and a herd in Yellowstone National Park. It was not until May of 1894 that an effective law for the preservation of the bison was passed by the United States Congress, and subsequently, the various herds were built up in the United States and Canada. By 1933 the total population of bison in North America was estimated at 21,000, of which the greater part (17,000) were in Canada on the Buffalo National Park near Wainwright, Alberta.

The bison of the western United States is normally a dweller of open prairies. The subspecies *B. b. athabascae* of Canada and the Old World relative (*Bos bonasus*), however, are forest animals. This, together with the fact that our plains bison lacks the keen eyesight of most plains dwellers but has a keen sense of smell, suggests that at some remote time in the past the plains bison, too, lived in woodland areas.

Bison are gregarious creatures that live together in herds, except for the old bulls which, especially in spring and early summer, lead a more or less solitary existence. During the period of rut in July and August, and again in winter, the old bulls tend to be more tolerant of the herd. Normally, bison are unobtrusive but when angered or when called upon to protect their calves they are vicious and dangerous. As with domestic cattle, old bulls are surly and may attack with slight provocation, as will cows with calves.

The daily activity of bison is much like that of domestic cattle. The chief feeding periods are early morning and late afternoon, with midday given over to cud-chewing, siesta, and wallowing. Normally, nighttime is a period of rest. Formerly, the plains bison migrated seasonally, going south as far as Florida and Texas in winter, and northward again in summer. Their normal gait is a plodding walk, which may break into a swinging trot or, when frightened or angered, a stiff-legged gallop.

Plains bison are predominantly grazers, feeding chiefly on grasses and secondarily on forbs. Browse species contribute slightly to their menu. Because of this, competition between bison and domestic cattle for range forage is so great that we cannot afford, for economic reasons, the return of the bison to anything like its former numbers.

The period of rut is July and August. The animals are promiscuous in mating habits but usually only the large, mature bulls do the breeding. Young and undersized bulls are driven from the herd to linger on the outskirts and await with anticipation the opportunity to participate whenever the herd bull is off guard. As with range cattle, a scale of social dominance is established with each bull next highest dominating those below him.

The period of gestation is 8½ - 9 months — the calves arriving in April, May, or early June. One calf at a time is the rule; twins are rare. The young one normally is weaned in late fall, but occasionally it continues to nurse until the arrival of the next calf. Sometimes cows breed only in alternate years. Sexual maturity is reached in the third year. According to Cahalane, cows have remained productive for 40 years indicating a life span of at least 45 years.

At present, the plains bison has little economic importance. There is some demand for its flesh as food for man, but the temperament of the beast will not permit its wide replacement of cattle.

MOUNTAIN SHEEP
Ovis canadensis Shaw

Description. A large, dark-brown sheep with heavy, tapering, curled brown horns in males (horns much smaller and less curled in females), and conspicuous white rump patch; pelage hairy, not woolly; four black hoofs on each foot; tail short; mammae two. Dental formula: I 0/3, C 0/1, Pm 3/3, M 3/3 X 2 = 32 (lower canine is shaped like an incisor). External measurements average: (males) total length, 1,763 mm; tail, 107 mm; hind foot, 439 mm; (females) 1,431-107-407 mm. Weight of rams, 75-150 kg; females, 45-65 kg.

Distribution. Formerly ranged throughout the isolated mountain ranges of the Trans-Pecos; however, native populations are now extirpated. The last native sheep were seen in the Sierra Diablo in 1959, when the total population was estimated at 14. Recent introductions of mountain sheep (or "bighorn sheep") in the Sierra Diablo, Van

Horn Mountains, Elephant Mountain Wildlife Management Area, and Baylor Mountains have resulted in small, wild populations in these areas.

Habits. In general, mountain sheep are inhabitants of rough, rocky, mountainous terrain. They are not forest dwellers but prefer bluffs and steep slopes where the vegetation is sparse and the view unobstructed.

Beds are conspicuous indicators of the presence of sheep. Two distinct types are utilized. The day bed, used during midday siestas, is a temporary affair constructed when and where the individual sheep decides to rest. Usually, each adult animal, particularly among the rams, excavates a shallow depression by executing three or four pawing scratches with each forefoot before lying down. Lambs and yearlings usually omit the pawing activity. The night beds are more elaborate structures. They are usually situated on steep, rocky slopes, on top of rocky rims, or on a slope between two bluffs. In such places the sheep receive adequate protection, for they have an unobstructed view in all directions except uphill, from which direction the approach of a predator would be signaled by rolling stones. The animals tend to bunch together at night. Individual beds are ovoid in shape with the long axis on the contour of the slope. Beds are typically 7-10 cm in depth, about 75 cm in length, and 60 cm in width. No bedding of any sort is utilized; the animals lie on the bare earth. Beds in constant use are rimmed with piles of feces and strong with the odor of urine.

The food of bighorn sheep depends on availability and season. In western Texas deer brush, sotol, and ocotillo were utilized extensively by bighorns. Vernon Bailey reported them as feeding on mountain mahogany, Mexican tea, trumpet flower, mock orange, prickly pear, wild onions, and penstemon. The fruits of datil (*Yucca*) and prickly pear are especially choice foods in the desert areas. Bighorns rarely need water.

Mountain Sheep (*Ovis canadensis*). Photo by John L. Tveten.

291

Apparently, they derive sufficient water from the green and succulent vegetation on which they feed.

The breeding season begins in November and continues for a period of approximately 6 weeks. The rams do considerable fighting at this period, and usually the larger and stronger ones prevent the weaker ones from mating. The bighorn ram does not assemble and guard a harem but moves from flock to flock seeking ewes that are ready to mate. Ewes become sexually mature in 2½ years and give birth to their first lambs at 3 years of age. Rams under 3 years of age appear to take little, if any, active part in breeding activities. The gestation period is approximately 180 days. The first lambs are born in mid-May with others appearing until about mid-June. Usually, only one lamb is produced, but twins are not infrequent. The lambs are weak and helpless at first but they develop rapidly and by the age of 1 week are able to follow the ewes about with ease.

Age in mountain sheep can be estimated by examination of the teeth. The formula at birth is I 0/3, C 0/1, Pm 2/2, M 0/0 (milk dentition); at 8 months, I 0/3, C 0/1, Pm 3/3, M 1/1 (molars permanent); at 15-18 months, I 0/3, C 0/1, Pm 3/3, M 2/2 (molars permanent); 24 months, first (middle) incisor is shed and replaced by permanent tooth; 36 months, first two premolars are shed and replaced by permanent teeth; 42 months, third molars are fully erupted, second milk incisor replaced, last premolars shed and replaced; 48 months, full set of permanent teeth.

At one time bighorn sheep were widespread in Trans-Pecos Texas but the advance of civilization and the inroads of domestic sheep upon the range of the wild animals led to a steady decline of the bighorn population. In spite of laws affording full protection to the sheep, they continued to decline in numbers. Today, the native population is extinct. The Texas Parks and Wildlife Department is attempting to establish wild-trapped sheep from other states in several Trans-Pecos mountain ranges. The 1990 population estimates for these herds were as follows: Van Horn, 25; Baylor, 18; Elephant Mountain, 31; Sierra Diablo, 127. In addition, 27 sheep were released on Beach Mountain in 1991.

BARBARY SHEEP*
Ammotragus lervia (Pallas)

Description. A relatively large sheep with horns curving outward, backward, and then inward and marked with strong transverse wrinkles; horns of females similar but somewhat smaller; tail relatively long, reaching nearly to hocks and with long hairs on terminal half; a conspicuous growth of long hair on throat, chest, and upperparts of front legs; no beard as is found in goats; upperparts and outer surface of legs uniform rufous or grayish brown; blackish mid-dorsal line from head to middle of back; flanks, inner surface of legs and belly whitish, but the chest colored like the sides; horns yellowish brown, darkening with age, set close together (nearly touching at the bases), and attaining a length of 50-80 cm. External measurements of a moderately large adult male: total length, 1,650 mm; tail, 141 mm; hind foot (tip of hoof to hock), 363 mm; ear, 116 mm; height at shoulder, 950 mm. Weight of males up to 145 kg; females to 65 kg. Dental formula: I 0/3, C 0/0, Pm 3/3, M 3/3 X 2 = 30.

Distribution. Native to the dry mountainous areas of northern Africa; introduced into the Palo Duro Canyon area of Texas in 1957-58, where it has become firmly established. Also present in the Edwards Plateau, Trans-Pecos, South Texas, Rolling Plains, and Post Oak Savannah regions as a result of private introductions.

Habits. This sheep, also called the aoudad, is adapted to a dry, rough, barren, and waterless habitat — much as is the native bighorn sheep of our southwestern deserts.

Consequently, it is quite likely that these two could not survive together in the same area because of competition between them.

These sheep live in small groups comprised of old and young animals of both sexes. They are expert climbers and can ascend and descend slopes so precipitous that man can negotiate them only with great difficulty. Consequently, they are difficult to hunt.

Their food consists of a wide variety of vegetation including grasses, forbs, and shrubs. Apparently, they are capable of producing metabolic water and can survive for long periods without access to fresh water. However, when water is available they utilize it for both drinking and bathing.

In studies conducted in New Mexico, Herman Ogren found that 79 species of plants were included in the diet of these sheep; of these, 13 were grasses, 20 were shrubs and the remainder forbs. Mountain mahogany (*Cercocarpus breviflorus*) was the most sought-for single plant. On a yearlong basis this species comprised nearly 22% of the items found in rumens of the sheep. Ogren found some seasonal variation in the diet. In winter, grasses comprised 86% of the rumen contents; browse, 11%; forbs, 3%. In spring, summer, and fall the browse species, mainly oaks and mountain mahogany, comprised about 60% of the diet; grasses, about 26%; and forbs (various species of "weeds") made up the balance. On a yearlong basis, browse species comprised 49% of the diet; grasses, 42%; forbs, 9%.

The breeding season appears to be rather extended, but most of the breeding is concentrated in the 2 months from mid-September to mid-November. The gestation period is about 160 days. Consequently, most of the lambs are born between late February and late April, but some lambs are born as late as November.

Barbary Sheep (*Ammotragus lervia*).

According to Ogren, females may become sexually mature at the age of 8 months, but normally they are older. All females 19 months of age or older that were collected in the fall and winter season were gravid, lactating, or ovulating.

Ogren developed a technique for aging these sheep by examination of the dentition in the lower jaw. The following scheme is adapted from his studies:

Age	Condition of Dentition
3 weeks	Deciduous dentition complete and consists of four pairs of deciduous incisiform teeth and three pairs of deciduous premolars.
8 months	First permanent molar erupted or erupting.
17 months	Second permanent molar erupting.
18 months	First (inner) permanent incisor erupts.
21 months	Third permanent molar erupting; deciduous premolars being replaced.
23 months	Second deciduous incisor shed.
27 months	Permanent dentition except for outer two pairs of incisiform teeth; last molar not fully exposed.
36 months	Third pair of permanent incisiform teeth present; last molar fully exposed but unworn.
48 months	Fourth (outer) pair of deciduous incisiform teeth (the canines) being replaced.
60 months	Full set of permanent teeth.

These sheep were first brought to the United States in about 1900 and have been reared in zoos and on private preserves for a number of years. They were first released in the wild in New Mexico in 1950 and in Texas in 1957, when 31 were released southwest of Claude in Armstrong County. Thirteen more were released near Quitaque. These introductions were highly successful in the Palo Duro Canyon area. By May of 1966 the population had increased to an estimated 400-500 sheep. By 1963, the population had increased to such a level that a controlled hunt was deemed advisable. Forty-two permits were issued; six rams and three ewes were harvested. In 1964, 50 permits were issued; eight rams and seven ewes were harvested. In 1965, 70 permits resulted in a harvest of eight rams and eight ewes. Statewide, the population in 1989 was estimated at over 20,000.

Whether this animal will eventually become a pest, as have most of the "successful" introduced animals, remains to be seen. There is some evidence that they compete directly with mule deer for food. They also have been observed feeding on winter wheat crops growing adjacent to Palo Duro Canyon. In the Trans-Pecos, Barbary sheep may have a deleterious impact on bighorn sheep reintroduction efforts.

BLACKBUCK*

Antilope cervicapra (Linnaeus)

Description. A medium-sized antelope with ringed, unbranched, "corkscrew" horns that rise above the head of males in a tall, V-shaped pattern. Measured from base to tip, horns reach up to 79 cm in length, although Texas blackbuck rarely have horns exceeding 58 cm. Normally, females are hornless.

Coloration in mature males is black dorsally, while females and young males are tan. All blackbuck have white eye rings, chin patch, chest, belly, and inner legs. In the nonbreeding season, after the spring molt, adult males may lighten considerably and retain their darkest coloration only on the face and legs.

In Texas, adult males average 38 kg in weight, with a range of 20-57 kg. Females weigh 20-33 kg, averaging 27 kg.

Distribution. Blackbuck antelope were originally released in Texas in the Edwards Plateau (Kerr County) in 1932. In 1988, only eight Texas counties had free-ranging blackbuck, but these antelope were confined on ranches in 86 counties. Of the total number of exotics confined on Texas ranches in 1988, only the axis deer outnumbered blackbuck antelope.

Habits. Blackbuck are native to India and Pakistan where they were widespread in plains and open woodlands; wet coastal areas, western deserts, and northern mountains limited their distribution. Today, extensive hunting and habitat destruction have restricted blackbuck to only small, isolated populations in their former native habitat.

More than 80% of the blackbuck in Texas inhabit the Edwards Plateau region, where the patchwork of open grassland and brush provides both excellent forage and cover. Their range is restricted to the north and west by cold winters, to the south by coyote predation, and to the east by parasitism.

Blackbuck prefer to graze on short to mid-length grasses but also browse on common brush species. Forage selection is primarily determined by availability with sedges, fall witchgrass, mesquite, and live oak commonly eaten. Forb use by blackbuck is low.

Adult males are highly territorial and defend areas ranging from 1.2 to 12 ha in size against trespass by other males. Female groups may graze through male territories, and breeding activity may take place at such times, but other males are excluded. Young males, and bucks without territories, form their own all male groups. At physical maturity (2 - 2$^1/_2$ years of age) young bucks may split from the all-male group to establish or win their own territory.

Breeding may take place at any time of the year; however, bucks are more active in spring and fall. Fawns are born at all seasons, but fewest births occur in winter. The length of gestation is about 5 months and within a month of parturition the female may breed again. A single fawn is the rule.

Females reach sexual maturity by 8 months of age, but usually do not breed until nearly 2 years of age. Physical maturity is reached at 1 year. Males mature later than females, and are able to breed at 18 month of age. The lifespan is up to 15 years.

Blackbuck (*Antilope cervicapra*). Photo by John L. Tveten.

ORDER SIRENIA
MANATEE AND ALLIES

The Sirenia are large, plump, torpedo-shaped mammals adapted to an aquatic habitat; they live in the bays and coastal waters in tropical regions of the world. Front limbs developed into paddles; hind limbs absent externally; tail expanded into a rounded, horizontal fluke; muzzle truncate; skin naked except for stiff bristles on the muzzle; nostrils separate and valvular; eyes and mouth small; bones dense and heavy; two mammary glands, pectoral in position; testes abdominal.

FAMILY TRICHECHIDAE (MANATEES)

WEST INDIAN MANATEE
Trichechus manatus Linnaeus

Description. A large, grayish, nearly hairless, aquatic mammal without hind limbs; tail broadened into a horizontal, rounded paddle; front limbs paddlelike. Dental formula: I 2/2 (nonfunctional), C 0/0, Pm 0/0, M 6/6 (variable and continuously being replaced) X 2 = 32. Total length of adults, up to 3.5 m; weight, up to 1,000 kg.

Distribution. West Indian manatees are found in rivers, estuaries, and coastal areas of the tropical and subtropical New World from the southeastern United States coast along Central America and the West Indies to the northern coastline of South America. Manatees are extremely rare in Texas although near the turn of the century they apparently were not uncommon in the Laguna Madre. Texas records also include specimens from Cow Bayou, near Sabine Lake, Copano Bay, the Bolivar Peninsula, and the mouth of the Rio Grande.

Habits. These animals occur chiefly in the larger rivers and brackish water bays. They are able to live in salt waters of the sea, however, and travel from one island to another or from place to place along the coast. They are extremely sensitive to cold and may be killed by a sudden drop in the temperature of the water to as low as 8°C. This intolerance doubtless limits their northward distribution in North America. Their irregular occurrence along the Texas coast suggests that they do considerable wandering — specimens from Texas probably represent migrants from coastal Mexico.

Sluggish and easily captured, West Indian manatees were once extensively exploited as a food source. Although now protected as an endangered mammal, manatees still face occasional losses from poaching and from collisions with speedboats. Additionally,

West Indian Manatee (*Trichechus manatus*). Illustration by Pieter A. Folkens

habitat loss to land development and channelization continues to pose problems for them. Conversely, in Florida the construction of power plants and industrial parks has apparently been beneficial in creating new warm water habitat that may be preferred by manatees in winter.

Manatees are opportunistic, aquatic herbivores that feed exclusively on aquatic vegetation, although captive animals have eaten lawn grass, dandelions, palmetto, and garden vegetables. Wild manatees seem to prefer submergent vegetation, followed by floating and emergent species. Manatees consume 30-50 kg of food per day. In saline waters, they feed on seagrasses.

Manatees occur in loosely knit groups, but are not gregarious by nature. Breeding and calving occurs year round with the gestation period lasting 12-13 months. Newborn manatees are about a meter long at birth and weigh 18-27 kg. One young is born.

Remarks. Stephanie Fernandez and Sherman Jones reported the recent (February, 1986) stranding of a manatee on the Texas coast. A local fisherman found the carcass of a male manatee, in an advanced state of decomposition, rolling in the surf about 1.5 km west of Caplen, Bolivar Peninsula. Parts of the anterior portion of the skull, the flipper bones, and sternum were exposed. The total length of the manatee was 274 cm. Along the right side of the abdomen were 10 golfball-sized holes, which penetrated, but did not pass through, the blubber. Seven holes formed a V-shaped figure, with the other three forming a straight line immediately beneath it. The cause of these holes was undetermined. A recent rope mark was also visible around the tail stock.

This was the first manatee stranding recorded by the Texas Marine Mammal Stranding Network since its inception in 1980.

ORDER CETACEA
WHALES, PORPOISES, AND DOLPHINS

Small to extremely large, hairless, fish-shaped mammals that are adapted strictly to an aquatic habitat; front limbs modified as flippers or fins, hind limbs absent, except for vestigial internal remnants; eyes and ears small, the latter valvular and lacking external parts; skull telescoped so that nostrils open on top of head through a single or double blowhole; no vocal apparatus, the so-called roar being produced by expelled air; soft palate and epiglottis so modified that nasal cavities connect directly with lungs and not with mouth; tail lengthened and dermal elements expanded into broad, flattened flukes; mammary glands situated on either side of vaginal opening, the single teat lodged in a slitlike recess; penis and testes contained within the body integument; skin glands, except for conjunctival and mammary, lacking; teeth present or absent.

This group contains the largest of all known mammals, living or extinct. The blue whale sometimes reaches a length of 33 m and may weigh up to 135 metric tons. As a group whales are slow breeders – one young every 2 years is generally the rule. The teat in a 15-m whale is no larger than a man's thumb, and the mouth of the young calf is so constructed that it cannot suck. Perhaps the milk is forced into the mouth of the baby by contraction of muscles over the udder or by the "butting" of the young one. In a freshly killed, lactating female palpation of the udder may force out jets of cream-colored milk.

Cetaceans have no voice but many produce distinct sounds used in mating rituals, communication, and echolocation. Such sounds are specific in character and many are audible for distances of a kilometer or more. Bats and cetaceans are the only mammals known to echolocate; they use sound emissions and echoes to form mental images of their surroundings.

Many of the whales have retained teeth in both jaws. Some have retained them in the lower jaw only, whereas others have lost them completely and have developed instead peculiar structures termed baleen or whalebone. These are elongated, flattened, leaflike modifications of the ridges in the roof of the mouth. Two series of plates, one on each side, hang from the roof of the mouth and the long, fibrous, hairlike structures on the inner edge of one plate overlap with those of its neighbor in such a way that an efficient sieve is produced. All whales with such structures feed on small organisms strained from the water. Toothed whales feed on larger animal life: fish, seals, or even other whales.

The spout is characteristic of many species. It is produced by expelling moisture-laden air from the lungs into the air. As the air escapes it cools, condenses, and becomes visible if the temperature of the outside air permits and then quickly dissipates. When not in use, the blowholes are closed by external flaps that prevent water from entering the lungs. All whales must come to the surface to breathe; if they are forced to remain submerged, they drown.

Many whales and porpoises live near the coast, frequenting shallow water, but a large number of them are pelagic and roam the open seas. Many of the latter perform regular migrations. In winter they inhabit temperate or tropical waters where they mate and give birth to their young a year later; in summer they move to the Arctic or Antarctic seas among the ice floes. Most of the food in the ocean is produced where cold and warm streams meet and it is there that whales flock in great numbers.

Twenty-nine species of cetaceans have been documented within the Gulf of Mexico. This assemblage includes approximately 40% of the genera and 35% of the cetacean species in the world. Twenty-six of the 29 Gulf species have either stranded on Texas beaches or been observed at sea in the waters of the western Gulf.

The terms whale, dolphin, and porpoise need explanation. As here used, the term whale is all-inclusive and may be applied to any cetacean. The term dolphin applies to those small whales that have a distinct snout or beak and numerous conical teeth that are roughly circular in cross-section. The term porpoise applies to those small, blunt-nosed whales that have flat, spade-shaped teeth. Based on these definitions, all the small, beaked whales in Texas waters with numerous conical teeth are dolphins. No porpoises are known to occur in Texas waters.

One of the more interesting biological aspects about marine mammals, especially cetaceans, is their propensity to strand — to ground or beach themselves out of water and be unable to return under their own power. Generally, there are two types of strandings — those of a single individual, which are by far the most prevalent, and multiple or mass (two or more animals) strandings, excluding parent/offspring combinations. The study of marine mammal strandings is a subject of considerable interest to scientists and the general public, and stranding studies have proven to be an undeniably good source of information, perhaps the only information, about aquatic mammals that exists.

A Texas Marine Mammal Stranding Network was organized in 1980, as a means of discovering, gathering, and reporting information of marine mammals stranded along the Texas coast. It also assists live stranded animals, administering first aid and transporting them to facilities where they can be treated. The network consists of scientists, students, federal and state agencies, marine veterinarians, and other interested individuals.

From October, 1980, through May, 1987, the Texas Marine Mammal Stranding Network documented a total of 501 cetacean strandings. Of these, 87% were represented by bottlenose dolphins, the most common inshore species. Live strandings accounted for only 7% of all strandings, and a majority of these occurred near Port Aransas where deeper waters are closer to shore. There was only one known instance of a mass stranding, that of a group of pygmy killer whales.

Although there has been much speculation and theorizing, scientists do not completely understand why cetaceans beach themselves. Oftentimes when live strandings are observed, attempts to return the animals to sea fail. Many, upon release, simply turn and head for shore once more. Undoubtedly, many factors may account for this "suicidal" form of behavior. Among the possible causes suggested for strandings are: parasites, disease, and illness; choking on ingested objects; wounds from gunshots and boat and ship encounters; difficulties in the birth process; starvation; bad or rough weather; seaquakes, tremors, and underwater explosions; pollution; net entanglements associated with commercial fishing; fouled sonar systems; and panic caused by the pursuit of other animals (predators). Social facilitation or as it is more commonly known, the "follow the leader" theory, is widely given as a reason for mass strandings. Social facilitation involves a cohesive group behavior whereby a dominant individual suddenly beaches itself causing the whole group to follow suite and do likewise.

KEY TO THE WHALES AND DOLPHINS OF THE TEXAS COAST

1. No teeth present; baleen plates in upper jaw; twin blowholes; skull symmetrical; no mandibular symphysis (baleen whales) 2

   Teeth present (although sometimes not erupted); no baleen plates; single blowhole; skull slightly to moderately asymmetrical; mandibular symphysis present (toothed whales) 8

2. Dorsal fin and ventral throat grooves present; no growths on top of head; upper jaw relatively flat when viewed from the side and broad from the top 3

No dorsal fin or ventral throat grooves; crusty growths (callosites) present on head; upper jaw arched when viewed from the side and relatively narrow from the top. *Eubalaena glacialis* (northern right whale), p. 303.

3. Throat grooves end well before navel 4

Throat grooves extend to or beyond navel 5

4. 50-70 ventral grooves, longest ending between flippers; 231-285 white or yellowish-white baleen plates per side, less than 21 cm long; conspicuous white bands on flippers; maximum body length 9 m. *Balaenoptera acutorostrata* (Minke whale), p. 304.

32-60 ventral grooves, longest ending well short of navel; 219-402 pairs of black baleen plates, less than 80 cm long; flippers totally dark; maximum body length 16 m. *Balaenoptera borealis* (Sei whale).[3]

5. Flippers more than 25% of body length, heavily scalloped on the leading edge, and marked on the underside with a variable pattern of white. *Megaptera novaeangliae* (humpback whale), p. 307.

Flippers less than 25% of body length, smooth on the leading edge, and without a distinct pattern of white on the underside 6

6. Head with only one prominent ridge from blowhole to snout; 55-100 ventral grooves; maximum body length more than 20 m 7

Head with series of three parallel ridges from blowhole to snout; 40-50 ventral grooves; maximum body length less than 15 m. *Balaenoptera edeni* (Bryde's whale), p. 305.

7. Head broad and almost U-shaped from above; dorsal fin very small (< 33 cm) and set in the last one-third of back; 270-295 black baleen plates per side; coloration of head symmetrical; body mottled gray; maximum body length 26 m. *Balaenoptera musculus* (blue whale), p. 306.

Head V-shaped and pointed at tip as viewed from above; dorsal fin up to 61 cm tall and set more than one-third forward from fluke notch; 260-480 white to gray baleen plates per side; head coloration asymmetrical (left side gray, much of right side white); back dark, with light streaks; maximum body length 24 m. *Balaenoptera physalus* (fin whale), p. 307.

8. Upper jaw extending well past lower jaw; lower jaw very narrow 9

Upper jaw not extending much or at all past lower jaw; lower and upper jaw about the same width 11

9. Body length 4-18 m; head squarish and large, up to one-third of body length; blowhole at left side of front of head; low roundish dorsal hump present, followed by a series of bumps; 18-25 teeth in each side of lower jaw, fitting into sockets in upper jaw. *Physeter macrocephalus* (sperm whale), p. 309.

---

[3] The Sei whale is not included in the species accounts because there are no confirmed records of this species from the Texas coast. However, it is possible that this species could occur in the region and has therefore been included in this key.

Body length less than 4 m; head much less than one-third of body length; blowhole set back from front of head; prominent dorsal fin present; 8-16 teeth in each side of lower jaw 10

10. Throat creases generally absent; dorsal fin small and located in last one-third of body; distance from tip of snout to blowhole greater than 10.3% of total length; 12-16 (rarely 10-11) teeth in each half of lower jaw. *Kogia breviceps* (pygmy sperm whale), p. 310.

Two small creases present on throat; dorsal fin generally tall and located near midpoint of back; distance from tip of snout to blowhole less than 10.2% of total length; 8-11 (rarely up to 13) teeth in each side of lower jaw. *Kogia simus* (dwarf sperm whale), p. 311.

11. Two conspicuous grooves on throat; notch between flukes absent or indistinct; enlarged teeth numbering no more than two pairs in lower jaw (beaked whales) 12

No conspicuous grooves present on throat; prominent median notch in flukes; teeth present in both upper and lower jaws (dolphins and toothed whales) 14

12. One or two pairs of teeth at or near tip of lower jaw, erupted only in some adults; beak indistinct; head small relative to body size; body to at least 7 m long. *Ziphius cavirostris* (Cuvier's beaked whale), p. 313.

One pair of teeth well behind tip of lower jaw, erupted only in adult males; moderate beak, not sharply demarcated from forehead; body to 4-5 m long ... 13

13. Tooth positioned approximately 7.5-10 cm from tip of mandible (one-third the length of mandible). *Mesoplodon europaeus* (Gervais' beaked whale), p. 313.

Tooth positioned at midpoint of mandible on bony prominences near corners of mouth. *Mesoplodon densirostris* (Blainville's beaked whale), p. 312.

14. Beak not sharply delineated from head by a distinct crease 15

Beak sharply delineated from head by a distinct crease 21

15. Head blunt, with no prominent beak 16

Head long and conical but beak runs smoothly into forehead, with no crease; body dark gray to black above and white below with narrow cape on back. *Steno bredanensis* (rough-toothed dolphin), p. 319.

16. Head divided medially by a heavy vertical crease; coloration gray with heavy scarring in the form of numerous scratches; no teeth in upper jaw (1-2 rarely present), 0-7 teeth present in each side of lower jaw. *Grampus griseus* (Risso's dolphin), p. 320.

Head not divided by a vertical, median crease; body coloration predominantly black with some white markings; teeth (7 or more pairs) in both upper and lower jaws 17

17. Striking black and white coloration, with white postocular patches, white lower jaw, and light gray saddle behind dorsal fin; dorsal fin tall and erect (up to 0.9 m in females and 1.8 m in males); flippers large and paddle-shaped; 10-12 large oval teeth (2.5 cm in diameter) in each tooth row; body to at least 9 m long. *Orcinus orca* (killer whale), p. 314.

Coloration predominantly black with little, if any, gray or white markings; dorsal fin less than 0.5 m in height; flippers long and pointed to slightly rounded at tips; body never more than 7 m long and often considerably less 18

18. Low, broad-based dorsal fin located on forward third of back; head bulbous; body black, with light anchor-shaped patch on belly and often light gray saddle-shaped flippers, one-fifth to one-sixth of body length; 7-9 pairs of teeth in front half of each tooth row; body to about 7 m long. *Globicephala macrorhynchus* (short-finned pilot whale), p. 317.

Dorsal fin located near midpoint of back; body never more than 5.5 m long .. 19

19. Flippers with distinct hump on leading edge giving S-shaped appearance; body predominantly black; 7-12 large teeth in each half of both jaws; body to at least 5.5 m long. *Pseudorca crassidens* (false killer whale), p. 315.

Flippers lack hump on leading edge and not S-shaped; body predominantly black but with some white markings on belly and chin or lips; 8-25 teeth in each half of the jaws; body considerably less than 5 m long 20

20. Fewer than 15 teeth in each half of both jaws; flippers rounded at tip; body mostly black with white belly patch which may extend onto sides in area of anus; head rounded from above; body to almost 3 m long. *Feresa attenuata* (pygmy killer whale), p. 316.

More than 15 teeth per side of each jaw; flippers sharply pointed at tip; body black to brownish black on back, light gray on sides, light gray to white on belly, lips often white; head triangular from above; body to at least 2.7 m long. *Peponocephala electra* (melon-headed whale), p. 318.

21. Body coloration dark gray on back, lighter gray on sides, with white to pink belly; no stripes or spots; beak relatively short and thick; 20 to 26 teeth present in each side of upper jaw and 18 to 24 teeth present in each side of lower jaw. *Tursiops truncatus* (bottlenose dolphin), p. 321.

Body coloration includes numerous spots, mottling, or stripes; beak relatively long and slender; up to 200 total teeth present in mouth 22

22. Body coloration heavily mottled with light or dark spots 23

Body coloration without spots but traversed by one or more longitudinal stripes 24

23. Coloration characterized by "spinal blaze" sweeping up and back below the dorsal fin; peduncle not divided into upper dark and lower light halves; no black stripes connecting eyes and flipper with jaws; background of dark ventral spots is white; total number of vertebrae, 67-72. *Stenella frontalis* (Atlantic spotted dolphin), p. 325.

Coloration not characterized by a "spinal blaze"; peduncle divided into upper dark and lower light halves; dark stripe from flipper to lower jaw; background of dark ventral spots is gray; total number of vertebrae, 74-84. *Stenella attenuata* (pantropical spotted dolphin), p. 323.

24. Light gray, tan, or yellow stripes crisscross on sides; palate with deep grooves bordering upper teeth. *Delphinus delphis* (common dolphin), p. 319.

Stripes do not crisscross; palatal groove shallow or absent 25

25. Black stripes extending from eye to anus, eye to flipper, and from above flipper toward belly; 43 to 50 teeth present in each side of both jaws. *Stenella coeruleoalba* (striped dolphin), p. 324.

Black side stripes absent 26

26. Dark-colored rostrum with gray or white "moustache" area; chin white to cream-colored; tip of upper jaw to apex of melon less than 12 cm; seldom more than 46 teeth in each side of the jaw. *Stenella clymene* (Clymene dolphin), p. 324.

Dark rostrum without "moustache"; tip of upper jaw to apex of melon more than 12 cm; chin gray to black; usually more than 46 teeth in each side of the jaw. *Stenella longirostris* (spinner dolphin), p. 326.

FAMILY BALAENIDAE (RIGHT WHALES)

NORTHERN RIGHT WHALE

Eubalaena glacialis Borowski

Description. A large, blackish whale with the following features: no dorsal fin; head huge, about one-fourth of total length; baleen (whalebone) about 2 m long, 30 cm wide, and between 200 and 250 in number on each side of mouth; closure of mouth highly arched; no furrows on the throat; prominent, large, wartlike areas (called bonnets), the one near tip of snout largest. Total length of adults, 14-17 m; weight, 20-30 metric tons.

Distribution. Worldwide in distribution but extremely rare. Only 3,000-4,000 remain in the world's oceans, with about 100 constituting the North Atlantic population. These whales are listed as "endangered." Known in Texas from a single individual that beached in February, 1972, at Surfside Beach near Freeport, Brazoria County.

Habits. Right whales were so named by early whalers because they were the "right" whale to kill — they are slow swimmers and were thus easily caught, floated when dead, and produced large quantities of oil and baleen. Consequently, right whales were decimated early by the world's whaling industries and have yet to recover.

Right whales spend spring, summer, and autumn at high latitude feeding grounds and migrate to more southerly, warmer waters in winter for mating and calving. Northern and southern populations do not interbreed due to asynchronous seasons between the hemispheres.

Right whales produce a variety of vocal sounds as well as percussive sounds of breaching, flipper slapping, and tail slapping. A distinctive clacking sound has been

Northern Right Whale (*Eubalaena glacialis*). Illustration by Pieter A. Folkens.

described for these whales as they feed at the surface. Termed the "baleen rattle," this sound is produced by small wavelets rattling the baleen plates when they are partially held out of water. Right whale sounds appear to differ with changing behavior and, thus, may be important in communication. As with other baleen whales, right whales probably do not echolocate.

Right whales feed by skimming through concentrations of krill. They have been seen feeding at depths ranging from the surface down to 10 m although they may also feed at deeper levels. Location of krill concentrations in the water column probably determines feeding depth.

After a one-year gestation period, females give birth to a single calf in winter. Calves are 5-6 m in length at birth but grow rapidly during the subsequent period of lactation, which lasts about 13 months. Calves remain with their mothers for 2-3 years following weaning and probably reach sexual maturity at about 10 years of age. Females give birth at 2 to 7 year intervals.

FAMILY BALAENOPTERIDAE
(RORQUALS OR BALEEN WHALES)

MINKE WHALE
Balaenoptera acutorostrata Lacepede

Description. Smallest of the baleen whales in the Gulf of Mexico, adult minkes only reach up to 10.2 m in length and 10 metric tons in weight. As with all baleen whales, females are slightly larger than males of comparable age. Minke whales have a very narrow and pointed rostrum and a broad white band on the dorsal surface of the flippers. Coloration is dark gray to black above and white below. The baleen plates are yellowish-white, or cream, colored. The dorsal fin, located in the latter third of the back, is tall and falcate and the throat grooves end just beyond the flippers.

Distribution. Worldwide in distribution, minke whales are the most numerous of baleen whales. They are not listed as endangered. Known in Texas on the basis of a single stranding from Matagorda Peninsula on March 29, 1988.

Habits. As with most other baleen whales, minke whales tend to be highly migratory and move to cold temperate and polar waters in spring and then return to warmer waters in autumn. The movements of minke whales in the North Atlantic are heavily influenced by spawning concentrations of capelin, upon which they feed. Also, seasonal segregation by sex and age is pronounced in these whales. Mature males tend to migrate farther north in spring and summer than do females and immatures.

Minke whales feed on krill; fish, including sand lace, sand eel, salmon, capelin, mackerel, cod, coal fish, whiting, sprat, wolffish, dogfish, pollack, haddock, and herring; and squid. Capelin are the dominant food item of North Atlantic minkes.

Minke Whale (*Balaenoptera acutorostrata*). Illustration by Pieter A. Folkens.

Although baleen whales are generally thought incapable of echolocation, minke whales are known to produce a variety of sounds including narrow band pulses suitable for echolocation. Such sounds are described as "series of clicks" and may aid in locating food concentrations. Other sounds of these whales are described as "grunts, pings, zips, ratchets, and clicks."

In the North Atlantic, mating occurs from October to March. Females give birth to a single calf in early winter. The gestation period is about 10 months. Newborn minke whales are 2.4-2.7 m in length and the lactation period is 4-5 months. Age at sexual maturity is approximately 6 years for males and 7 years for females.

Remarks. The minke whale that stranded on the Texas coast was an immature female that was alive when first observed. This not only was the first of its kind known for Texas, but its physical features were particularly interesting in that the white bands usually present on the dorsal surface of the flippers were absent, and the baleen plates were partially black and numbered only approximately 240 per side. Typically, minke whales have about 300 baleen plates on each side of the mouth and they are cream-white in color. These features initially caused confusion in the identification of the whale; however, measurements of the tympanic bullae confirmed that, indeed, it was a minke whale.

BRYDE'S WHALE
Balaenoptera edeni Anderson

Description. Bryde's whales are the second smallest of rorquals and only average 12.2-13.1 m in length and 12 metric tons in weight. As with all rorquals, females tend to be a little larger than males. Maximum length is about 15.5 m.

Bryde's whales are unique in having three head ridges extending from the blowholes to the end of the rostrum. This is the only baleen whale with this feature, although several have one such ridge, and the presence of three head ridges will always distinguish *B. edeni*. Coloration is a dark, bluish-gray overall but somewhat lighter in the throat area. The dorsal fin is only about 46 cm in height and rises abruptly from the back. Bryde's whales have ventral pleats extending to, or slightly beyond, the navel.

Distribution. Bryde's whales are not yet known from Texas, but have stranded on nearby beaches in Louisiana. It is probable that one of these whales will one day strand along the Texas coast.

Habits. Bryde's whales appear to be near-shore, year-round residents of tropical and subtropical waters. Although most commonly seen in groups of five to six, large groups of 30-40 have been observed in areas of food concentrations. This whale frequently feeds on pelagic fishes such as pilchard, mackerel, herring, mullet, and anchovies; however, cephalopods and pelagic crustaceans (krill) are also eaten.

Bryde's whales are believed to breed year round and their gestation period is estimated to be 12 months. Calves are about 4 m long at birth and weigh 1 metric ton. Sexual maturity is reached at 8-10 years and the animals are about 12 m long at this time.

Bryde's Whale (*Balaenoptera edeni*). Illustration by Pieter A. Folkens.

Remarks. Bryde's whales are one of the more frequently observed baleen whales from the Gulf of Mexico. These whales have stranded on Gulf beaches in winter, spring, and summer, indicating that they may be year-round residents of these waters.

BLUE WHALE
Balaenoptera musculus (Linnaeus)

Description. Largest of the whales; upperparts slate gray with bluish cast, darker on head, lips, and throat; paler on sides; underparts often yellowish, sometimes spotted with white; dorsal fin small, located posterior to vent; pectoral fin small, about one-tenth of total length; commissure of mouth nearly straight, except for downward curve near corner; grooves on underparts numerous and extending posteriorly past navel; whalebone black, broad basally, short (60-80 cm), and averaging 370 to each side; snout broad and U-shaped. External measurements of one reported by Scammon: length, 29 m; girth, 12 m; length of jawbone, 6.4 m. Estimated weight, up to 100 metric tons.

Distribution. Blue whales occur in all oceans of the world. There are only two records from the Gulf of Mexico; one stranded near Sabine Pass, Louisiana, in 1924 and one stranded on the Texas coast between Freeport and San Luis Pass in 1940. Both of these identifications have been questioned, however, and the occurrence of the blue whale in the Gulf of Mexico is problematical. The current worldwide population is only 11,000-12,000, with the current North Atlantic population numbering 100-1,500 animals. Blue whales are classified as "endangered."

Habits. Spring and summer finds northern hemisphere blue whales migrating northward to arctic feeding grounds. In fall and winter the whales move back to temperate waters where mating and parturition take place. This trend is also exhibited by southern hemisphere blue whales although feeding grounds are in the Antarctic. As the seasons are reversed between the two hemispheres, northern and southern blue whales do not interbreed in temperate and equatorial waters.

Feeding occurs mainly in higher latitudes but is also common during migration. In the North Pacific, for example, blue whales stop to feed off California every fall of the year, on their way towards northern waters. Small, shrimp-like crustaceans known as "krill" predominate in the diet, tremendous amounts of which are required to sustain a single whale. An adult blue whale must consume about 3,000-5,000 kg of krill daily to meet its energy requirements.

Female blue whales give birth to a single calf in temperate or equatorial waters during the winter months. Gestation is about 11 months and females bear young every other year. The birth of a blue whale has never been observed, but records from past whaling activities indicate that a newborn blue whale is about 8 m in length and weighs 2-3 metric tons. The baby whale nurses for about 8 months and during this time gains 90 kg per day, or 3.75 kg per <u>hour</u>! Sexual maturity is reached at 5-6 years and the lifespan is unknown.

Blue Whale (*Balaenoptera musculus*). Illustration by Pieter A. Folkens.

FIN WHALE

Balaenoptera physalus (Linnaeus)

Description. A large, slender whale similar to the blue whale but head V-shaped in dorsal view, rather than U-shaped; dorsal fin high and placed even with or posterior to anus, on posterior one-fourth of body; pectoral fin about one-ninth of total length; head flattened, with right side more whitish than left; right lower jaw white, left grayish to black; upperparts gray, underparts pure white; grooves on throat numerous and extending beyond navel; whalebone lead color with whitish or yellowish fringes, 45-90 cm long, and more than 400 blades on each side. External measurements of an immature animal: total length, 18 m; tip of snout to corner of mouth, 3.6 m; expansion of flukes, 4.3 m. Old individuals attain a length of 25 m or more; females average slightly larger than males. Weight of a 21-m female, 59.4 metric tons.

Distribution. Cosmomarine, but rare in Texas waters. One young individual, 5.5 m long, was stranded on the beach at Gilchrist, Chambers County, on February 21, 1951. This is the only known Texas record. Fin whales are classified as "endangered."

Habits. Fin whales are highly migratory. The whales move to high latitude feeding grounds during spring and summer and return to southerly, temperate waters for mating and calving during autumn and winter. As with other migratory baleen whales, northern and southern hemisphere populations do not interbreed due to asynchronous seasons.

Fin whales feed mainly on krill but also eat schooling fish including herring, cod, mackerel, pollock, sardine, and capelin. Fish are eaten more often in winter.

The reproductive habits of these whales remain largely unknown; however, females are thought to give birth only at 3-year intervals. Mating and calving occur from November to March in temperate waters. The gestation period is approximately 11 months and newborn fin whales are about 6.4 m in length and weigh 1.8 metric tons. The period of lactation lasts 6-7 months and after weaning the young whales are approximately 12.2 m long. Sexual maturity is reached at 6-12 years of age.

Fin Whale (*Balaenoptera physalus*). Illustration by Pieter A. Folkens.

HUMPBACK WHALE

Megaptera novaeangliae (Borowski)

Description. Humpback whales typically reach lengths of 14.6-15.2 m and weights of 31-41 metric tons. Females are usually slightly larger than males and an exceptional individual may be up to 18.9 m in length and weigh 48 metric tons. For their length, humpbacks tend to be greater in girth than the other balaenopterid whales.

Coloration is black overall with irregular white markings on the throat, sides, and abdomen. In some individuals the belly may be entirely white, or there may be white patterns dorsally. The flippers are very long (up to 4.6 m) but are narrow. The flippers typically are white below but range from black to patterns of black and white dorsally,

Humpback Whale (*Megaptera novaeangliae*). Illustration by Pieter A. Folkens.

or even entirely white. The tail flukes are broad, serrated on the free edge, and black above with black and white coloration ventrally. Distinctive tail flukes may serve to identify individual humpback whales in many cases.

As with other balaenopterid whales, humpbacks have a dorsal fin, which may be up to 31 cm in height, and is falcate to rounded in profile. Although the humpback does have throat pleats, they are fewer and spaced wider apart than is typical for balaenopterids. Humpbacks, therefore, are not usually classed as rorquals. Other differences of the humpback whale include lack of a median head ridge, enormous flippers , and the presence of numerous knobby structures, or "dermal tubercles," about the dorsal surface of the snout, chin, and mandible. The number and location of these head tubercles vary between individuals. Each tubercle contains a sensory hair.

Humpbacks typically submerge for 6-7 minutes at a time with occasional dives of 15-30 minutes. The blow may be up to 3 m high and is not a slender plume but rather bushy. When diving, humpbacks arch the back steeply, thus the common name. The flukes rarely show in shallow dives but when a deep dive is accomplished the flukes may be lifted well above the water's surface.

Distribution. Humpback whales occur in all oceans of the world. In the western North Atlantic these whales are distributed from north of Iceland, Disko Bay and west of Greenland south to Venezuela and around the tropical islands of the West Indies. Population estimates indicate that the worldwide, prewhaling population of humpbacks was approximately 100,000. The present stock numbers 5,200-5,600 with about 800-1,000 occurring in the western North Atlantic. Humpback whales are listed as endangered by the U.S. Fish and Wildlife Service.

In the Gulf of Mexico humpback whales have been captured in the Florida Keys and northern Cuba. Sightings have occurred off the west coast of Florida and Alabama. The only known occurrence along the Texas Coast is of a young, immature animal observed by Victor Cockraft and David Weller at the inshore side of Bolivar Jetty near Galveston on 19 February 1992. No population estimates are available for Gulf humpbacks.

Humpbacks are highly migratory. In the western North Atlantic these whales occupy high latitude feeding grounds from Cape Cod to Iceland during spring, summer, and fall. In late autumn and winter the whales then move into Caribbean waters for mating and calving.

Habits. Humpbacks often congregate in groups of 20-30 to perhaps 100-200. These are among the most acrobatic and visible of whales and breach completely out of water in spectacular displays of strength. Humpbacks commonly slap their tail flukes or flippers on the water's surface and occasionally lift their huge heads above water to peer about, a behavior known as "spyhopping." Tail slapping, breaching, and other such behaviors may serve in communication between the whales, possibly as warnings or a means of indicating location.

Humpbacks also produce a number of unusual sounds described variously as moans, groans, cries, squeals, chirps, and clicks. Sounds may be arranged into complex and predictable patterns known as "songs." Humpback songs may be repeated for long periods of time and have been most often recorded on low latitude breeding grounds. Although yet to be proven, songs are thought to be broadcast by sexually mature, lone males and may have some purpose in mating rituals.

Humpback whales eat krill, mackerel, sand lance, capelin, herring, pollock, smelt, cod, sardines, salmon, and anchovies. These whales are lunge-feeders but use several different techniques to concentrate their food before lunging. An especially interesting technique is known as "bubble netting." In bubble netting, one or more humpbacks exhale while circling below a food source. The resulting bubble column effectively forms a net to concentrate food items through which the whales lunge with open mouths.

Females give birth to a single calf in tropical or subtropical waters in winter. The gestation period is approximately 11 months. Newborn humpbacks are 4.6 m in length and weigh about 1.3 metric tons. The period of lactation lasts approximately 5 months. Sexual maturity is reached at 2-5 years, at which time the young whales measure about 12 m in length. Physical maturity occurs at 12-15 years of age. Females breed every other year.

FAMILY PHYSETERIDAE (SPERM WHALES)

SPERM WHALE
Physeter macrocephalus Linnaeus

Description. A large, blackish-brown whale with huge head and truncate snout; lower jaw small, long, and slender, the symphysis extending half the length of rami; the single blowhole on anterior left edge of snout; no dorsal fin, but conspicuous hump; eye very small, low, and near angle of mouth; pectoral fin short and relatively broad; upper jaw lacking functional teeth; lower jaw with 22-24 large, sharp teeth on each side. Total length of males, up to 20 m; females much smaller. Weight of a male 13 m long, 39 metric tons.

Distribution. Sperm whales are worldwide in distribution and occur in all oceans, including Arctic and Antarctic waters, but are primarily found in temperate and tropical waters of the Atlantic and Pacific Oceans. Sperm whales are the most numerous of the great whales in the Gulf of Mexico and sightings near the Texas coast are relatively common. They are classified as "endangered."

Habits. Sperm whales are highly migratory, especially the males. Adult males move into high latitude temperate waters during summer, leading a solitary lifestyle, while females remain grouped in tropical or subtropical waters. In winter, the bulls return to lower latitudes for mating.

Sperm Whale (*Physeter macrocephalus*). Illustration by Pieter A. Folkens.

These whales regularly dive to depths of 1,000 m but are known to reach depths of over 2,100 m and may be capable of dives to 3,000 m. At such depths these remarkable animals hunt their primary prey — squid. Much speculation has arisen concerning the feeding method of sperm whales as no light penetrates to the depths these whales dive, and squid are highly elusive swimmers. The whales may feed by ambushing prey as they lie relatively motionless near the ocean floor, attracting squid with a bioluminescent glow emanating from their mouth, or perhaps by stunning prey with ultrasonic sounds. Due to the great depths at which these animals feed, the exact method of the sperm whale's feeding habits has yet to be determined. These whales are known to produce a variety of "click sounds" occurring in sequence and termed "codas." Such sounds are probably used in echolocation and may play an important role in locating prey while feeding.

Up to 1 metric ton of squid per day is required to sustain a single sperm whale. Other than squid, these whales occasionally consume other deepwater prey including octopus, lobsters, crabs, jellyfish, sponges, and several varieties of fish.

Breeding behavior in sperm whales is similar to harem formation — a single, dominant male accompanies a group of females and defends the group against competing males. During this time, smaller males are driven off to form their own "bachelor groups" and battles between rival males for control of the harem may occur. Twenty to thirty females may comprise a harem but many of them may already be pregnant or tending young. The gestation period is approximately 15 months, the period of lactation is 1-2 years, and there is a "resting period" of up to 10 months following weaning before the females will mate again. The breeding cycle therefore, may take as long as 5-7 years.

Newborn sperm whales are about 4 m in length and weigh approximately 1 metric ton. Although twin calves are known, a single calf per female is believed the rule. Sexual maturity is reached at about 10 years of age.

Sperm whales were once the mainstay of the pelagic whaling industry. Prior to the advent of cannon harpoons, diesel-powered catcher boats, and massive factory ships, the hunting of sperm whales was a dangerous occupation. Sperm whales are known to have effectively fought back on occasion — one even sank an American whaler, the *Essex*, in 1820. In spite of the danger, sperm whales were hunted the world over for the array of valuable products these whales contained — whale oil for lamps and lubricants; spermaceti (oil from the forehead) for high quality, smokeless candles; and ambergris, a waxy by-product of digestion which was used in the manufacture of fragrances. By the early twentieth century, whaling had become an efficient, "wide open" business that threatened not only the sperm whale, but all of the great whales, with extinction. Finally, in the 1970s whaling was banned worldwide.

PYGMY SPERM WHALE
Kogia breviceps (Blainville)

Description. A small, toothed whale; upperparts, top of pectoral fins, and flukes blackish; underparts and upper lip, white; dorsal fin small, situated posterior to the mid-point on back, the tip pointing backwards; pectoral fin short and "spear-shaped"; blowhole an oblique crescent left of midline; mouth small and subterminal; snout blunt; skull short, broad, spongy, and markedly asymmetrical; left naris large, right one degenerate, as in the sperm whale; front part of skull deeply bowl-shaped; teeth small, slender, and widely spaced, 12-16 in each lower jaw; total length 2-4 m. Measurements of one whale: total length, 3.2 m; snout to anterior edge of dorsal fin, 1.7 m; height of dorsal fin, 76 mm; length of pectoral fin, 495 mm. Weight of adults, more than 300 kg.

Pygmy Sperm Whale (*Kogia breviceps*). Illustration by Pieter A. Folkens.

Distribution. These whales are found in warm waters worldwide. In the western North Atlantic they occur from Nova Scotia to Cuba and as far westward as the Texas coast, where strandings occur relatively frequently. These whales were once thought to be quite rare, but stranding records indicate they may be more common than originally believed.

Habits. This is a deep water, pelagic species about which very little is known. They occur in small groups of three to six individuals and appear slow and deliberate in their actions. Low frequency, low intensity, pulsed sounds have been recorded from these whales, suggesting that they may be capable of echolocation.

Their food habits are not well-known. Stomachs that have been examined contained carapaces and appendages of green crabs, shrimp, and beaks of squid.

Information available suggests that mating takes place in late summer and the young are born the following spring after a gestation period of some 9 months. The young calf stays with its mother during its first year, as judged from records of capture of pregnant females accompanied by offspring of the previous year. Newborns are about 1.2 m long and weigh 54 kg. Strandings of these whales may often be related to calving, as females with newborn young often strand, as well as females whose reproductive tract shows evidence of parturition just prior to stranding.

DWARF SPERM WHALE
Kogia simus (Owen)

Description. Similar to *Kogia breviceps* but smaller (rarely reaching 3 m in length); dorsal fin higher (relatively and actually) and located near center of back; number of teeth in the lower jaw normally 8-11, rarely as many as 13; usually three rudimentary teeth in each upper jaw. Total length of adults usually less than 2.5 m, rarely to 2.7 m. Weight, less than 300 kg.

Dwarf Sperm Whale (*Kogia simus*). Illustration by Pieter A. Folkens.

Distribution. Like *Kogia breviceps,* the dwarf sperm whale is probably cosmomarine and is found in warm water oceans. In the western North Atlantic, these whales are known from Virginia to the Lesser Antilles and the Gulf of Mexico. They strand fairly frequently but not so often as *K. breviceps.*

Habits. Until the mid 1960's, dwarf sperm whales were routinely grouped with *K. breviceps* in stranding and sighting reports. This has resulted in little available data on the natural history of these whales.

Dwarf sperm whales make deep and prolonged dives in quest of food. Squid and fish are known to occur in the diet.

The reproductive habits of *K. simus* are almost completely unknown. At birth, calves are estimated to be about 1 m in length and 45 kg in weight. The young reach maturity when they are about 2 m in length.

FAMILY ZIPHIIDAE (BEAKED WHALES)

BLAINVILLE'S BEAKED WHALE
Mesoplodon densirostris (Blainville)

Description. A medium-sized whale that reaches lengths of 4.6-4.9 m and weighs about 1 metric ton. Slender in form; flippers short and set low on body; dorsal fin present. Rostrum slender and pointed. Coloration dark gray to black dorsally and somewhat lighter ventrally. Typically mottled with grayish scars left by parasites, squid "sucker marks," and scratches incurred in intraspecific fighting. Males have a single large tooth at the midpoint of each side of the mandible. This tooth may be up to 20 cm in total length and is imbedded in a large hump of supporting bone that gives a high, arching contour to the lower jaw. Females do not have so prominent a tooth and crested jaw.

Distribution. These whales are uncommon residents of warm waters worldwide. In the western North Atlantic they are rare but occur from Nova Scotia to Florida and the Gulf of Mexico. Known in Texas on the basis of a single individual stranded on Padre Island on February 29, 1980.

Habits. Little natural history information is available for these rare and secretive whales. They are normally observed in small groups of three to six and are known to feed on squid.

Sounds recorded from a young male stranded in Florida were described as "chirps" and "whistles." Sound spectrograms showed that at least some of these sounds were pulsed, indicating that echolocation by these whales may occur.

The reproductive habits of these whales are completely unknown.

Blainville's Beaked Whale (*Mesoplodon densirostris*). Illustration by Pieter A. Folkens.

GERVAIS' BEAKED WHALE
Mesoplodon europaeus (Gervais)

Description. A rather small whale with a prominent beak and only one large tooth in each lower jaw, placed about 15 cm back from the tip and beside the posterior end of the symphysis of the lower jaws. In males this tooth is large, protrudes from the closed mouth, and fits into a groove in the skin of the upper lip; in females the tooth usually does not project above the gums so that the animal appears to be toothless. No teeth in upper jaw. Upperparts of body described as dark slate black; lowerparts lighter; no special or distinctive markings. External measurements of an adult male reported by J.C. Moore: total length, 4.3 m; circumference immediately in front of flipper, 1.85 m; width across flukes, 91.5 cm; height of dorsal fin, 18.7 cm; distance from corner of eye to corner of mouth, 20 cm. Maximum known length, 5.45 m. Skulls of females are larger than those of males so the assumption is that females are also larger in body size than males.

Distribution. Gervais' beaked whales are known primarily from the western North Atlantic. They are the most commonly stranded beaked whale in the Gulf of Mexico with several strandings on Texas beaches known. Although there are no population estimates for these whales, they are thought to be rare.

Habits. Almost nothing is known about the life history of these whales. They are believed to inhabit deep waters close to shore but little information is available on movements. They are known to feed on squid and fish.

Strandings of these whales are believed to be associated with calving, which probably takes place in shallow waters. A 4-meter female with a 2-meter calf stranded in Jamaica and a pregnant female with a near term fetus stranded along the Texas coast.

Specific data on the reproductive habits are not available.

Gervais' Beaked Whale (*Mesoplodon europaeus*). Illustration by Pieter A. Folkens.

CUVIER'S BEAKED WHALE
Ziphius cavirostris G. Cuvier

Description. A moderately small beaked whale with upperparts ranging in color from dark brown to lead gray or blackish in color; underparts paler, but not whitish; occasionally head and upper back whitish; beak moderately prominent and the forehead rising rather sharply; lower jaw longer than upper; pectoral fin relatively small and the dorsal fin placed on posterior third of body; prominent keel extends from dorsal fin to tail; skull with length of rostrum less than twice its breadth at notch; lower jaw of males with one large tooth (about 7 cm in length and 4 cm in diameter) at the tip; in females the teeth are small and seldom break through the gums so that the animal appears to be toothless; two converging grooves on throat. Total length of adults, 5-7 m. Weight, 2.5-4.5 metric tons.

Cuvier's Beaked Whale (*Ziphius cavirostris*). Illustration by Pieter A. Folkens.

Distribution. Sparsely distributed throughout tropical and subtropical waters of the world. In the western North Atlantic, these whales are found from Massachusetts to Florida and the Gulf of Mexico.

Habits. Little is known of this whale beyond information revealed by stranded specimens. They are often observed in groups of 10-25. These whales are deep divers and may remain below water for 30 minutes or longer. They are known to eat squid, fish, crabs, and starfish.

The reproductive habits are almost unknown. There does not seem to be a distinct breeding season as calves are born year round. Calves are about 2.1 m long at birth. The length of gestation is unknown.

FAMILY DELPHINIDAE
(TOOTHED WHALES AND DOLPHINS)

KILLER WHALE
Orcinus orca (Linnaeus)

Description. Killer whales are the largest of the dolphin family. Adult males reach up to 9.4 m in length although 8.2 m is average. Females typically reach 7 m in length with the maximum about 8.5 m. Maximum weight is about 7 metric tons. Body form is stocky, the snout is blunt, and the flippers are large and paddle-shaped. In males the dorsal fin may be up to 1.8 m tall, but is considerably shorter in females. Coloration is black dorsally and white ventrally from the chin to slightly behind the anus. An area of white extends up the side posterior to the dorsal fin and an oval white patch is located just above and behind the eye. Each side of both jaws has 10-12 slightly curved teeth that are about 13 cm in length and interlock when the mouth is closed. The teeth are oval in cross section.

Distribution. Killer whales are distributed worldwide, including polar seas. They are rare in the Gulf of Mexico. Known in Texas on the basis of one stranding on South Padre Island and one sighting in waters off of Port Aransas.

Habits. Killer whales are most often observed as gentle giants of marine aquariums but they are, in fact, the supreme carnivore of the world's oceans. At sea they are usually seen in "pods" of 5-20, although up to 150 have been seen together at one time. Large groups probably consist of several pods which have temporarily aggregated. Pods themselves appear very stable for many years, with little emigration or immigration. They are highly cooperative and the group functions as a unit when hunting, making these delphinids extremely efficient predators. Groups usually contain adults of both sexes but sometimes females with young will form their own groups.

Killer Whale (*Orcinus orca*). Illustration by Pieter A. Folkens.

Food items include squid, fish, skates, rays, sharks, sea turtles, sea birds, seals, sea lions, walrus, dolphins, porpoises, and large whales such as fin whales, humpback whales, right whales, minke whales, and gray whales. They are even known to attack the sperm whale and blue whale. On the Atlantic coast of South America, as well as on islands of the Indian Ocean, killer whales have been observed lunging through the surf — and coming right onto the beach — in pursuit of elephant seals and sea lions. After such an attack the whales have to wriggle and slide back into depths adequate for swimming. In captivity, killer whales eat about 45 kg of food per day but free ranging animals probably require much more. Although these are obviously proficient and voracious hunters, killer whales are not known to have ever attacked a human.

The reproductive habits of these whales are poorly known. The males may mate with more than one female and mating may occur throughout the year, although most calves seem to appear in autumn or winter in shallow waters. Their period of gestation is about 12 months. Calves are approximately 2.4 m long at birth and reach sexual maturity when 4.9-6.1 m in length.

FALSE KILLER WHALE
Pseudorca crassidens Owen

Description. A small, entirely black delphinid; no beak, the head slopes gradually from tip of snout to the blowhole; dorsal fin small, narrow, placed slightly forward of midpoint of the back and directed backward; pectoral fins small, about one-eighth of total length and tapering; teeth large, conical, elliptical in cross section, 15-25 mm in diameter, the largest ones projecting 30 mm or so above the gums (40 mm above jawbone), and 8-11 in each tooth row. Adult males reach a length of 5.7 m; females, 4.9 m. Superficially resembles the short-finned pilot whale (*Globicephala*) but lacks the bulbous forehead, and the teeth are nearly twice as large.

Distribution. Found throughout deep tropical, subtropical, and warm temperate waters of the world. Known in Texas on the basis of two strandings from the upper Texas coast.

Habits. Groups of these whales may number from two to several hundred with both sexes and all age groups represented. These delphinids are known to emit "whistling" sounds audible to humans and probably are good echolocators. They eat squid and fish.

False Killer Whale (*Pseudorca crassidens*). Illustration by Pieter A. Folkens.

For unknown reasons false killer whales often strand, sometimes *en masse*. There are three known mass strandings of these whales in the Gulf of Mexico, but the best known such stranding occurred on the Atlantic coast of southern Florida. On January 11, 1970, 150-175 false killer whales beached themselves and refused to return seaward, despite the best efforts of volunteers. All of the whales subsequently died and the cause of this mysterious event was never determined.

Their reproductive habits are poorly known. Breeding probably occurs the year round and the gestation period lasts approximately 15 months. Newborn false killer whales are about 1.5 m in length and weigh 80 kg.

PYGMY KILLER WHALE
Feresa attenuata Gray

Description. A small, blunt-nosed, toothed cetacean similar to the false killer whale (*Pseudorca*), but dorsal fin larger and teeth considerably smaller; body color black with white patches around mouth and on chest and abdomen; dorsal fin about 220 mm high, 375 mm long at base, and located near midpoint of back; teeth about 8 mm in diameter at alveolus, less than 30 mm in length, and with 9-13 in each toothrow; 68-71 vertebrae (50 in *Pseudorca*). Total length about 2.5 m.

Distribution. Deep tropical, subtropical, and warm temperate waters of the world. Known in Texas on the basis of three strandings and one sighting of 20-25 animals about 130 km off the South Texas coast in November, 1980.

Habits. One of the best accounts of this whale to date is that by Taylor Pryor, Karen Pryor, and Kenneth Norris that appeared in the "Journal of Mammalogy" in 1965. The following account is excerpted from their report.

On July 6, 1963, a school of about 50 pygmy killer whales of several sizes (lengths varying from 1 to 2.5 m or so) was sighted from a boat off the island of Hawaii in waters

Pygmy Killer Whale (*Feresa attenuata*). Illustration by Pieter A. Folkens.

about 600 fathoms deep. The school was resting quietly at the surface in a roughly circular group. The whales were aware of the approach of the boat but they did not flee; instead, they circled and dived in the same general area. When the crew of the boat netted an adult animal, the others made no attempt to assist the struggling captive although they remained within 30 or so meters of it.

The captive animal was unusually aggressive, as compared with other cetaceans its size, when it was being handled. It snapped at its captors and emitted a "blatting or growling" noise by forcing air through its blowhole. When released in the training tank at Sea Life Park, it made almost no attempt to avoid an observer, but instead acted as if it expected the observer to move. The day after capture, the animal was once observed to swim quickly with its mouth open toward the arm and hand of a man who was reaching into the tank to check a water input. The man withdrew his arm when the whale was about 2 m away, whereupon the animal closed its mouth and swam past. Ten days after capture the animal was moved to a tank containing an adult and an immature pilot whale (*Globicephala*). The pygmy killer became much more active than usual and swam ceaselessly. It was attracted to the small pilot whale and frequently chased it. One morning the small blackfish was found dead. Autopsy revealed that it had been killed by a single powerful blow — possibly a lethal butt from the pygmy killer whale to the temporal region of the cranium. The animal also exhibited aggressive behavior toward spotted dolphins (*Stenella*).

While in captivity, the pygmy killer whale learned to feed readily on mackerel and it consumed as much as 5 kg of such food a day. It also accepted squid.

Nothing seems to be known regarding reproduction and development in this species.

SHORT-FINNED PILOT WHALE
Globicephala macrorhynchus Gray

Description. A rather large, black delphinid with globose head, no beak, and a bulbous swelling on the forehead in adults; dorsal fin far forward on body, beginning about on plane with back of pectoral fins; pectoral fins long and narrow, about 1/5 of body length; mouth oblique; teeth large, about 10 mm in diameter, 20 mm high, conical, incurved, placed only in anterior part of jaw, and numbering 8-10 in each tooth row. External measurements: total length of male, 4.72 m; tip of snout to dorsal fin, 1.37 m; tip of snout to pectoral fin, 838 mm; length of pectoral fin, 864 mm; breadth of flukes, 1.07 m.

Distribution. Common inhabitants of offshore tropical, subtropical, and warm temperate waters of the world. They are common in the Gulf of Mexico and numerous stranding and sighting records are available from Texas.

Short-finned Pilot Whale (*Globicephala macrorhynchus*). Illustration by Pieter A. Folkens.

Habits. Short-finned pilot whales may congregate in large numbers offshore — schools of several hundred have been observed — but group size usually ranges from 10 to 60. They are seen inshore at infrequent intervals and occasionally become stranded by severe storms. In fact, these are among the most frequently stranded of cetaceans, and often mass strand. These dolphins have mass stranded 15 times in the Gulf of Mexico, although none of these events occurred in Texas. Pilot whales are highly communicative and make a variety of sounds, including noises described as "squealing, whistling, loud smacking, whining, and snores." They probably are excellent echolocators.

The food habits of pilot whales are not well known. In the wild they feed on squid and fish; a captive whale consumed 20 kg of squid per day. This particular whale showed no interest in the fish fed to dolphins in the same tank.

Breeding and calving take place in winter. Gestation lasts about 12 months. Calves are about 1.4 m long at birth and weigh approximately 59 kg. Females are believed to give birth only once every three years.

MELON-HEADED WHALE
Peponocephala electra Gray

Description. Melon-headed whales are about the same size as pygmy killer whales (*Feresa attenuata*), with adult males up to 2.7 m and adult females up to 2.6 m in length. Maximum weight is about 225 kg. The profile of the melon-headed whale is not unlike that of the pygmy killer whale; however, while the pygmy killer whale has a totally rounded, bulbous head, that of the melon-headed whale is rounded in profile and on the top, flat below, and seen from bottom or top, forms a distinct triangle between the eyes and the tip of the snout. The dorsal fin is distinct and falcate, and located at the middle of the back. The flippers are long and, unlike those of the pygmy killer whale, pointed at the tips. Each upper jaw has 20-25 sharp-pointed teeth, while there are 22-24 in each lower jaw. This is about twice the number found in the pygmy killer whale and the false killer whale (*Pseudorca crassidens*), and is a firm identification mark for even decomposed animals.

Coloration is black except on the belly and around the mouth, with the white lips resembling those of pygmy killer whales. Although the belly may be very white, it is usually a light gray and not as distinct as the white belly patch of the pygmy killer whale.

Distribution. Worldwide in tropical and subtropical waters but most numerous in the Philippine sea. They appear to favor warm, pelagic waters and rarely stray over the continental shelf. Known in Texas on the basis of one animal that stranded alive on Matagorda Peninsula in June, 1990. Previously, the nearest record of occurrence was from the island of St. Vincents in the Caribbean.

Melon-headed Whale (*Peponocephala electra*). Illustration by Pieter A. Folkens.

Habits. Melon-headed whales travel in groups of 100-1,000, although even larger groups have been reported. In the tropical Atlantic, Pacific, and Indian Ocean they have been reported traveling with Fraser's dolphin (*Lagenodelphis hosei*) and with spinner and spotted dolphins (*Stenella* spp.).

Little is known about their reproductive habits. Calving appears to peak in early spring in the low latitudes of both hemispheres. The length of gestation is not known, but is probably about 12 months. Migration is unknown, and strandings occur year round in tropical and subtropical waters. Melon-headed whales feed mainly on squid and fish.

ROUGH-TOOTHED DOLPHIN
Steno bredanensis (Lesson)

Description. A small, grayish-black dolphin with the forehead rising gradually from the beak; 20-27 fairly large teeth in each toothrow, the crowns of which have many fine, vertical wrinkles (from which feature the name rough-toothed dolphin is derived); length of rostrum of skull about three times its width. Total length, 2-2.5 m; weight, 100-135 kg.

Distribution. Tropical and warm temperate waters of the world. In the western North Atlantic they are sparsely distributed from Virginia to the northeastern coast of South America. Known in Texas on the basis of two strandings near Galveston.

Habits. Little is known about the life history of these dolphins. They occasionally travel in groups of 50 or more, but smaller groups are normal. They are probably good echolocators and are easily trained.

A mass stranding of these dolphins occurred on the upper Gulf coast of Florida in May, 1961. Sixteen of these dolphins ran aground in a shallow, marshy area but the cause was never determined.

Food habits are almost unknown. They are known to eat octopus, squid, and fish. Nothing is known about their reproductive habits; in captivity, they have mated with bottlenose dolphins and produced hybrid offspring.

Rough-toothed Dolphin (*Steno bredanensis*). Illustration by Pieter A. Folkens.

COMMON DOLPHIN
Delphinus delphis Linnaeus

Description. This is a small, slender dolphin with a long, well defined beak. Average length is 2.1 m with a maximum of about 2.6 m. Weight may be up to 135 kg. Coloration is distinctive. The back is brownish-gray to black and the belly is white. A crisscross, or "hourglass" pattern of light gray, yellow, or tan bands occurs on the sides

Common Dolphin (*Delphinus delphis*). Illustration by Pieter A. Folkens.

and a black stripe extends from the lower jaw to the flipper. The rostrum is black with a white tip and the eyes are set in a black, circular patch from which black lines run forward to the base of the snout. Although varying in extent between individuals, the black dorsal coloration extends down the sides below the dorsal fin giving the impression of a saddle.

Distribution. Worldwide in tropical, subtropical, and warm temperate waters. Known in Texas on the basis of a single animal that stranded at Galveston.

Habits. These are highly social, deep water dolphins; groups contain 20 to several hundred members but huge concentrations numbering into the hundreds of thousands have been observed. They commonly travel above submarine ridges where they dive to feed on squid and fishes including lantern fish, anchovies, and hake.

Breeding appears to have seasonal peaks in spring and fall. The period of gestation is 10-11 months. Newborns are about a meter long and sexual maturity is reached at approximately 3 years of age.

RISSO'S DOLPHIN
Grampus griseus (Cuvier)

Description. This is a medium-sized dolphin that averages 3 m in length and 300 kg in weight. Maximum size is about 4.3 m in length and 680 kg in weight. Body form is stocky from the dorsal fin forward but the tailstock is slender. The head is blunt, beakless, and divided medially by a heavy crease. Coloration is dark gray with lighter gray patches ventrally. In older individuals the face and area just forward of the dorsal fin is also light gray. They are often heavily scarred by parasites and by wounds inflicted by other Risso's dolphins. The blunt, creased head and extensive scarring are noticeable as the animals ride boat bow waves, or spyhop, and are probably the best field character for distinguishing these dolphins. Stranded specimens are distinguished by the unique head shape and crease, and by the teeth. There are up to seven teeth in each side of the lower jaw and none in the upper jaw.

Distribution. Worldwide in warm temperate and tropical waters. They are uncommon in the Gulf of Mexico and are most frequently observed in the eastern part of these waters. There is only one stranding from Texas; a group of nine Risso's dolphins was seen in the Gulf waters off the South Texas coast in November, 1980.

Habits. Risso's dolphins have been observed in large groups of several hundred but smaller groups of three to 30 are more common. They seem to prefer deep offshore waters and in the Gulf they are probably rare over the shallow waters of the continental shelf. They eat squid and fishes.

Risso's Dolphin (*Grampus griseus*). Illustration by Pieter A. Folkens.

Their reproductive habits are poorly known. They probably calve in winter. Newborns are about 1.4 m long at birth and these dolphins may live as long as 24 years. A well-known Risso's dolphin called "Pelorus Jack" was sighted in a New Zealand harbor for over 20 years.

Pelagic sightings of Risso's dolphins in the Gulf of Mexico show that these dolphins appear to prefer deep offshore waters; they have been sighted at ocean depths of 200-1,530 m. They are probably rare near the northern Gulf coast where the continental shelf is broad and the nearshore waters are relatively shallow. In deep, offshore waters of the Gulf these dolphins may be more common than previously thought; however, additional data are needed to effectively assess their status in the Gulf.

BOTTLENOSE DOLPHIN
Tursiops truncatus (Montague)

Description. A rather stout, short-beaked (seldom more than 75 mm long) dolphin with sloping forehead and projecting lower jaw; dorsal fin high, falcate, and situated about midway from snout to flukes; pectoral fin broad at base, obtusely rounded at tip; upperparts plumbeous gray, more or less tinged with purplish, becoming black soon after death; sides pale gray, belly white; teeth 23/23, large, nearly round in cross section in adults, and conical; height above jawbone, 12-17 mm, diameter, 5-9 mm. Total length of adults may reach 3.5 m. A sub-adult male measured: total length, 2.9 m; length of mouth, 319 mm; tip of snout to dorsal fin, 1,275 mm; length of pectoral fin, 395 mm; vertical height of dorsal fin, 229 mm; breadth of flukes, 612 mm.

Distribution. Bottlenose dolphins are distributed worldwide in tropical and temperate waters. In the western North Atlantic, these dolphins occur as far north as Nova Scotia but are most common in coastal waters from New England to Florida, the Gulf of Mexico, the Caribbean, and south to Venezuela. This is the most common cetacean of the Gulf of Mexico and along the Texas coast.

Habits. Bottlenose dolphins may be seen in groups numbering up to several hundred but smaller social units of two to 15 are more common. Group size is affected by habitat structure and tends to increase with water depth. Group members interact closely and are highly cooperative in feeding, protective, and nursery activities. These dolphins make numerous sounds and are probably both good echolocators and highly communicative.

Bottlenose dolphins eat a wide variety of food items depending on what is available and abundant at a given time. In Texas waters they eat fishes including tarpon, sailfish, sharks, speckled trout, pike, rays, mullet, and catfish. They are also known to eat anchovies, menhaden, minnows, shrimp, and eel. They eat about 18-36 kg of fish each day.

Commonly observed feeding behaviors include foraging around shrimp boats, either working or not, to feed on fish attracted to the boats. The dolphins also eat "bycatch" dumped from working trawlers. Groups of these dolphins have been observed cooperating in prey capture, with several dolphins herding fish into tight schools that are more easily exploited. Bottlenoses are also known to chase prey into very shallow water and may lunge onto mud banks and shoals in pursuit of panicked fish.

Of 15 females captured in Texas waters, six that were pregnant were taken between December 17 and March 19. On the first date the fetus was 78 cm long and weighed 5 kg; on the last date fetuses were almost as large as some of the small calves. Nursing females were all taken between April 20 and September 11. These data suggest that breeding occurs in the summer and that the young are born the following March to May. At birth the calf is more than a third as long as its mother. The longest fetus recorded was 1.1 m in a female 2.8 m long; the smallest calf also was 1.1 m in length. Females give birth to a single calf and only give birth every 2-3 years. Males mature at 10-13 years of age and females at 5-12 years, when about 2.4 m in length. That the family group may remain intact for nearly a year is suggested by the capture on February 24 of a pregnant female and a young male approximately 1.5 m in length. These two animals were traveling together and were presumably mother and son.

Bottlenose dolphins are the most widespread and common cetacean of the coastal Gulf of Mexico and are commonly seen in bays, estuaries, and ship channels. Two distinct forms may occur in the Gulf. These are inshore animals that inhabit shallow lagoons, bays, and inlets and oceanic, or offshore, populations that remain in deeper, offshore waters. Interaction between the two populations is thought to be minimal. Populations of these dolphins in the southern and central portions of the Texas coast appear to increase dramatically in fall and winter. Either offshore dolphins move into nearshore waters during these seasons, or dolphins from adjacent bay systems move into these coastal sections. There is some evidence of a winter decline in dolphin numbers off Galveston.

The bottlenose dolphin is the only cetacean for which census techniques have yielded useful population estimates in the Gulf of Mexico. Nevertheless, these estimates do not include offshore dolphins, which are difficult to census, and therefore underestimate the total Gulf population. A cumulative summation of aerial surveys estimates 35,000-45,000 bottlenose dolphins in the Gulf of Mexico.

All cetaceans, including bottlenose dolphins, are protected from hunting by strict laws, but are affected by other human-caused activities. In the Gulf these include petroleum resource development, heavy boating traffic, and the pollution of Gulf waters, but the cumulative effects of these factors on dolphins are difficult to determine. Bottlenoses have been observed swimming through heavy oil spills and superficially

Bottlenose Dolphin (*Tursiops truncatus*). Illustration by Pieter A. Folkens.

show no ill effects. Bottlenoses may be able to adapt to man's activities but probably are readily affected by pollution and would make a good "indicator species" signalling the overuse and excessive pollution of Gulf waters.

PANTROPICAL SPOTTED DOLPHIN
Stenella attenuata Gray

Description. A small dolphin with a relatively short, black beak, blackish back, grayish sides, and white underparts; eyes usually encircled with black rings joined by a black stripe across base of rostrum; dorsal fin, flipper, and flukes black; the pale sides and abdomen often covered with small blackish spots; posterior to the dorsal fin the blackish upperparts and the flippers often covered with grayish white dots. Teeth small (diameter at alveolus 2.5-3.0 mm) and 38-42 in each toothrow. Total length, 1.5-2.0 m. Similar to *S. frontalis* but upperparts blackish, general size smaller, beak narrower, and the teeth smaller and more numerous.

Distribution. Occurs in the tropical and subtropical oceans of the world. Known in Texas from three individuals that were beached near Yarborough Pass on Padre Island during Hurricane Fern in September, 1971, and two separate individual strandings near Port Aransas in 1989 and 1990.

Habits. These dolphins are usually seen in groups of five to 30, although large herds of 1,000 or more are occasionally observed. Unlike many other dolphins, groups of pantropical spotted dolphins do not appear to be segregated by sex and age. These dolphins feed at or near the surface on fish, including mackerel and flying fish, squid, and shrimp.

In the eastern tropical Pacific, the following reproductive data are known. The gestation period lasts 11.5 months and lactation lasts about 11 months. At birth the calves average 80 cm in length and at 1 year are 1.4 m long. Males attain sexual maturity at about 6 years of age while females reach maturity at 5 years. The calving interval is 26 months. No data on reproductive habits are available for the Gulf of Mexico.

In the Pacific, these dolphins are killed incidentally in the course of seining for tuna. In 1970, about 400,000 were killed by U.S. vessels alone but that figure was reduced to 15,000-20,000 by 1978. Currently, incidental catch is limited by U.S. law to 20,500 per year but is usually lower than that due to declining tuna seining efforts and the recent adoption of a porpoise mortality reduction program; this international agreement by all major tuna seining countries has a goal of reducing total incidental catch to less than 5,000 dolphins per year by 1999. In the Atlantic and Gulf of Mexico, the problem of incidental catch is limited and was never as great as in the Pacific.

Remarks. This dolphin was previously known as *Stenella frontalis* (Cuvier).

Pantropical Spotted Dolphin (*Stenella attenuata*). Illustration by Pieter A. Folkens.

CLYMENE DOLPHIN
Stenella clymene (Gray)

Description. This is a small dolphin that averages about 1.8 m in length and 75 kg in weight. It can be distinguished by its moderately short beak; triparite color pattern (white belly, light gray sides, dark cape that dips in two points - above the eye and below the dorsal fin); and distinctive facial markings (black eye ring, dark lips and snout tip, and dark line on top of snout, sometimes incorporating a "moustache" near the apex of the melon). The cape is sometimes obscured by blotchy patches on the sides and, occasionally, a faint spinal blaze may be present. The dorsal fin is gray but bordered with dark margins. Average total number of teeth is 200.

Distribution. Found only in the tropical and subtropical waters of the Atlantic Ocean. Known in Texas from four strandings, including three recent strandings along Padre and Mustang Islands.

Habits. This dolphin was not described as a distinct species until 1981 and is rarely observed alive. Consequently, it is one of the most poorly known dolphins of the world.

Stenella clymene has been observed at sea only in deep water. These dolphins eat small fishes and squid and appear to feed at night or in mid-water depths. Squid remains found in their stomachs are of species that characteristically live at intermediate depths and surface at night.

These dolphins may leap and spin out of water but their movements are not so high or complex as those of the spinner dolphin, *S. longirostris*. Stranding records from the Gulf of Mexico indicate that they are probably year-round residents of this region.

The Clymene dolphin is not found outside of Atlantic waters, an unusual distribution for a tropically distributed cetacean. This dolphin may possibly have evolved in the Atlantic.

Clymene Dolphin (*Stenella clymene*). Illustration by Pieter A. Folkens.

STRIPED DOLPHIN
Stenella coeruleoalba (Meyen)

Description. A slender dolphin that reaches lengths of about 2.4 m and averages 100 kg in weight. Maximum size is approximately 3 m in length and 129 kg in weight. Strikingly colored in shades of gray or brown. Dark dorsally fading to lighter sides and white ventrally with black stripes extending from the eye to the anus and from the eye to the flipper. Dorsal fin tall, beak relatively short and uniformly dark. There are 43-50 teeth in each side of both jaws, average total is 200. Only *Stenella longirostris* has more average total teeth (224).

Distribution. Worldwide in tropical and temperate waters. Although they are occasionally seen in the western Gulf of Mexico near Texas, and have stranded on Texas beaches, these dolphins are better known from waters around Florida.

Habits. Striped dolphins may be observed in herds of several hundred to several thousand with such groups usually segregated by sex and age. In the Gulf of Mexico group size ranges from one to 130 and averages 16 dolphins per group. They are usually found in deep, offshore waters where they feed on small pelagic fishes, squid, and shrimp.

Adult females bear young once every 3 years and the gestation period is 12 months. Calves are approximately a meter long at birth. In the Gulf of Mexico, calves have been seen in June, August, October, and February, indicating that there may not be a sharply defined breeding season. Males reach maturity at about 9 years of age and females at 7 years.

Striped Dolphin (*Stenella coeruleoalba*). Illustration by Pieter A. Folkens.

ATLANTIC SPOTTED DOLPHIN
Stenella frontalis (Cuvier)

Description. A rather small, long-snouted, spotted dolphin; ground color purplish gray, appearing blackish at a distance, usually with numerous small white or gray spots on sides and back; sides paler, belly whitish; young grayish, unspotted; dorsal fin high and strongly recurved, strongly concave at rear; beak deeper than wide and about 6% of total length of animal; teeth small and slightly incurved, especially toward tip of snout in upper jaw, varying in number from 31/31 to 37/34; height of teeth above jawbones seldom over 10 mm; diameters of largest tooth at alveolus, 5.5 by 4.0 mm; total length, 2.2 m; girth in front of dorsal fin, 1.2 m; length of anterior edge of dorsal fin, 431 mm; width of flukes, 661 mm. Weight, 125 kg.

Distribution. These dolphins are a common, offshore resident of tropical and warm temperate waters of the Atlantic Ocean. Not known outside of the Atlantic. In the Gulf of Mexico, this dolphin is second in abundance only to the bottlenose dolphin, *Tursiops truncatus*.

Habits. Atlantic spotted dolphins may be seen in groups of up to 50 animals, but smaller groups of six to 10 are more common. They eat small fishes including herring, anchovies, and flounder, as well as squid.

These dolphins make a variety of sounds used in echolocation and communication. Sounds are described as "loud whistles, chirps, low intensity click trains, squawks, barks, growls, and cracks."

These dolphins mate and calve in summer. Sexual behavior has been observed in the Gulf of Mexico in mid-May. The gestation period lasts 12 months and calves are born in offshore waters.

Although this dolphin is a common offshore resident of the Gulf of Mexico, the dolphins may move into nearshore waters in late spring and summer in Florida. This movement may be related to the movements of certain prey species for the dolphins; such migrations are not known for Texas waters.

Remarks. This dolphin was previously known as *Stenella plagiodon*.

Atlantic Spotted Dolphin (*Stenella frontalis*). Illustration by Pieter A. Folkens.

SPINNER DOLPHIN
Stenella longirostris (Gray)

Description. These are small dolphins that average less than 1.8 m in length and 75 kg in weight. Maximum size is about 2.1 m and 95 kg. These dolphins are very slender and have a long, slender beak that is black above and white below. Coloration is dark gray dorsally fading to lighter gray on the sides and the belly is white. A dark stripe extends from the flipper to the eye. Average total teeth, 224, is greater than for any other Texas cetacean.

Distribution. Worldwide in tropical and warm temperate waters. Known in Texas from strandings along Padre Island National Seashore.

Habits. Spinner dolphins derive their name from a habit of leaping from the water and warping their bodies into graceful curves, or spinning lengthwise before splashing back. The motives for this behavior are not known but such actions are often in themselves enough to distinguish this species.

Spinner Dolphin (*Stenella longirostris*). Illustration by Pieter A. Folkens.

326

They usually occur in groups of 30 to several hundred but may number into the thousands. Spinner dolphins feed on mesopelagic fishes, squid, and shrimp.

Adult females give birth to a single calf at 2-year intervals. Parturition usually occurs in early summer but can occur in any season. Their period of gestation is 11 months and calves are about 75 cm long at birth.

Spinner dolphins have mass stranded twice in the Gulf of Mexico. One stranding of 36 animals occurred on Dog Island, Florida, in 1961, and the other was near Sarasota, Florida, in 1976. The latter stranding involved 50-150 spinners that beached themselves at several points during an extremely low tide. The dolphins came ashore with much "squealing and crying" but this later subsided and the animals were quite passive on the beach. Several of the animals were returned, apparently successfully, to the sea; however, others merely stranded again and at least 10 died.

In the eastern tropical Pacific this species is often caught and drowned in large numbers by the tuna fishing industry. Over the last 20 years the total population in those waters has declined about 80%, from 2 million to 400,000, due to incidental catch. Gulf of Mexico populations do not receive this pressure, but data for population estimates are unavailable and population trends are not known in Gulf waters.

Appendix I.
The measurement system.

Previous editions of *The Mammals of Texas* used the old Roman system of measurements (foot-pound-inch, etc.) with the metric system equivalent recorded in parentheses. In this edition, we present only the metric system which is the official standard of measurement for scientific communication. For those who are less familiar with the metric system, the following table of metric-to-Roman conversion factors may be helpful.

To Convert	Multiply by
millimeters to inches	0.039
centimeters to inches	0.394
meters to feet	3.281
meters to yards	1.094
kilometers to miles	0.621
hectares to acres	2.471
hectares to square miles	0.004
liters to quarts	1.057
grams to ounces	0.035
kilograms to pounds	2.205
metric tons to tons	1.102

Appendix II.
Observing and collecting mammals.

Whether to satisfy the interest of the casual outdoorsman or to fulfill the needs of scientific research, the observation and collection of mammals are exciting occupations. Practically all that is needed to make interesting and useful observations of mammals is a good pair of binoculars, and the inclination to rise early and stay late. Unlike birds, most mammals are either crepuscular (twilight active) or nocturnal (night active) in nature, making prolonged observation of behavior, feeding habits, and other aspects of natural history more difficult. Additionally, many species are fossorial (dwell underground) and cannot be directly observed except during the rare and brief moments these animals may appear at their burrow entrances.

For these reasons, the observation of mammals is often done indirectly, by evaluating the tracks, scats, scrapes, rubs, and other such "sign" that mammals leave behind as evidence of their activities. Locating sign and drawing accurate deductions of animal activity is an art that for the most part has been lost as people rely less and less on understanding nature to fulfill basic needs. Nevertheless, "reading sign" is a fascinating occupation, many aspects of which can be learned simply through interest and perseverance. Acquiring one or more of the numerous field guides now available on this subject will speed up the learning process and allow for a more complete understanding of the outdoors.

For scientific purposes, collections of mammals are sometimes made. The collection of mammals and their subsequent preparation as museum specimens is a complicated process that often requires a great deal of equipment and planning. Numerous techniques and types of traps are available depending on the animals to be taken, the region studied, and the type of information being sought. For smaller mammals, such as mice, mouse traps of the variety that snap shut on the animal can be purchased in almost every hardware store. However, the larger "Museum Special" is best because the wire that strikes and kills the mouse is far enough from the treadle to keep the head of the mouse from being struck and crushed. For study purposes, broken skulls are less desirable than unbroken ones.

The still larger rat trap is stocked in most hardware stores and is suitable for taking animals the size of wood rats and small ground squirrels. Steel traps in sizes 0 to 4 are used in many areas to secure other animals. McAbee gopher traps are the best yet devised for taking pocket gophers. Several mole traps are on the market; the stabbing variety is preferred by most collectors.

Many specimens are most effectively taken by shooting. For smaller and medium-sized kinds, a shotgun is recommended but shot of small size should be used in order to avoid unnecessary mutilation of the animal. Nets of silk or nylon may be useful to the mammal collector, especially in capturing bats. Pitfall traps are often set for shrews by burying a can up to the rim in mammal runways and other likely spots.

In addition to traps that kill the mammal, numerous styles and sizes of live traps are offered for sale by various manufacturers. These include the popular "Sherman" live trap frequently used for mouse and rat-sized mammals, up to the equally popular "Havahart" traps useful for capturing racoon-sized mammals. Large drive nets, drop nets, and similar traps, often used in conjunction with other equipment such as helicopters and immobilizing drugs, are used by specialists to capture larger mammals for study, such as deer and even elk.

Properly preparing mammals as museum specimens requires skill, patience, and training. The labeling, skinning, and stuffing of mammal skins, as well as preparing skeletal material, are demanding, sometimes tedious tasks that require attention to detail and a lot of practice. Several handbooks and guides are available to introduce the mammal enthusiast to this necessary aspect of mammalogy.

For safely storing prepared mammal specimens in accessible fashion a museum cabinet that excludes insects, dust, and light is essential. A visit to the nearest museum known to maintain a collection of study specimens of mammals, or a letter of inquiry addressed there, will yield all needed information about the type of container best suited to the needs of the collector. Advice concerning the preparation of mammals as specimens, including the preparing of skins and cleaning of skeletal material, can be obtained from the same sources.

The trapping of mammals, even for scientific purposes, requires a scientific collecting permit. Every state has its own laws relating to hunting and trapping, and the collector should obtain and read these laws so as to carry on collecting in conformance with the law. In Texas, scientific collecting permits are issued by the Texas Parks and Wildlife Department; advice and clarification on collecting regulations can also be obtained from this department. Collecting on federal lands, such as national parks and monuments, requires a permit from federal authorities. Government personnel at the site to be studied should be contacted for information on obtaining federal collecting permits. Of course, if mammal collecting is to be done on private lands the permission of the landowner is also required.

Next to conducting mammal collection and observation activities in a lawful and responsible manner, the most important obligation of the mammalogist is to take accurate and complete field notes. Only in this way can new information eventually be provided for the benefit of others. Field notes can usefully be divided into a catalog of specimens, itinerary or journal, and accounts of species. For convenience all three sections of the notes ordinarily are kept in a single binder, but separate binders may be used. Enter the name of the collector and the year in the upper left-hand corner of every page but far enough from the margin to permit binding of the pages. Each page should be filled before another page is started.

In the catalog, all specimens of vertebrate animals should be given consecutive numbers. Never repeat a number; for instance, do not begin a new series each year. One line of the notebook page should be devoted to the precise locality. Include airline distance from some well-established town. Include also elevation, county, and state. Devote one line to each specimen. If not a conventional specimen, indicate the nature by entry directly above the field number — whether (if) skeleton, skull-only, skin-only, or alcoholic. Toward the end of line it may be desirable to enter, on occasion, color of iris and soft parts. Use the vernacular name of the species if you are not sure of the scientific name.

On the first line of the itinerary enter date and locality. Follow with a concise account of route and travel area and habitats studied, and record number and kinds of traps set, distance between traps, number of vertebrates collected, as well as other pertinent information. For example, record number of traps set in each type of vegetation and numbers and kinds of animals caught therein. Section, township, and range comprise useful information.

Accounts of species should be headed either with the scientific or common name, as preferred. The date and locality for the account should be given on the first line. Only one species should be written about on a single page. Information in the account should not be a repetition of material given in the itinerary or journal. Include not only facts but also interpretations and generalizations. The accounts should be written in a style suitable for quoting in any publication. Accounts of species need not be restricted to kinds collected. If the account is about animals collected it is wise to refer to the animals by your field numbers.

Head each and every notebook page with collector's name and year, page number (if number system is used), locality (in detail the first time used), and date. Write full notes, even at risk of entering much information of seemingly little value. One cannot anticipate the needs of the future when notes and collections are worked up. The following are suggested topics, but do not restrict yourself to these alone. Be alert for new ideas and new facts. Special data sheets may be helpful.

Describe vegetation (saving plant-press samples of species not positively known), nature of ground, slope, exposure, and drainage in each belt of animal life sampled. Describe exact location of trap lines, referring to your topographic maps, and also enter a sketch, in profile or surface view or both, to illustrate the location and relations of the different habitats crossed. Properly marked maps for each region worked should ultimately be bound in with the field notes of at least one member of your field party.

Keep record of closeness of settings of traps, distance covered, and results of each night's trappings; give number and type of traps put out in each habitat and number of animals of each species captured in each habitat (whether or not preserved). It is advisable to record the sex, age, and breeding condition of each animal. We have found special data sheets helpful.

Keep full record of breeding data; number and approximate size (crown-rump length) of embryos, or of young found in nests. Dig out burrows if practicable; make drawings to scale, plan, and elevation; describe fully.

Record food plants; keep specimens for identification where not known by a definite name; preserve contents of cheek pouches and stomachs. If these are not saved, identify and record contents.

Note regularly in notebook all "pick-up," that is, odd skulls or fragments of animals of whatever sort or source, serially numbered along with specimens of the more usual sort. Give full information, as with odd skulls secured from trappers. Label all such specimens adequately, as elsewhere described.

Keep frequent censuses of diurnal mammals, with habitat preferences indicated. These censuses, if short, need not be entered on formal census sheets. When leaving a well-worked locality, enter a summary of species observed, with remarks of a general nature, such as relate to local conditions of terrain, human activities, and other pertinent conditions.

Where feasible interview residents, trappers, state wildlife biologists, National Forest and National Park rangers at each locality visited. Always record accurately the name, official position, or occupation and address of each person giving information; give also your opinion as to his/her reliability. Note general attitude of person interviewed as to game laws, conservation, and effects of settlement by man, and record specific comments, complaints, and criticisms.

Ascertain present numbers and distribution of large mammals as compared with former status. As far as possible get definite statements expressing ratio of abundance now, compared with a definite number of years back. Seek such information where feasible, by indirect query. Do not risk influencing your informant's statements by leading questions. Record fully all evidence as to human influence upon original or "natural" balance. Record present economic relations of vertebrate animal life; that is, effect on agriculture and stock raising, with full details. Note opinions of persons interviewed as to whether species should be protected or destroyed. Describe local methods of capture or destruction; give your opinion as to their effectiveness and justification.

Opportunity offering, record detailed observations on effects upon mammals of severe storms; floods; forest, brush or prairie fires; overgrazing; tree cutting; road-building; or tree-planting.

Appendix III.
Selected references on mammals from Texas and adjoining states.

ad hoc Committee on Acceptable Field Methods in Mammalogy. 1987. Acceptable field methods in mammalogy: preliminary guidelines approved by the American Society of Mammalogists. *J. Mamm.* 68 (supplement):1-18.

Alvarez, T. 1963. The Recent mammals of Tamaulipas, Mexico. *Univ. Kansas Publ., Mus. Nat. Hist.* 14:363-473.

Anderson, S. 1972. Mammals of Chihuahua: taxonomy and distribution. *Bull. Amer. Mus. Nat. Hist.* 148:151-410.

Baker, R. H. 1956. Mammals of Coahuila, Mexico. *Univ. Kansas Publ., Mus. Nat. Hist.* 9:125-335.

Burt, W. H., and R. P. Grossenheider. 1964. *A field guide to the mammals.* 2nd ed. Peterson Field Guide Series No. 5. Boston: Houghton Mifflin Co. 284 pp.

Caire, W., J. D. Tyler, B. P. Glass, and M. A. Mares. 1989. *Mammals of Oklahoma.* Norman: Univ. Oklahoma Press.

Dalquest, W. W., and N. V. Horner. 1984. *Mammals of northcentral Texas.* Wichita Falls: Midwestern State Univ. Press.

DeBlase, A. F., and R. E. Martin. 1981. *A manual of mammalogy, with keys to families of the world.* Dubuque, Iowa: Wm. C. Brown Co. Publishers.

Findley, J. S. 1987. *The natural history of New Mexican mammals.* Albuquerque: Univ. New Mexico Press.

Findley, J. S., A. H. Harris, D. E. Wilson, and C. Jones. 1975. *Mammals of New Mexico.* Albuquerque: Univ. New Mexico Press.

Hall, E. R. 1962. Collecting and preparing study specimens of vertebrates. *Univ. Kansas, Mus. Nat. Hist. Misc. Publ.* 30:1-46.

Hall, E. R. 1981. *The mammals of North America.* 2 vols. New York: John Wiley & Sons.

Hoffmeister, D. F. 1986. *Mammals of Arizona.* Tucson: Univ. Arizona Press.

Jones, J. K., Jr., and J. A. Homan. 1976. Contribution to a bibliography of Recent Texas mammals, 1961-1970. *Occas. Pap. Mus. Texas Tech Univ.* 41:1-21.

Jones, J. K., Jr., and C. Jones. 1992. Revised checklist of Recent land mammals of Texas, with annotations. *Texas J. Sci.* 44(1):53-74.

Jones, J. K., Jr., C. J. Young, and D. J. Schmidly. 1985. Contribution to a bibliography of Recent Texas mammals, 1971-1980. *Occas. Pap. Mus. Texas Tech Univ.* 95:1-44.

Jones, J. K., Jr., C. Jones, and D. J. Schmidly. 1988. Annotated checklist of Recent land mammals of Texas. *Occas. Papers Mus. Texas Tech Univ.* 119:1-26.

Jones, J. K., Jr., R. S. Hoffman, D. W. Rice, C. Jones, R. J. Baker, and M. D. Engstom. 1992. Revised checklist of North American mammals north of Mexico, 1991. *Occas. Papers Mus. Texas Tech Univ.* 146:1-23.

Lowery, G. H., Jr. 1974. *The mammals of Louisiana and its adjacent waters.* Baton Rouge: Louisiana State Univ. Press.

Murie, O. J. 1954. *A field guide to animal tracks.* Peterson Field Guide Series No. 9. Boston: Houghton Mifflin Co. 374 pp.

Raun, G. G. 1962. A bibliography of the Recent mammals of Texas. *Tex. Mem. Mus. Bull.* 3:1-81.

Schmidly, D. J. 1977. *The mammals of Trans-Pecos Texas.* College Station: Texas A&M Univ. Press. 225 pp.

Schmidly, D. J. 1983. *Texas mammals east of the Balcones Fault Zone.* College Station: Texas A&M Univ. Press. 400 pp.

Schmidly, D. J. 1984. *The furbearers of Texas.* Bull. Texas Parks Wildl. Dept. 111:vii 55 pp.

Schmidly, D. J. 1991. *The bats of Texas.* College Station: Texas A&M Univ. Press. 188 pp.

Sealander, J. A. 1979. *A guide to Arkansas mammals.* Conway: River Road Press.

Vaughan, T. A. 1986. *Mammalogy.* 3rd ed. Philadelphia: Saunders College Publishing.

Whitaker, J. O., Jr. 1980. *The Audubon Society field guide to North American mammals.* New York: Alfred A. Knopf. 745 pp.

Wilson, D.E., and D.M. Reeder, eds. 1993. *Mammal species of the world.* 2nd ed. Washington, D.C.: Smithsonian Institution Press. 1206 pp.

Appendix IV.
Scientific names.

The scientific name of a mammal as here used consists of two Latinized words followed by the name of a person. The first word designates the GENUS to which the animal is assigned; the second is the name of the SPECIES; and the third, the name of the AUTHORITY for the specific epithet (species name). If the person's name is enclosed in parentheses, it indicates that he/she described the species under a generic name different from that in current use. For example, when Linnaeus described our mole in 1758 and gave it the specific name *aquaticus* he placed it in the genus *Sorex*. We now reserve the genus *Sorex* for a certain group of shrews and place the Texas moles in the genus *Scalopus*. Consequently, the scientific name of Texas moles is written *Scalopus aquaticus* (Linnaeus). On the other hand, when he described our fox squirrel in 1758 and gave it the specific epithet *niger*, he placed it in the genus *Sciurus*. We currently accept that arrangement so the scientific name of the fox squirrel appears as *Sciurus niger* Linnaeus — parentheses are omitted.

Appendix V.
Standard measurements of study specimens.

Each species account in this book includes under the heading "Description" a number of standard measurements that may be helpful in identifying species in the field or specimens in the hand. Measurements are usually recorded in millimeters and weights in grams, although measurements for larger species may be recorded in meters and weights in kilograms.

Explanations of the most common standard measurements for mammals are as follows:

> Total length – length from tip of nose pad to tip of fleshy part of tail, excluding hairs that project beyond tip.
>
> Length of tail – with tail held at right angle to body, the length from bend on back to tip of fleshy part of tail, excluding hairs that project beyond tip.
>
> Length of hind foot – distance from tip of longest claw to heel.
>
> Height of ear from notch – distance from notch at front base of ear to distalmost border of fleshy part of ear.

Some mammal descriptions include other measurements appropriate for the species, such as: length of the forearm of bats; length of the metatarsal gland of ungulates; height at shoulder of large mammals such as bears and artiodactyls; length of pectoral fin, height of dorsal fin, and girth of cetaceans.

Measurements of the skull are also useful for identifying specimens, particularly those of small mammals. The figure below illustrates some of the more common identifying features of the skull and selected standard measurements.

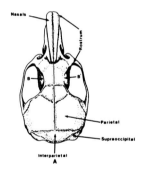

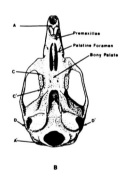

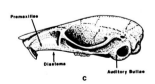

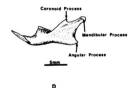

Views of the skull and lower jaw of the white-ankled mouse, *Peromyscus pectoralis*, showing the bones and indicating the measurements used in identifying species. Point A to Point A' – condylobasal length; Point B to Point B' – interorbital breadth; Point C to Point C' – length of molar tooth row; Point D to Point D' – mastoidal breadth.

Appendix VI.
Basis for distribution of species.

Each species account in this book includes a description of the distribution of the species in Texas, and most accounts include a map of the distribution in Texas based on known county records. The distribution for each species is based on the following types of data:

1) Specimens collected in Texas and held in various museums.
2) Records in published scientific literature.
3) Survey response records of trappers in Texas (furbearers).
4) Texas Department of Health records (bats).
5) Texas Parks and Wildlife Department distribution files and field biologists' reports.
6) Records of the Texas Marine Mammal Stranding Network (cetaceans).

GLOSSARY

allopatric — Of populations or species occupying mutually exclusive, but usually adjacent, geographical areas.

annulation — A circular or ringlike formation, as of the dermal scales on the tail of a mammal where one ring of scales that extends entirely around the tail is succeeded, posteriorly, by other rings.

aquatic — Inhabiting or frequenting water.

arboreal — Inhabiting or frequenting trees — contrasted with fossorial, aquatic, or cursorial.

canine — Of, pertaining to, or designating the tooth next to the incisors in mammals; fang.

carnivore — An animal that preys on other animals; especially any mammal of the Order Carnivora.

cheek-teeth — Teeth behind the canines.

conch — The external ear of a mammal; sometimes the spelling is concha (plural conchae); the origin of both spellings is conch or konch, originally a bivalve shell of a marine mollusk.

cursorial — Adapted or modified for running, such as are deer.

dental formula (plural, formulae) — A brief method for expressing the number and kind of teeth of mammals. The abbreviations I (incisor), C (canine), P or Pm (premolar), and M (molar) indicate the kinds in the permanent dentition. The number of teeth in each jaw is written like a fraction; the figure in front of the diagonal line showing the number in the upper jaw and that after, the number in the lower jaw. The dental formula of an adult coyote is I 3/3, C 1/1, Pm 4/4, M 2/3 X 2 = 42.

dentition — The teeth, considered collectively, of an animal.

diurnal — Active by day; as opposed to nocturnal.

electrophoresis — A process by which enzymes are separated based on differences in electrical charge. Observed differences between or within species indicate mutation and genetic divergence over long periods of time, thus elucidating the inter-relationships of organisms.

fossorial — Fitted for digging.

gestation period — The period of carrying young in the uterus, as applied to placental mammals; the period of pregnancy.

guard hairs — The stiffer, longer hairs which grow up through the limber, shorter hairs (fur) of a mammal's pelage.

habitat — The kind of environment in which a species or organism is normally found.

hibernation — Of an animal, torpidity especially in winter; the body temperature approximates that of the surroundings; the rate of respiration and the heart beat ordinarily are much slower than in an active mammal.

incisor — The front or cutting teeth between the canines.

inguinal — Pertaining to or in the region of the groin.

insectivorous — Eating insects; preying or feeding on insects.

interfemoral membrane — In a bat, the fold of skin stretching from hind legs to tail.

karyotype — An arrangement of chromosomes by size and morphology to detect changes in chromosomal structure and arrangement; used to aid in identification of species and subspecies within a species.

litter — The two or more young brought forth at one birth by a female mammal.

molar — Of, or pertaining to, a molar tooth. One of the teeth behind the premolar teeth; for example, in the opossum three on each side in upper jaw and in lower jaw, making 12 in all. A molar tooth is not preceded in embryological development by a deciduous (milk) tooth.

molt (moult) — In a mammal, the act or process of shedding or casting off the hair, outer layer of skin, or horns; most mammals shed the hair once, twice, or three times annually. The castoff covering (obsolete). As a verb; To be shed or to shed.

nocturnal — Active by night; as opposed to diurnal.

opposable — Capable of being placed opposite something else; said of the first toe of the hind foot in an opossum in the sense that it can be placed opposite each of the other toes on that same foot.

overhair — The longer hairs of the pelage of a mammal that project above the fur (shorter hairs).

parapatric — Pertaining to the ranges of species that are contiguous but not overlapping.

pastern — That part of the foot of a hoofed mammal from the fetlock to the hoof.

pectoral — Of, pertaining to, situated, or occurring in or on the chest.

premolar — Designating, or pertaining to, one of the teeth (a maximum of four on each side of upper jaw and lower jaw of placental mammals, or 16 in all) in front of the true molars. When canine teeth are present, premolars are behind these teeth; premolars are preceded by deciduous teeth, and in the upper jaw are confined to the maxillary bone.

rut — The breeding period, as in deer.

species — Groups of actually (or potentially) interbreeding natural populations that are reproductively isolated from other such groups. Reproductive isolation implies that interbreeding between individuals of two species normally is prevented by intrinsic factors.

subspecies — Geographically defined aggregate of local populations which differs taxonomically from other such subdivisions of the species.

sympatric — Pertaining to two or more populations which occupy overlapping geographical areas.

tarsus — The ankle.

tibia — The inner and usually the larger of the two bones of the hind limb (leg) between the knee and ankle.

torpid — Having lost most of the power of exertion; dormant. A ground squirrel is torpid when it is hibernating.

tricolor — Having three colors. Said of hair on the back of a mammal when the hair has three bands each of a different color.

underfur — The short hair of a mammal; in temperate and boreal climates the underfur ordinarily is denser, made up of more hairs, than the longer and coarser overhair.

underpart — The underneath (ventral) side of a mammal (not the back or sides), as of a wood mouse with white underparts.

upperpart — The top (dorsal) surface and all of the sides (not belly, chest or throat), as of a wood mouse with reddish-brown upperparts.

uropatagium — The interfemoral membrane of a bat; that is to say, the fold of skin that stretches from the hind legs to the tail.

Notes

Notes

Notes

Notes